ROMEO & JULIET

ALSO IN THE NO FEAR SHAKESPEARE GRAPHIC NOVELS SERIES:

HAMLET
MACBETH

NO FEAR SHAKESPEARE | Graphic Novels

ROMEO & JULIET

ILLUSTRATED BY MATT WIEGLE

SPARKNOTES

SPARKNOTES IS A REGISTERED TRADEMARK OF SPARKNOTES LLC.

SPARK PUBLISHING
120 FIFTH AVENUE
NEW YORK, NY 10011
WWW.SPARKNOTES.COM

ISBN: 978-1-4114-9874-7

LIBRARY OF CONGRESS CATALOGING-IN-PUBLICATION DATA

WIEGLE, MATT, 1978-
  ROMEO & JULIET / [ILLUSTRATED BY MATT WIEGLE].
    P. CM.—(NO FEAR SHAKESPEARE GRAPHIC NOVELS)
  ADAPTATION OF ROMEO AND JULIET BY WILLIAM SHAKESPEARE.
  ISBN: 978-1-4114-9874-7
  1. GRAPHIC NOVELS. I. SHAKESPEARE, WILLIAM, 1564-1616. ROMEO AND JULIET. II. TITLE.
PN6727.W4555R66 2008
741.5'973DC22

                                                        2007061805

PLEASE SUBMIT CHANGES OR REPORT ERRORS TO WWW.SPARKNOTES.COM/ERRORS.

PRINTED AND BOUND IN THE UNITED STATES OF AMERICA

20 19 18 17

ACKNOWLEDGMENTS

THANKS TO THE FOLLOWING PEOPLE AND INSTITUTIONS: KATE; PARTYKA; JOHN M.; NINA, JOHN C., AND KEVIN AT SPARKNOTES; THE BROOKLYN LIBRARY AND THE GREEN VALLEY BOOK FAIR FOR REFERENCE MATERIAL (ALSO, THE INTERNET... THANKS, THE INTERNET); AND CAROL AND HERB, WHO REARED ME.

Characters

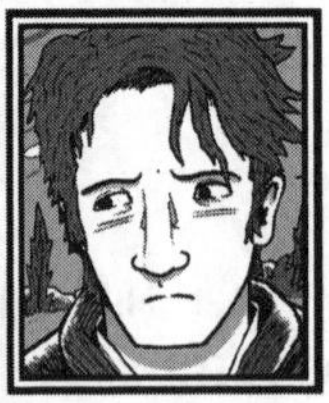

ROMEO:
THE SON OF MONTAGUE AND LADY MONTAGUE

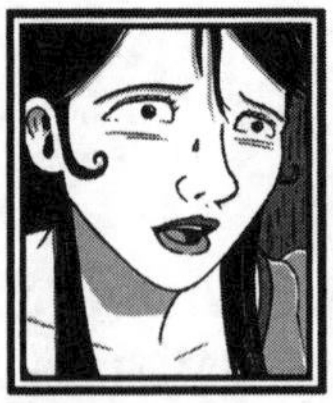

JULIET:
THE DAUGHTER OF CAPULET AND LADY CAPULET

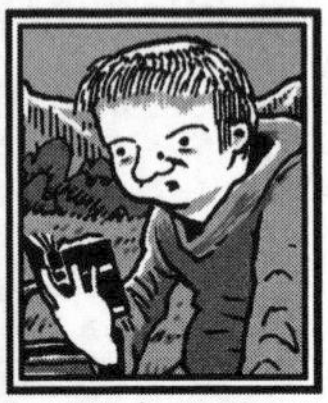

FRIAR LAWRENCE:
A FRANCISCAN FRIAR, FRIEND TO BOTH ROMEO AND JULIET

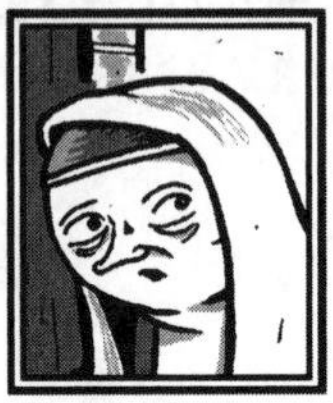

NURSE:
JULIET'S NURSE

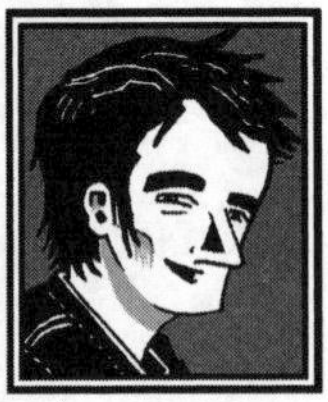

MERCUTIO:
A KINSMAN TO THE PRINCE, AND ROMEO'S CLOSE FRIEND

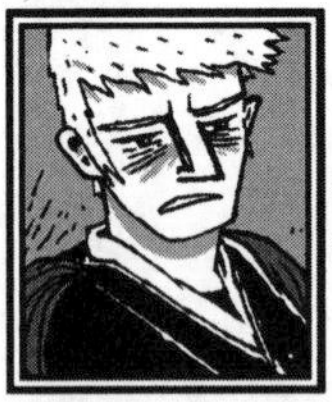

TYBALT:
CAPULET, JULIET'S COUSIN ON HER MOTHER'S SIDE

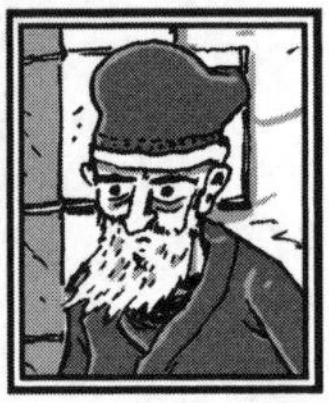

MONTAGUE:
THE PATRIARCH OF THE MONTAGUE FAMILY

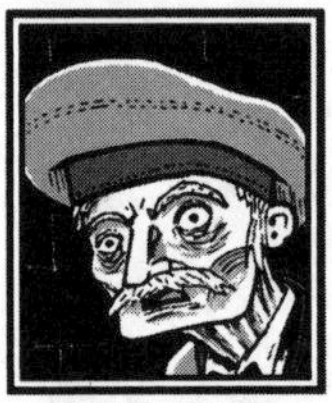

CAPULET:
THE PATRIARCH OF THE CAPULET FAMILY

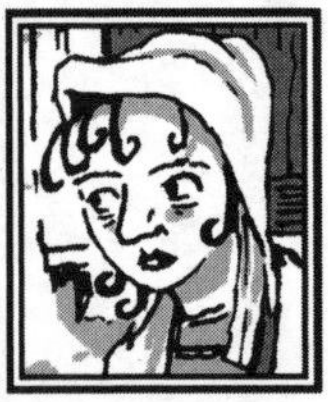

LADY MONTAGUE:
ROMEO'S MOTHER, MONTAGUE'S WIFE

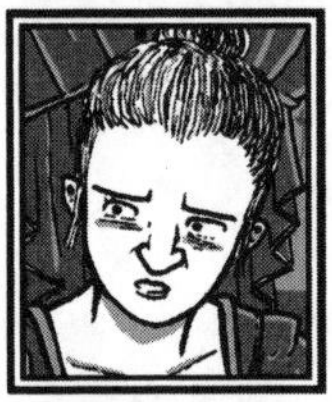

LADY CAPULET:
JULIET'S MOTHER, CAPULET'S WIFE

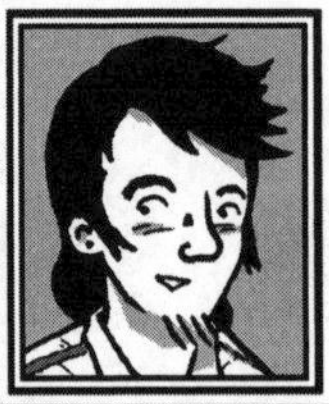

BENVOLIO:
MONTAGUE'S NEPHEW, ROMEO'S COUSIN AND FRIEND

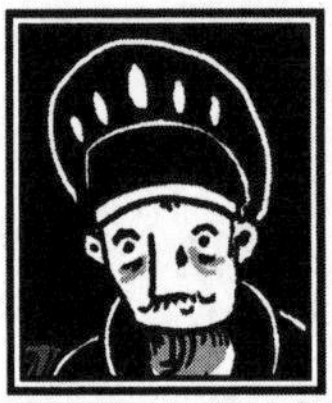

PARIS:
A KINSMAN OF THE PRINCE, AND THE SUITOR OF JULIET MOST PREFERRED BY CAPULET

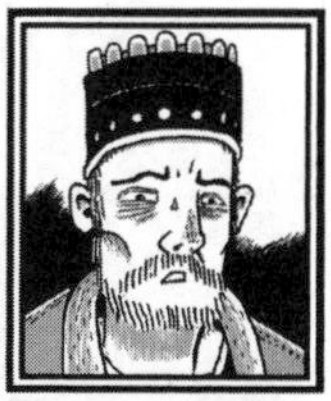

PRINCE ESCALUS:
THE PRINCE OF VERONA

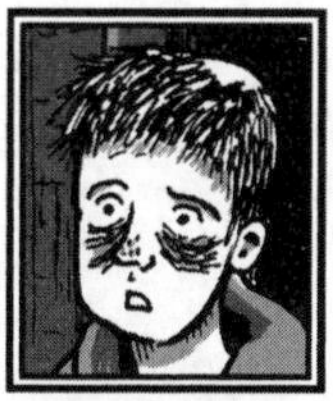

FRIAR JOHN:
A FRANCISCAN FRIAR

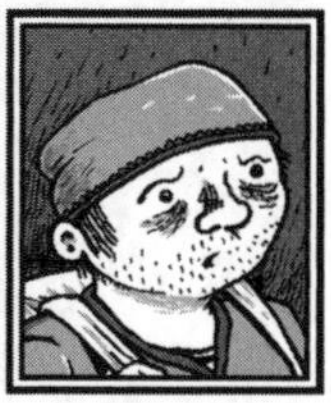

BALTHASAR:
ROMEO'S SERVANT

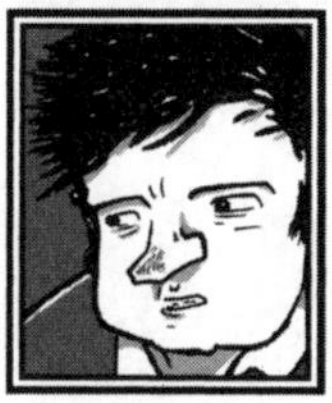

SAMPSON:
A CAPULET SERVANT

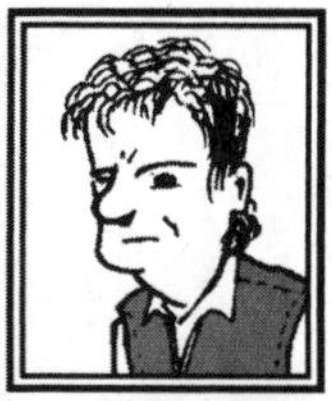

ABRAHAM:
A MONTAGUE SERVANT

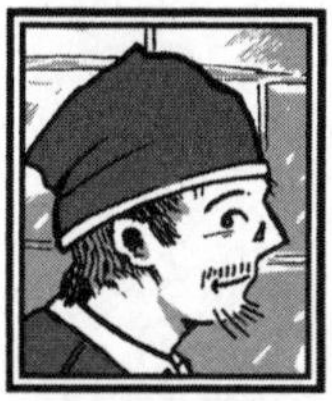

GREGORY:
A CAPULET SERVANT

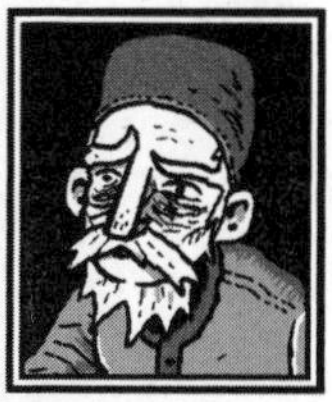

THE APOTHECARY:
A POOR APOTHECARY IN MANTUA

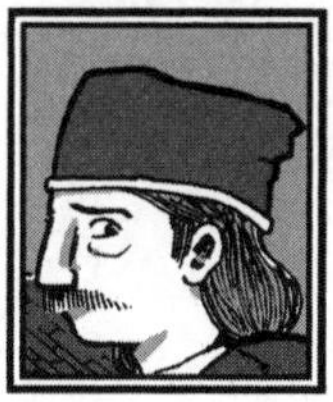

PETER:
A CAPULET SERVANT

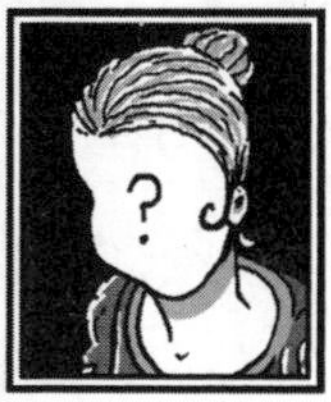

ROSALINE:
ROMEO'S BELOVED BEFORE JULIET

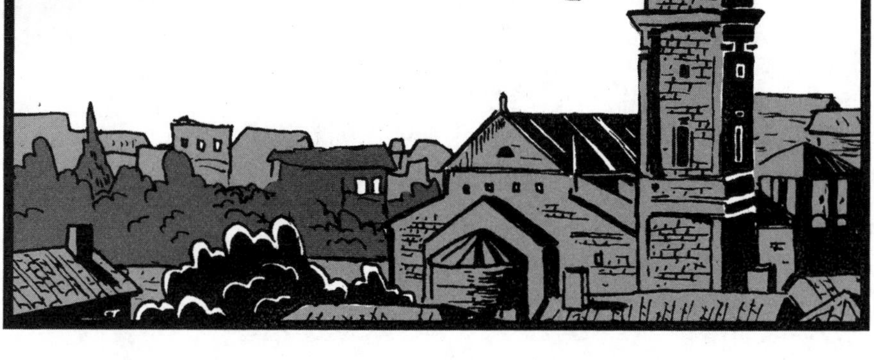

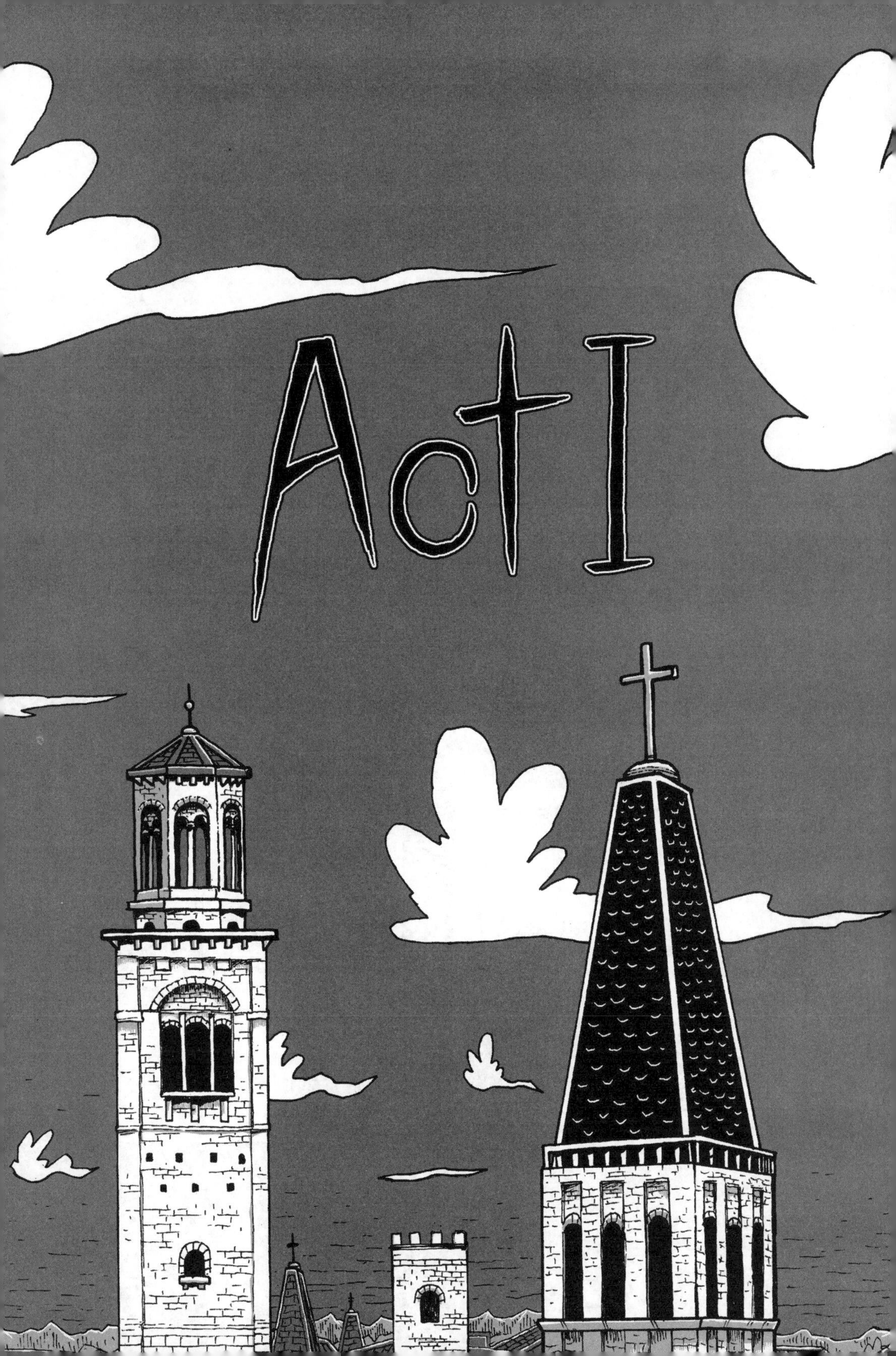
Act I

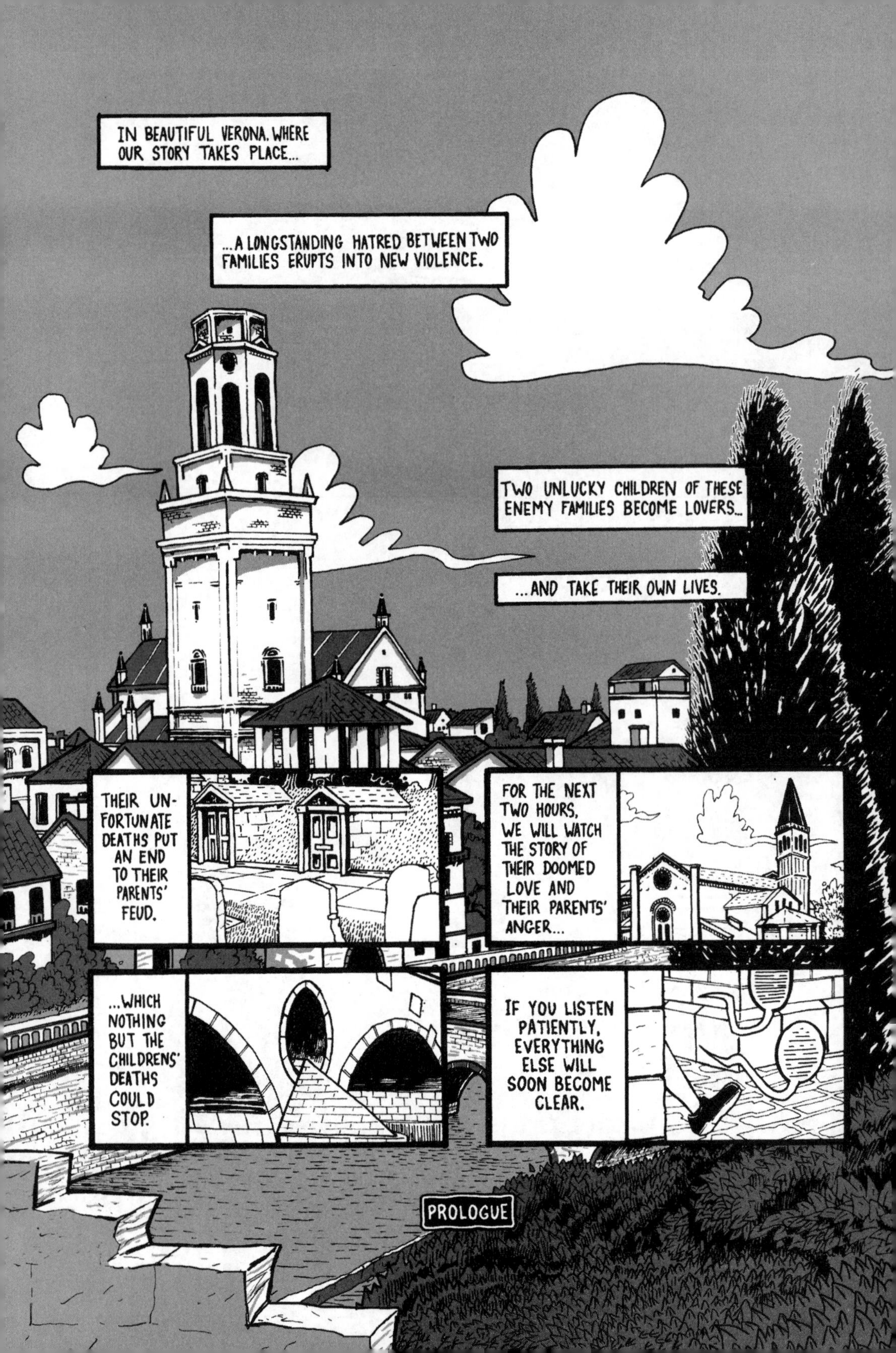
IN BEAUTIFUL VERONA, WHERE OUR STORY TAKES PLACE...
...A LONGSTANDING HATRED BETWEEN TWO FAMILIES ERUPTS INTO NEW VIOLENCE.
TWO UNLUCKY CHILDREN OF THESE ENEMY FAMILIES BECOME LOVERS...
...AND TAKE THEIR OWN LIVES.
THEIR UNFORTUNATE DEATHS PUT AN END TO THEIR PARENTS' FEUD.
FOR THE NEXT TWO HOURS, WE WILL WATCH THE STORY OF THEIR DOOMED LOVE AND THEIR PARENTS' ANGER...
...WHICH NOTHING BUT THE CHILDRENS' DEATHS COULD STOP.
IF YOU LISTEN PATIENTLY, EVERYTHING ELSE WILL SOON BECOME CLEAR.
PROLOGUE

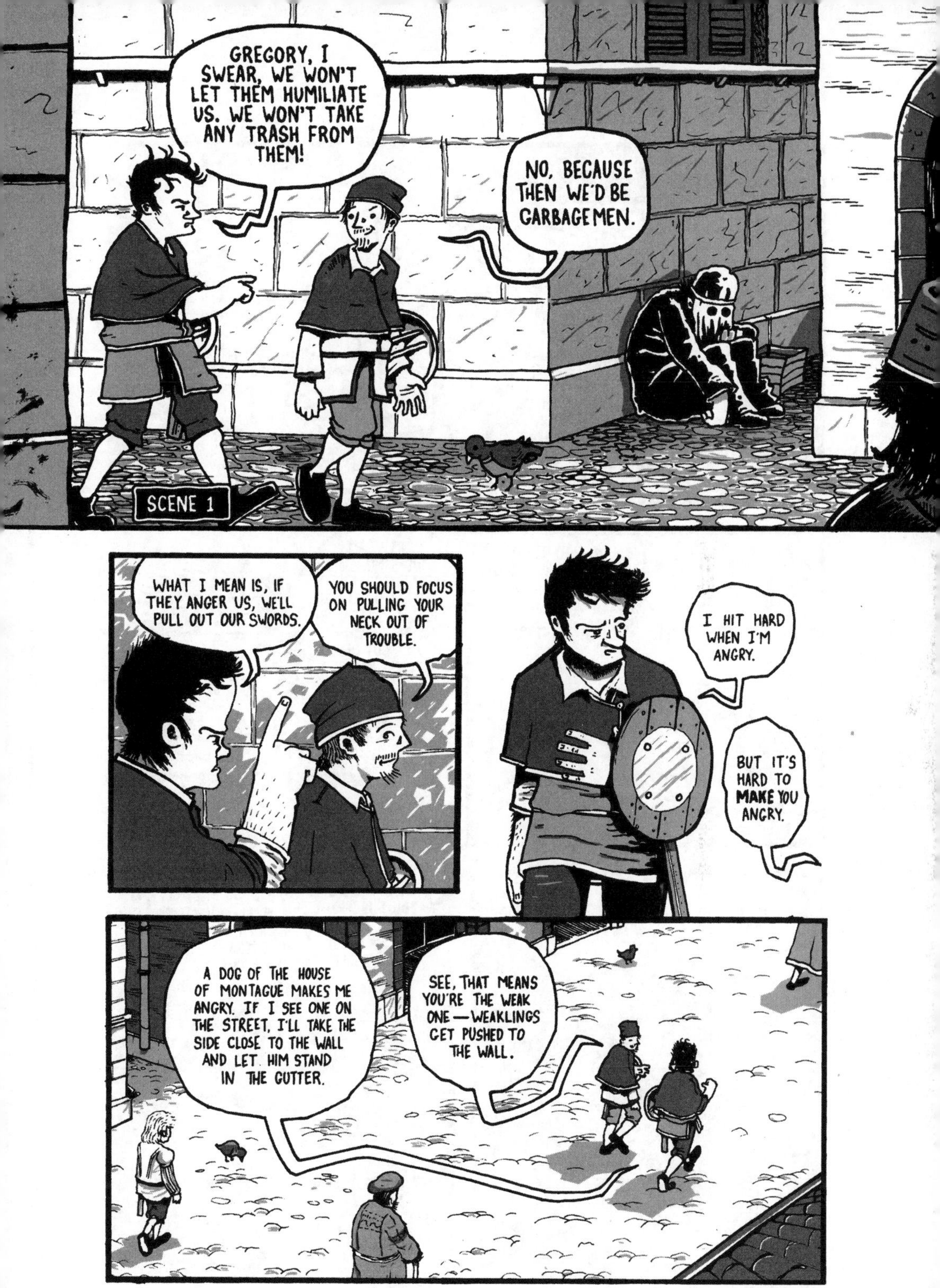
GREGORY, I SWEAR, WE WON'T LET THEM HUMILIATE US. WE WON'T TAKE ANY TRASH FROM THEM!
NO, BECAUSE THEN WE'D BE GARBAGEMEN.
SCENE 1
WHAT I MEAN IS, IF THEY ANGER US, WE'LL PULL OUT OUR SWORDS.
YOU SHOULD FOCUS ON PULLING YOUR NECK OUT OF TROUBLE.
I HIT HARD WHEN I'M ANGRY.
BUT IT'S HARD TO MAKE YOU ANGRY.
A DOG OF THE HOUSE OF MONTAGUE MAKES ME ANGRY. IF I SEE ONE ON THE STREET, I'LL TAKE THE SIDE CLOSE TO THE WALL AND LET HIM STAND IN THE GUTTER.
SEE, THAT MEANS YOU'RE THE WEAK ONE — WEAKLINGS GET PUSHED TO THE WALL.

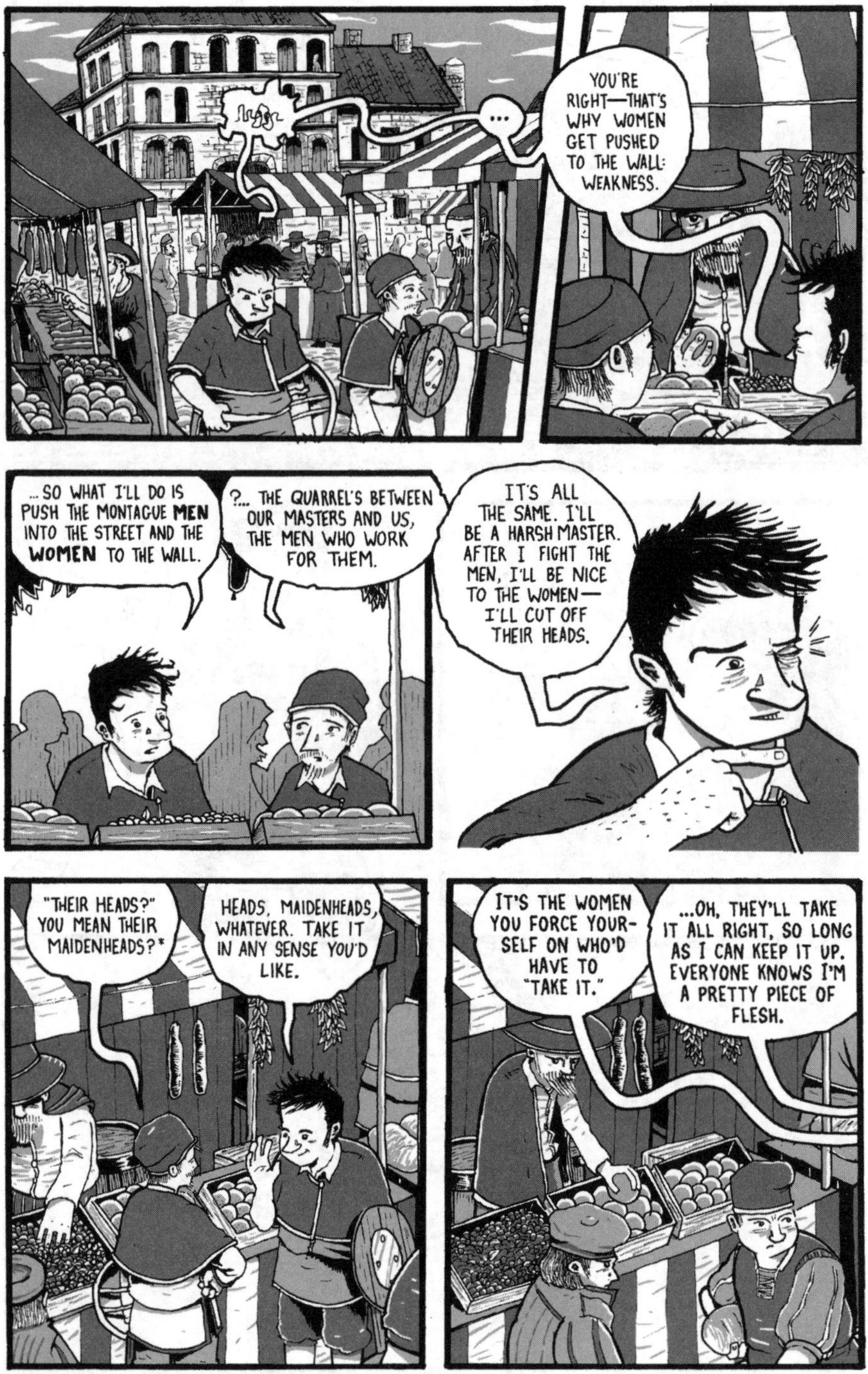
YOU'RE RIGHT—THAT'S WHY WOMEN GET PUSHED TO THE WALL: WEAKNESS.
...SO WHAT I'LL DO IS PUSH THE MONTAGUE MEN INTO THE STREET AND THE WOMEN TO THE WALL.
?... THE QUARREL'S BETWEEN OUR MASTERS AND US, THE MEN WHO WORK FOR THEM.
IT'S ALL THE SAME. I'LL BE A HARSH MASTER. AFTER I FIGHT THE MEN, I'LL BE NICE TO THE WOMEN— I'LL CUT OFF THEIR HEADS.
"THEIR HEADS?" YOU MEAN THEIR MAIDENHEADS?*
HEADS, MAIDENHEADS, WHATEVER. TAKE IT IN ANY SENSE YOU'D LIKE.
IT'S THE WOMEN YOU FORCE YOURSELF ON WHO'D HAVE TO "TAKE IT."
...OH, THEY'LL TAKE IT ALL RIGHT, SO LONG AS I CAN KEEP IT UP. EVERYONE KNOWS I'M A PRETTY PIECE OF FLESH.

*MAIDENHEADS = VIRGINITY

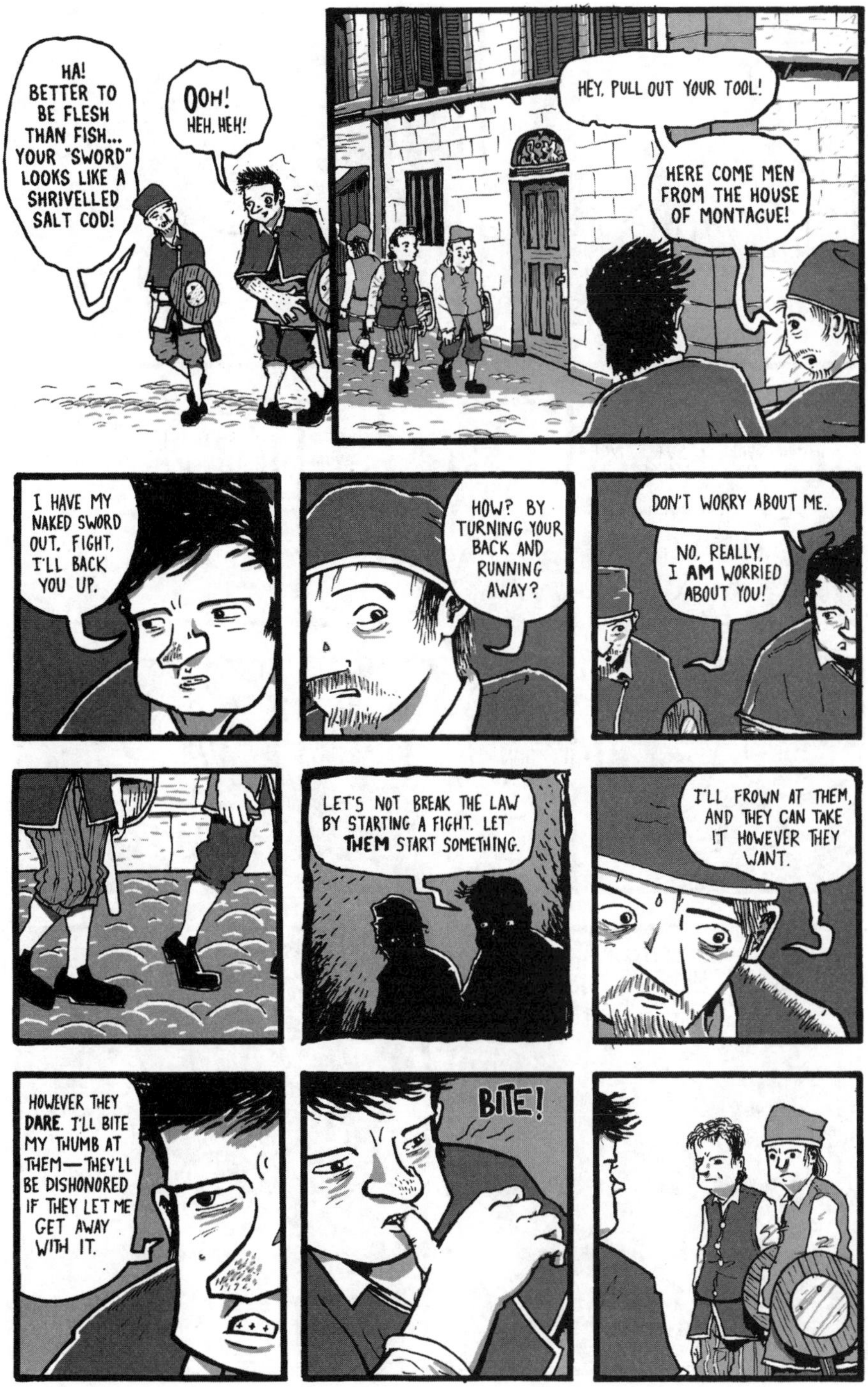
HA! BETTER TO BE FLESH THAN FISH... YOUR "SWORD" LOOKS LIKE A SHRIVELLED SALT COD!
OOH! HEH, HEH!
HEY, PULL OUT YOUR TOOL!
HERE COME MEN FROM THE HOUSE OF MONTAGUE!
I HAVE MY NAKED SWORD OUT. FIGHT, I'LL BACK YOU UP.
HOW? BY TURNING YOUR BACK AND RUNNING AWAY?
DON'T WORRY ABOUT ME.
NO, REALLY, I AM WORRIED ABOUT YOU!
LET'S NOT BREAK THE LAW BY STARTING A FIGHT. LET THEM START SOMETHING.
I'LL FROWN AT THEM, AND THEY CAN TAKE IT HOWEVER THEY WANT.
HOWEVER THEY DARE. I'LL BITE MY THUMB AT THEM—THEY'LL BE DISHONORED IF THEY LET ME GET AWAY WITH IT.
BITE!

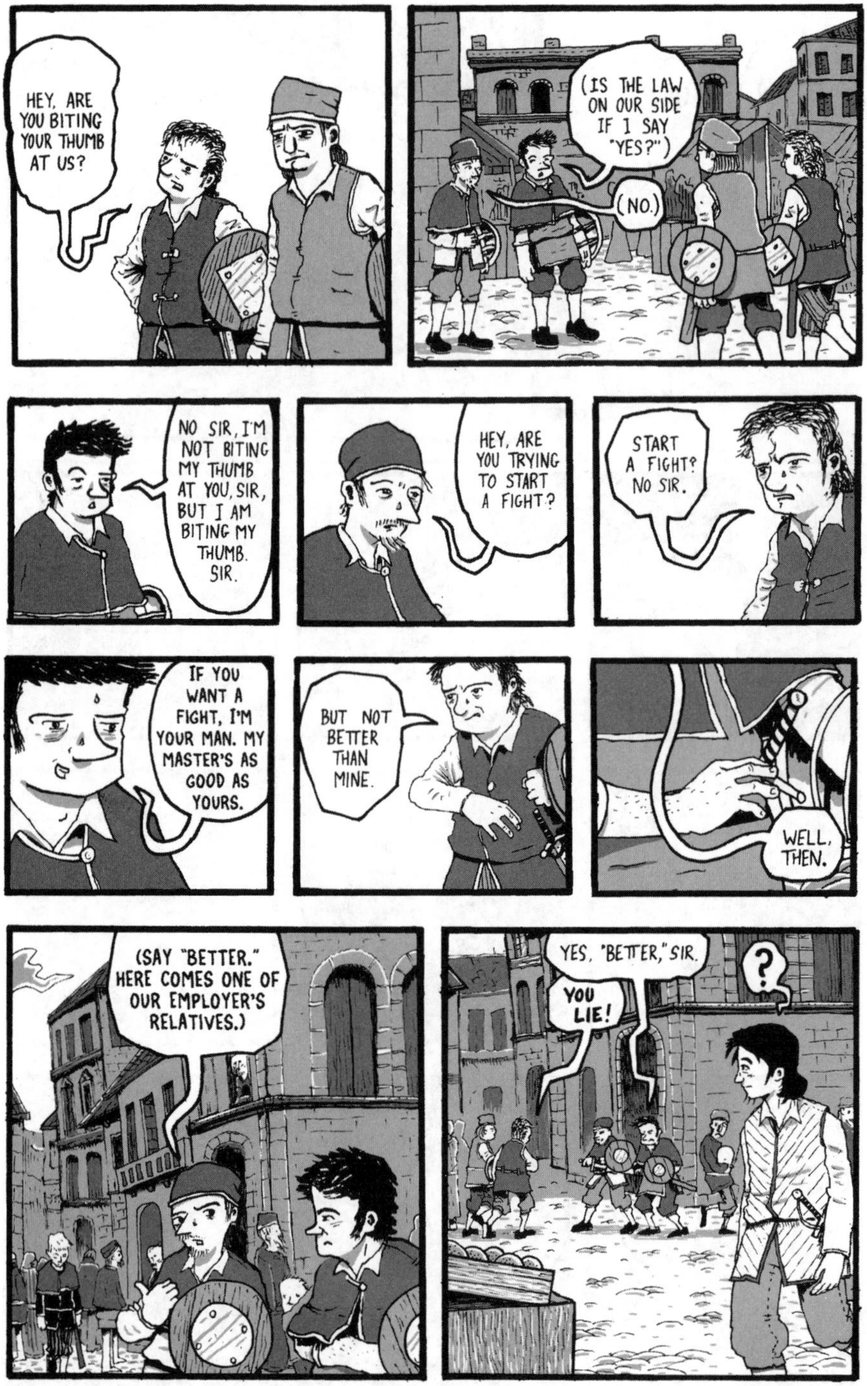
HEY, ARE YOU BITING YOUR THUMB AT US?
(IS THE LAW ON OUR SIDE IF I SAY "YES?")
(NO.)
NO SIR, I'M NOT BITING MY THUMB AT YOU, SIR, BUT I AM BITING MY THUMB. SIR.
HEY, ARE YOU TRYING TO START A FIGHT?
START A FIGHT? NO SIR.
IF YOU WANT A FIGHT, I'M YOUR MAN. MY MASTER'S AS GOOD AS YOURS.
BUT NOT BETTER THAN MINE.
WELL, THEN.
(SAY "BETTER." HERE COMES ONE OF OUR EMPLOYER'S RELATIVES.)
YES, "BETTER," SIR.
YOU LIE!
?

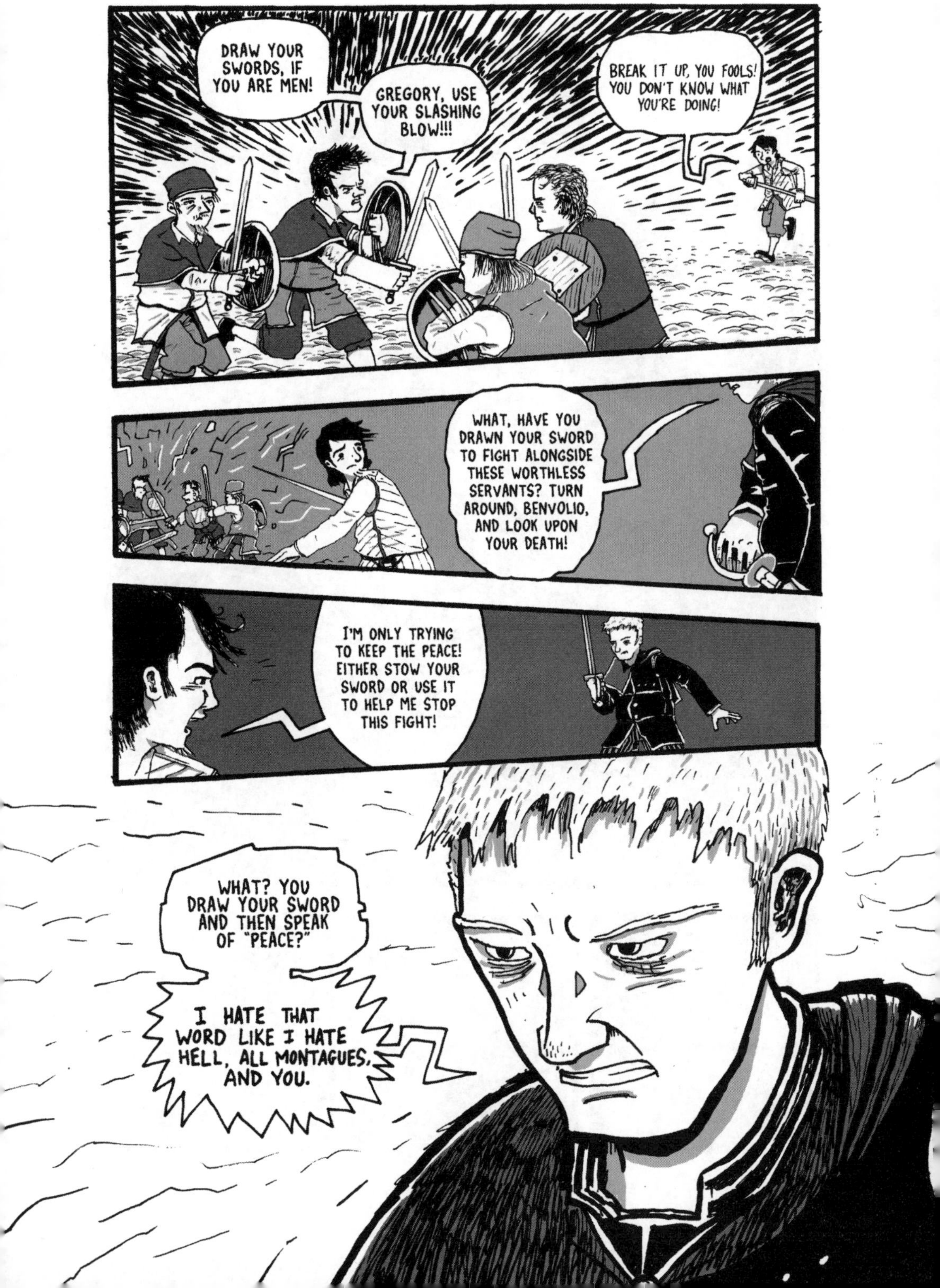
DRAW YOUR SWORDS, IF YOU ARE MEN!
GREGORY, USE YOUR SLASHING BLOW!!!
BREAK IT UP, YOU FOOLS! YOU DON'T KNOW WHAT YOU'RE DOING!
WHAT, HAVE YOU DRAWN YOUR SWORD TO FIGHT ALONGSIDE THESE WORTHLESS SERVANTS? TURN AROUND, BENVOLIO, AND LOOK UPON YOUR DEATH!
I'M ONLY TRYING TO KEEP THE PEACE! EITHER STOW YOUR SWORD OR USE IT TO HELP ME STOP THIS FIGHT!
WHAT? YOU DRAW YOUR SWORD AND THEN SPEAK OF "PEACE?"
I HATE THAT WORD LIKE I HATE HELL, ALL MONTAGUES, AND YOU.

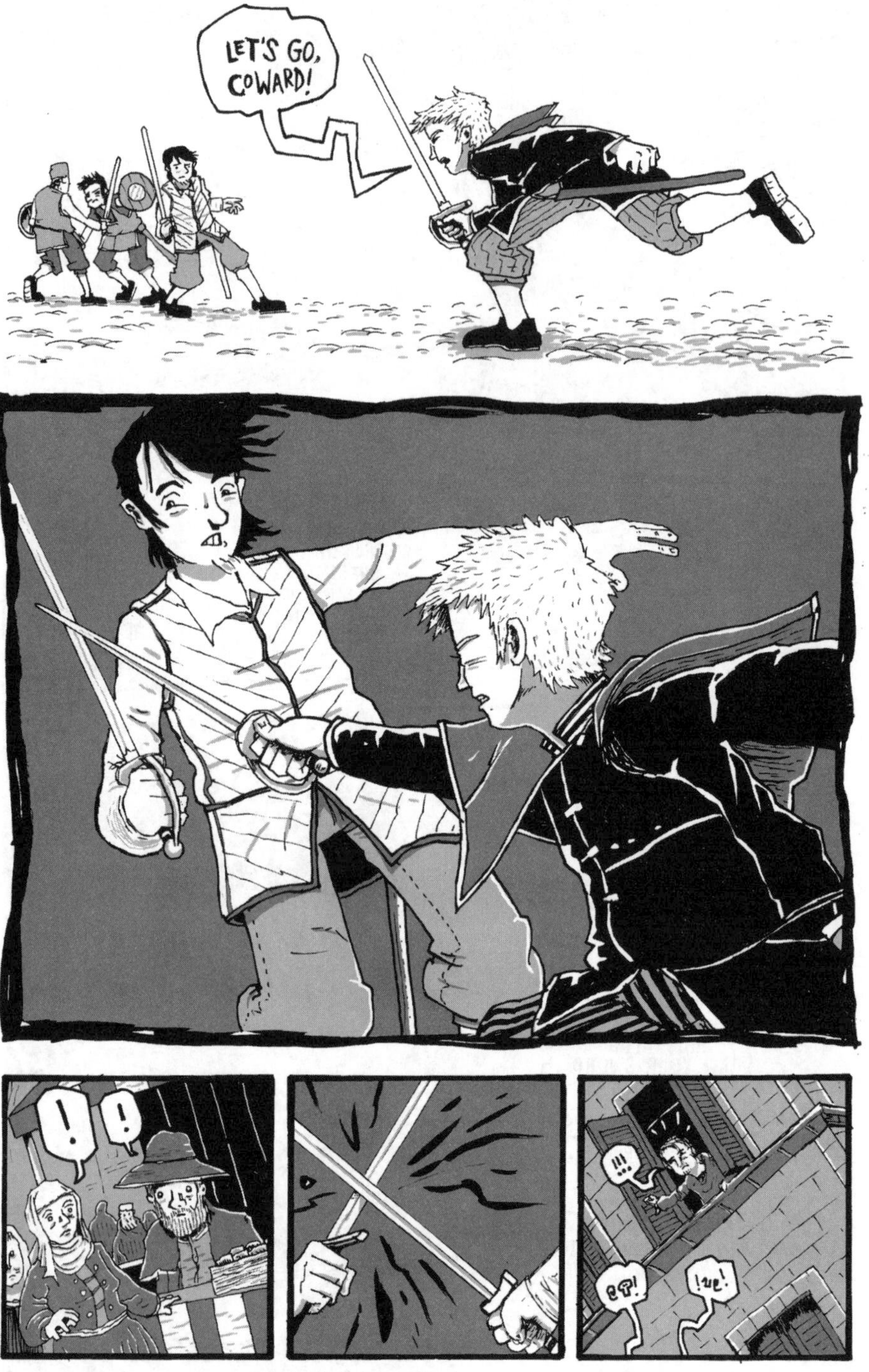
LET'S GO, COWARD!
!
!
!!!

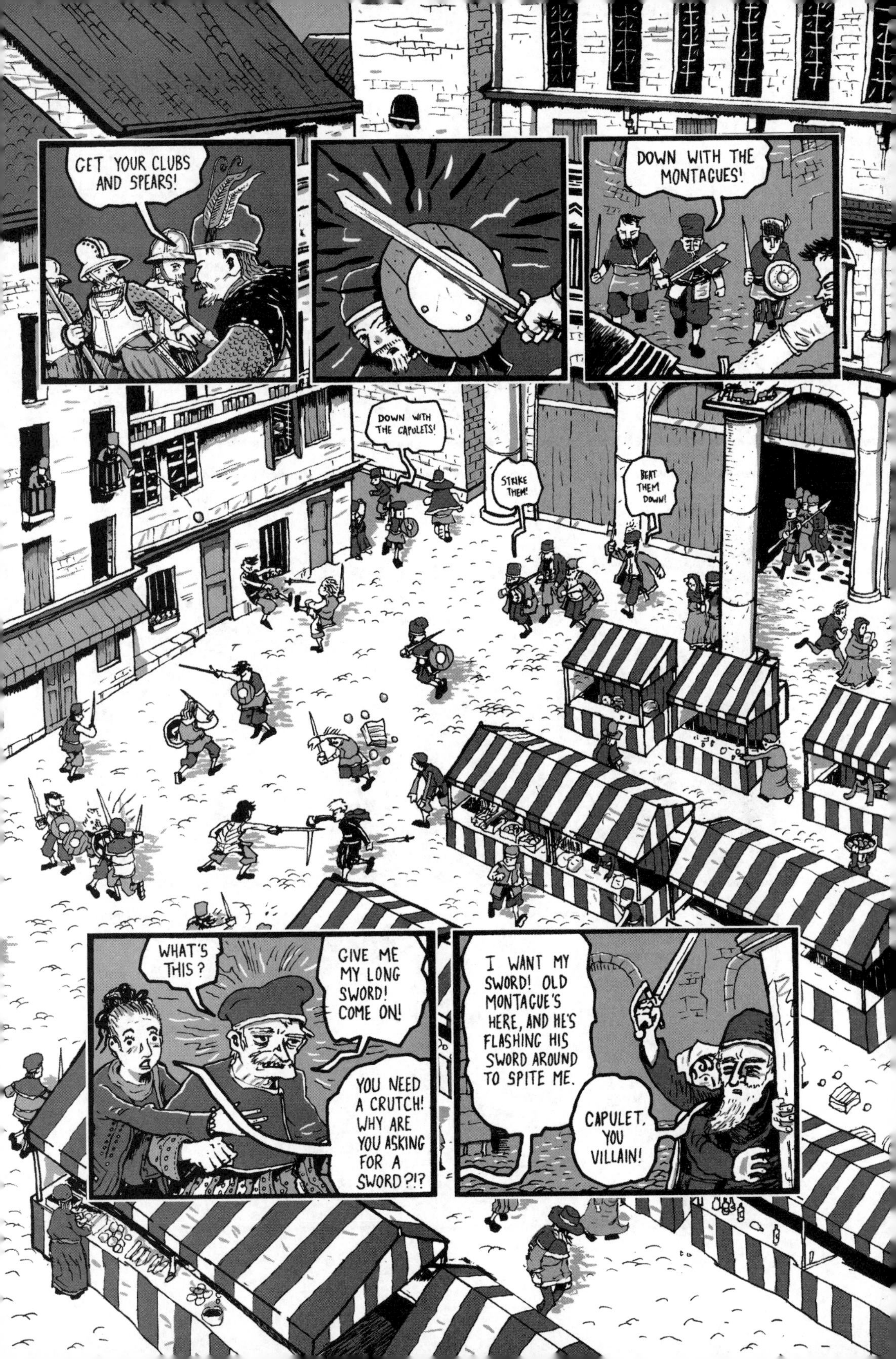
GET YOUR CLUBS AND SPEARS!
DOWN WITH THE MONTAGUES!
DOWN WITH THE CAPULETS!
STRIKE THEM!
BEAT THEM DOWN!
WHAT'S THIS?
GIVE ME MY LONG SWORD! COME ON!
YOU NEED A CRUTCH! WHY ARE YOU ASKING FOR A SWORD?!?
I WANT MY SWORD! OLD MONTAGUE'S HERE, AND HE'S FLASHING HIS SWORD AROUND TO SPITE ME.
CAPULET, YOU VILLAIN!

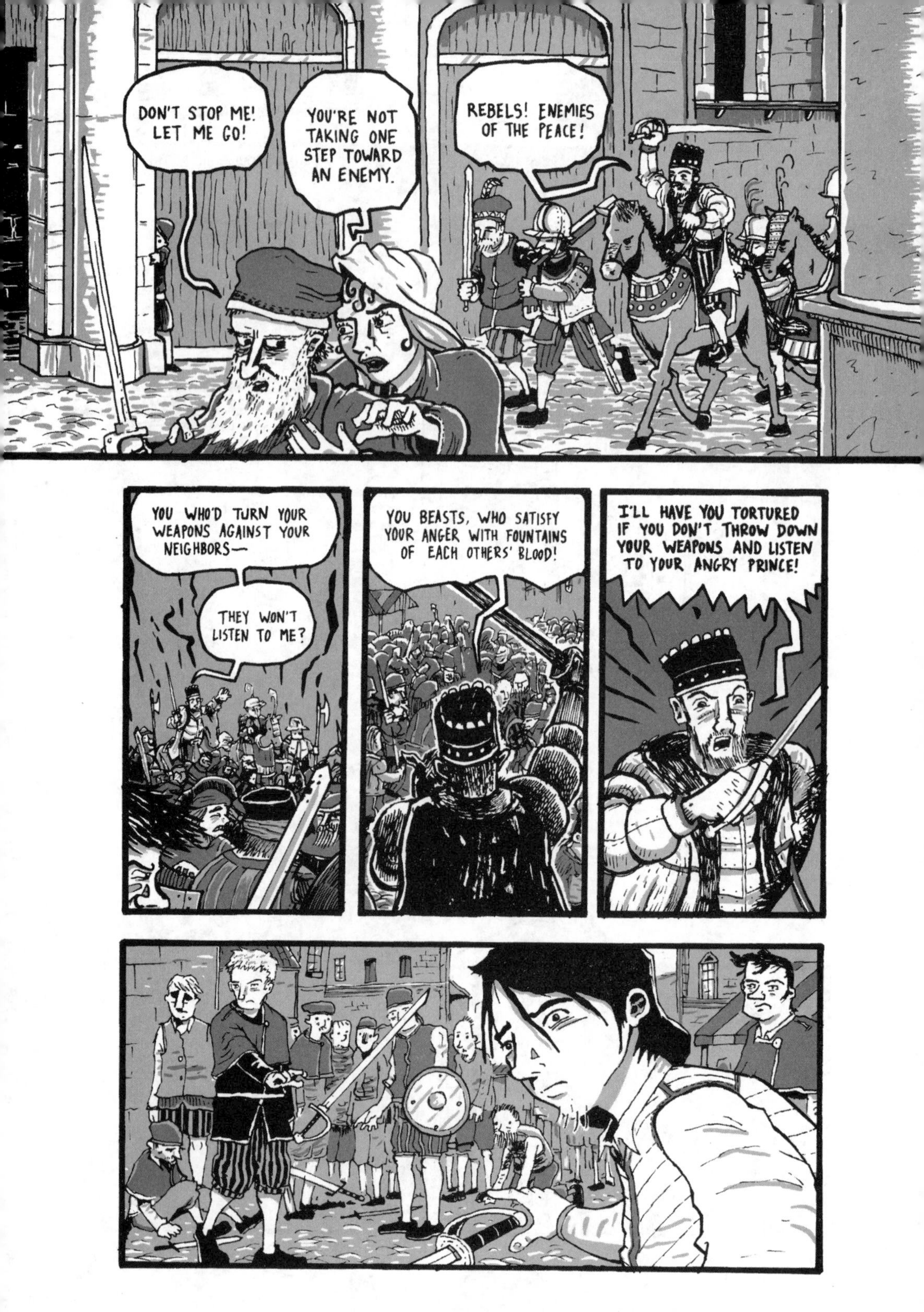
DON'T STOP ME! LET ME GO!
YOU'RE NOT TAKING ONE STEP TOWARD AN ENEMY.
REBELS! ENEMIES OF THE PEACE!
YOU WHO'D TURN YOUR WEAPONS AGAINST YOUR NEIGHBORS—
THEY WON'T LISTEN TO ME?
YOU BEASTS, WHO SATISFY YOUR ANGER WITH FOUNTAINS OF EACH OTHERS' BLOOD!
I'LL HAVE YOU TORTURED IF YOU DON'T THROW DOWN YOUR WEAPONS AND LISTEN TO YOUR ANGRY PRINCE!

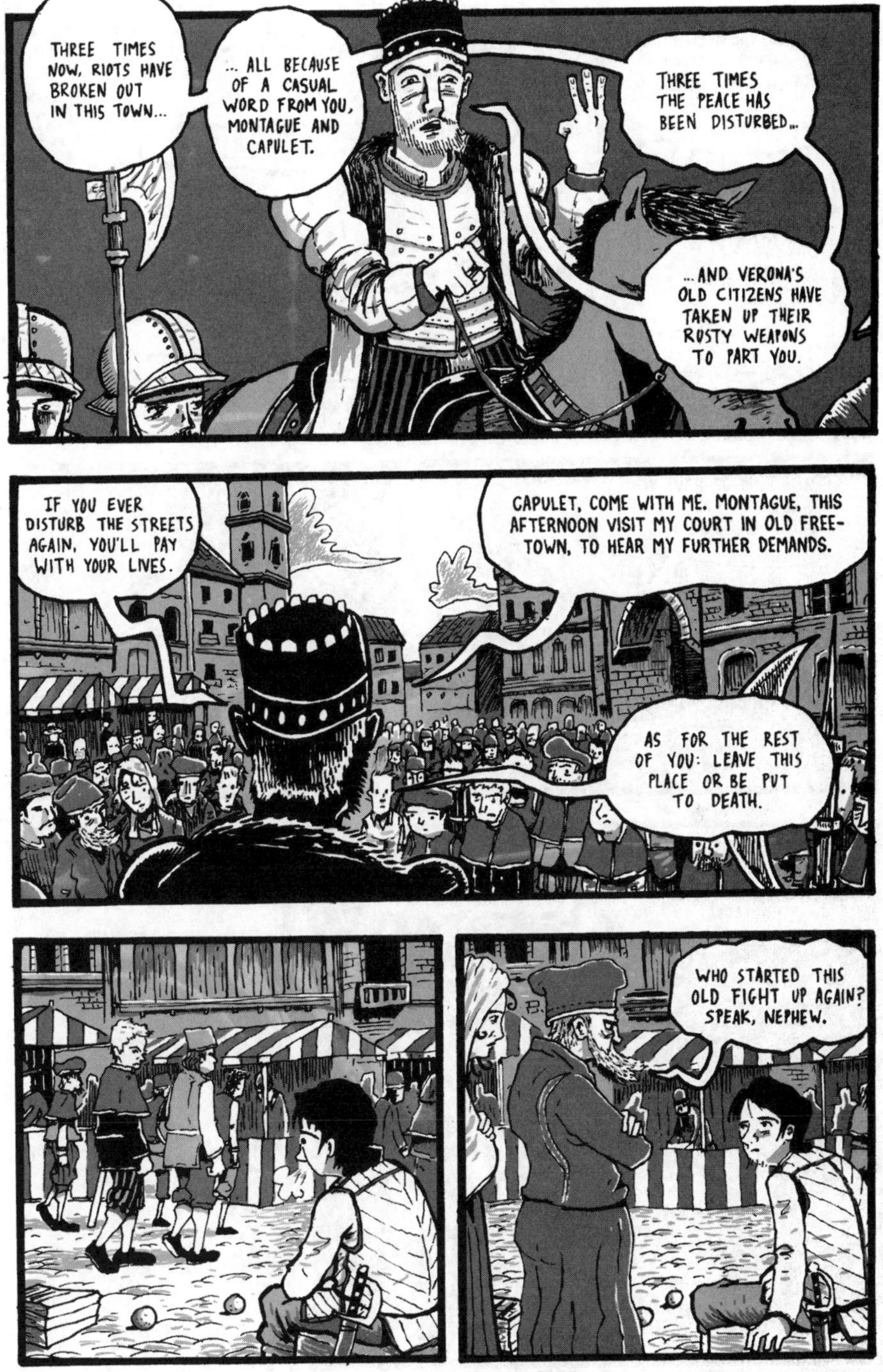
THREE TIMES NOW, RIOTS HAVE BROKEN OUT IN THIS TOWN...
... ALL BECAUSE OF A CASUAL WORD FROM YOU, MONTAGUE AND CAPULET.
THREE TIMES THE PEACE HAS BEEN DISTURBED...
...AND VERONA'S OLD CITIZENS HAVE TAKEN UP THEIR RUSTY WEAPONS TO PART YOU.
IF YOU EVER DISTURB THE STREETS AGAIN, YOU'LL PAY WITH YOUR LIVES.
CAPULET, COME WITH ME. MONTAGUE, THIS AFTERNOON VISIT MY COURT IN OLD FREE-TOWN, TO HEAR MY FURTHER DEMANDS.
AS FOR THE REST OF YOU: LEAVE THIS PLACE OR BE PUT TO DEATH.
WHO STARTED THIS OLD FIGHT UP AGAIN? SPEAK, NEPHEW.

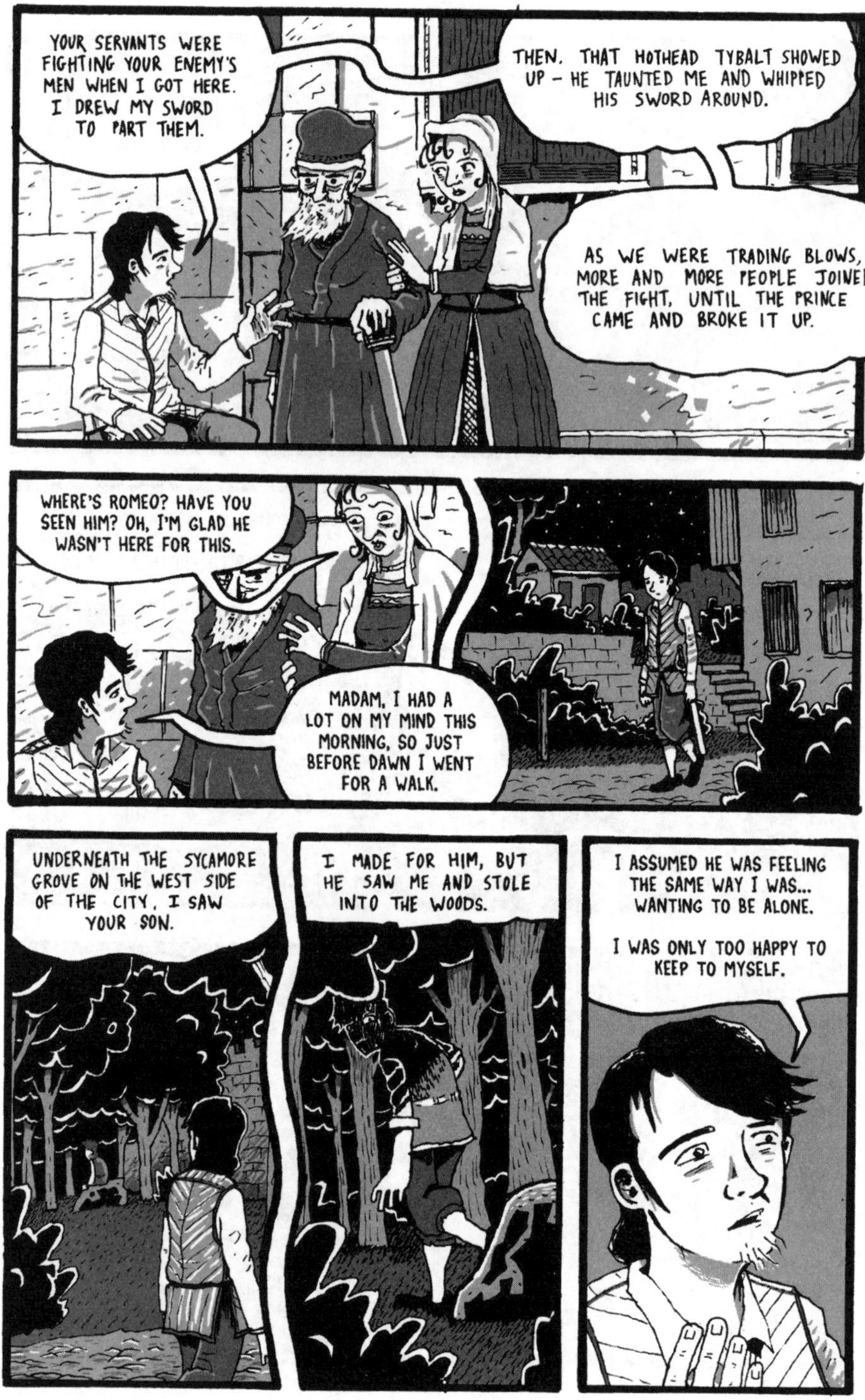
YOUR SERVANTS WERE FIGHTING YOUR ENEMY'S MEN WHEN I GOT HERE. I DREW MY SWORD TO PART THEM.
THEN, THAT HOTHEAD TYBALT SHOWED UP – HE TAUNTED ME AND WHIPPED HIS SWORD AROUND.
AS WE WERE TRADING BLOWS, MORE AND MORE PEOPLE JOINED THE FIGHT, UNTIL THE PRINCE CAME AND BROKE IT UP.
WHERE'S ROMEO? HAVE YOU SEEN HIM? OH, I'M GLAD HE WASN'T HERE FOR THIS.
MADAM, I HAD A LOT ON MY MIND THIS MORNING, SO JUST BEFORE DAWN I WENT FOR A WALK.
UNDERNEATH THE SYCAMORE GROVE ON THE WEST SIDE OF THE CITY, I SAW YOUR SON.
I MADE FOR HIM, BUT HE SAW ME AND STOLE INTO THE WOODS.
I ASSUMED HE WAS FEELING THE SAME WAY I WAS... WANTING TO BE ALONE.
I WAS ONLY TOO HAPPY TO KEEP TO MYSELF.

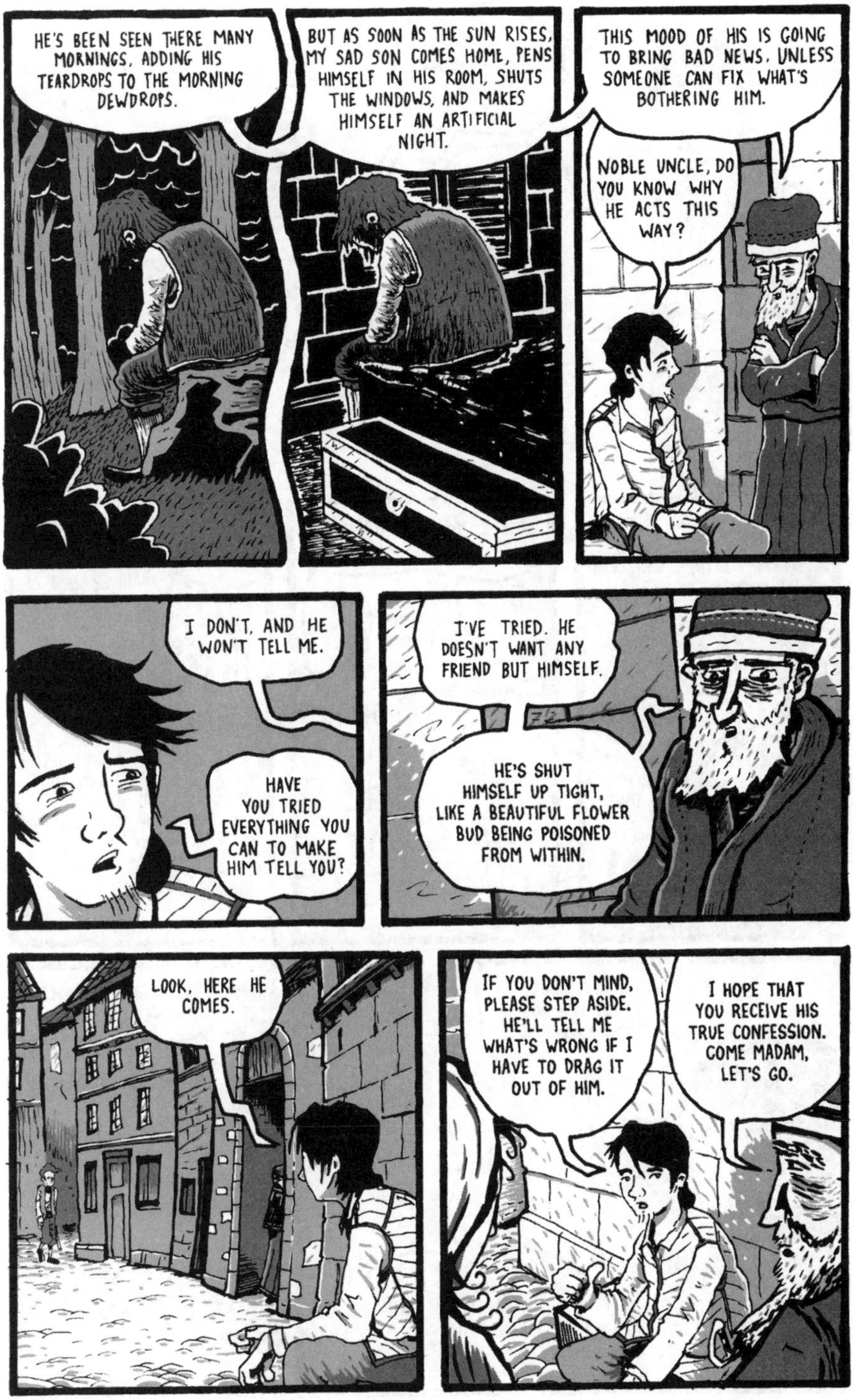
HE'S BEEN SEEN THERE MANY MORNINGS, ADDING HIS TEARDROPS TO THE MORNING DEWDROPS.
BUT AS SOON AS THE SUN RISES, MY SAD SON COMES HOME, PENS HIMSELF IN HIS ROOM, SHUTS THE WINDOWS, AND MAKES HIMSELF AN ARTIFICIAL NIGHT.
THIS MOOD OF HIS IS GOING TO BRING BAD NEWS. UNLESS SOMEONE CAN FIX WHAT'S BOTHERING HIM.
NOBLE UNCLE, DO YOU KNOW WHY HE ACTS THIS WAY?
I DON'T. AND HE WON'T TELL ME.
HAVE YOU TRIED EVERYTHING YOU CAN TO MAKE HIM TELL YOU?
I'VE TRIED. HE DOESN'T WANT ANY FRIEND BUT HIMSELF.
HE'S SHUT HIMSELF UP TIGHT, LIKE A BEAUTIFUL FLOWER BUD BEING POISONED FROM WITHIN.
LOOK, HERE HE COMES.
IF YOU DON'T MIND, PLEASE STEP ASIDE. HE'LL TELL ME WHAT'S WRONG IF I HAVE TO DRAG IT OUT OF HIM.
I HOPE THAT YOU RECEIVE HIS TRUE CONFESSION. COME MADAM, LET'S GO.

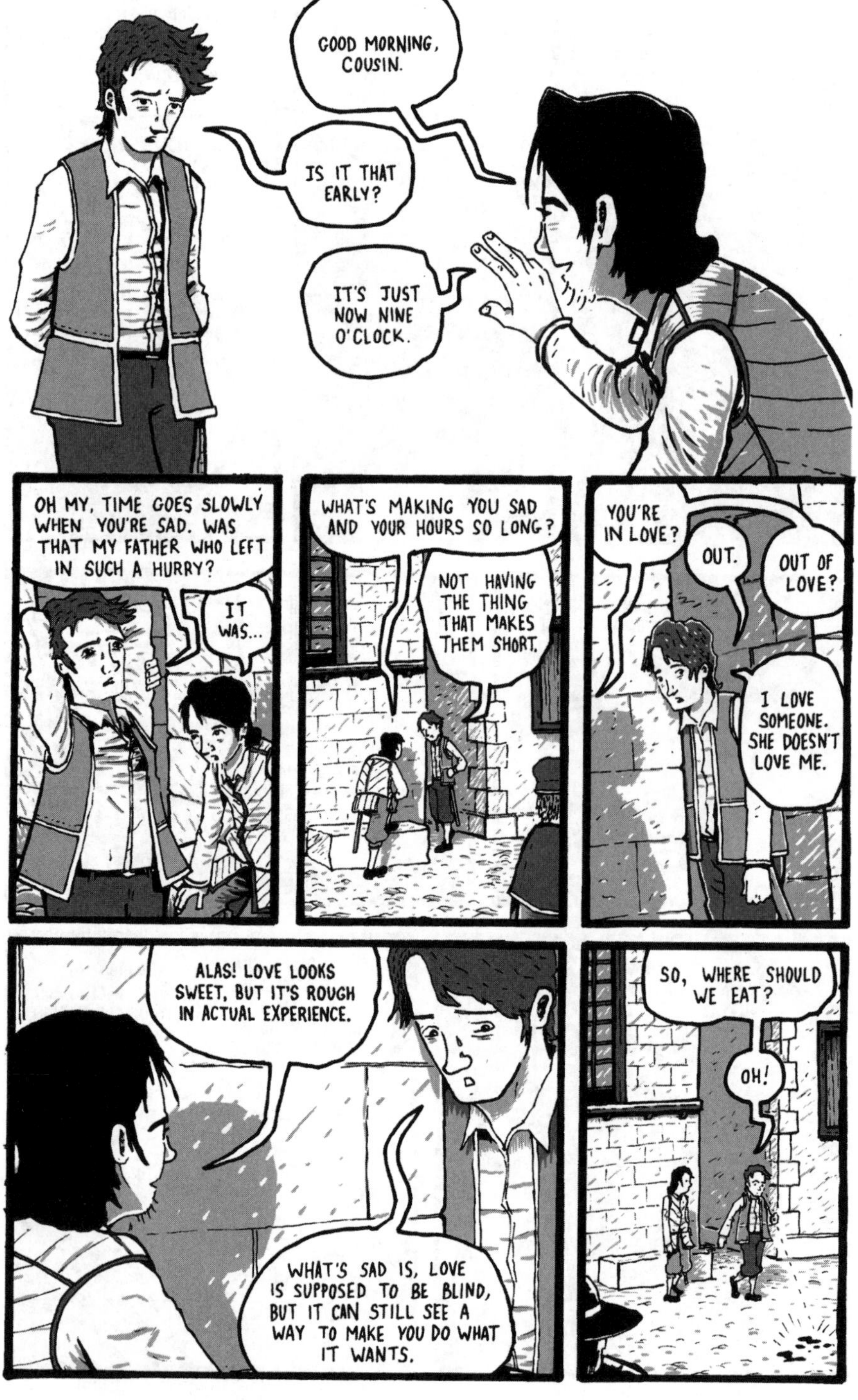
GOOD MORNING, COUSIN.
IS IT THAT EARLY?
IT'S JUST NOW NINE O'CLOCK.
OH MY, TIME GOES SLOWLY WHEN YOU'RE SAD. WAS THAT MY FATHER WHO LEFT IN SUCH A HURRY?
IT WAS...
WHAT'S MAKING YOU SAD AND YOUR HOURS SO LONG?
NOT HAVING THE THING THAT MAKES THEM SHORT.
YOU'RE IN LOVE?
OUT.
OUT OF LOVE?
I LOVE SOMEONE. SHE DOESN'T LOVE ME.
ALAS! LOVE LOOKS SWEET, BUT IT'S ROUGH IN ACTUAL EXPERIENCE.
WHAT'S SAD IS, LOVE IS SUPPOSED TO BE BLIND, BUT IT CAN STILL SEE A WAY TO MAKE YOU DO WHAT IT WANTS.
SO, WHERE SHOULD WE EAT?
OH!

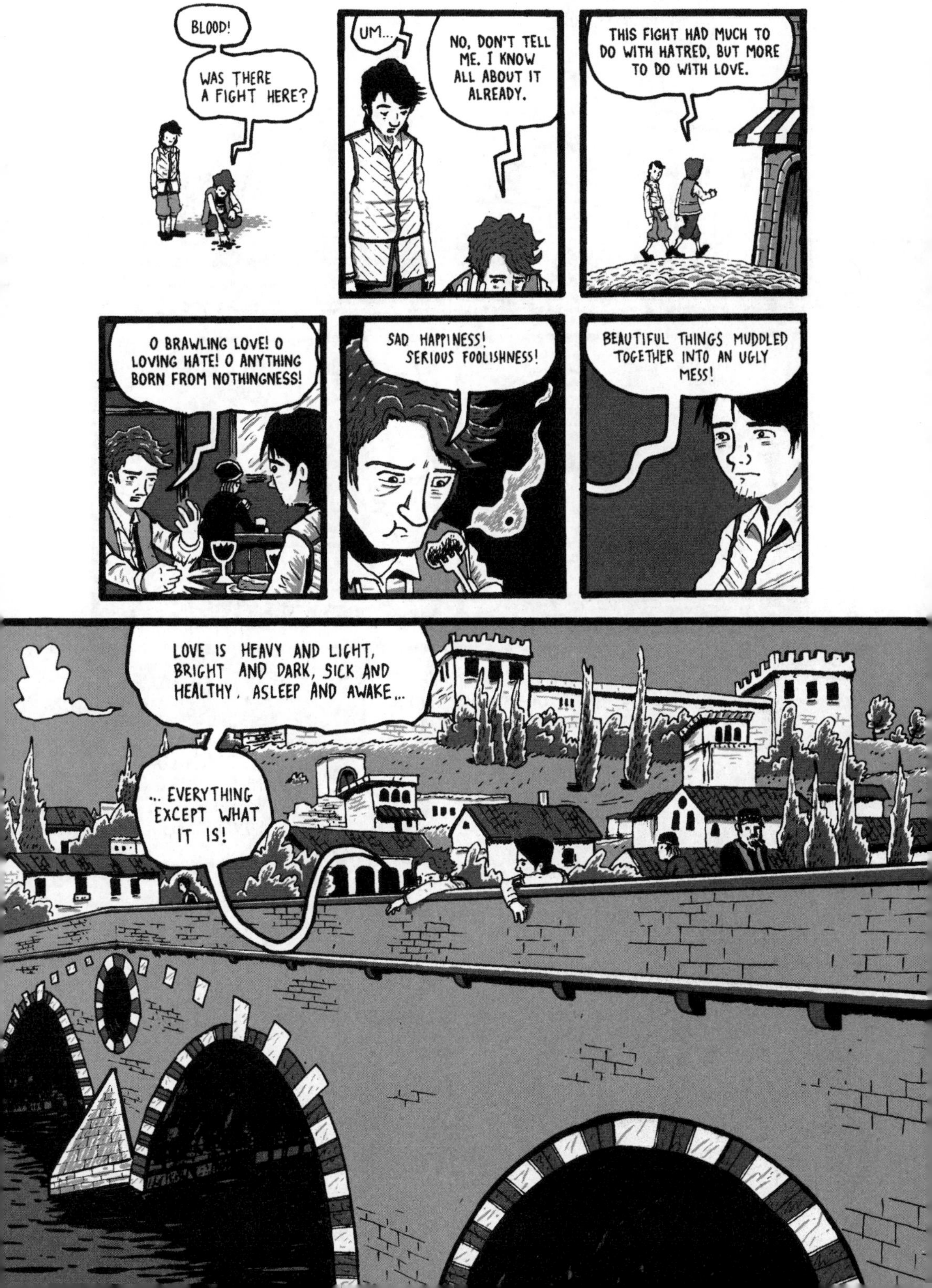
BLOOD!
WAS THERE A FIGHT HERE?
UM...
NO, DON'T TELL ME. I KNOW ALL ABOUT IT ALREADY.
THIS FIGHT HAD MUCH TO DO WITH HATRED, BUT MORE TO DO WITH LOVE.
O BRAWLING LOVE! O LOVING HATE! O ANYTHING BORN FROM NOTHINGNESS!
SAD HAPPINESS! SERIOUS FOOLISHNESS!
BEAUTIFUL THINGS MUDDLED TOGETHER INTO AN UGLY MESS!
LOVE IS HEAVY AND LIGHT, BRIGHT AND DARK, SICK AND HEALTHY, ASLEEP AND AWAKE...
... EVERYTHING EXCEPT WHAT IT IS!

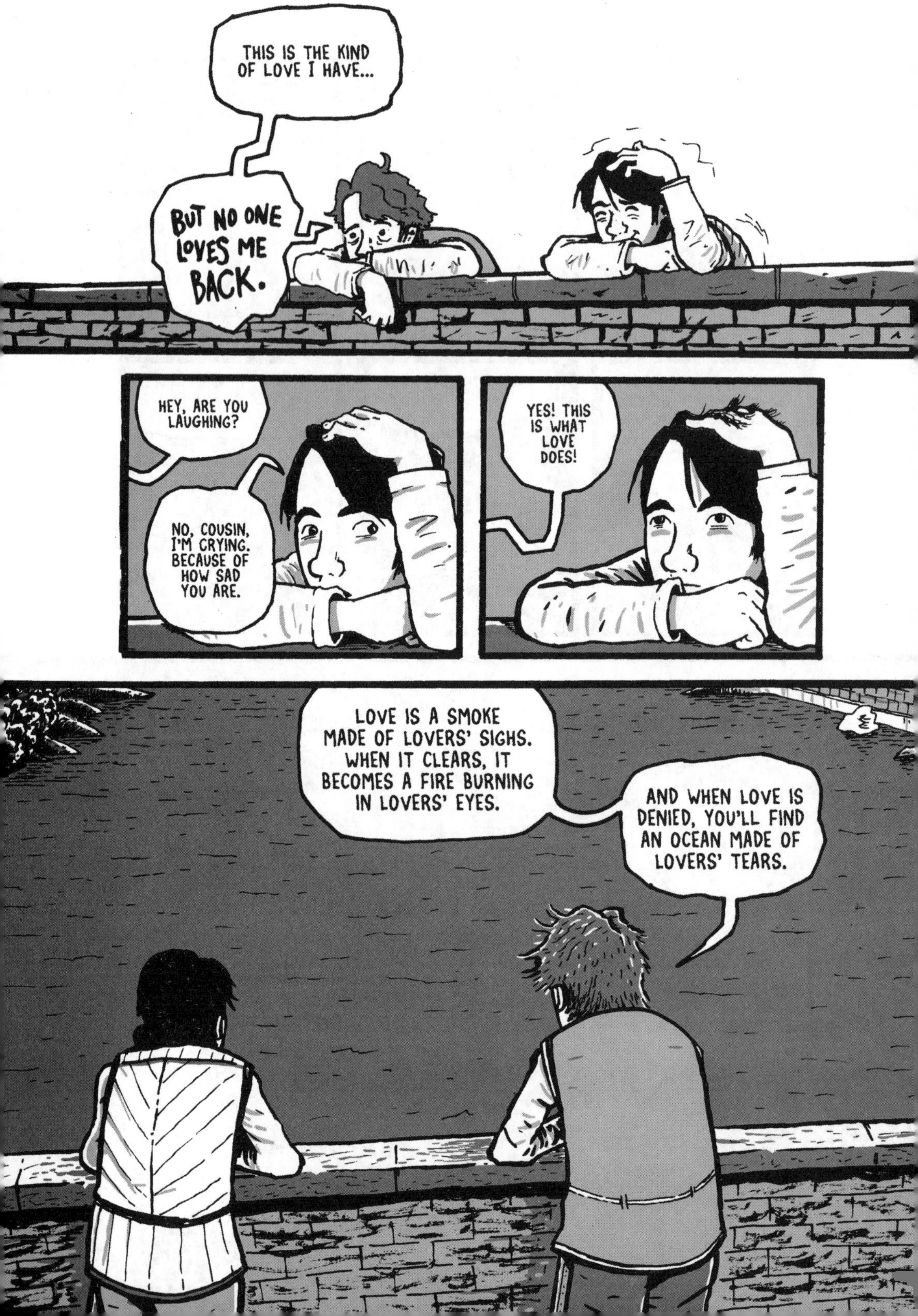
THIS IS THE KIND OF LOVE I HAVE...
BUT NO ONE LOVES ME BACK.
HEY, ARE YOU LAUGHING?
NO, COUSIN, I'M CRYING. BECAUSE OF HOW SAD YOU ARE.
YES! THIS IS WHAT LOVE DOES!
LOVE IS A SMOKE MADE OF LOVERS' SIGHS. WHEN IT CLEARS, IT BECOMES A FIRE BURNING IN LOVERS' EYES.
AND WHEN LOVE IS DENIED, YOU'LL FIND AN OCEAN MADE OF LOVERS' TEARS.

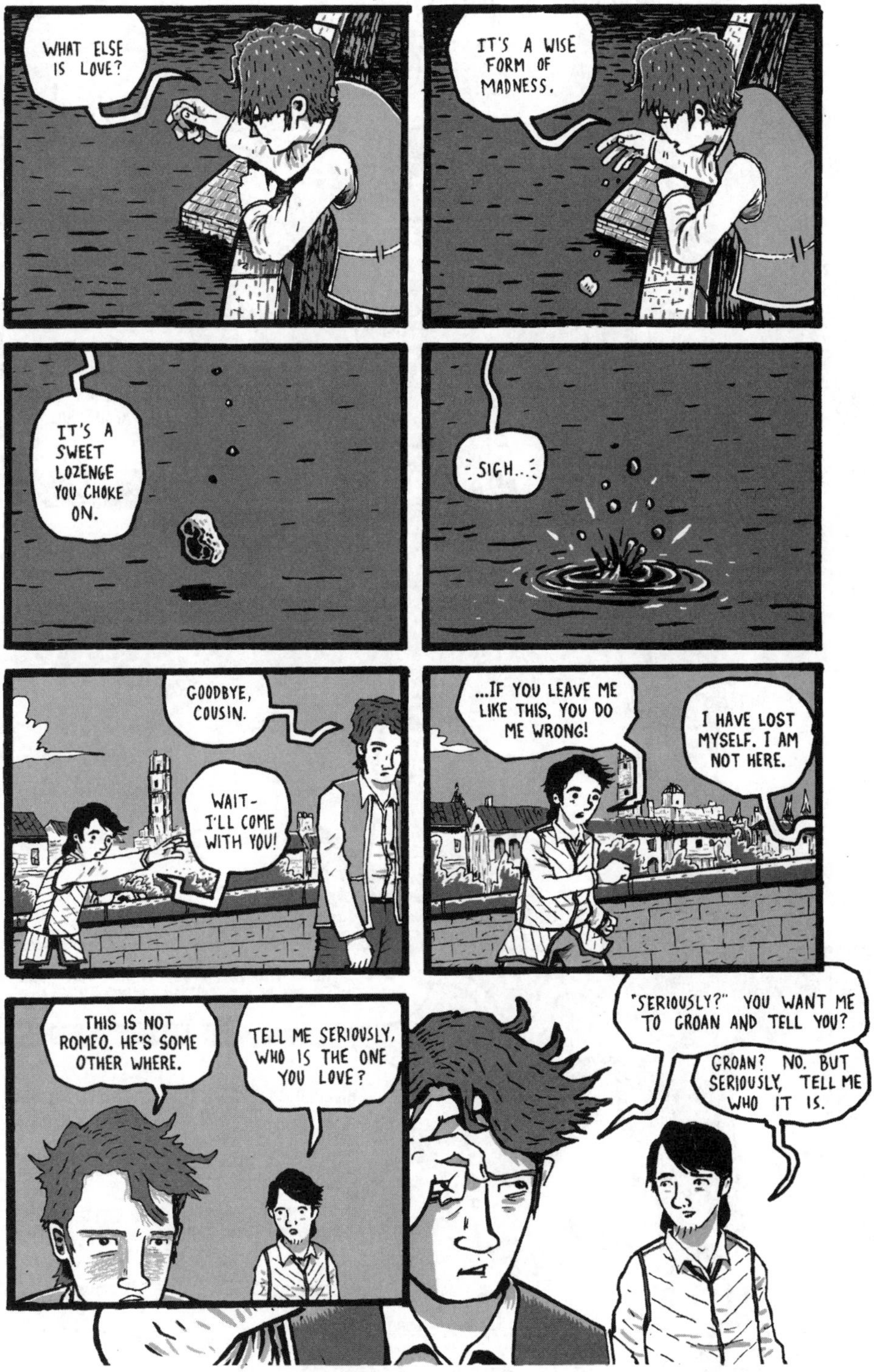
WHAT ELSE IS LOVE?
IT'S A WISE FORM OF MADNESS.
IT'S A SWEET LOZENGE YOU CHOKE ON.
SIGH...
GOODBYE, COUSIN.
WAIT- I'LL COME WITH YOU!
...IF YOU LEAVE ME LIKE THIS, YOU DO ME WRONG!
I HAVE LOST MYSELF. I AM NOT HERE.
THIS IS NOT ROMEO. HE'S SOME OTHER WHERE.
TELL ME SERIOUSLY, WHO IS THE ONE YOU LOVE?
"SERIOUSLY?" YOU WANT ME TO GROAN AND TELL YOU?
GROAN? NO. BUT SERIOUSLY, TELL ME WHO IT IS.

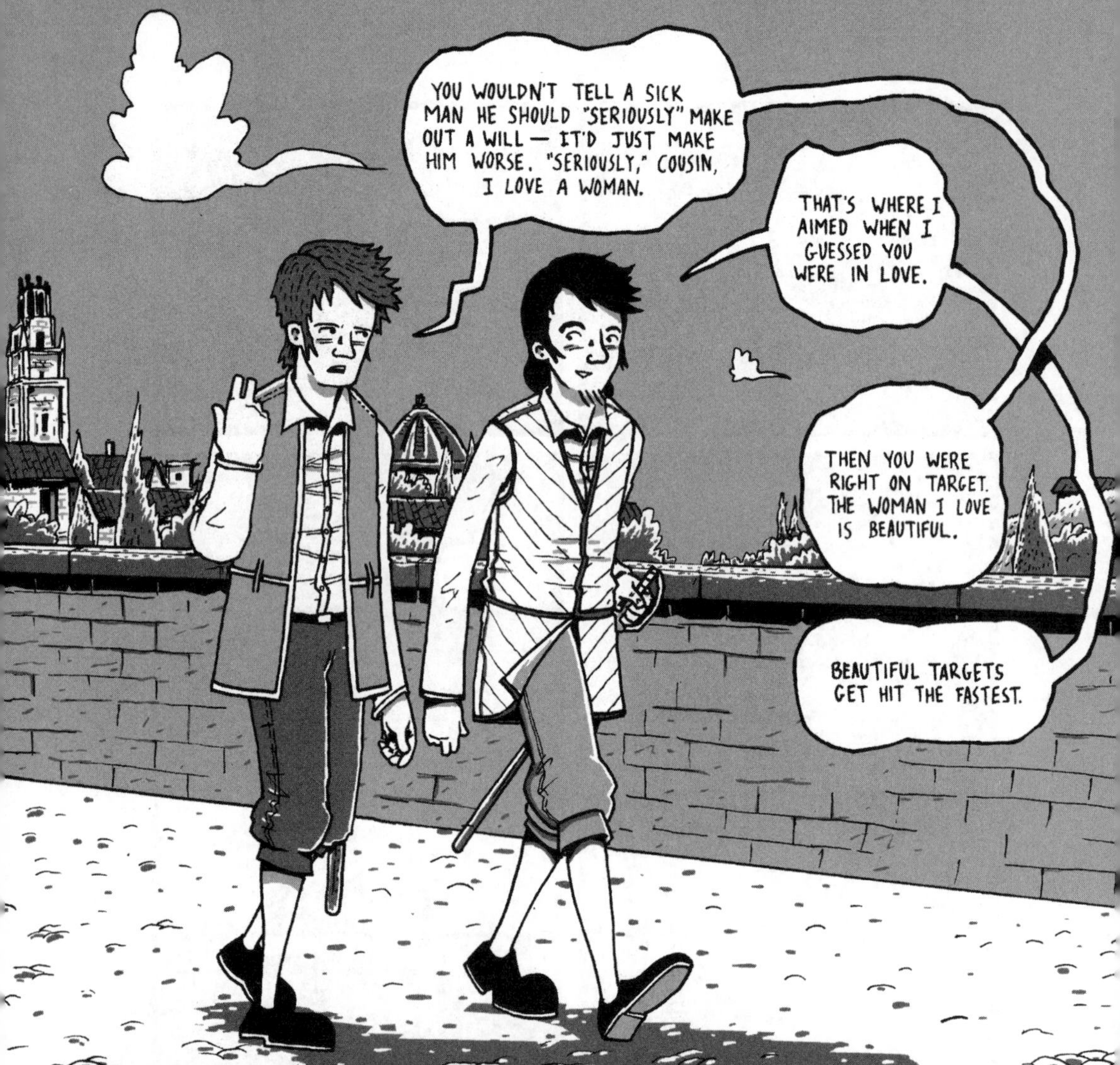
YOU WOULDN'T TELL A SICK MAN HE SHOULD "SERIOUSLY" MAKE OUT A WILL — IT'D JUST MAKE HIM WORSE. "SERIOUSLY," COUSIN, I LOVE A WOMAN.
THAT'S WHERE I AIMED WHEN I GUESSED YOU WERE IN LOVE.
THEN YOU WERE RIGHT ON TARGET. THE WOMAN I LOVE IS BEAUTIFUL.
BEAUTIFUL TARGETS GET HIT THE FASTEST.
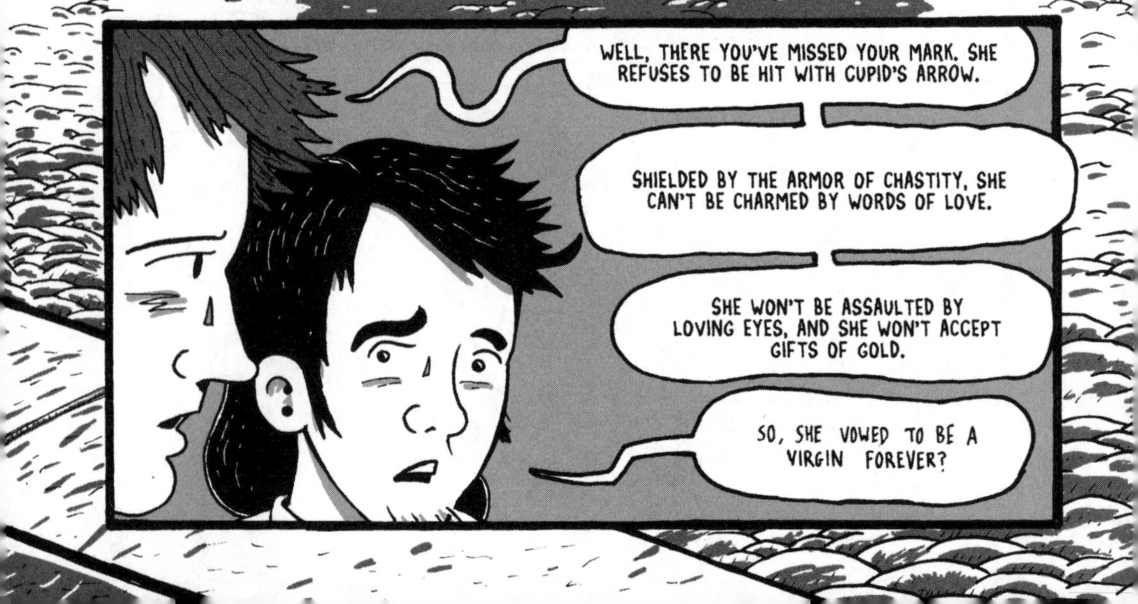
WELL, THERE YOU'VE MISSED YOUR MARK. SHE REFUSES TO BE HIT WITH CUPID'S ARROW.
SHIELDED BY THE ARMOR OF CHASTITY, SHE CAN'T BE CHARMED BY WORDS OF LOVE.
SHE WON'T BE ASSAULTED BY LOVING EYES, AND SHE WON'T ACCEPT GIFTS OF GOLD.
SO, SHE VOWED TO BE A VIRGIN FOREVER?

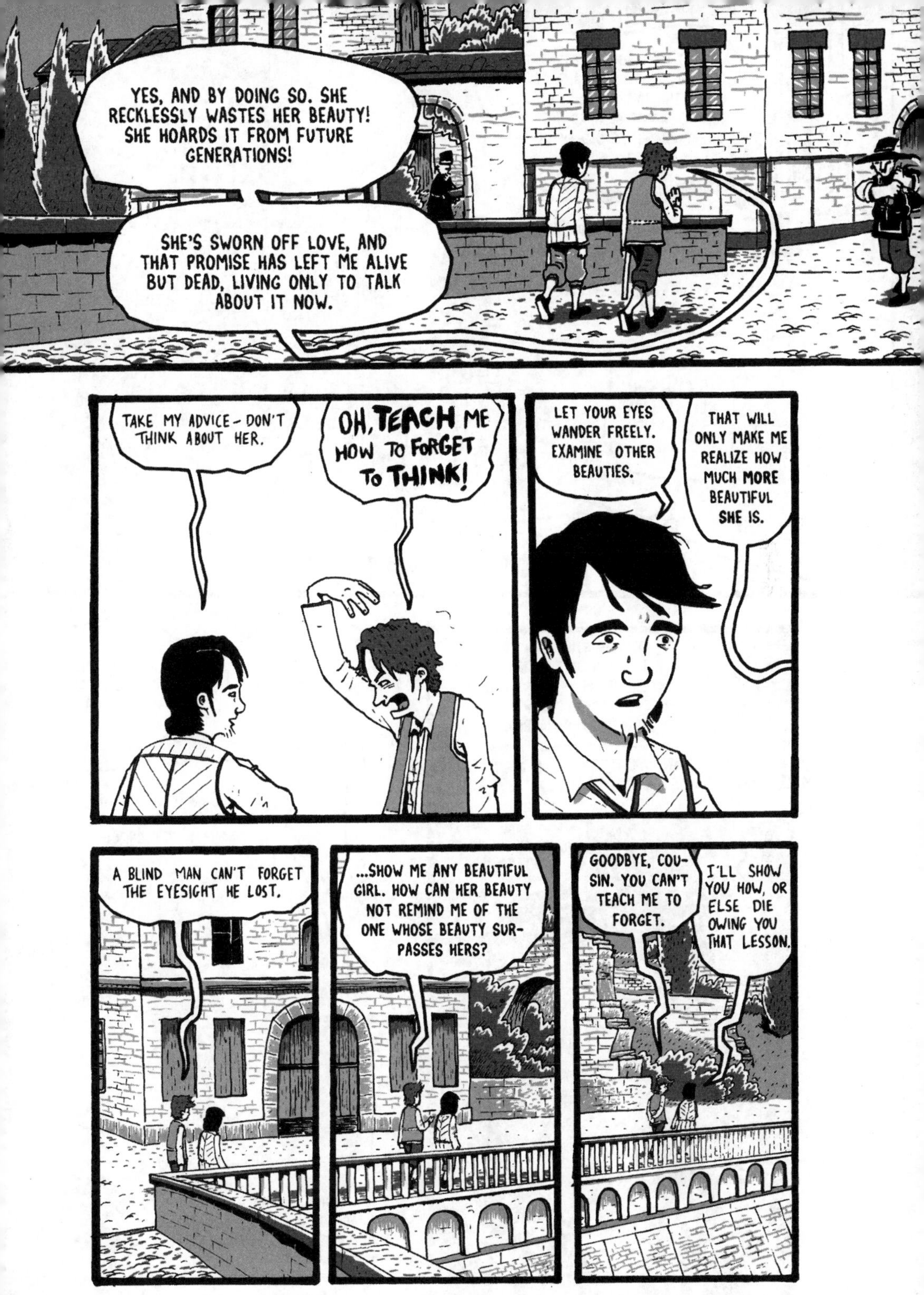
YES, AND BY DOING SO. SHE RECKLESSLY WASTES HER BEAUTY! SHE HOARDS IT FROM FUTURE GENERATIONS!
SHE'S SWORN OFF LOVE, AND THAT PROMISE HAS LEFT ME ALIVE BUT DEAD, LIVING ONLY TO TALK ABOUT IT NOW.
TAKE MY ADVICE - DON'T THINK ABOUT HER.
OH, TEACH ME HOW TO FORGET TO THINK!
LET YOUR EYES WANDER FREELY. EXAMINE OTHER BEAUTIES.
THAT WILL ONLY MAKE ME REALIZE HOW MUCH MORE BEAUTIFUL SHE IS.
A BLIND MAN CAN'T FORGET THE EYESIGHT HE LOST.
...SHOW ME ANY BEAUTIFUL GIRL. HOW CAN HER BEAUTY NOT REMIND ME OF THE ONE WHOSE BEAUTY SURPASSES HERS?
GOODBYE, COUSIN. YOU CAN'T TEACH ME TO FORGET.
I'LL SHOW YOU HOW, OR ELSE DIE OWING YOU THAT LESSON.

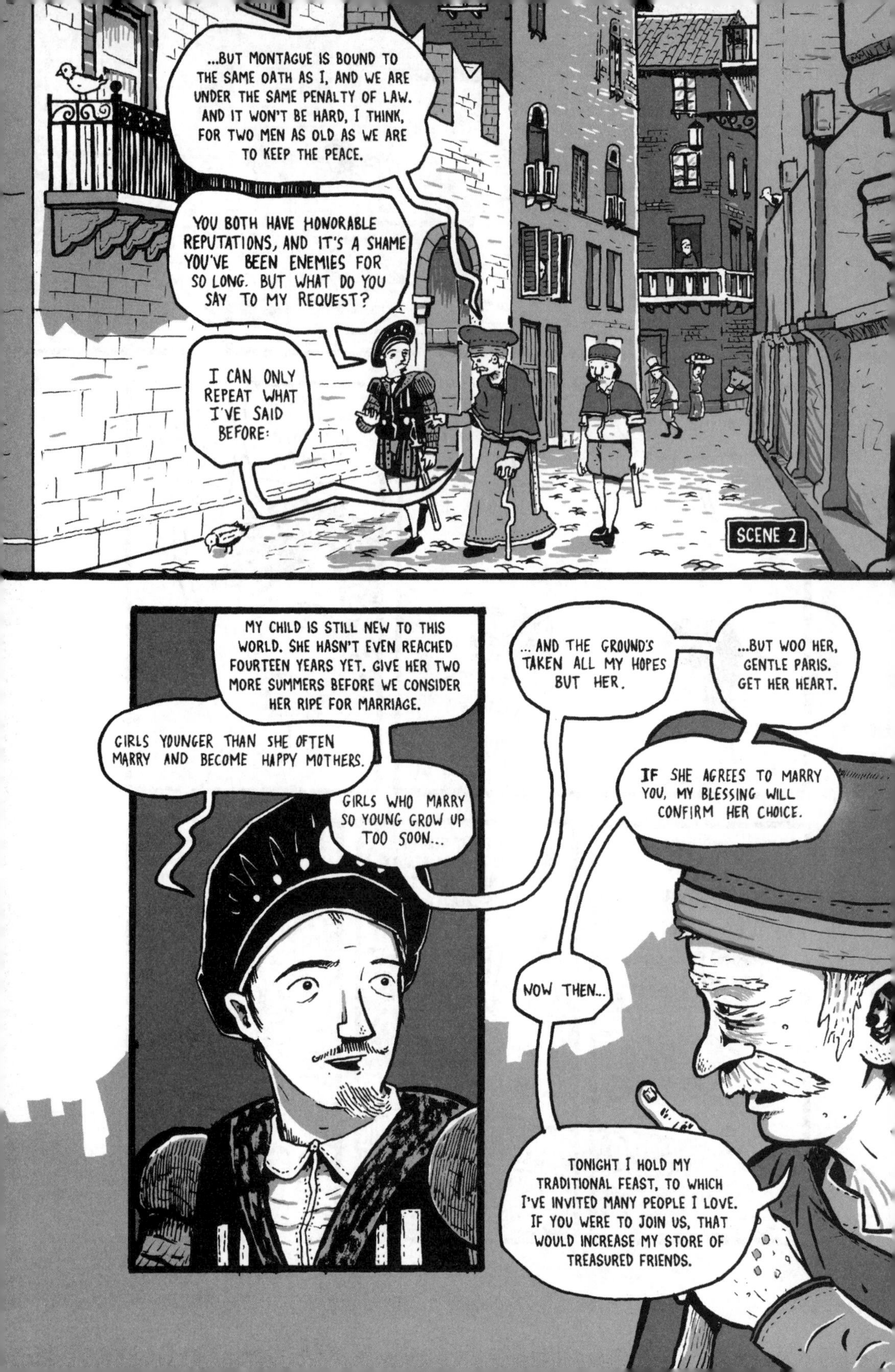
...BUT MONTAGUE IS BOUND TO THE SAME OATH AS I, AND WE ARE UNDER THE SAME PENALTY OF LAW. AND IT WON'T BE HARD, I THINK, FOR TWO MEN AS OLD AS WE ARE TO KEEP THE PEACE.
YOU BOTH HAVE HONORABLE REPUTATIONS, AND IT'S A SHAME YOU'VE BEEN ENEMIES FOR SO LONG. BUT WHAT DO YOU SAY TO MY REQUEST?
I CAN ONLY REPEAT WHAT I'VE SAID BEFORE:
SCENE 2
MY CHILD IS STILL NEW TO THIS WORLD. SHE HASN'T EVEN REACHED FOURTEEN YEARS YET. GIVE HER TWO MORE SUMMERS BEFORE WE CONSIDER HER RIPE FOR MARRIAGE.
GIRLS YOUNGER THAN SHE OFTEN MARRY AND BECOME HAPPY MOTHERS.
GIRLS WHO MARRY SO YOUNG GROW UP TOO SOON...
... AND THE GROUND'S TAKEN ALL MY HOPES BUT HER.
...BUT WOO HER, GENTLE PARIS. GET HER HEART.
IF SHE AGREES TO MARRY YOU, MY BLESSING WILL CONFIRM HER CHOICE.
NOW THEN...
TONIGHT I HOLD MY TRADITIONAL FEAST, TO WHICH I'VE INVITED MANY PEOPLE I LOVE. IF YOU WERE TO JOIN US, THAT WOULD INCREASE MY STORE OF TREASURED FRIENDS.

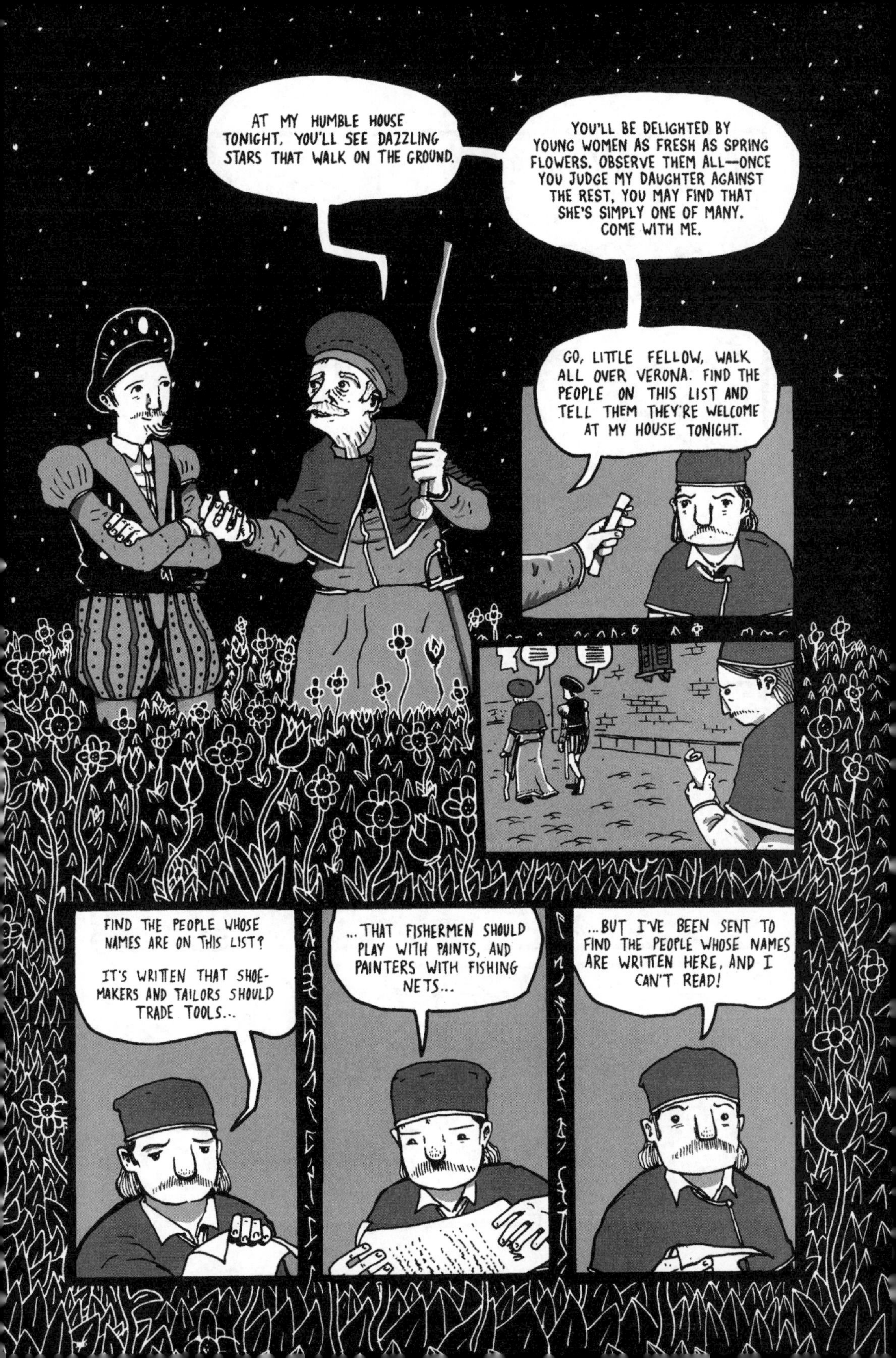
AT MY HUMBLE HOUSE TONIGHT, YOU'LL SEE DAZZLING STARS THAT WALK ON THE GROUND.
YOU'LL BE DELIGHTED BY YOUNG WOMEN AS FRESH AS SPRING FLOWERS. OBSERVE THEM ALL—ONCE YOU JUDGE MY DAUGHTER AGAINST THE REST, YOU MAY FIND THAT SHE'S SIMPLY ONE OF MANY. COME WITH ME.
GO, LITTLE FELLOW, WALK ALL OVER VERONA. FIND THE PEOPLE ON THIS LIST AND TELL THEM THEY'RE WELCOME AT MY HOUSE TONIGHT.
FIND THE PEOPLE WHOSE NAMES ARE ON THIS LIST?
IT'S WRITTEN THAT SHOEMAKERS AND TAILORS SHOULD TRADE TOOLS...
...THAT FISHERMEN SHOULD PLAY WITH PAINTS, AND PAINTERS WITH FISHING NETS...
...BUT I'VE BEEN SENT TO FIND THE PEOPLE WHOSE NAMES ARE WRITTEN HERE, AND I CAN'T READ!

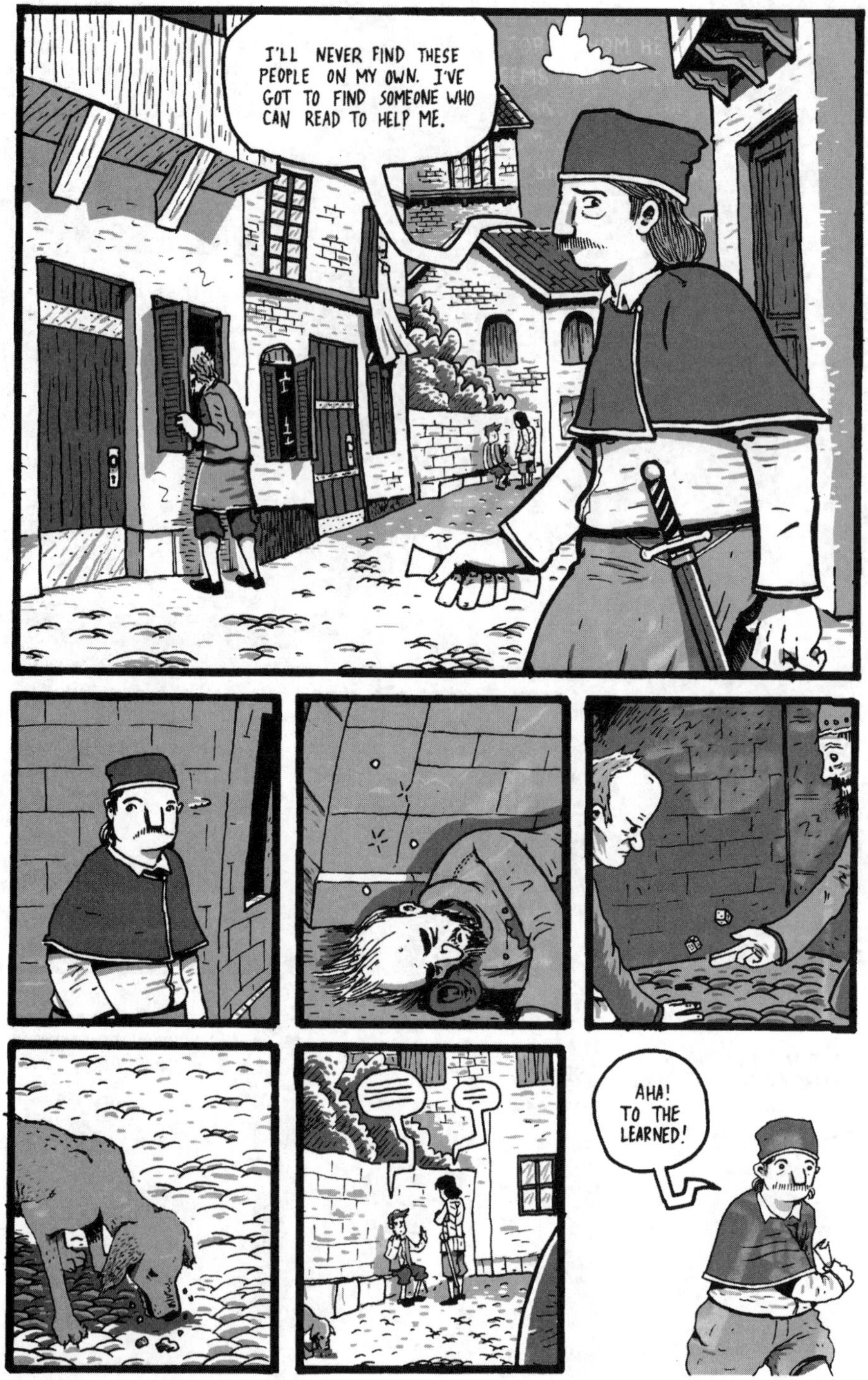
I'LL NEVER FIND THESE PEOPLE ON MY OWN. I'VE GOT TO FIND SOMEONE WHO CAN READ TO HELP ME.
AHA! TO THE LEARNED!

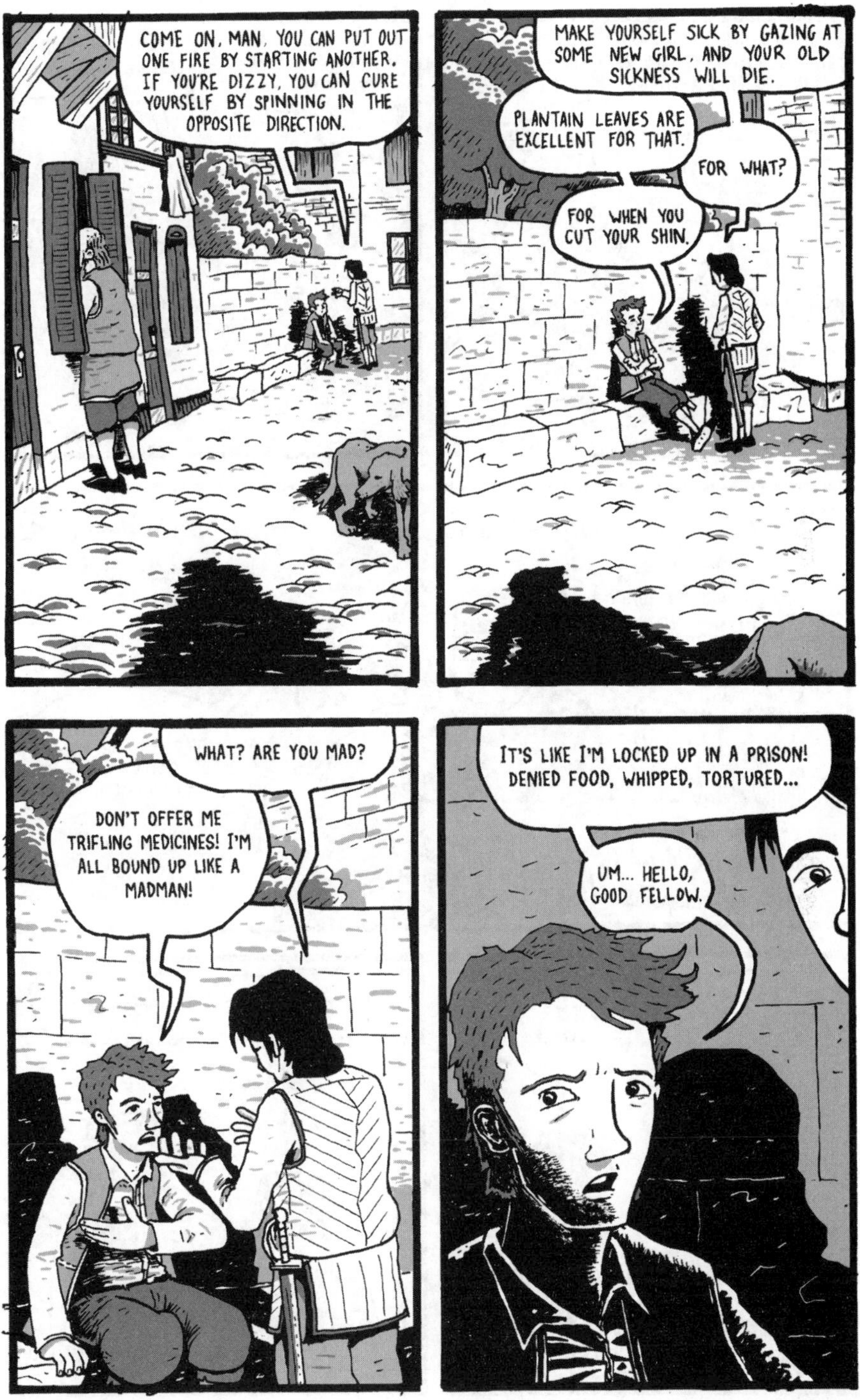
COME ON, MAN, YOU CAN PUT OUT ONE FIRE BY STARTING ANOTHER. IF YOU'RE DIZZY, YOU CAN CURE YOURSELF BY SPINNING IN THE OPPOSITE DIRECTION.
MAKE YOURSELF SICK BY GAZING AT SOME NEW GIRL, AND YOUR OLD SICKNESS WILL DIE.
PLANTAIN LEAVES ARE EXCELLENT FOR THAT.
FOR WHAT?
FOR WHEN YOU CUT YOUR SHIN.
WHAT? ARE YOU MAD?
DON'T OFFER ME TRIFLING MEDICINES! I'M ALL BOUND UP LIKE A MADMAN!
IT'S LIKE I'M LOCKED UP IN A PRISON! DENIED FOOD, WHIPPED, TORTURED...
UM... HELLO, GOOD FELLOW.

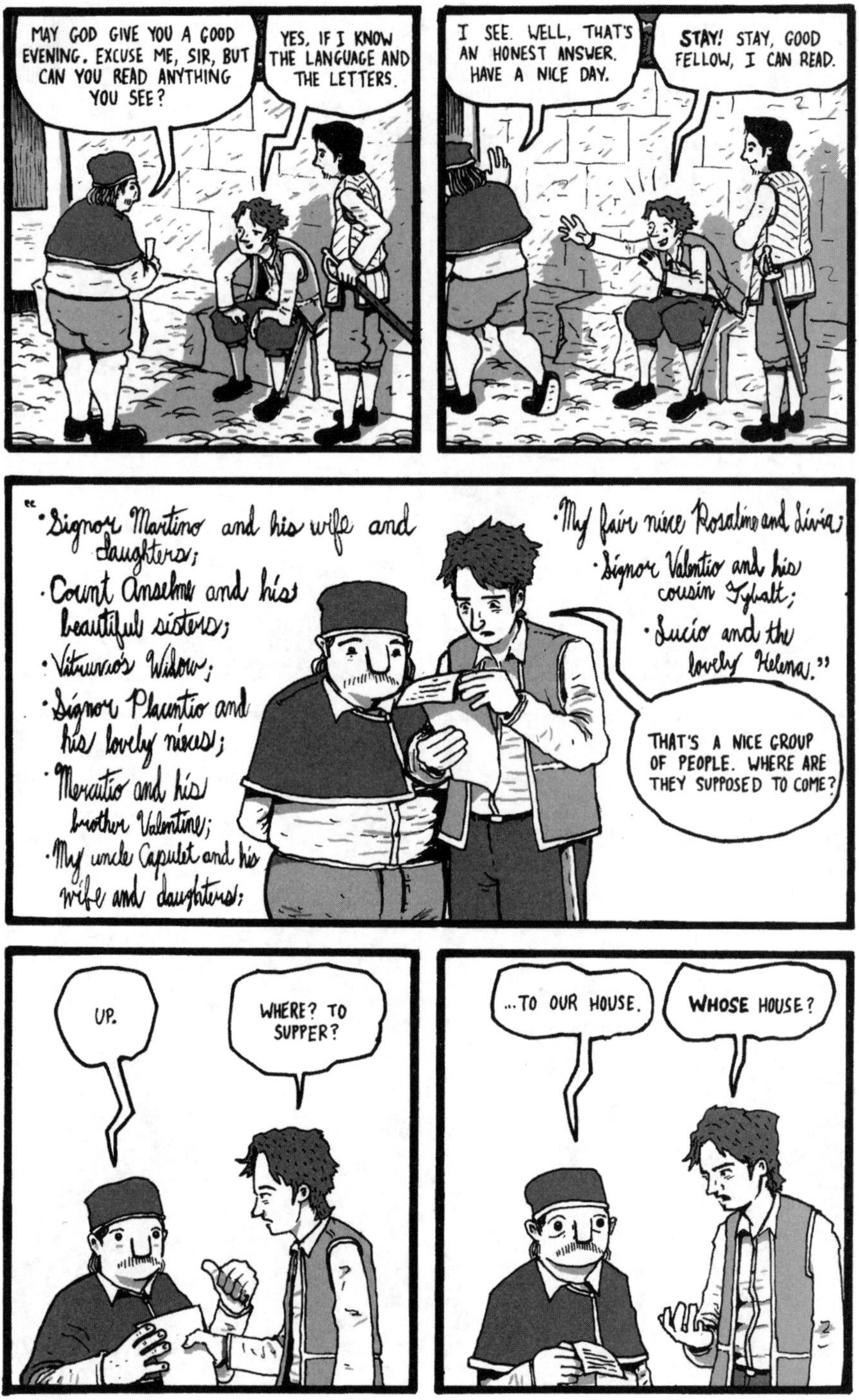
MAY GOD GIVE YOU A GOOD EVENING. EXCUSE ME, SIR, BUT CAN YOU READ ANYTHING YOU SEE?
YES, IF I KNOW THE LANGUAGE AND THE LETTERS.
I SEE. WELL, THAT'S AN HONEST ANSWER. HAVE A NICE DAY.
STAY! STAY, GOOD FELLOW, I CAN READ.
"·Signor Martino and his wife and daughters;
·Count Anselme and his beautiful sisters;
·Vitruvio's Widow;
·Signor Placentio and his lovely nieces;
·Mercutio and his brother Valentine;
·My uncle Capulet and his wife and daughters;
·My fair niece Rosaline and Livia;
·Signor Valentio and his cousin Tybalt;
·Lucio and the lovely Helena."
THAT'S A NICE GROUP OF PEOPLE. WHERE ARE THEY SUPPOSED TO COME?
UP.
WHERE? TO SUPPER?
...TO OUR HOUSE.
WHOSE HOUSE?

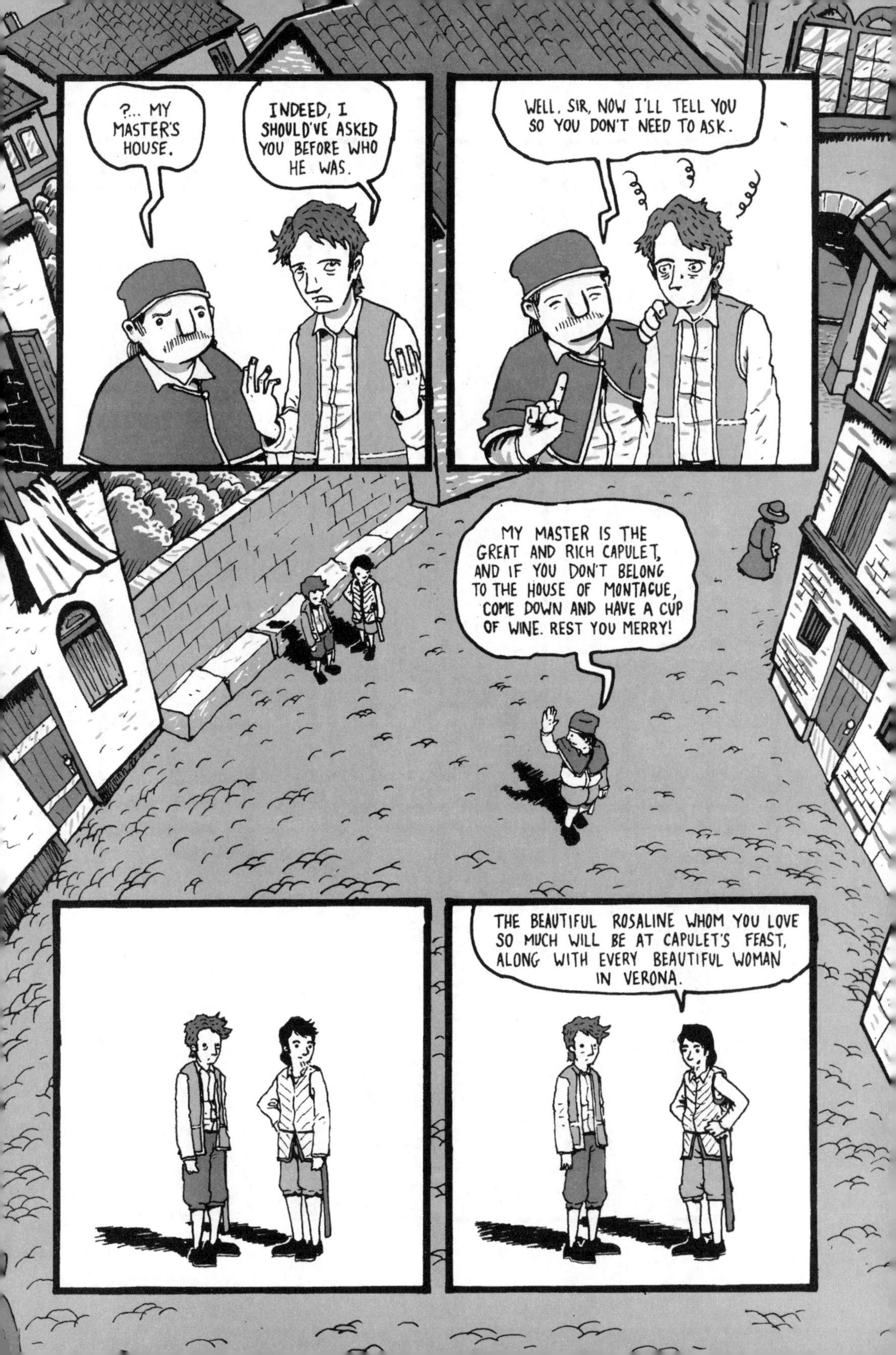
?... MY MASTER'S HOUSE.
INDEED, I SHOULD'VE ASKED YOU BEFORE WHO HE WAS.
WELL, SIR, NOW I'LL TELL YOU SO YOU DON'T NEED TO ASK.
MY MASTER IS THE GREAT AND RICH CAPULET, AND IF YOU DON'T BELONG TO THE HOUSE OF MONTAGUE, COME DOWN AND HAVE A CUP OF WINE. REST YOU MERRY!
THE BEAUTIFUL ROSALINE WHOM YOU LOVE SO MUCH WILL BE AT CAPULET'S FEAST, ALONG WITH EVERY BEAUTIFUL WOMAN IN VERONA.

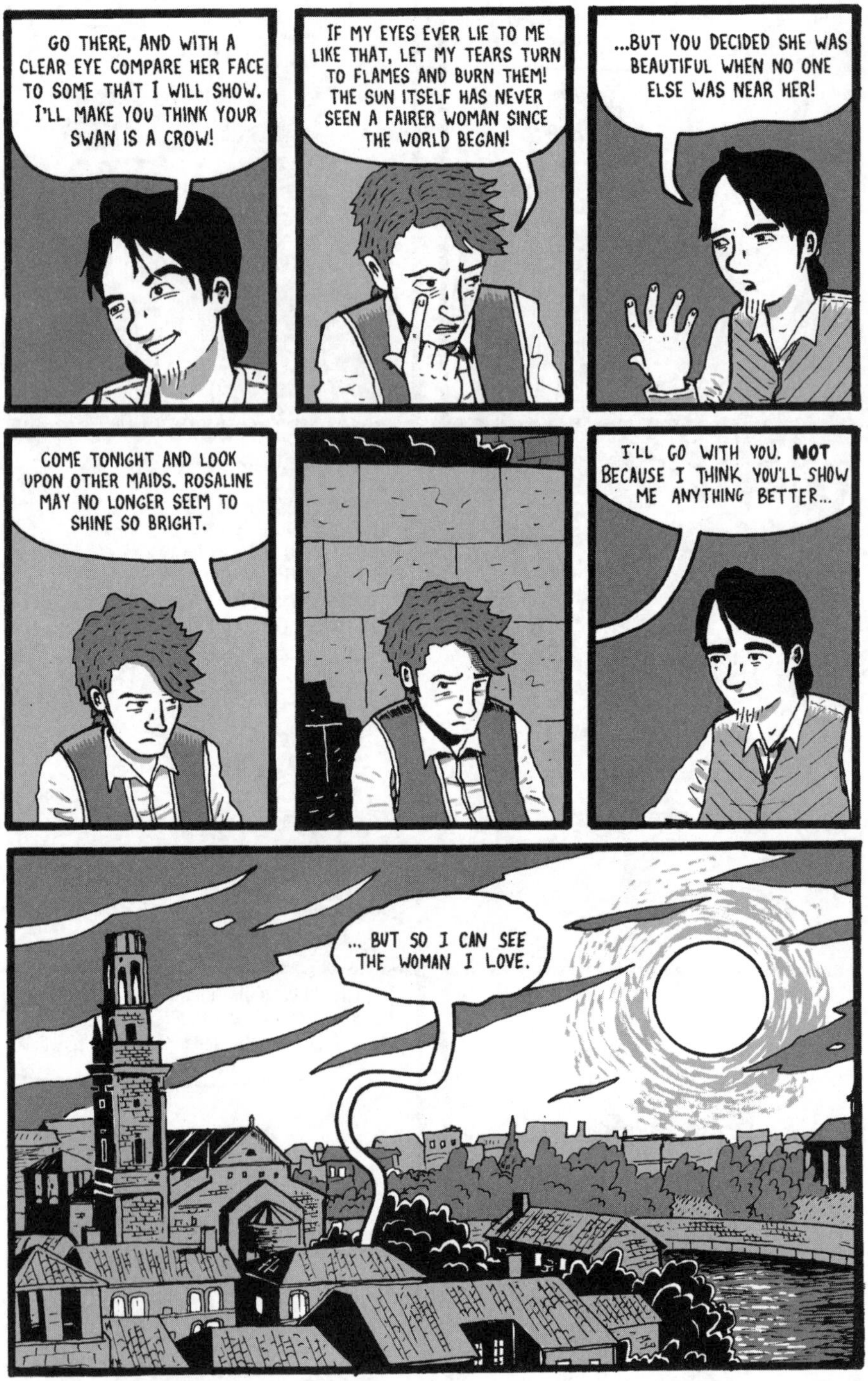
GO THERE, AND WITH A CLEAR EYE COMPARE HER FACE TO SOME THAT I WILL SHOW. I'LL MAKE YOU THINK YOUR SWAN IS A CROW!
IF MY EYES EVER LIE TO ME LIKE THAT, LET MY TEARS TURN TO FLAMES AND BURN THEM! THE SUN ITSELF HAS NEVER SEEN A FAIRER WOMAN SINCE THE WORLD BEGAN!
...BUT YOU DECIDED SHE WAS BEAUTIFUL WHEN NO ONE ELSE WAS NEAR HER!
COME TONIGHT AND LOOK UPON OTHER MAIDS. ROSALINE MAY NO LONGER SEEM TO SHINE SO BRIGHT.
I'LL GO WITH YOU. NOT BECAUSE I THINK YOU'LL SHOW ME ANYTHING BETTER...
... BUT SO I CAN SEE THE WOMAN I LOVE.

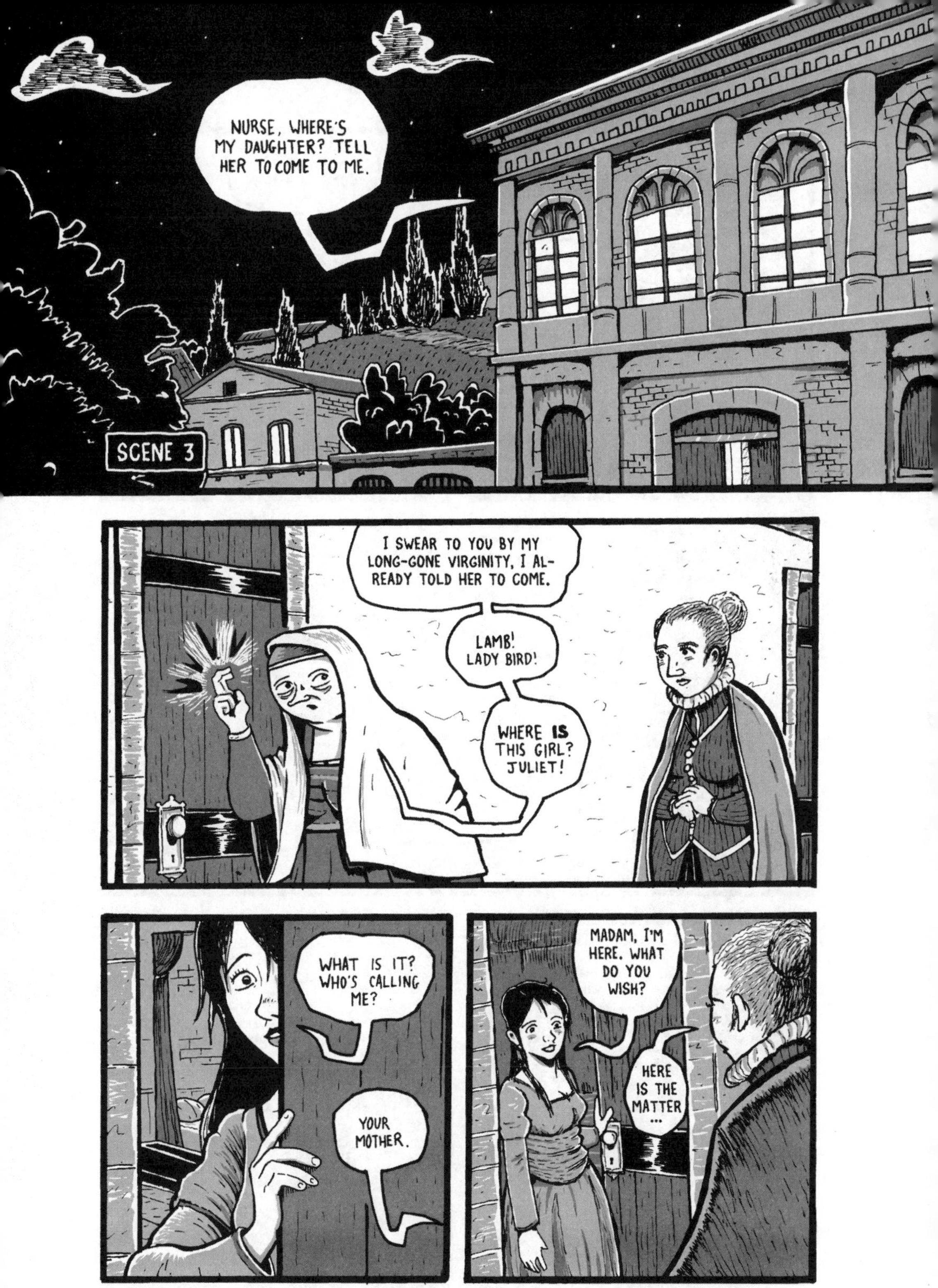
NURSE, WHERE'S MY DAUGHTER? TELL HER TO COME TO ME.
SCENE 3
I SWEAR TO YOU BY MY LONG-GONE VIRGINITY, I ALREADY TOLD HER TO COME.
LAMB! LADY BIRD!
WHERE **IS** THIS GIRL? JULIET!
WHAT IS IT? WHO'S CALLING ME?
YOUR MOTHER.
MADAM, I'M HERE. WHAT DO YOU WISH?
HERE IS THE MATTER ...

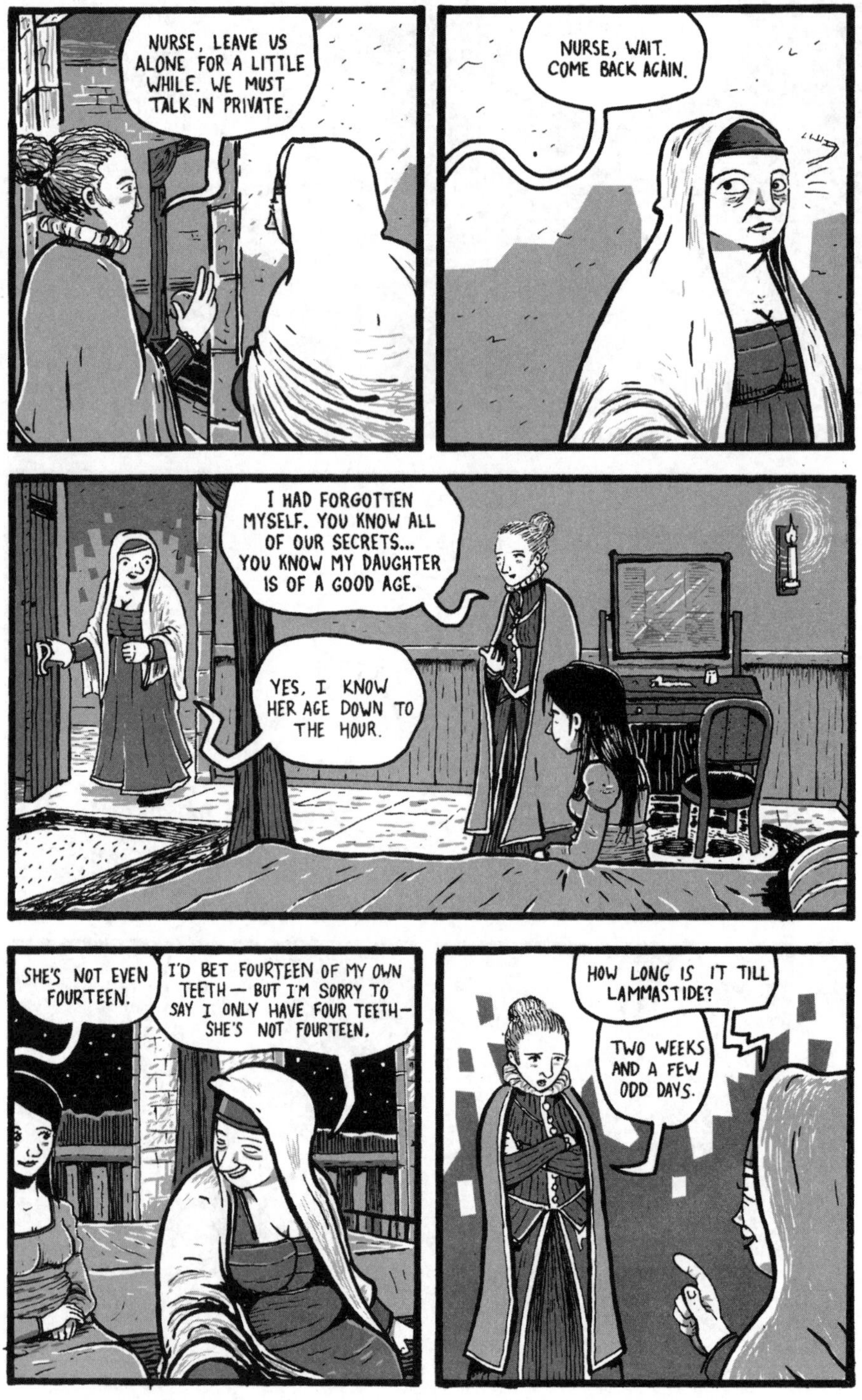
NURSE, LEAVE US ALONE FOR A LITTLE WHILE. WE MUST TALK IN PRIVATE.
NURSE, WAIT. COME BACK AGAIN.
I HAD FORGOTTEN MYSELF. YOU KNOW ALL OF OUR SECRETS... YOU KNOW MY DAUGHTER IS OF A GOOD AGE.
YES, I KNOW HER AGE DOWN TO THE HOUR.
SHE'S NOT EVEN FOURTEEN.
I'D BET FOURTEEN OF MY OWN TEETH — BUT I'M SORRY TO SAY I ONLY HAVE FOUR TEETH— SHE'S NOT FOURTEEN.
HOW LONG IS IT TILL LAMMASTIDE?
TWO WEEKS AND A FEW ODD DAYS.

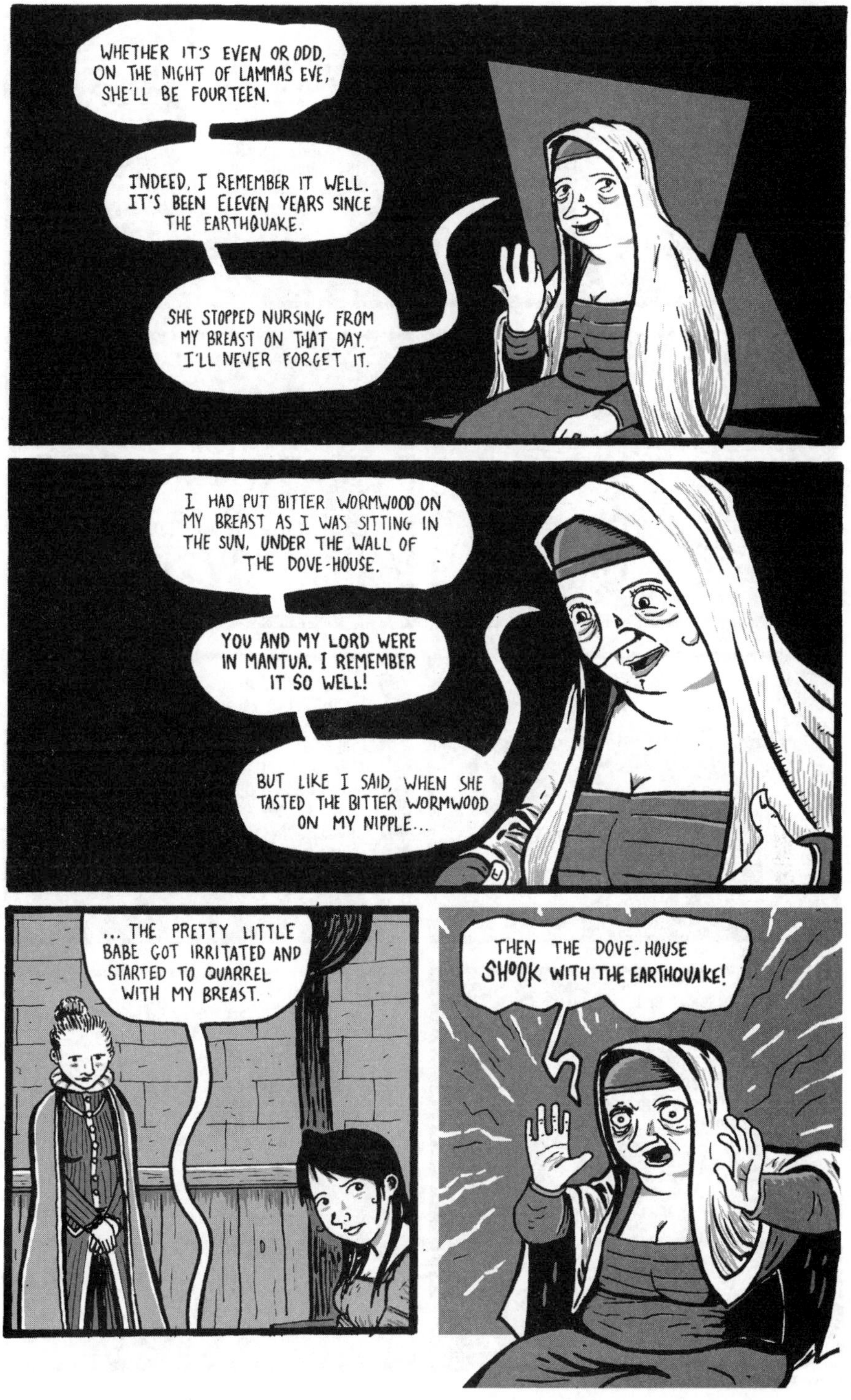
WHETHER IT'S EVEN OR ODD, ON THE NIGHT OF LAMMAS EVE, SHE'LL BE FOURTEEN.
INDEED, I REMEMBER IT WELL. IT'S BEEN ELEVEN YEARS SINCE THE EARTHQUAKE.
SHE STOPPED NURSING FROM MY BREAST ON THAT DAY. I'LL NEVER FORGET IT.
I HAD PUT BITTER WORMWOOD ON MY BREAST AS I WAS SITTING IN THE SUN, UNDER THE WALL OF THE DOVE-HOUSE.
YOU AND MY LORD WERE IN MANTUA. I REMEMBER IT SO WELL!
BUT LIKE I SAID, WHEN SHE TASTED THE BITTER WORMWOOD ON MY NIPPLE...
... THE PRETTY LITTLE BABE GOT IRRITATED AND STARTED TO QUARREL WITH MY BREAST.
THEN THE DOVE-HOUSE SHOOK WITH THE EARTHQUAKE!

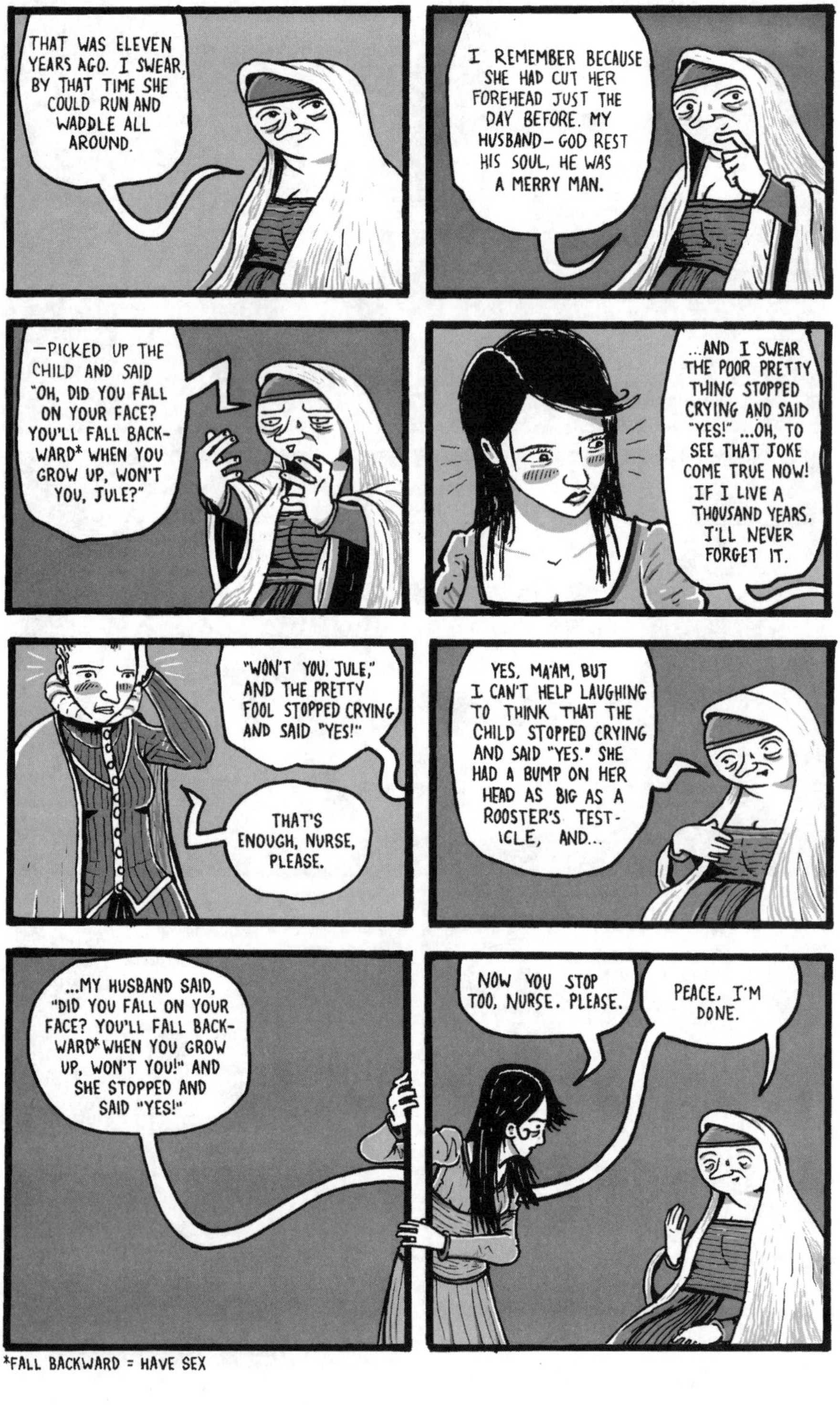
THAT WAS ELEVEN YEARS AGO. I SWEAR, BY THAT TIME SHE COULD RUN AND WADDLE ALL AROUND.
I REMEMBER BECAUSE SHE HAD CUT HER FOREHEAD JUST THE DAY BEFORE. MY HUSBAND— GOD REST HIS SOUL, HE WAS A MERRY MAN.
—PICKED UP THE CHILD AND SAID "OH, DID YOU FALL ON YOUR FACE? YOU'LL FALL BACKWARD* WHEN YOU GROW UP, WON'T YOU, JULE?"
...AND I SWEAR THE POOR PRETTY THING STOPPED CRYING AND SAID "YES!" ...OH, TO SEE THAT JOKE COME TRUE NOW! IF I LIVE A THOUSAND YEARS, I'LL NEVER FORGET IT.
"WON'T YOU, JULE," AND THE PRETTY FOOL STOPPED CRYING AND SAID "YES!"
THAT'S ENOUGH, NURSE, PLEASE.
YES, MA'AM, BUT I CAN'T HELP LAUGHING TO THINK THAT THE CHILD STOPPED CRYING AND SAID "YES." SHE HAD A BUMP ON HER HEAD AS BIG AS A ROOSTER'S TESTICLE, AND...
...MY HUSBAND SAID, "DID YOU FALL ON YOUR FACE? YOU'LL FALL BACKWARD* WHEN YOU GROW UP, WON'T YOU!" AND SHE STOPPED AND SAID "YES!"
NOW YOU STOP TOO, NURSE. PLEASE.
PEACE, I'M DONE.

*FALL BACKWARD = HAVE SEX

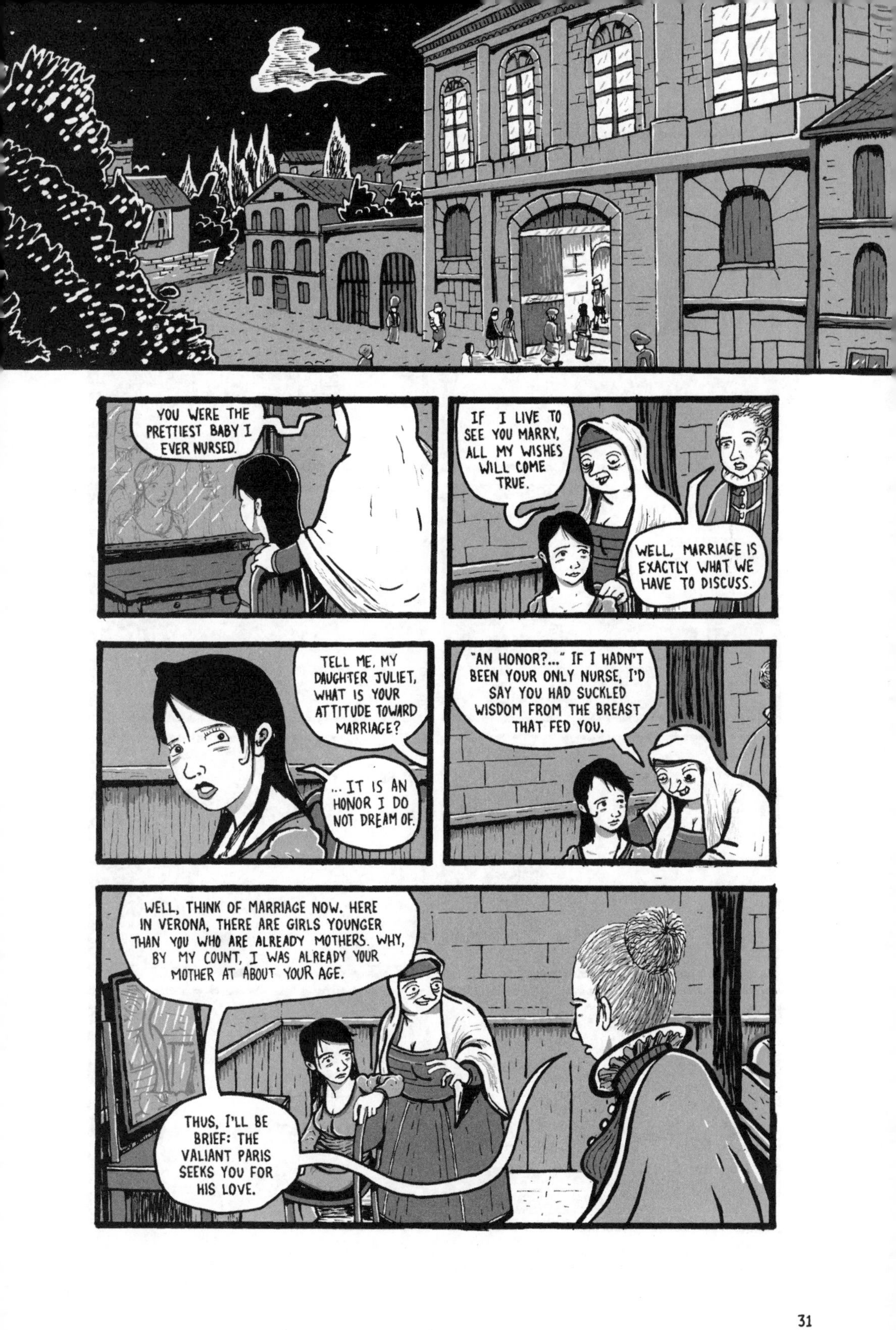
YOU WERE THE PRETTIEST BABY I EVER NURSED.
IF I LIVE TO SEE YOU MARRY, ALL MY WISHES WILL COME TRUE.
WELL, MARRIAGE IS EXACTLY WHAT WE HAVE TO DISCUSS.
TELL ME, MY DAUGHTER JULIET, WHAT IS YOUR ATTITUDE TOWARD MARRIAGE?
... IT IS AN HONOR I DO NOT DREAM OF.
"AN HONOR?..." IF I HADN'T BEEN YOUR ONLY NURSE, I'D SAY YOU HAD SUCKLED WISDOM FROM THE BREAST THAT FED YOU.
WELL, THINK OF MARRIAGE NOW. HERE IN VERONA, THERE ARE GIRLS YOUNGER THAN YOU WHO ARE ALREADY MOTHERS. WHY, BY MY COUNT, I WAS ALREADY YOUR MOTHER AT ABOUT YOUR AGE.
THUS, I'LL BE BRIEF: THE VALIANT PARIS SEEKS YOU FOR HIS LOVE.

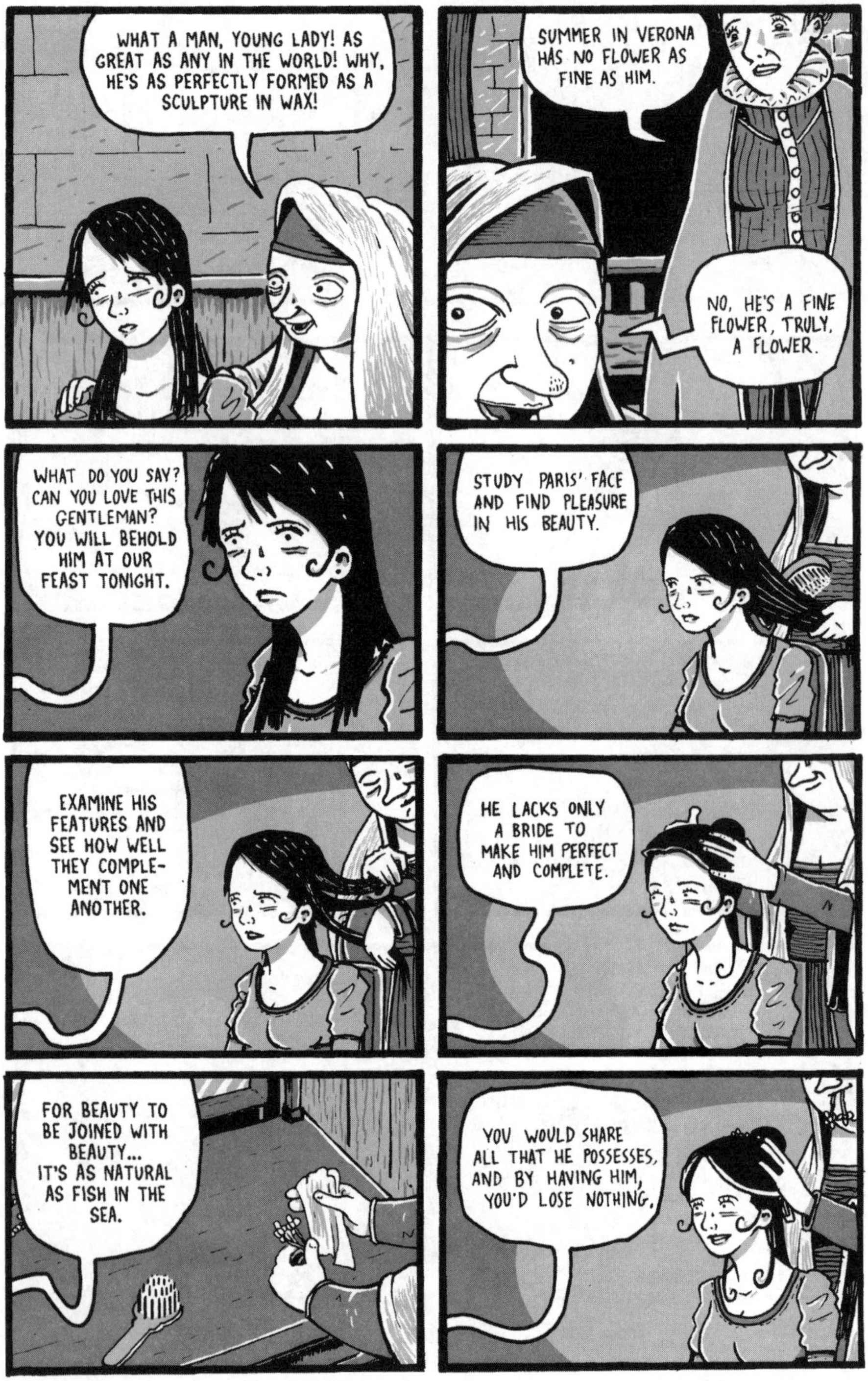
WHAT A MAN, YOUNG LADY! AS GREAT AS ANY IN THE WORLD! WHY, HE'S AS PERFECTLY FORMED AS A SCULPTURE IN WAX!
SUMMER IN VERONA HAS NO FLOWER AS FINE AS HIM.
NO, HE'S A FINE FLOWER, TRULY, A FLOWER.
WHAT DO YOU SAY? CAN YOU LOVE THIS GENTLEMAN? YOU WILL BEHOLD HIM AT OUR FEAST TONIGHT.
STUDY PARIS' FACE AND FIND PLEASURE IN HIS BEAUTY.
EXAMINE HIS FEATURES AND SEE HOW WELL THEY COMPLEMENT ONE ANOTHER.
HE LACKS ONLY A BRIDE TO MAKE HIM PERFECT AND COMPLETE.
FOR BEAUTY TO BE JOINED WITH BEAUTY... IT'S AS NATURAL AS FISH IN THE SEA.
YOU WOULD SHARE ALL THAT HE POSSESSES, AND BY HAVING HIM, YOU'D LOSE NOTHING.

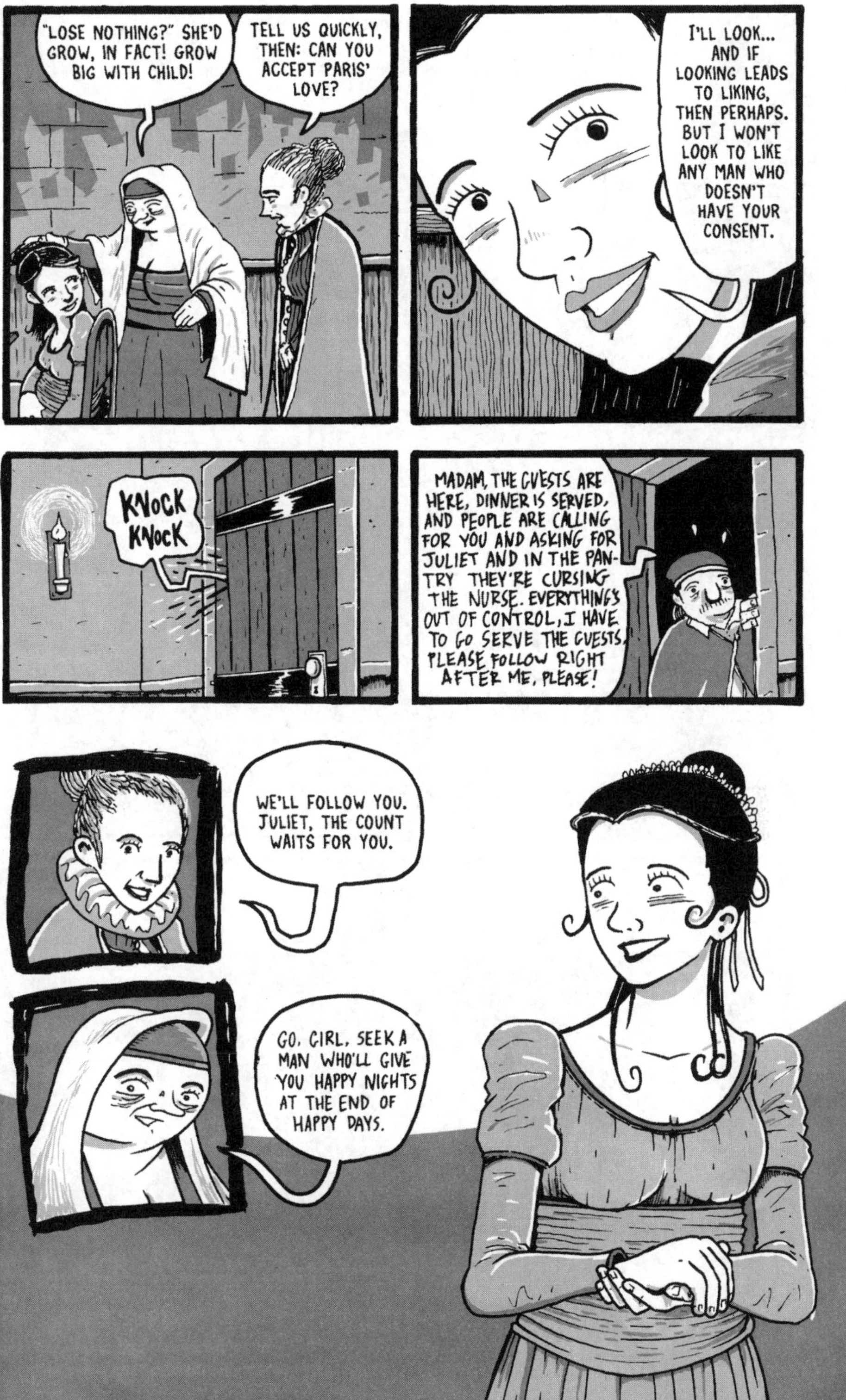
"LOSE NOTHING?" SHE'D GROW, IN FACT! GROW BIG WITH CHILD!
TELL US QUICKLY, THEN: CAN YOU ACCEPT PARIS' LOVE?
I'LL LOOK... AND IF LOOKING LEADS TO LIKING, THEN PERHAPS. BUT I WON'T LOOK TO LIKE ANY MAN WHO DOESN'T HAVE YOUR CONSENT.
KNOCK KNOCK
MADAM, THE GUESTS ARE HERE, DINNER IS SERVED, AND PEOPLE ARE CALLING FOR YOU AND ASKING FOR JULIET AND IN THE PANTRY THEY'RE CURSING THE NURSE. EVERYTHING'S OUT OF CONTROL, I HAVE TO GO SERVE THE GUESTS. PLEASE FOLLOW RIGHT AFTER ME, PLEASE!
WE'LL FOLLOW YOU. JULIET, THE COUNT WAITS FOR YOU.
GO, GIRL, SEEK A MAN WHO'LL GIVE YOU HAPPY NIGHTS AT THE END OF HAPPY DAYS.

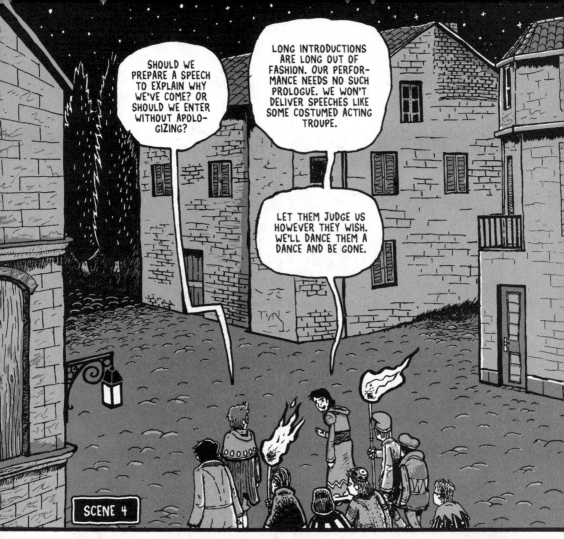

SHOULD WE PREPARE A SPEECH TO EXPLAIN WHY WE'VE COME? OR SHOULD WE ENTER WITHOUT APOLOGIZING?

LONG INTRODUCTIONS ARE LONG OUT OF FASHION. OUR PERFORMANCE NEEDS NO SUCH PROLOGUE. WE WON'T DELIVER SPEECHES LIKE SOME COSTUMED ACTING TROUPE.

LET THEM JUDGE US HOWEVER THEY WISH. WE'LL DANCE THEM A DANCE AND BE GONE.

SCENE 4

GIVE ME A TORCH. I DON'T WANT TO DANCE. MY HEART IS **HEAVY**, SO LET ME JUST CARRY THE **LIGHT**.

NO, NOBLE ROMEO, WE MUST HAVE YOU DANCE.

NOT I, BELIEVE ME. YOU HAVE DANCING SHOES WITH NIMBLE SOLES. I HAVE A **SOUL** OF LEAD THAT STAKES ME TO THE GROUND.

YOU'RE A LOVER! BORROW CUPID'S WINGS AND USE THEM TO SOAR ABOVE THE COMMON MAN.

34

ARROWS TO SOAR WITH HIS WINGS. BEING **BOUND** BY LOVE, I CANNOT **BOUND** AWAY FROM MY SORROWS. I SINK UNDER LOVE'S HEAVY WEIGHT.

IF YOU SINK, THEN YOU DRAG LOVE DOWN... TOO ROUGH A TREATMENT FOR SUCH A TENDER THING.

IS LOVE A TENDER THING? IT IS ROUGH, ROWDY, AND PRICKS LIKE A THORN.

IF LOVE PLAYS ROUGH WITH YOU, PLAY ROUGH WITH LOVE. IF YOU PRICK LOVE WHEN LOVE PRICKS YOU, YOU'LL BEAT LOVE DOWN.

GIVE ME A MASK TO PUT MY FACE IN; A MASK TO PUT OVER MY OTHER MASK.

WHAT DO I CARE IF SOME CURIOUS EYE SEES MY FLAWS? LET THIS MASK, WITH ITS BLACK EYEBROWS, BLUSH FOR ME!

COME, KNOCK AND ENTER. AS SOON AS WE'RE IN, LET EVERY MAN TAKE TO DANCING.

I'LL TAKE A TORCH.

35

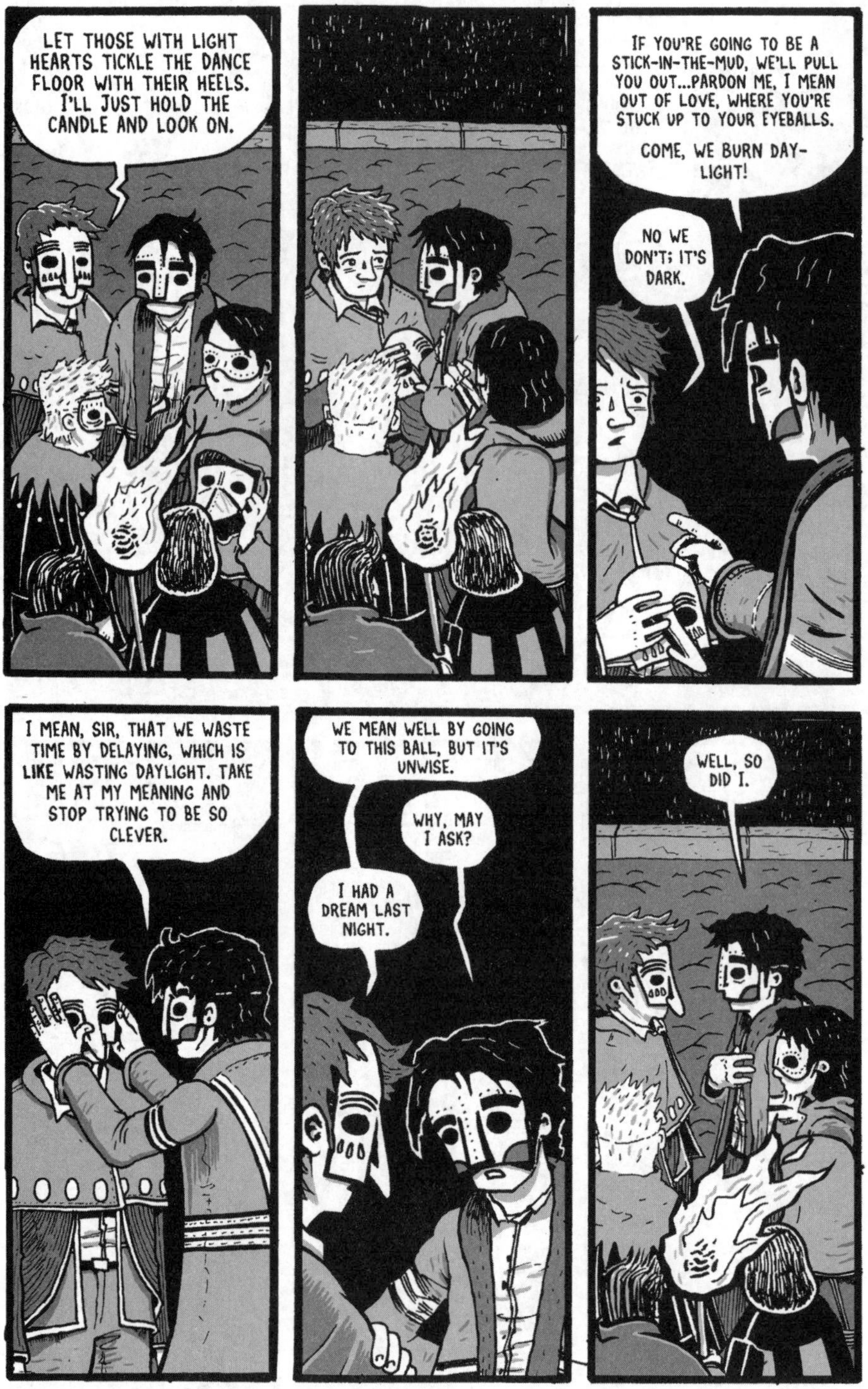
LET THOSE WITH LIGHT HEARTS TICKLE THE DANCE FLOOR WITH THEIR HEELS. I'LL JUST HOLD THE CANDLE AND LOOK ON.
IF YOU'RE GOING TO BE A STICK-IN-THE-MUD, WE'LL PULL YOU OUT...PARDON ME, I MEAN OUT OF LOVE, WHERE YOU'RE STUCK UP TO YOUR EYEBALLS.
COME, WE BURN DAY-LIGHT!
NO WE DON'T; IT'S DARK.
I MEAN, SIR, THAT WE WASTE TIME BY DELAYING, WHICH IS LIKE WASTING DAYLIGHT. TAKE ME AT MY MEANING AND STOP TRYING TO BE SO CLEVER.
WE MEAN WELL BY GOING TO THIS BALL, BUT IT'S UNWISE.
WHY, MAY I ASK?
I HAD A DREAM LAST NIGHT.
WELL, SO DID I.

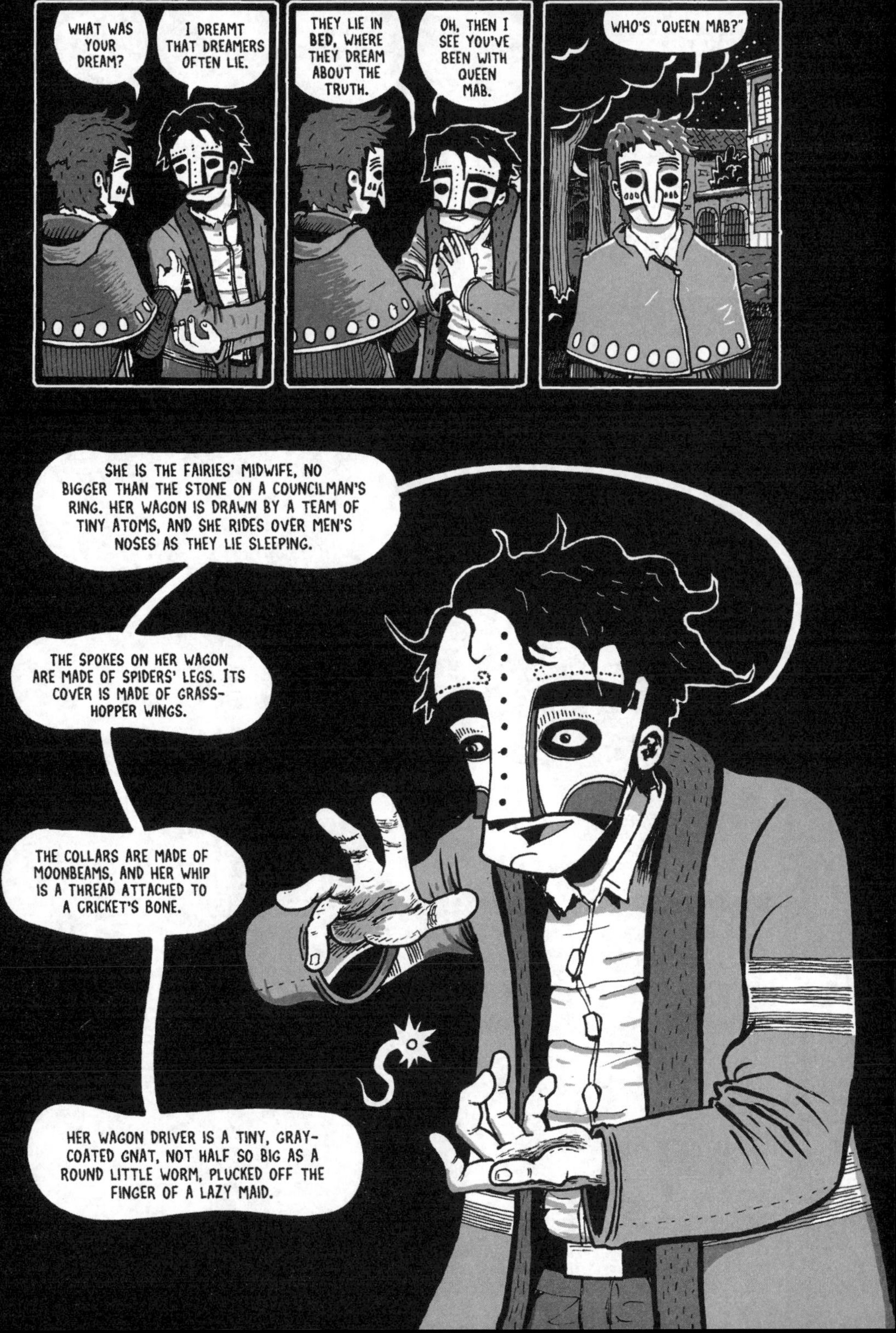
WHAT WAS YOUR DREAM?
I DREAMT THAT DREAMERS OFTEN LIE.
THEY LIE IN BED, WHERE THEY DREAM ABOUT THE TRUTH.
OH, THEN I SEE YOU'VE BEEN WITH QUEEN MAB.
WHO'S "QUEEN MAB?"
SHE IS THE FAIRIES' MIDWIFE, NO BIGGER THAN THE STONE ON A COUNCILMAN'S RING. HER WAGON IS DRAWN BY A TEAM OF TINY ATOMS, AND SHE RIDES OVER MEN'S NOSES AS THEY LIE SLEEPING.
THE SPOKES ON HER WAGON ARE MADE OF SPIDERS' LEGS. ITS COVER IS MADE OF GRASS-HOPPER WINGS.
THE COLLARS ARE MADE OF MOONBEAMS, AND HER WHIP IS A THREAD ATTACHED TO A CRICKET'S BONE.
HER WAGON DRIVER IS A TINY, GRAY-COATED GNAT, NOT HALF SO BIG AS A ROUND LITTLE WORM, PLUCKED OFF THE FINGER OF A LAZY MAID.

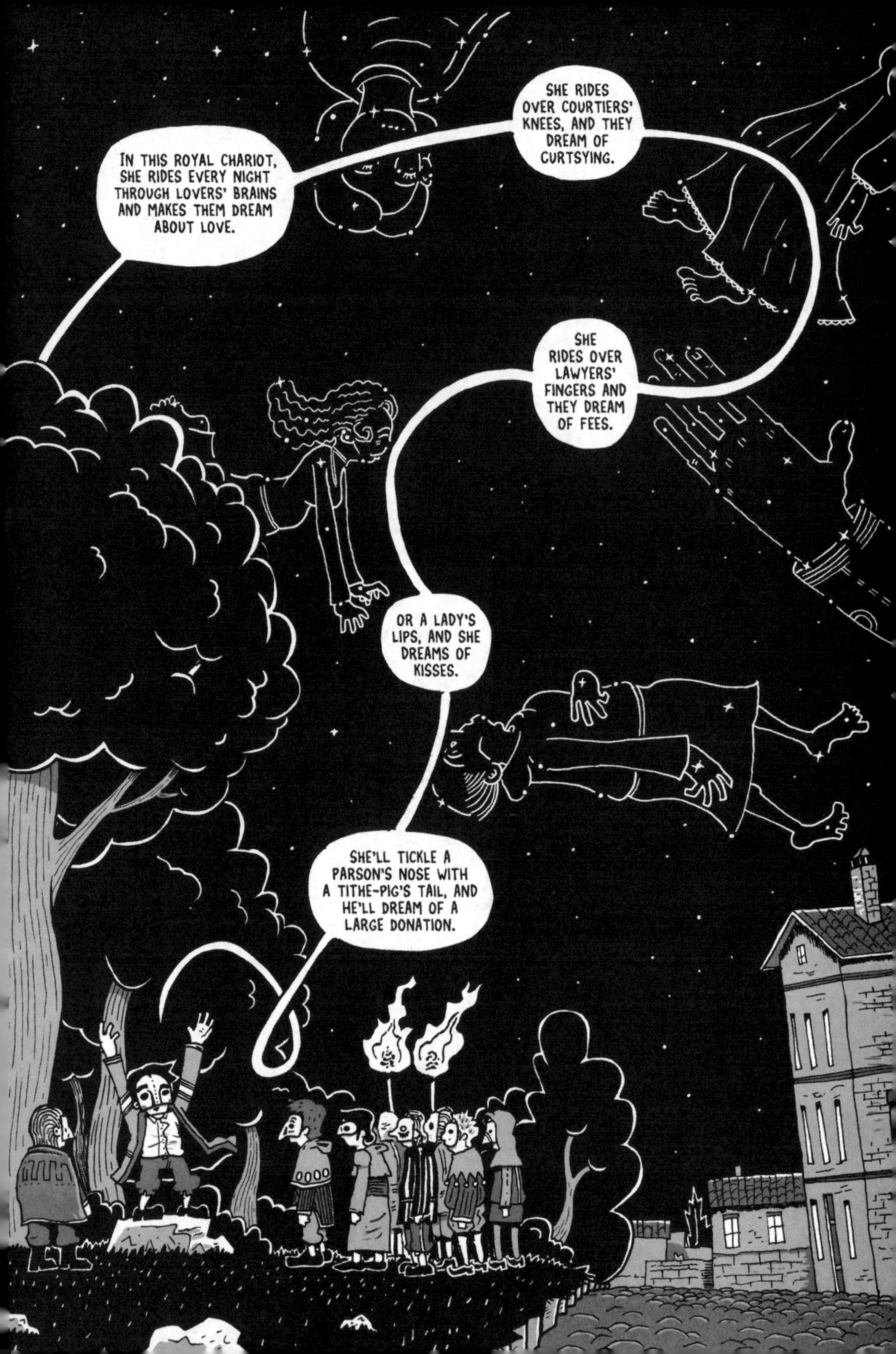
IN THIS ROYAL CHARIOT, SHE RIDES EVERY NIGHT THROUGH LOVERS' BRAINS AND MAKES THEM DREAM ABOUT LOVE.
SHE RIDES OVER COURTIERS' KNEES, AND THEY DREAM OF CURTSYING.
SHE RIDES OVER LAWYERS' FINGERS AND THEY DREAM OF FEES.
OR A LADY'S LIPS, AND SHE DREAMS OF KISSES.
SHE'LL TICKLE A PARSON'S NOSE WITH A TITHE-PIG'S TAIL, AND HE'LL DREAM OF A LARGE DONATION.

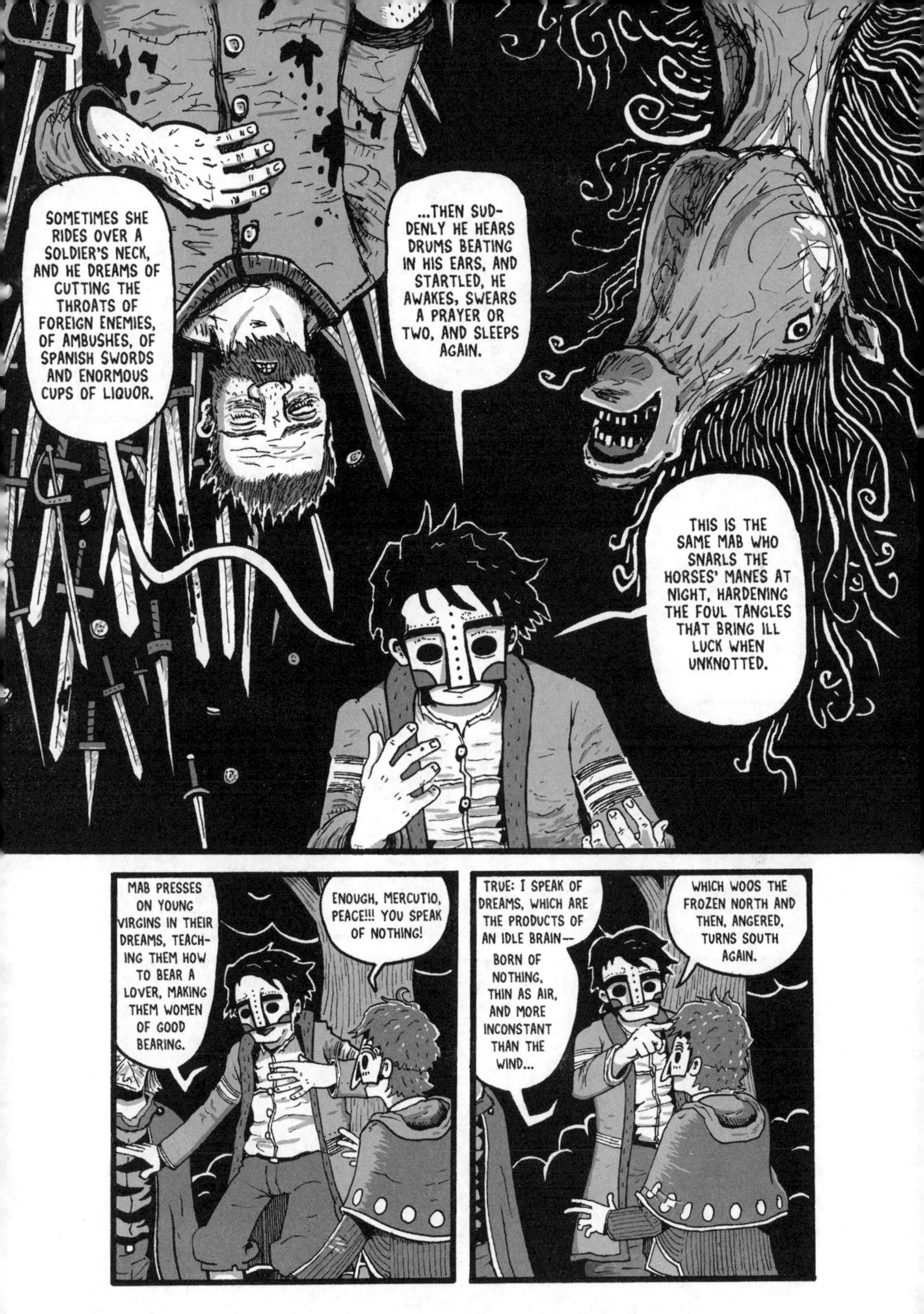
SOMETIMES SHE RIDES OVER A SOLDIER'S NECK, AND HE DREAMS OF CUTTING THE THROATS OF FOREIGN ENEMIES, OF AMBUSHES, OF SPANISH SWORDS AND ENORMOUS CUPS OF LIQUOR.
...THEN SUDDENLY HE HEARS DRUMS BEATING IN HIS EARS, AND STARTLED, HE AWAKES, SWEARS A PRAYER OR TWO, AND SLEEPS AGAIN.
THIS IS THE SAME MAB WHO SNARLS THE HORSES' MANES AT NIGHT, HARDENING THE FOUL TANGLES THAT BRING ILL LUCK WHEN UNKNOTTED.
MAB PRESSES ON YOUNG VIRGINS IN THEIR DREAMS, TEACHING THEM HOW TO BEAR A LOVER, MAKING THEM WOMEN OF GOOD BEARING.
ENOUGH, MERCUTIO, PEACE!!! YOU SPEAK OF NOTHING!
TRUE: I SPEAK OF DREAMS, WHICH ARE THE PRODUCTS OF AN IDLE BRAIN—
BORN OF NOTHING, THIN AS AIR, AND MORE INCONSTANT THAN THE WIND...
WHICH WOOS THE FROZEN NORTH AND THEN, ANGERED, TURNS SOUTH AGAIN.

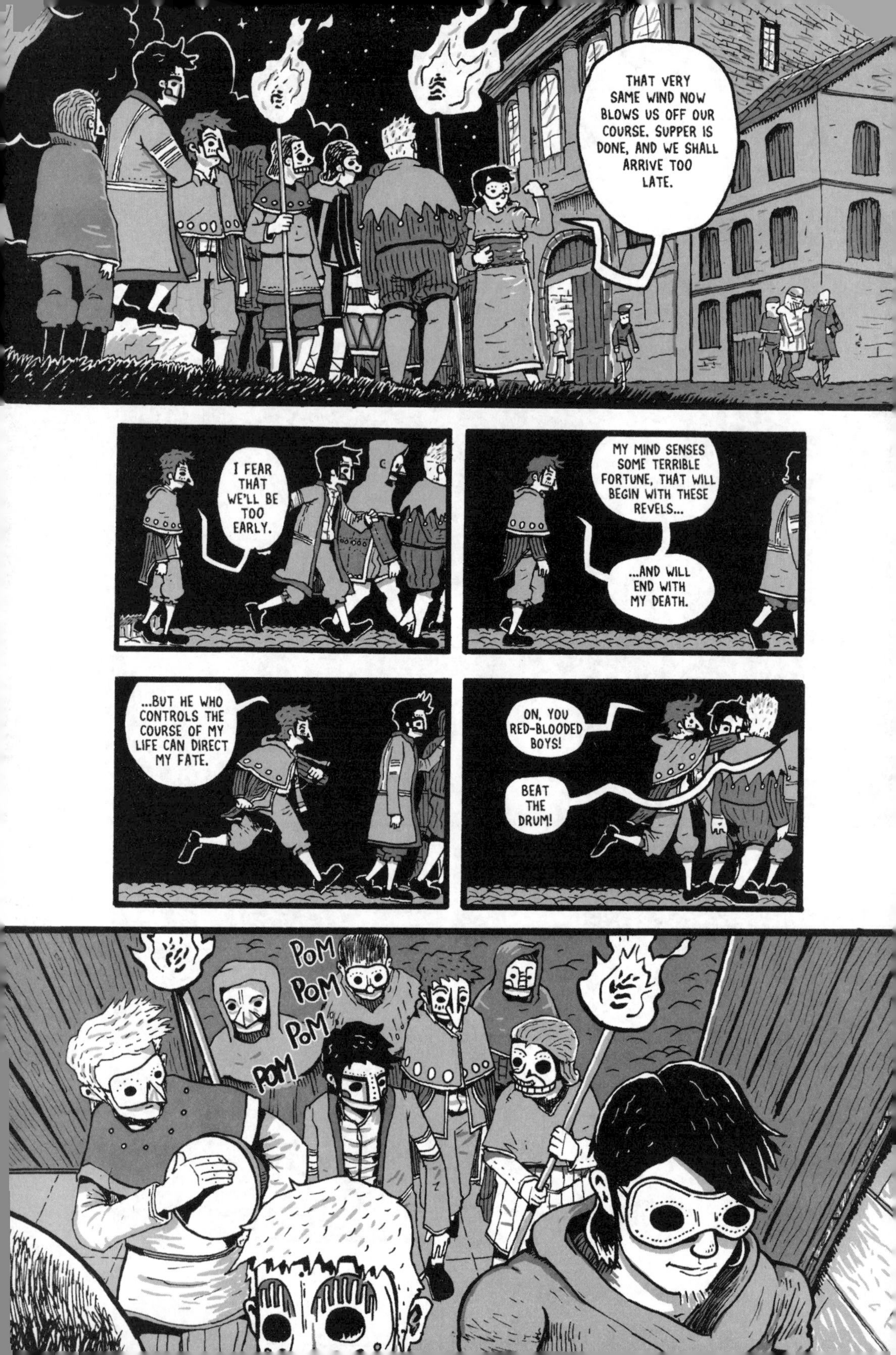

THAT VERY SAME WIND NOW BLOWS US OFF OUR COURSE. SUPPER IS DONE, AND WE SHALL ARRIVE TOO LATE.
I FEAR THAT WE'LL BE TOO EARLY.
MY MIND SENSES SOME TERRIBLE FORTUNE, THAT WILL BEGIN WITH THESE REVELS...
...AND WILL END WITH MY DEATH.
...BUT HE WHO CONTROLS THE COURSE OF MY LIFE CAN DIRECT MY FATE.
ON, YOU RED-BLOODED BOYS!
BEAT THE DRUM!
POM
POM
POM
POM

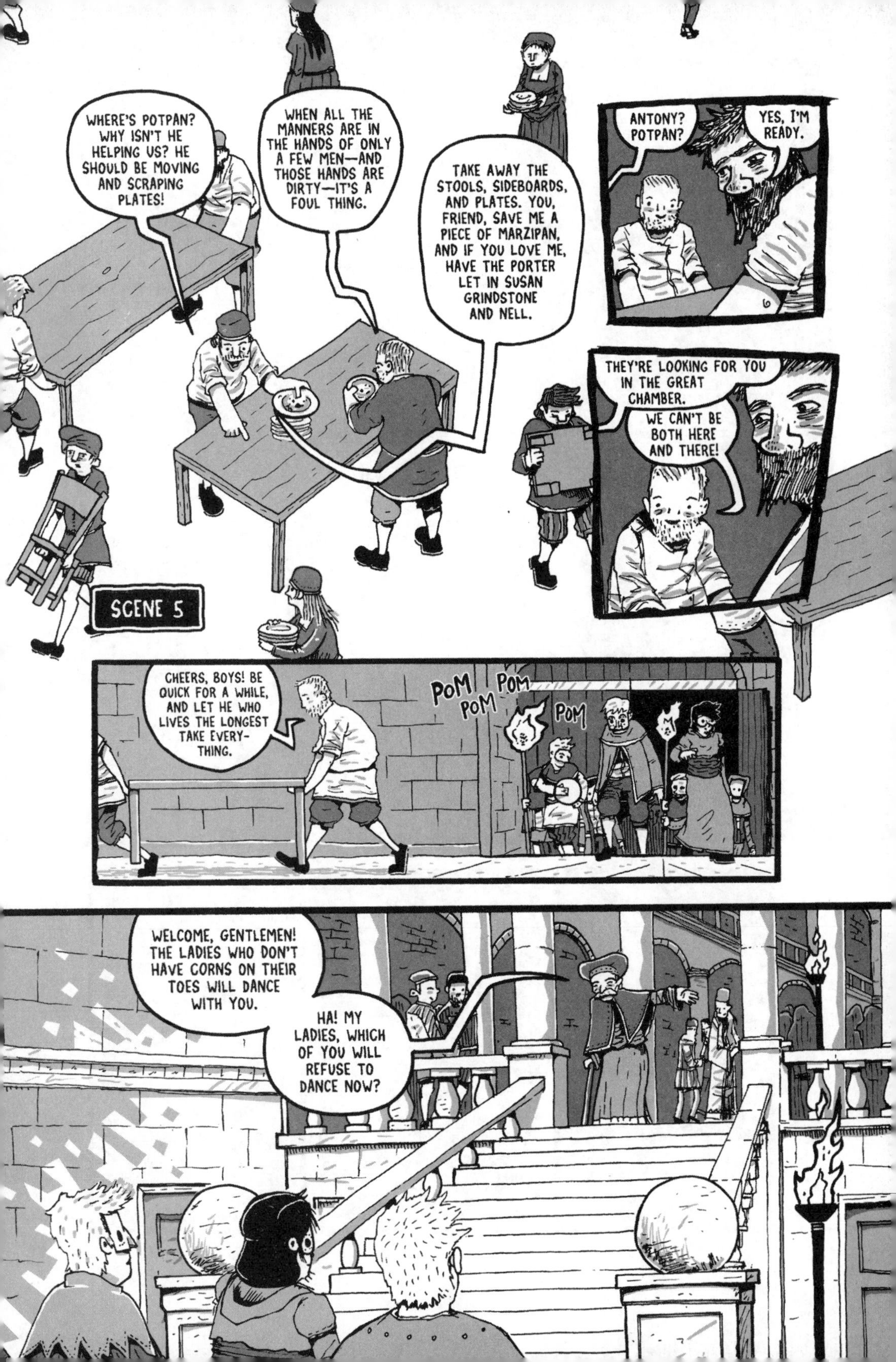
WHERE'S POTPAN? WHY ISN'T HE HELPING US? HE SHOULD BE MOVING AND SCRAPING PLATES!
WHEN ALL THE MANNERS ARE IN THE HANDS OF ONLY A FEW MEN—AND THOSE HANDS ARE DIRTY—IT'S A FOUL THING.
TAKE AWAY THE STOOLS, SIDEBOARDS, AND PLATES. YOU, FRIEND, SAVE ME A PIECE OF MARZIPAN, AND IF YOU LOVE ME, HAVE THE PORTER LET IN SUSAN GRINDSTONE AND NELL.
ANTONY? POTPAN?
YES, I'M READY.
THEY'RE LOOKING FOR YOU IN THE GREAT CHAMBER.
WE CAN'T BE BOTH HERE AND THERE!
SCENE 5
CHEERS, BOYS! BE QUICK FOR A WHILE, AND LET HE WHO LIVES THE LONGEST TAKE EVERY-THING.
POM POM POM POM
WELCOME, GENTLEMEN! THE LADIES WHO DON'T HAVE CORNS ON THEIR TOES WILL DANCE WITH YOU.
HA! MY LADIES, WHICH OF YOU WILL REFUSE TO DANCE NOW?

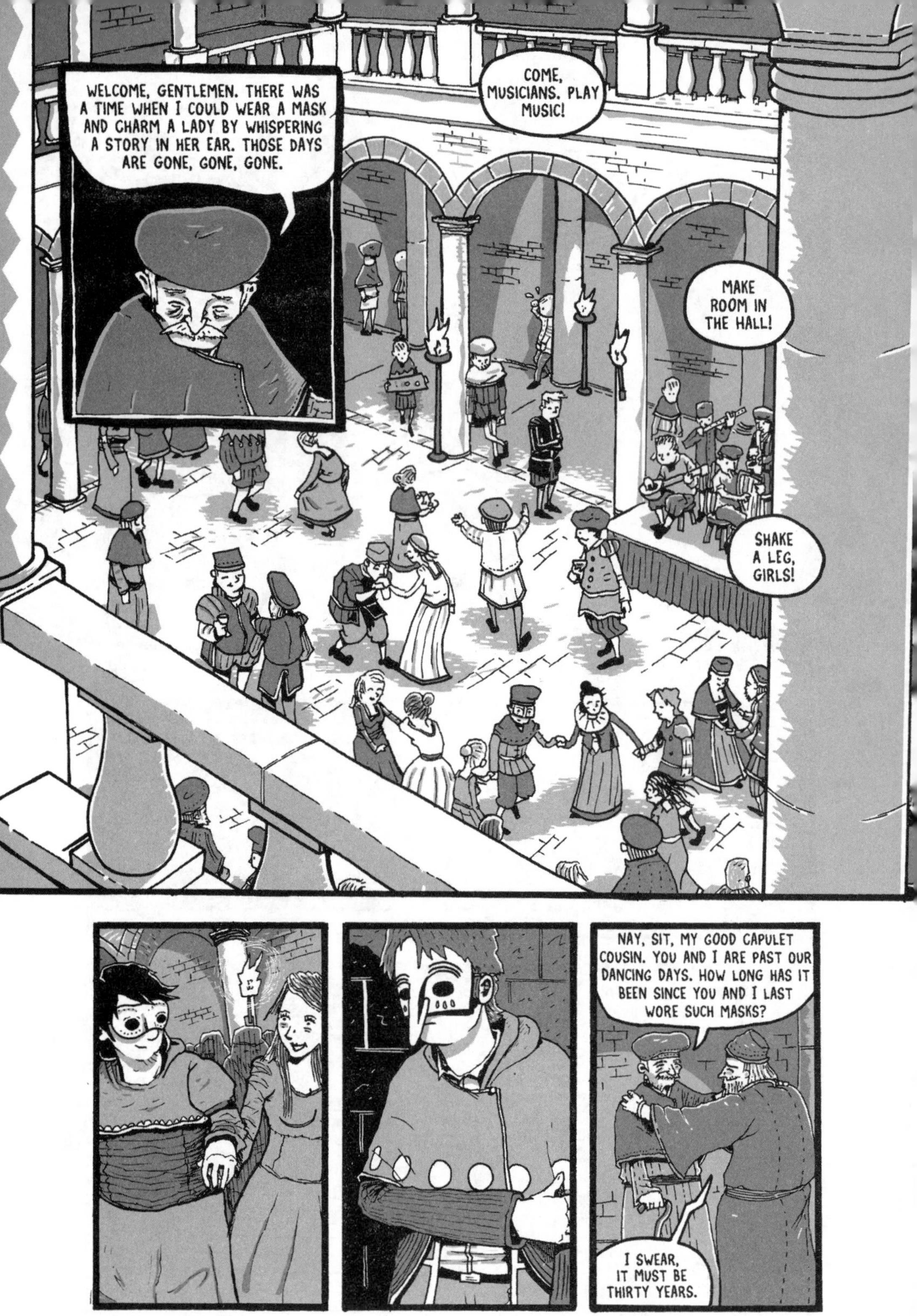
WELCOME, GENTLEMEN. THERE WAS A TIME WHEN I COULD WEAR A MASK AND CHARM A LADY BY WHISPERING A STORY IN HER EAR. THOSE DAYS ARE GONE, GONE, GONE.
COME, MUSICIANS. PLAY MUSIC!
MAKE ROOM IN THE HALL!
SHAKE A LEG, GIRLS!
NAY, SIT, MY GOOD CAPULET COUSIN. YOU AND I ARE PAST OUR DANCING DAYS. HOW LONG HAS IT BEEN SINCE YOU AND I LAST WORE SUCH MASKS?
I SWEAR, IT MUST BE THIRTY YEARS.

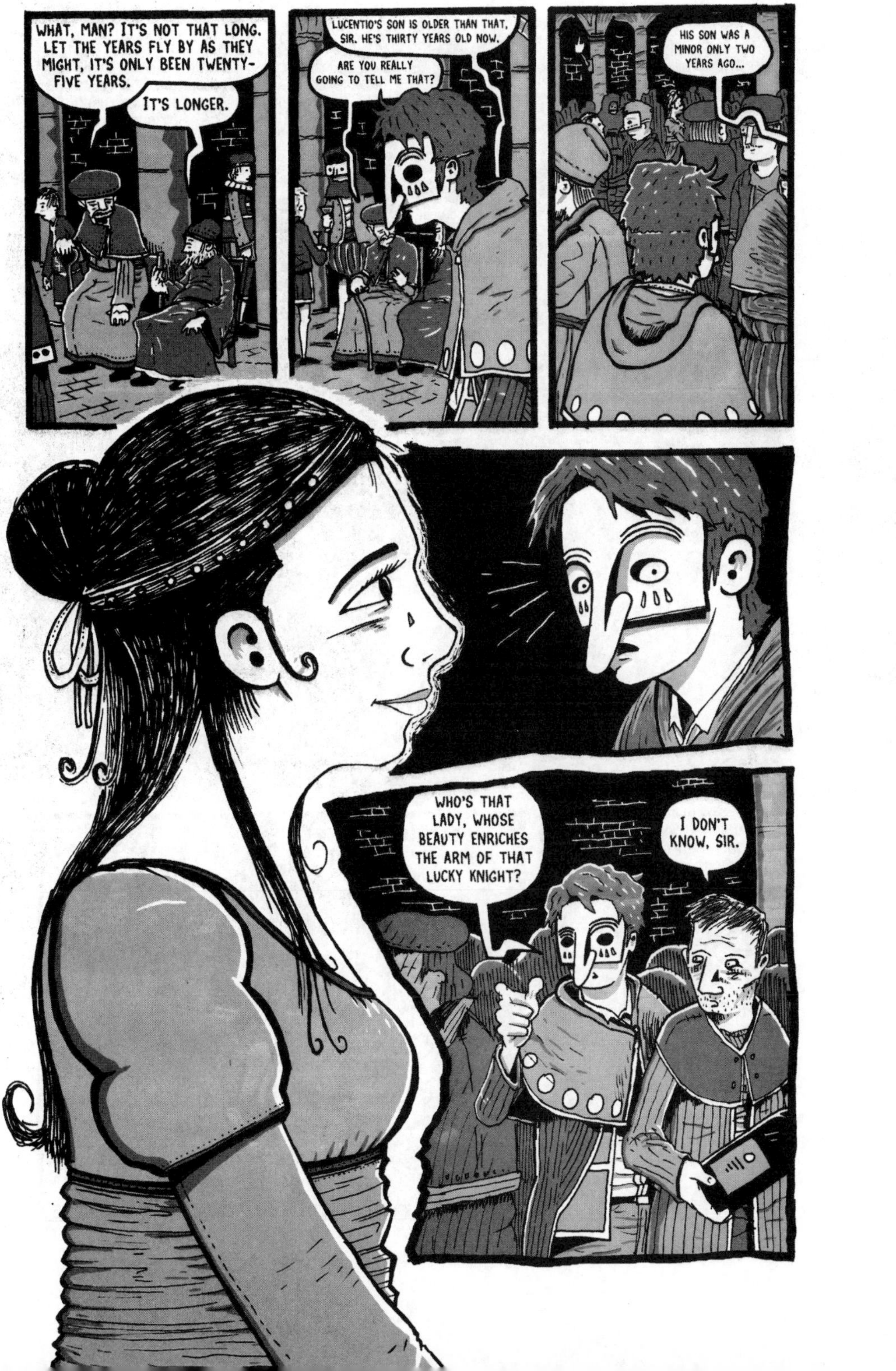
WHAT, MAN? IT'S NOT THAT LONG. LET THE YEARS FLY BY AS THEY MIGHT, IT'S ONLY BEEN TWENTY-FIVE YEARS.
IT'S LONGER.
LUCENTIO'S SON IS OLDER THAN THAT, SIR. HE'S THIRTY YEARS OLD NOW.
ARE YOU REALLY GOING TO TELL ME THAT?
HIS SON WAS A MINOR ONLY TWO YEARS AGO...
WHO'S THAT LADY, WHOSE BEAUTY ENRICHES THE ARM OF THAT LUCKY KNIGHT?
I DON'T KNOW, SIR.

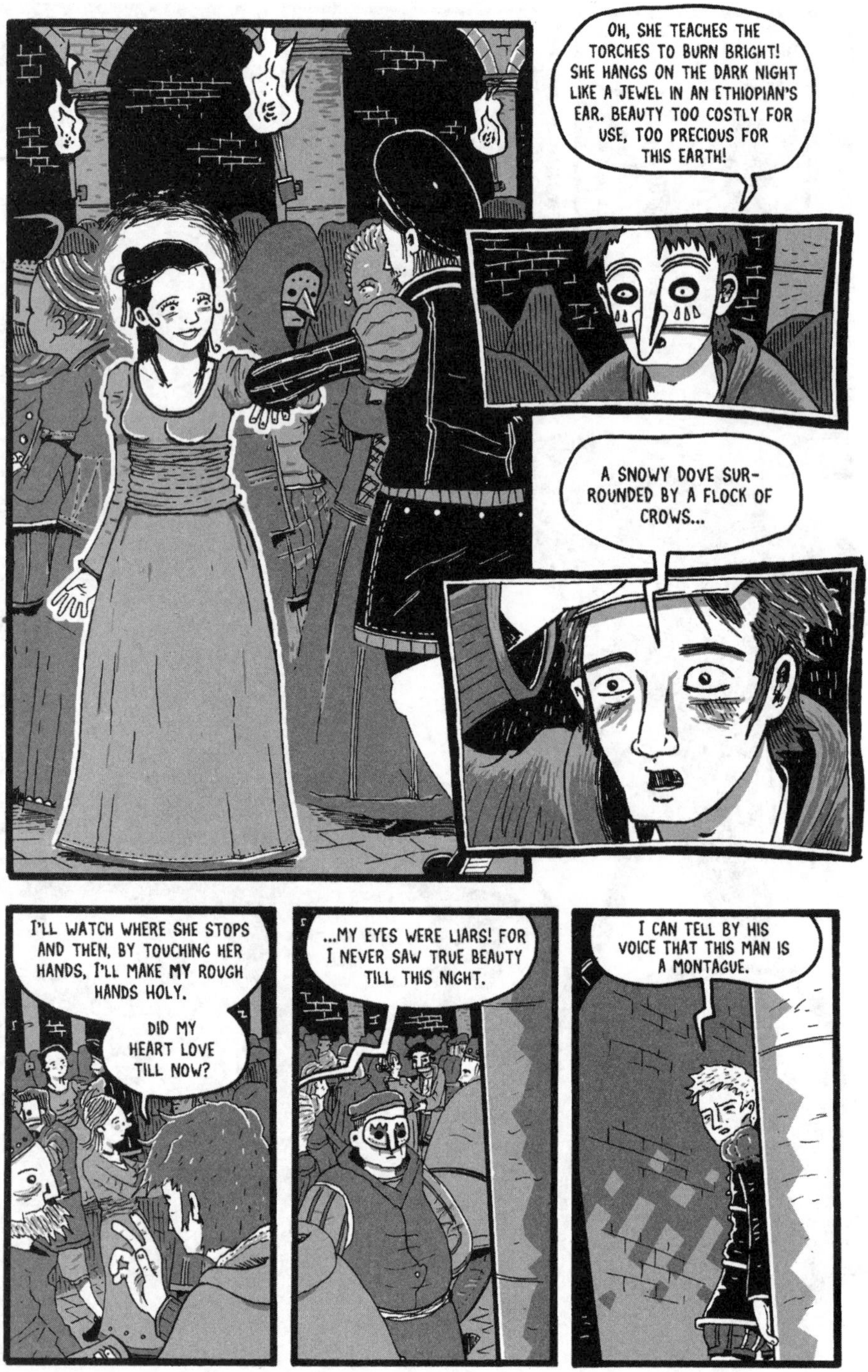
OH, SHE TEACHES THE TORCHES TO BURN BRIGHT! SHE HANGS ON THE DARK NIGHT LIKE A JEWEL IN AN ETHIOPIAN'S EAR. BEAUTY TOO COSTLY FOR USE, TOO PRECIOUS FOR THIS EARTH!
A SNOWY DOVE SURROUNDED BY A FLOCK OF CROWS...
I'LL WATCH WHERE SHE STOPS AND THEN, BY TOUCHING HER HANDS, I'LL MAKE MY ROUGH HANDS HOLY.
DID MY HEART LOVE TILL NOW?
...MY EYES WERE LIARS! FOR I NEVER SAW TRUE BEAUTY TILL THIS NIGHT.
I CAN TELL BY HIS VOICE THAT THIS MAN IS A MONTAGUE.

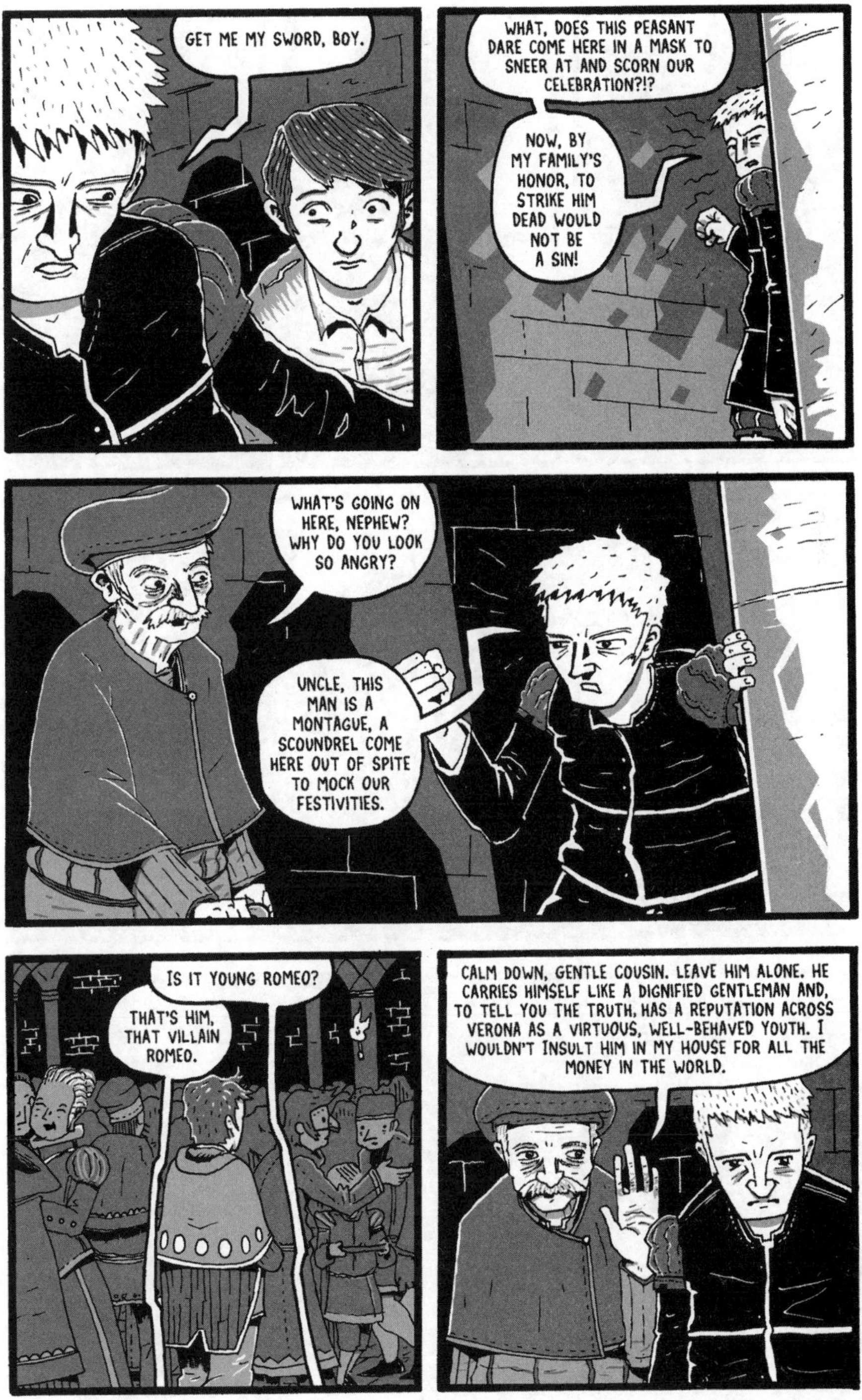
GET ME MY SWORD, BOY.
WHAT, DOES THIS PEASANT DARE COME HERE IN A MASK TO SNEER AT AND SCORN OUR CELEBRATION?!?
NOW, BY MY FAMILY'S HONOR, TO STRIKE HIM DEAD WOULD NOT BE A SIN!
WHAT'S GOING ON HERE, NEPHEW? WHY DO YOU LOOK SO ANGRY?
UNCLE, THIS MAN IS A MONTAGUE, A SCOUNDREL COME HERE OUT OF SPITE TO MOCK OUR FESTIVITIES.
IS IT YOUNG ROMEO?
THAT'S HIM, THAT VILLAIN ROMEO.
CALM DOWN, GENTLE COUSIN. LEAVE HIM ALONE. HE CARRIES HIMSELF LIKE A DIGNIFIED GENTLEMAN AND, TO TELL YOU THE TRUTH, HAS A REPUTATION ACROSS VERONA AS A VIRTUOUS, WELL-BEHAVED YOUTH. I WOULDN'T INSULT HIM IN MY HOUSE FOR ALL THE MONEY IN THE WORLD.

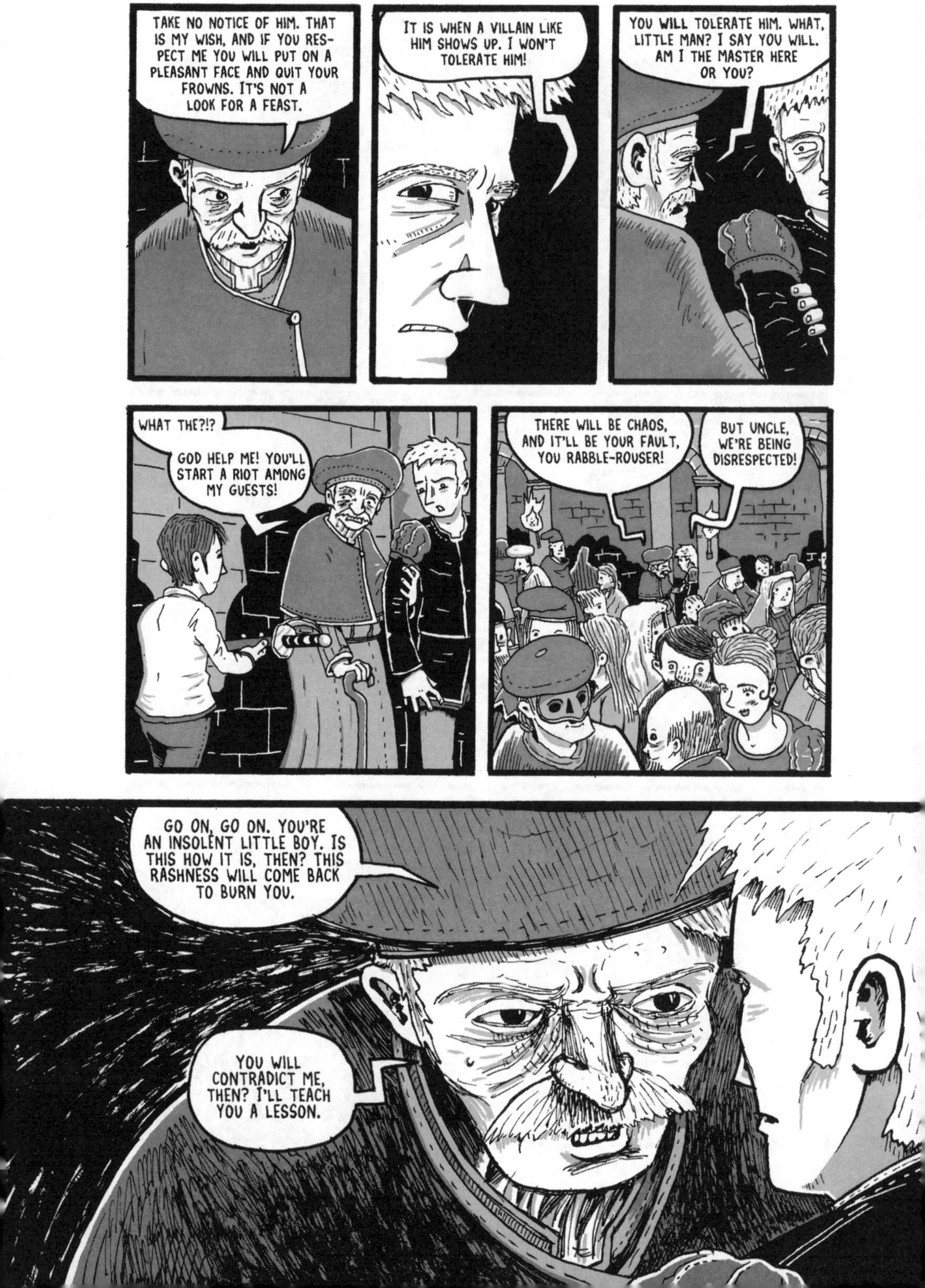
TAKE NO NOTICE OF HIM. THAT IS MY WISH, AND IF YOU RESPECT ME YOU WILL PUT ON A PLEASANT FACE AND QUIT YOUR FROWNS. IT'S NOT A LOOK FOR A FEAST.
IT IS WHEN A VILLAIN LIKE HIM SHOWS UP. I WON'T TOLERATE HIM!
YOU WILL TOLERATE HIM. WHAT, LITTLE MAN? I SAY YOU WILL. AM I THE MASTER HERE OR YOU?
WHAT THE?!?
GOD HELP ME! YOU'LL START A RIOT AMONG MY GUESTS!
THERE WILL BE CHAOS, AND IT'LL BE YOUR FAULT, YOU RABBLE-ROUSER!
BUT UNCLE, WE'RE BEING DISRESPECTED!
GO ON, GO ON. YOU'RE AN INSOLENT LITTLE BOY. IS THIS HOW IT IS, THEN? THIS RASHNESS WILL COME BACK TO BURN YOU.
YOU WILL CONTRADICT ME, THEN? I'LL TEACH YOU A LESSON.

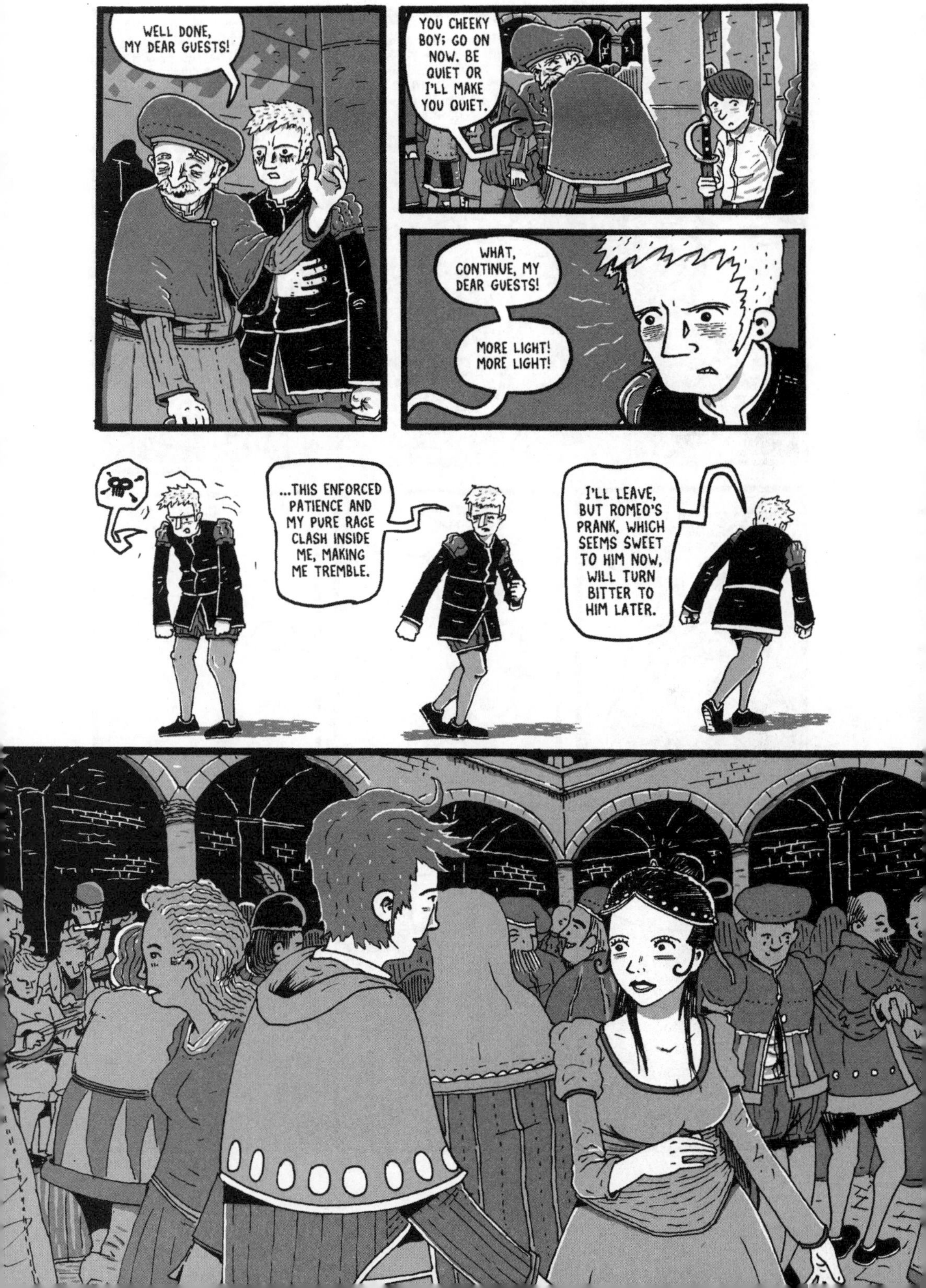
WELL DONE, MY DEAR GUESTS!
YOU CHEEKY BOY; GO ON NOW. BE QUIET OR I'LL MAKE YOU QUIET.
WHAT, CONTINUE, MY DEAR GUESTS!
MORE LIGHT! MORE LIGHT!
...THIS ENFORCED PATIENCE AND MY PURE RAGE CLASH INSIDE ME, MAKING ME TREMBLE.
I'LL LEAVE, BUT ROMEO'S PRANK, WHICH SEEMS SWEET TO HIM NOW, WILL TURN BITTER TO HIM LATER.

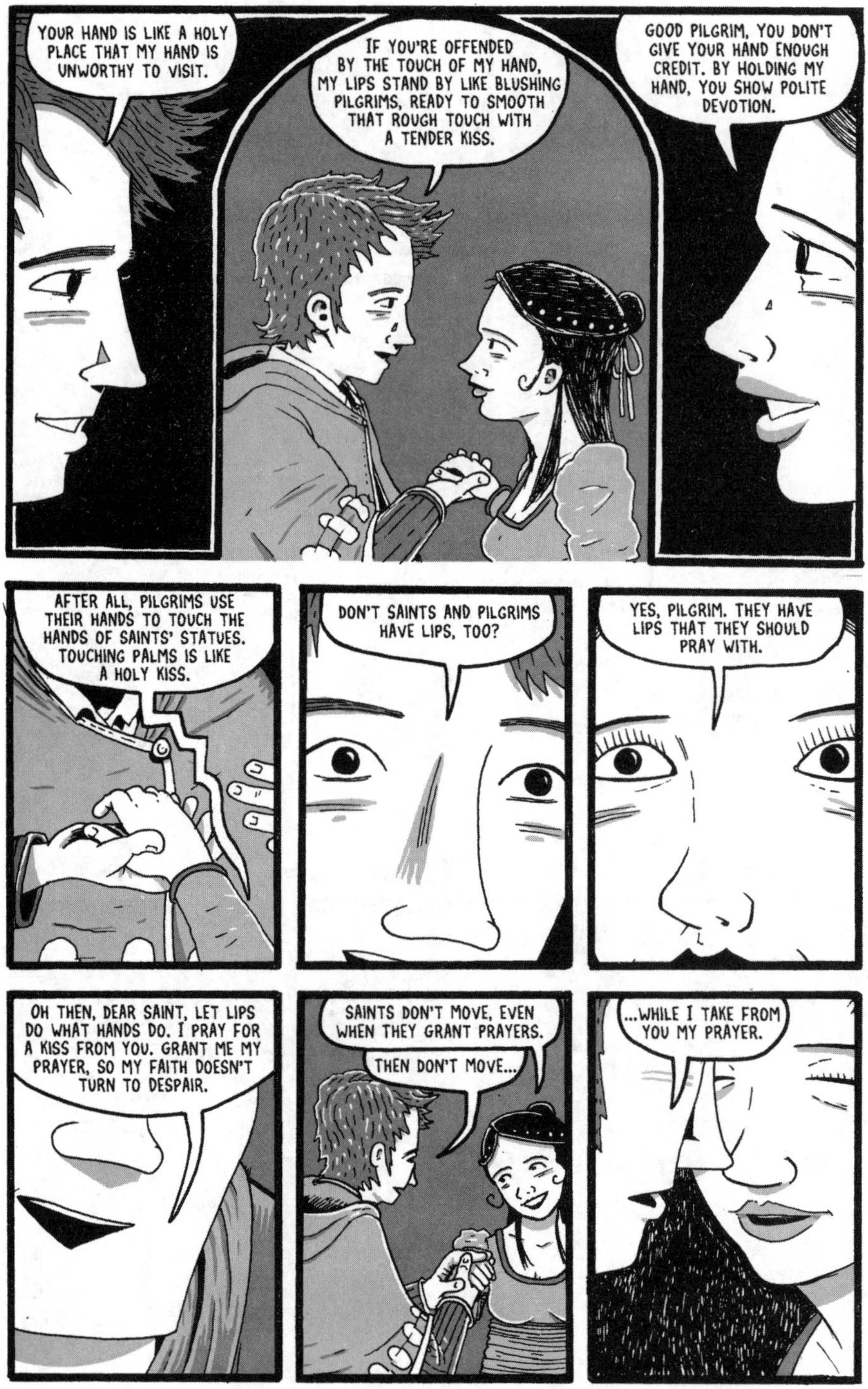
YOUR HAND IS LIKE A HOLY PLACE THAT MY HAND IS UNWORTHY TO VISIT.
IF YOU'RE OFFENDED BY THE TOUCH OF MY HAND, MY LIPS STAND BY LIKE BLUSHING PILGRIMS, READY TO SMOOTH THAT ROUGH TOUCH WITH A TENDER KISS.
GOOD PILGRIM, YOU DON'T GIVE YOUR HAND ENOUGH CREDIT. BY HOLDING MY HAND, YOU SHOW POLITE DEVOTION.
AFTER ALL, PILGRIMS USE THEIR HANDS TO TOUCH THE HANDS OF SAINTS' STATUES. TOUCHING PALMS IS LIKE A HOLY KISS.
DON'T SAINTS AND PILGRIMS HAVE LIPS, TOO?
YES, PILGRIM. THEY HAVE LIPS THAT THEY SHOULD PRAY WITH.
OH THEN, DEAR SAINT, LET LIPS DO WHAT HANDS DO. I PRAY FOR A KISS FROM YOU. GRANT ME MY PRAYER, SO MY FAITH DOESN'T TURN TO DESPAIR.
SAINTS DON'T MOVE, EVEN WHEN THEY GRANT PRAYERS.
THEN DON'T MOVE...
...WHILE I TAKE FROM YOU MY PRAYER.

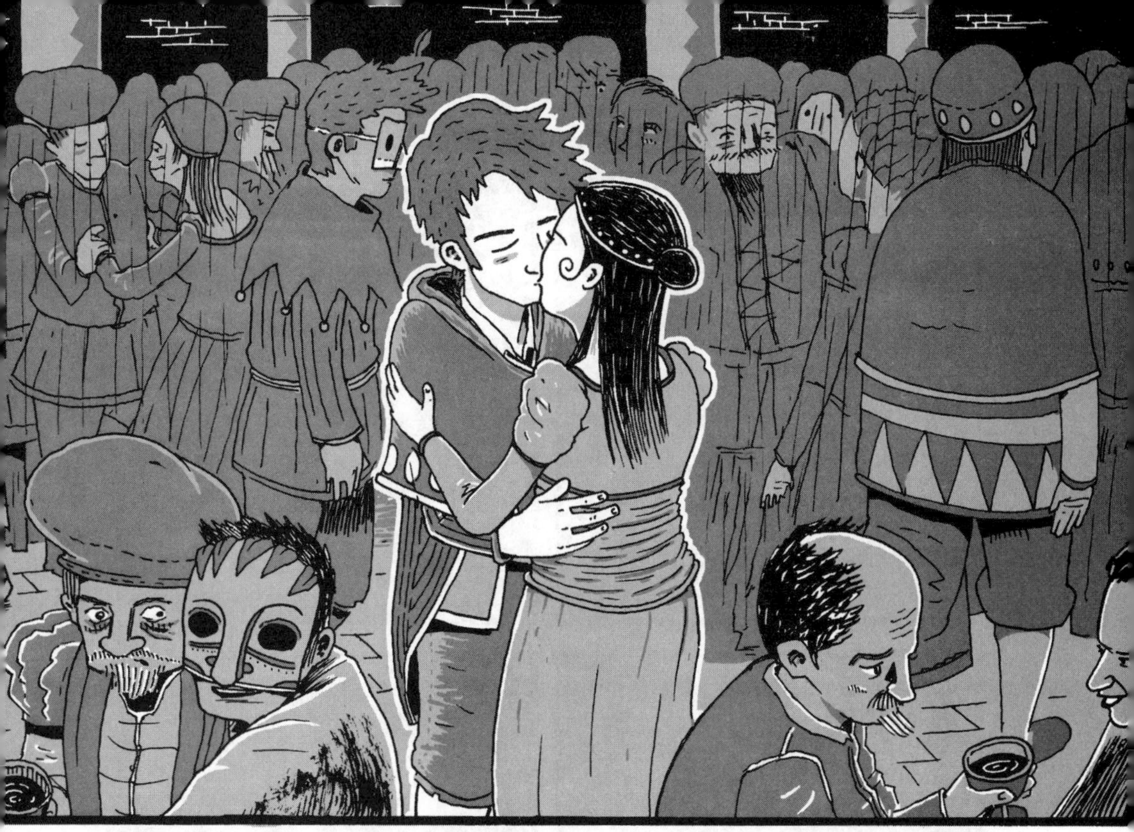

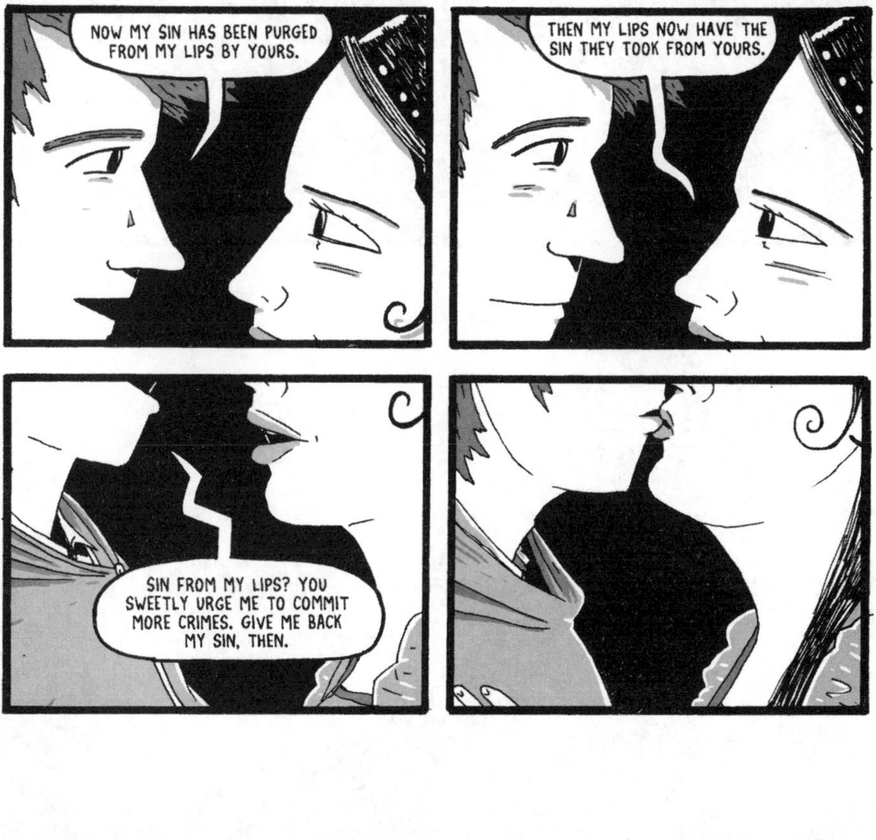
NOW MY SIN HAS BEEN PURGED FROM MY LIPS BY YOURS.
THEN MY LIPS NOW HAVE THE SIN THEY TOOK FROM YOURS.
SIN FROM MY LIPS? YOU SWEETLY URGE ME TO COMMIT MORE CRIMES. GIVE ME BACK MY SIN, THEN.

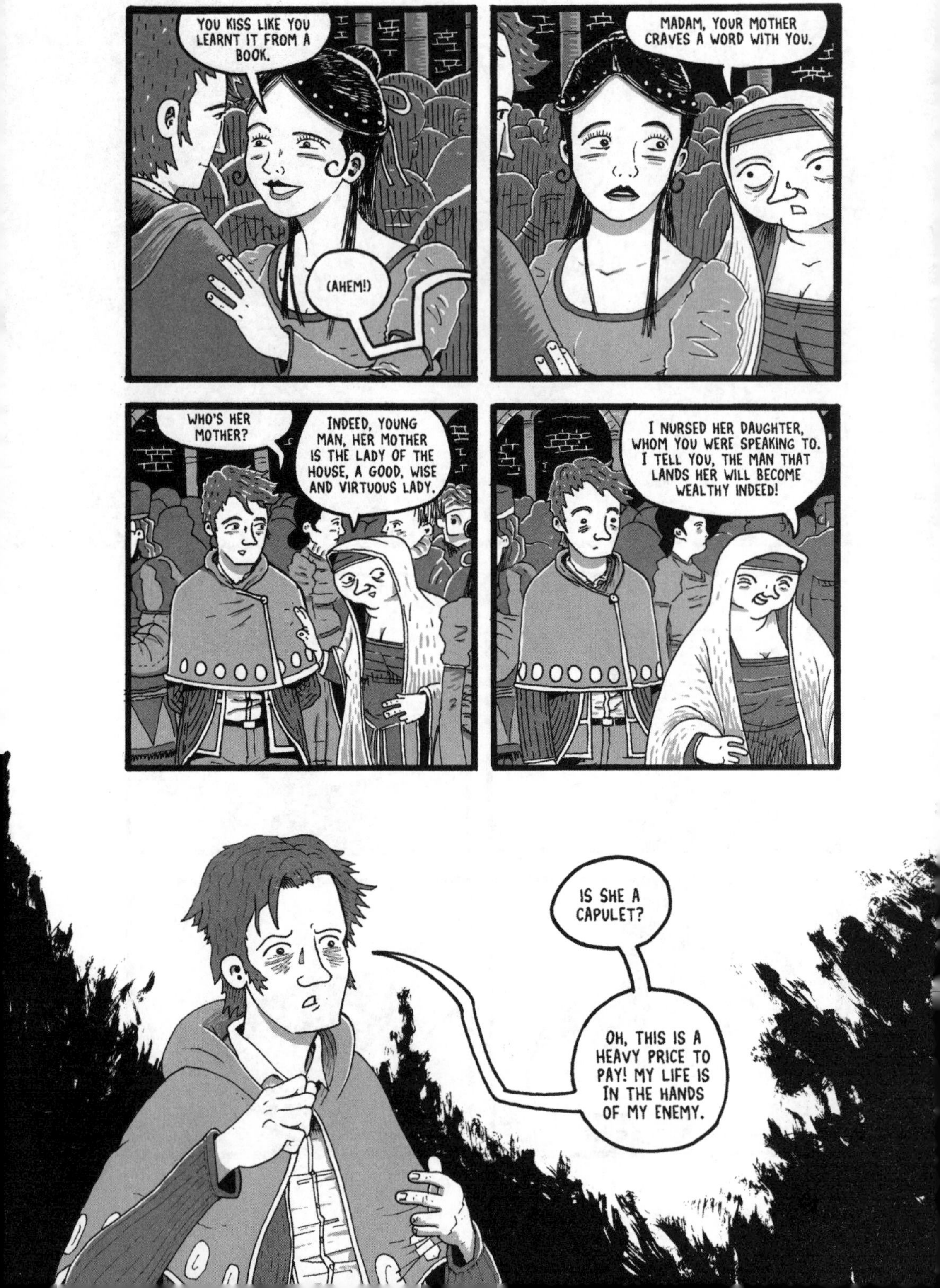
YOU KISS LIKE YOU LEARNT IT FROM A BOOK.
(AHEM!)
MADAM, YOUR MOTHER CRAVES A WORD WITH YOU.
WHO'S HER MOTHER?
INDEED, YOUNG MAN, HER MOTHER IS THE LADY OF THE HOUSE, A GOOD, WISE AND VIRTUOUS LADY.
I NURSED HER DAUGHTER, WHOM YOU WERE SPEAKING TO. I TELL YOU, THE MAN THAT LANDS HER WILL BECOME WEALTHY INDEED!
IS SHE A CAPULET?
OH, THIS IS A HEAVY PRICE TO PAY! MY LIFE IS IN THE HANDS OF MY ENEMY.

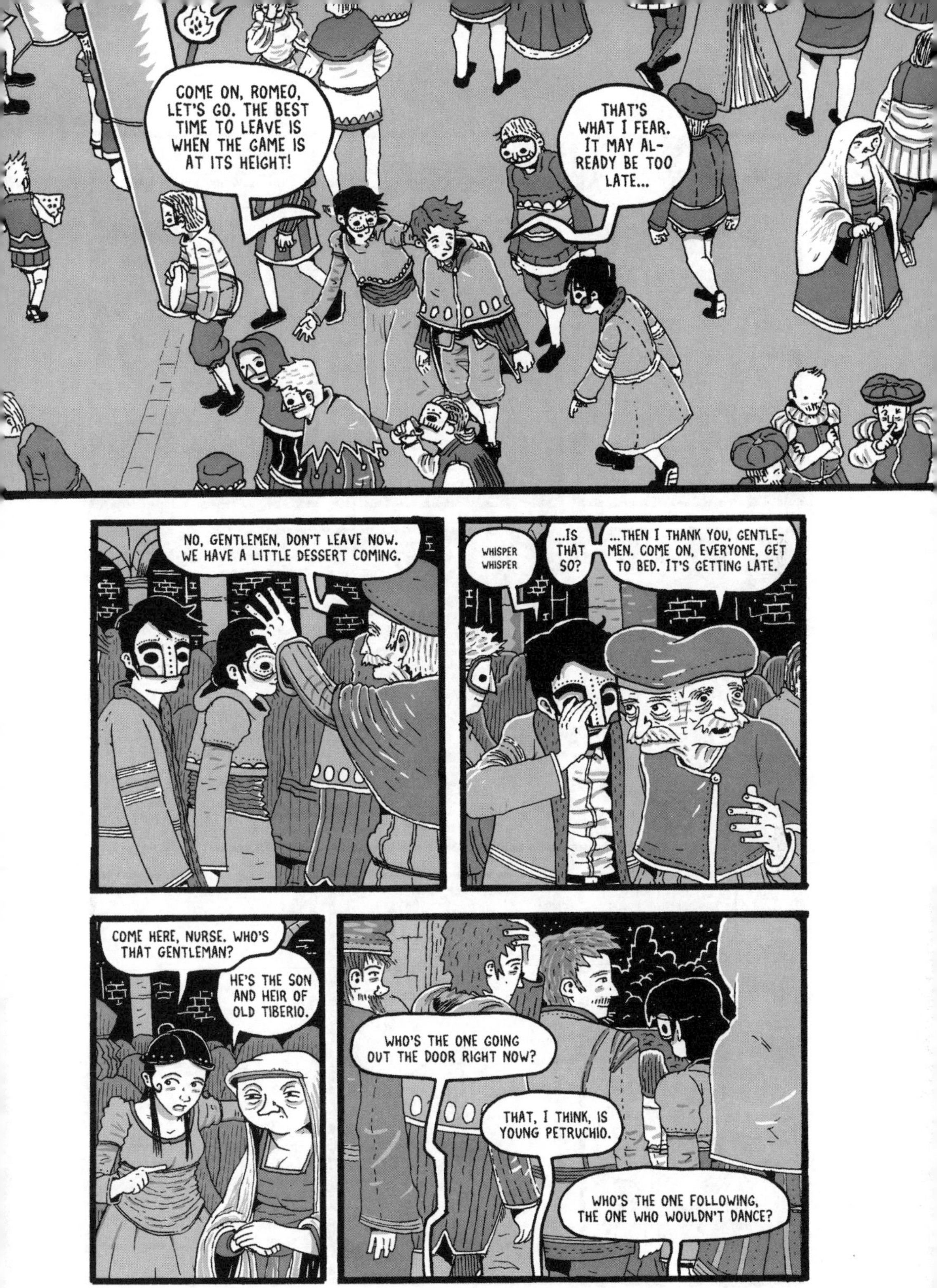
COME ON, ROMEO, LET'S GO. THE BEST TIME TO LEAVE IS WHEN THE GAME IS AT ITS HEIGHT!
THAT'S WHAT I FEAR. IT MAY ALREADY BE TOO LATE...
NO, GENTLEMEN, DON'T LEAVE NOW. WE HAVE A LITTLE DESSERT COMING.
WHISPER WHISPER
...IS THAT SO?
...THEN I THANK YOU, GENTLEMEN. COME ON, EVERYONE, GET TO BED. IT'S GETTING LATE.
COME HERE, NURSE. WHO'S THAT GENTLEMAN?
HE'S THE SON AND HEIR OF OLD TIBERIO.
WHO'S THE ONE GOING OUT THE DOOR RIGHT NOW?
THAT, I THINK, IS YOUNG PETRUCHIO.
WHO'S THE ONE FOLLOWING, THE ONE WHO WOULDN'T DANCE?

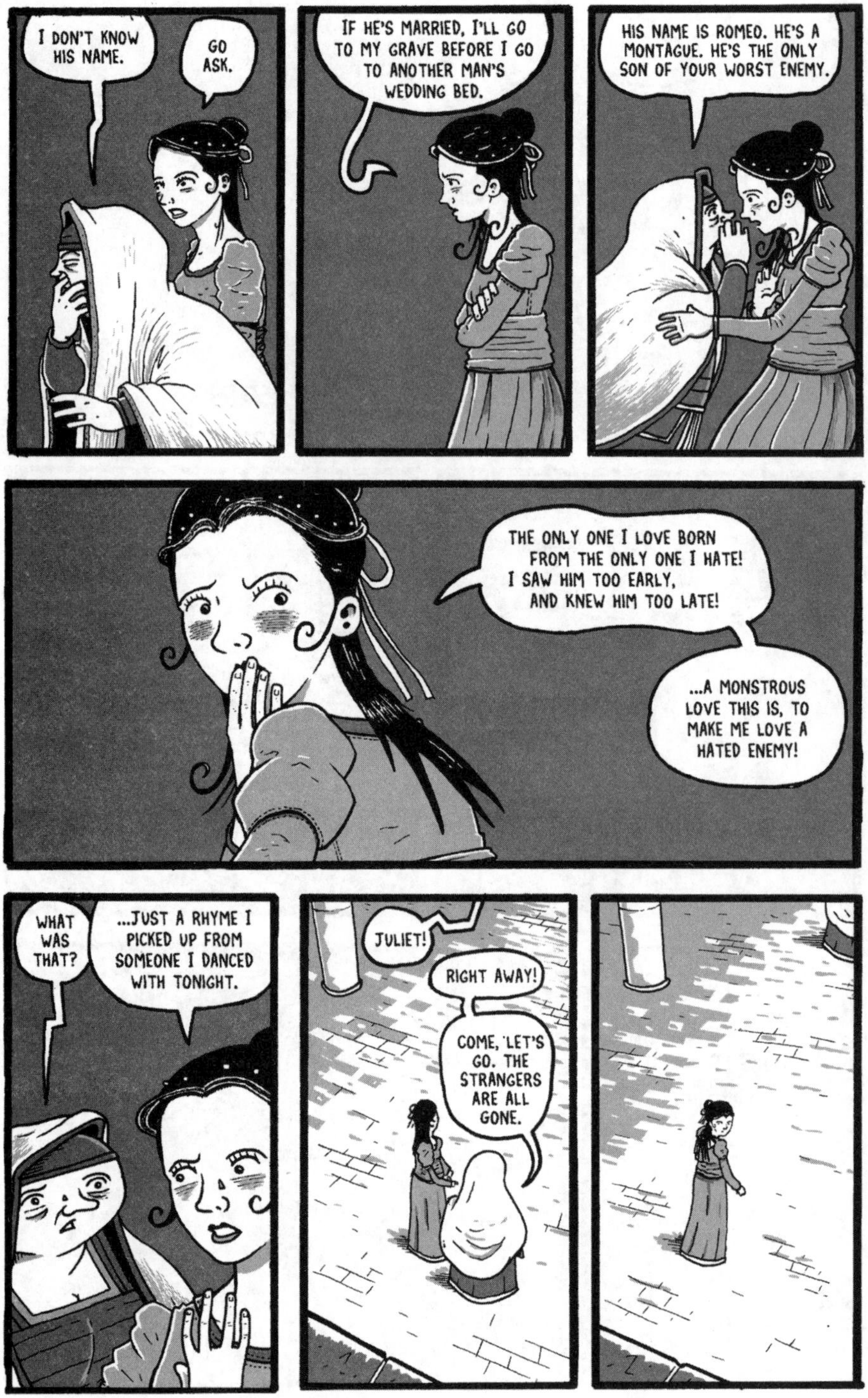
I DON'T KNOW HIS NAME.
GO ASK.
IF HE'S MARRIED, I'LL GO TO MY GRAVE BEFORE I GO TO ANOTHER MAN'S WEDDING BED.
HIS NAME IS ROMEO. HE'S A MONTAGUE. HE'S THE ONLY SON OF YOUR WORST ENEMY.
THE ONLY ONE I LOVE BORN FROM THE ONLY ONE I HATE! I SAW HIM TOO EARLY, AND KNEW HIM TOO LATE!
...A MONSTROUS LOVE THIS IS, TO MAKE ME LOVE A HATED ENEMY!
WHAT WAS THAT?
...JUST A RHYME I PICKED UP FROM SOMEONE I DANCED WITH TONIGHT.
JULIET!
RIGHT AWAY!
COME, LET'S GO. THE STRANGERS ARE ALL GONE.

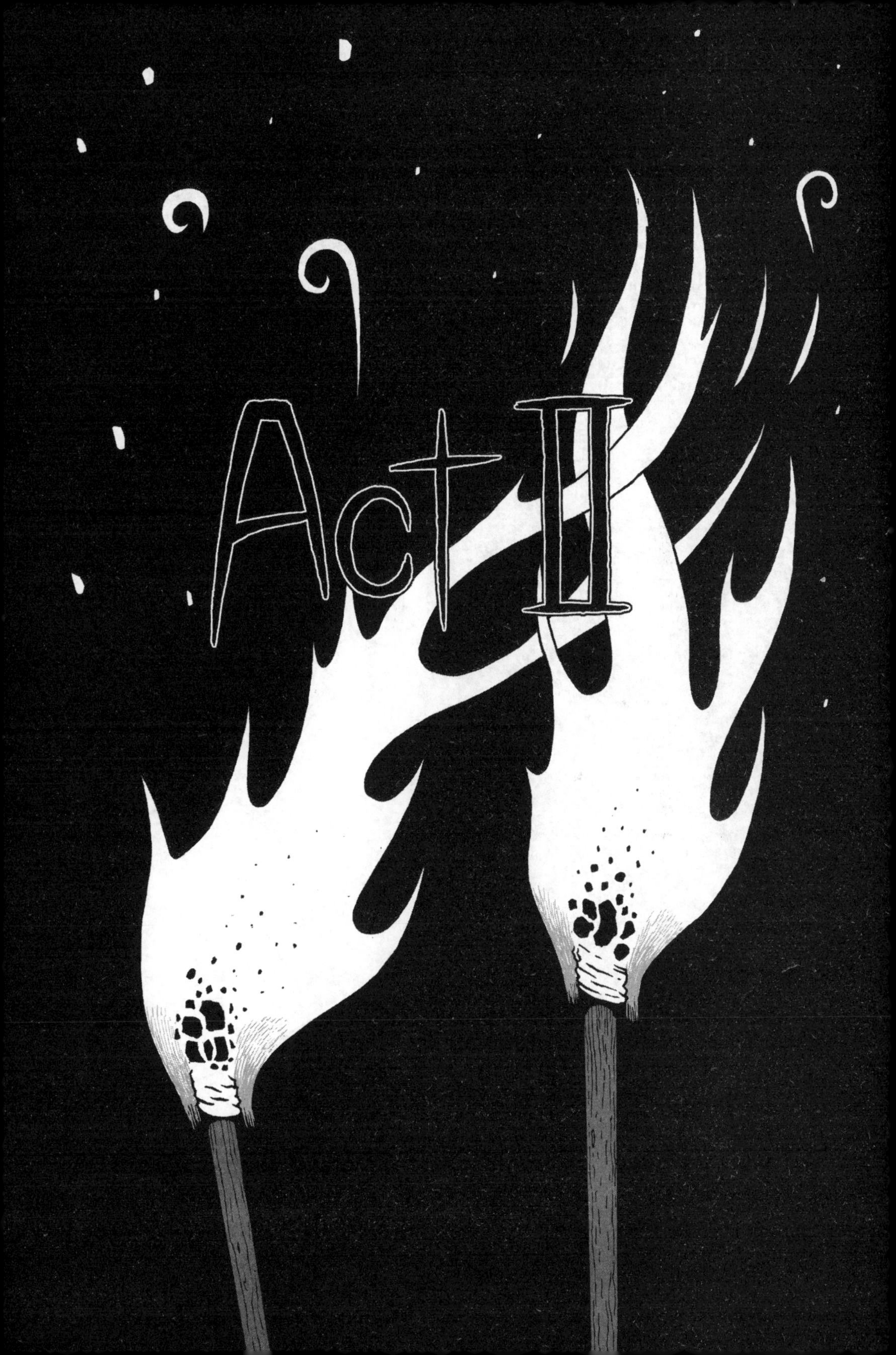
Act II

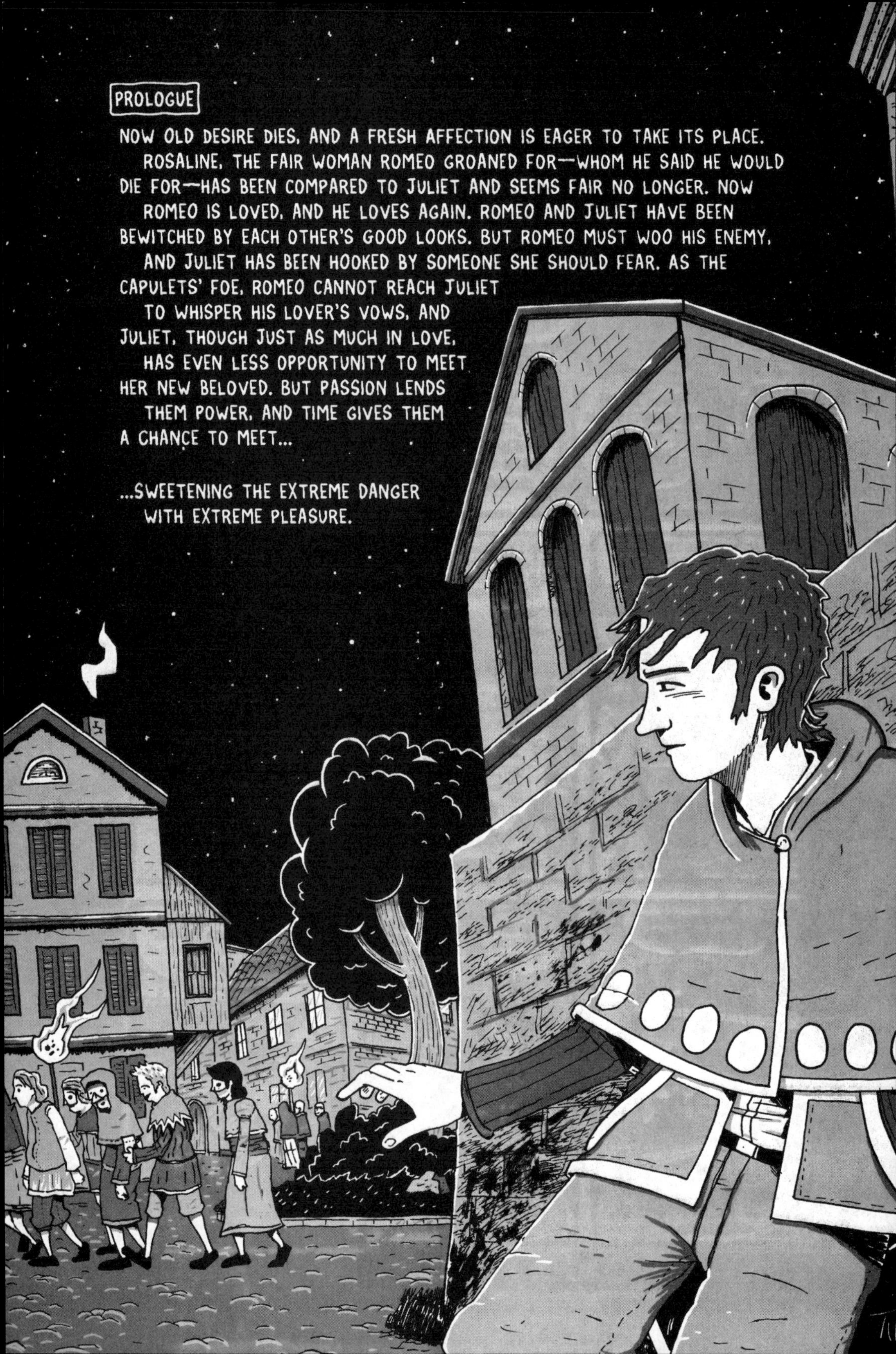
PROLOGUE
NOW OLD DESIRE DIES, AND A FRESH AFFECTION IS EAGER TO TAKE ITS PLACE. ROSALINE, THE FAIR WOMAN ROMEO GROANED FOR—WHOM HE SAID HE WOULD DIE FOR—HAS BEEN COMPARED TO JULIET AND SEEMS FAIR NO LONGER. NOW ROMEO IS LOVED, AND HE LOVES AGAIN. ROMEO AND JULIET HAVE BEEN BEWITCHED BY EACH OTHER'S GOOD LOOKS. BUT ROMEO MUST WOO HIS ENEMY, AND JULIET HAS BEEN HOOKED BY SOMEONE SHE SHOULD FEAR. AS THE CAPULETS' FOE, ROMEO CANNOT REACH JULIET TO WHISPER HIS LOVER'S VOWS, AND JULIET, THOUGH JUST AS MUCH IN LOVE, HAS EVEN LESS OPPORTUNITY TO MEET HER NEW BELOVED. BUT PASSION LENDS THEM POWER, AND TIME GIVES THEM A CHANCE TO MEET...
...SWEETENING THE EXTREME DANGER WITH EXTREME PLEASURE.

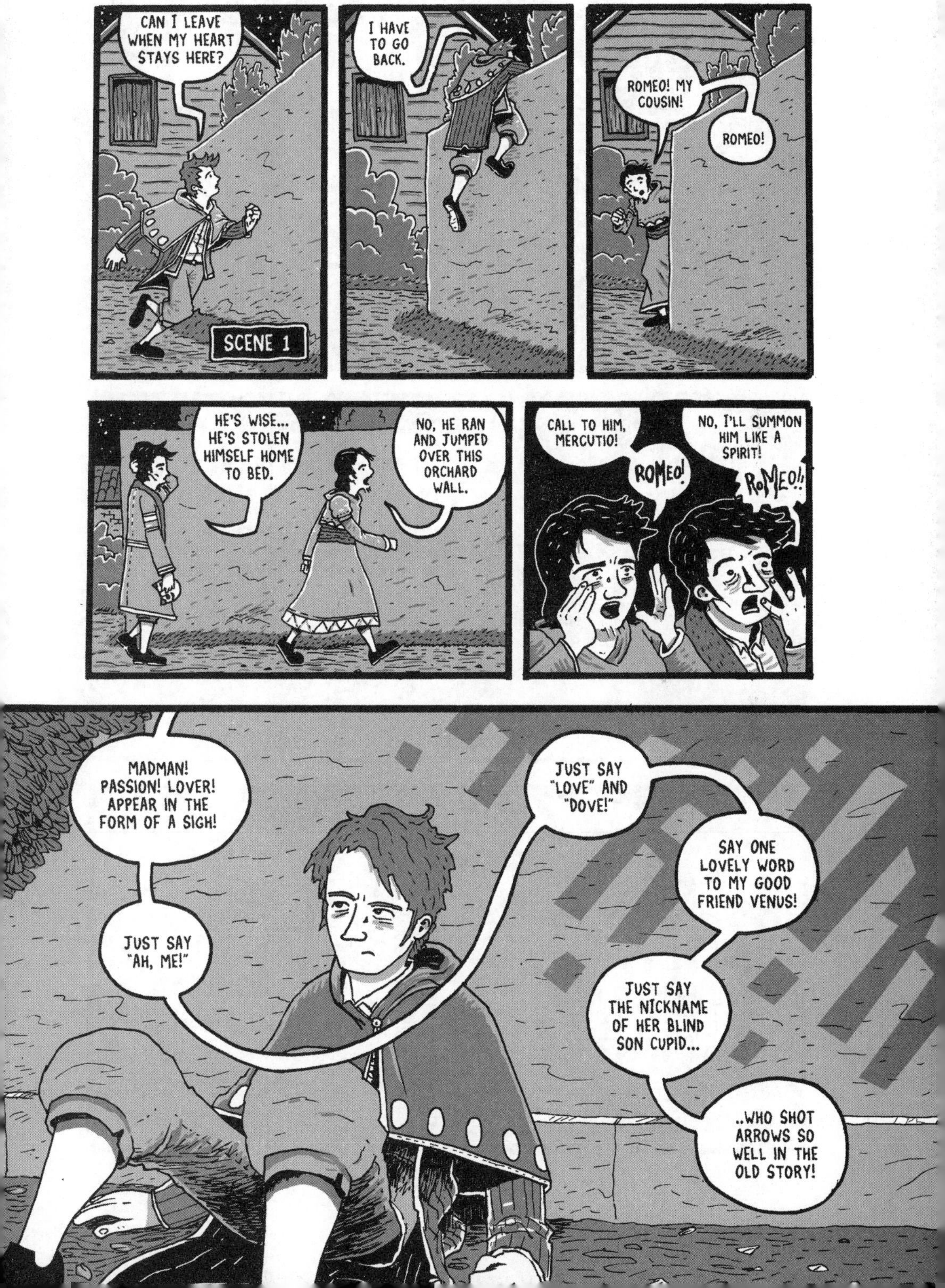
CAN I LEAVE WHEN MY HEART STAYS HERE?
SCENE 1
I HAVE TO GO BACK.
ROMEO! MY COUSIN!
ROMEO!
HE'S WISE... HE'S STOLEN HIMSELF HOME TO BED.
NO, HE RAN AND JUMPED OVER THIS ORCHARD WALL.
CALL TO HIM, MERCUTIO!
ROMEO!
NO, I'LL SUMMON HIM LIKE A SPIRIT!
ROMEO!!
MADMAN! PASSION! LOVER! APPEAR IN THE FORM OF A SIGH!
JUST SAY "AH, ME!"
JUST SAY "LOVE" AND "DOVE!"
SAY ONE LOVELY WORD TO MY GOOD FRIEND VENUS!
JUST SAY THE NICKNAME OF HER BLIND SON CUPID...
..WHO SHOT ARROWS SO WELL IN THE OLD STORY!

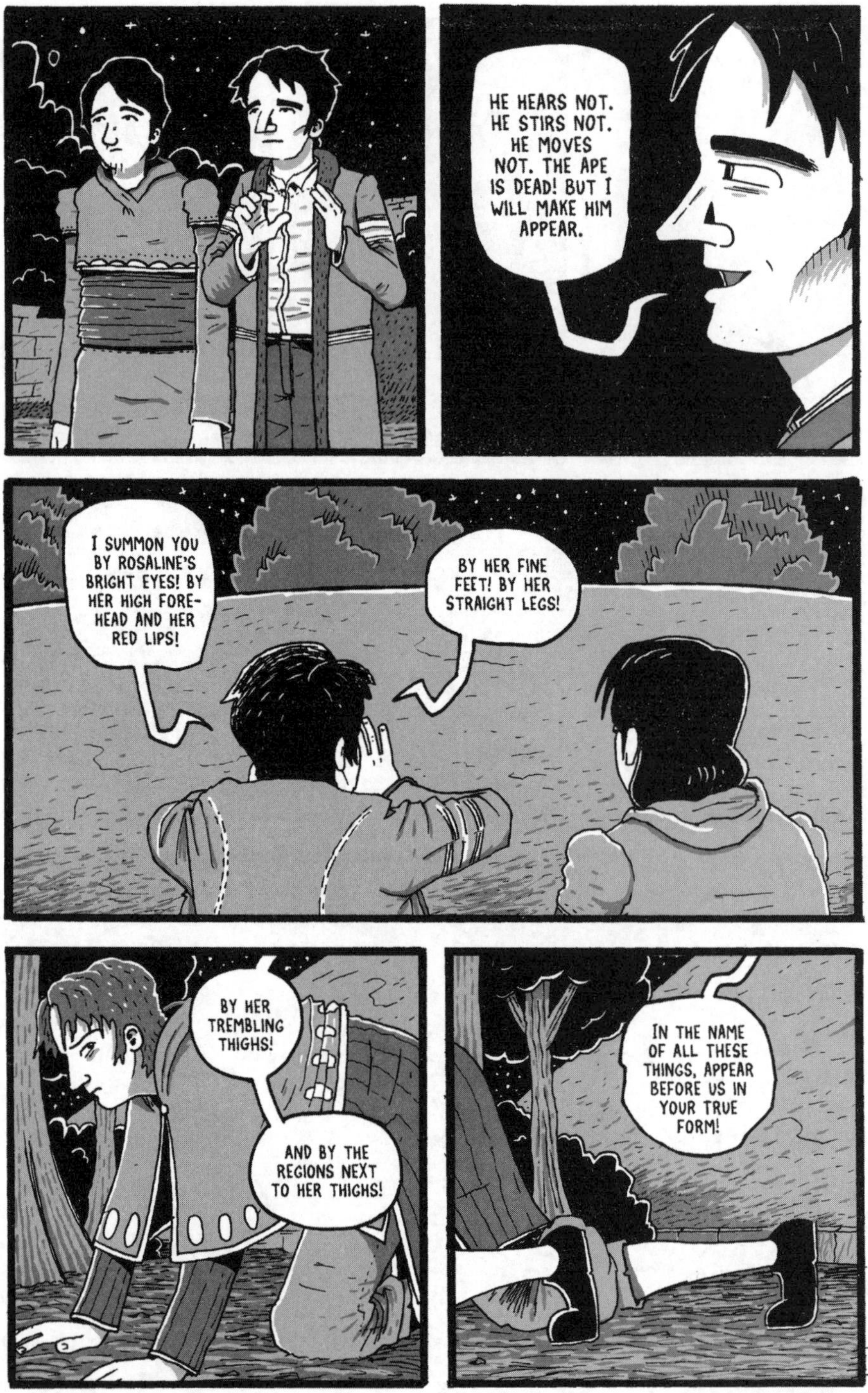
HE HEARS NOT. HE STIRS NOT. HE MOVES NOT. THE APE IS DEAD! BUT I WILL MAKE HIM APPEAR.
I SUMMON YOU BY ROSALINE'S BRIGHT EYES! BY HER HIGH FORE-HEAD AND HER RED LIPS!
BY HER FINE FEET! BY HER STRAIGHT LEGS!
BY HER TREMBLING THIGHS!
AND BY THE REGIONS NEXT TO HER THIGHS!
IN THE NAME OF ALL THESE THINGS, APPEAR BEFORE US IN YOUR TRUE FORM!

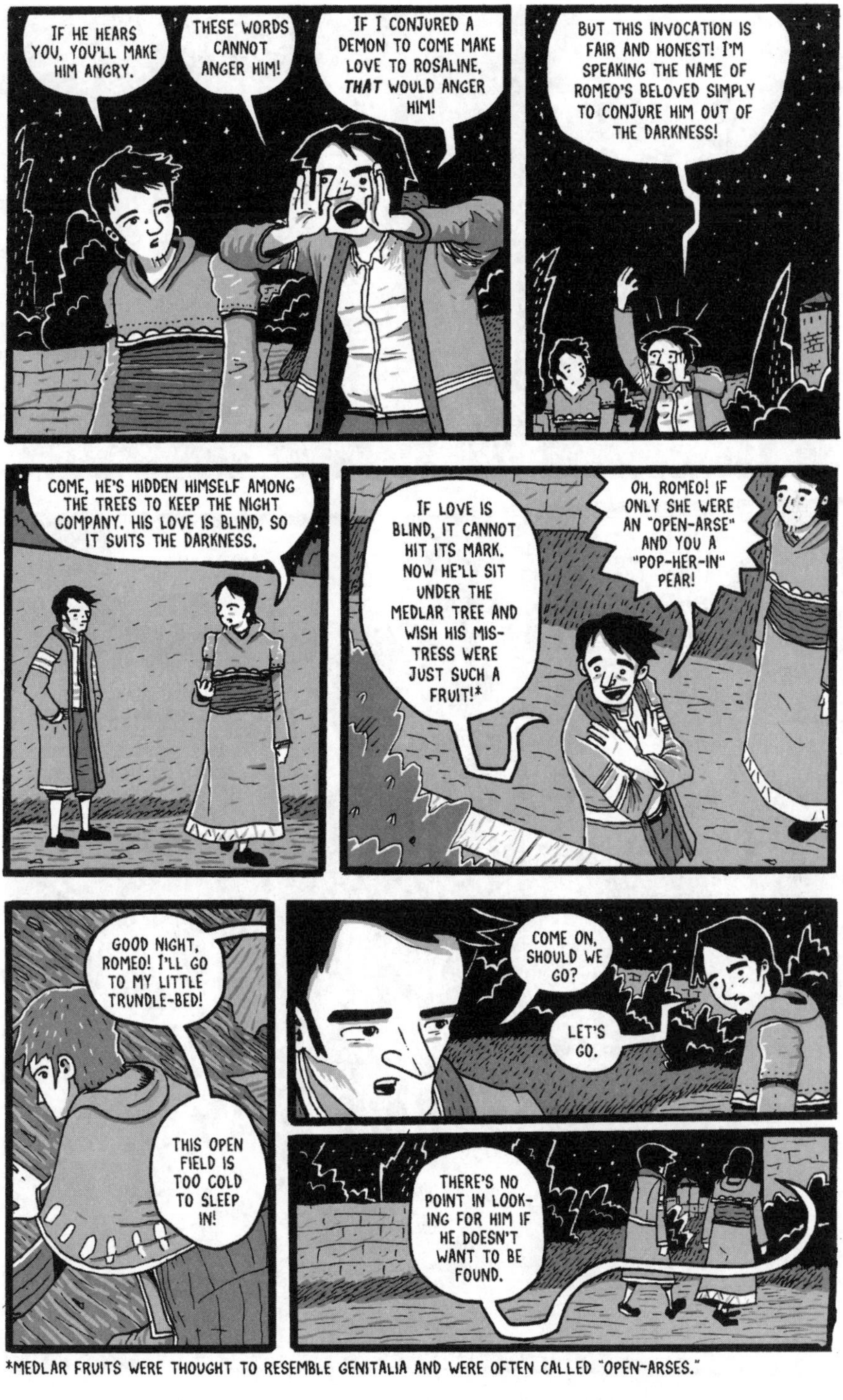
IF HE HEARS YOU, YOU'LL MAKE HIM ANGRY.
THESE WORDS CANNOT ANGER HIM!
IF I CONJURED A DEMON TO COME MAKE LOVE TO ROSALINE, *THAT* WOULD ANGER HIM!
BUT THIS INVOCATION IS FAIR AND HONEST! I'M SPEAKING THE NAME OF ROMEO'S BELOVED SIMPLY TO CONJURE HIM OUT OF THE DARKNESS!
COME, HE'S HIDDEN HIMSELF AMONG THE TREES TO KEEP THE NIGHT COMPANY. HIS LOVE IS BLIND, SO IT SUITS THE DARKNESS.
IF LOVE IS BLIND, IT CANNOT HIT ITS MARK. NOW HE'LL SIT UNDER THE MEDLAR TREE AND WISH HIS MISTRESS WERE JUST SUCH A FRUIT!*
OH, ROMEO! IF ONLY SHE WERE AN "OPEN-ARSE" AND YOU A "POP-HER-IN" PEAR!
GOOD NIGHT, ROMEO! I'LL GO TO MY LITTLE TRUNDLE-BED!
THIS OPEN FIELD IS TOO COLD TO SLEEP IN!
COME ON, SHOULD WE GO?
LET'S GO.
THERE'S NO POINT IN LOOKING FOR HIM IF HE DOESN'T WANT TO BE FOUND.

*MEDLAR FRUITS WERE THOUGHT TO RESEMBLE GENITALIA AND WERE OFTEN CALLED "OPEN-ARSES."

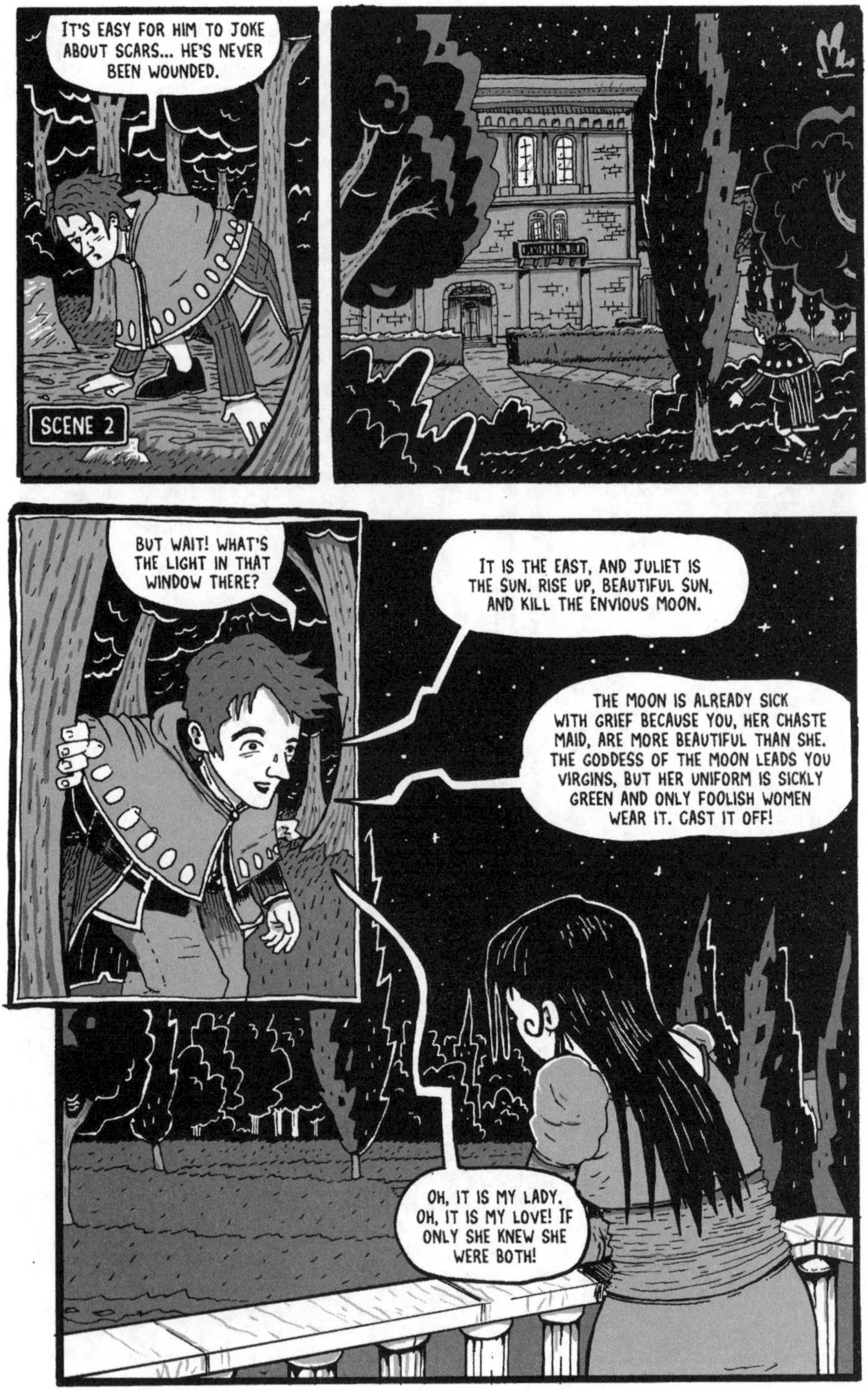
IT'S EASY FOR HIM TO JOKE ABOUT SCARS... HE'S NEVER BEEN WOUNDED.
SCENE 2
BUT WAIT! WHAT'S THE LIGHT IN THAT WINDOW THERE?
IT IS THE EAST, AND JULIET IS THE SUN. RISE UP, BEAUTIFUL SUN, AND KILL THE ENVIOUS MOON.
THE MOON IS ALREADY SICK WITH GRIEF BECAUSE YOU, HER CHASTE MAID, ARE MORE BEAUTIFUL THAN SHE. THE GODDESS OF THE MOON LEADS YOU VIRGINS, BUT HER UNIFORM IS SICKLY GREEN AND ONLY FOOLISH WOMEN WEAR IT. CAST IT OFF!
OH, IT IS MY LADY. OH, IT IS MY LOVE! IF ONLY SHE KNEW SHE WERE BOTH!

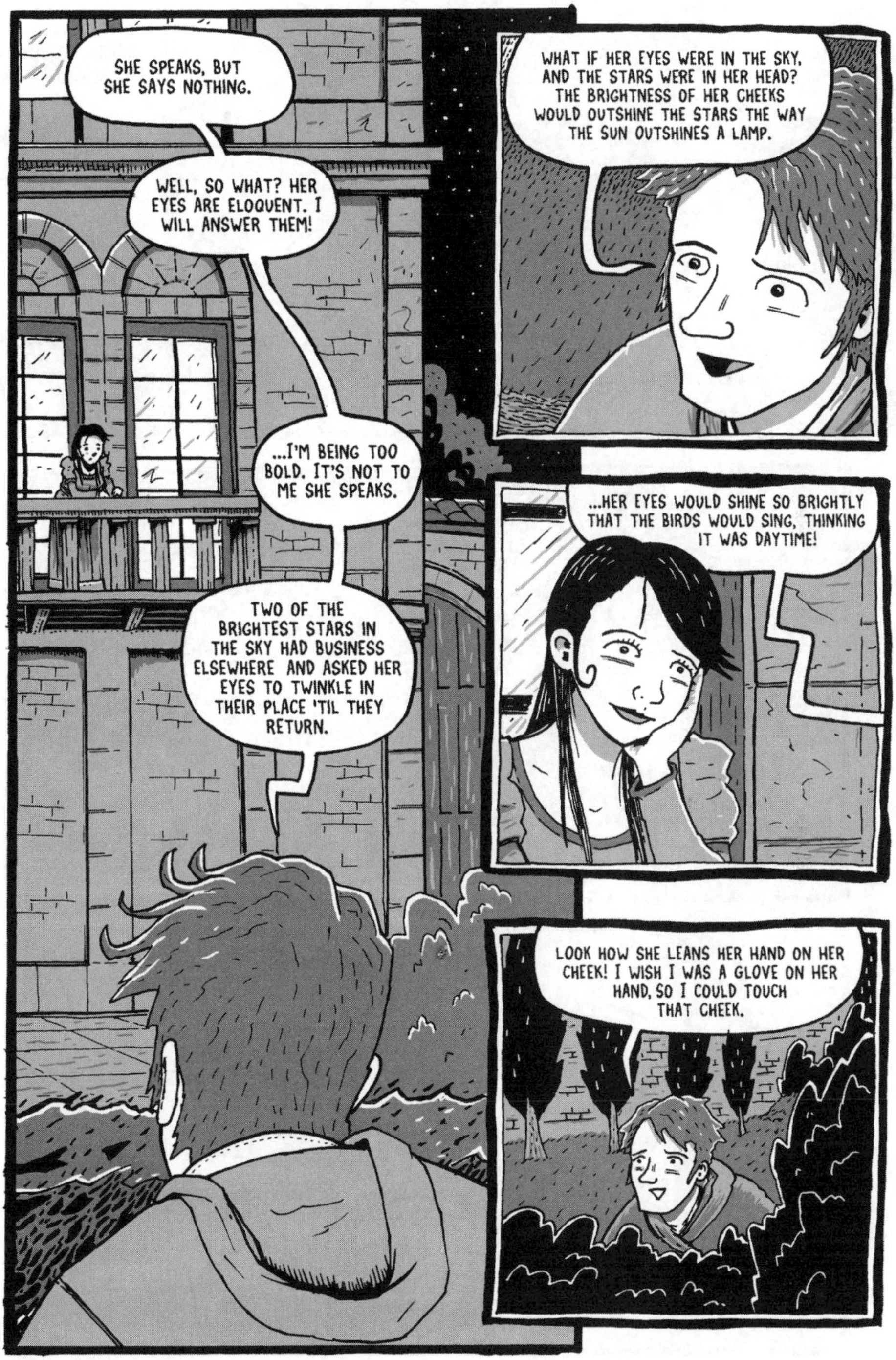
SHE SPEAKS, BUT SHE SAYS NOTHING.
WELL, SO WHAT? HER EYES ARE ELOQUENT. I WILL ANSWER THEM!
...I'M BEING TOO BOLD. IT'S NOT TO ME SHE SPEAKS.
TWO OF THE BRIGHTEST STARS IN THE SKY HAD BUSINESS ELSEWHERE AND ASKED HER EYES TO TWINKLE IN THEIR PLACE 'TIL THEY RETURN.
WHAT IF HER EYES WERE IN THE SKY, AND THE STARS WERE IN HER HEAD? THE BRIGHTNESS OF HER CHEEKS WOULD OUTSHINE THE STARS THE WAY THE SUN OUTSHINES A LAMP.
...HER EYES WOULD SHINE SO BRIGHTLY THAT THE BIRDS WOULD SING, THINKING IT WAS DAYTIME!
LOOK HOW SHE LEANS HER HAND ON HER CHEEK! I WISH I WAS A GLOVE ON HER HAND, SO I COULD TOUCH THAT CHEEK.

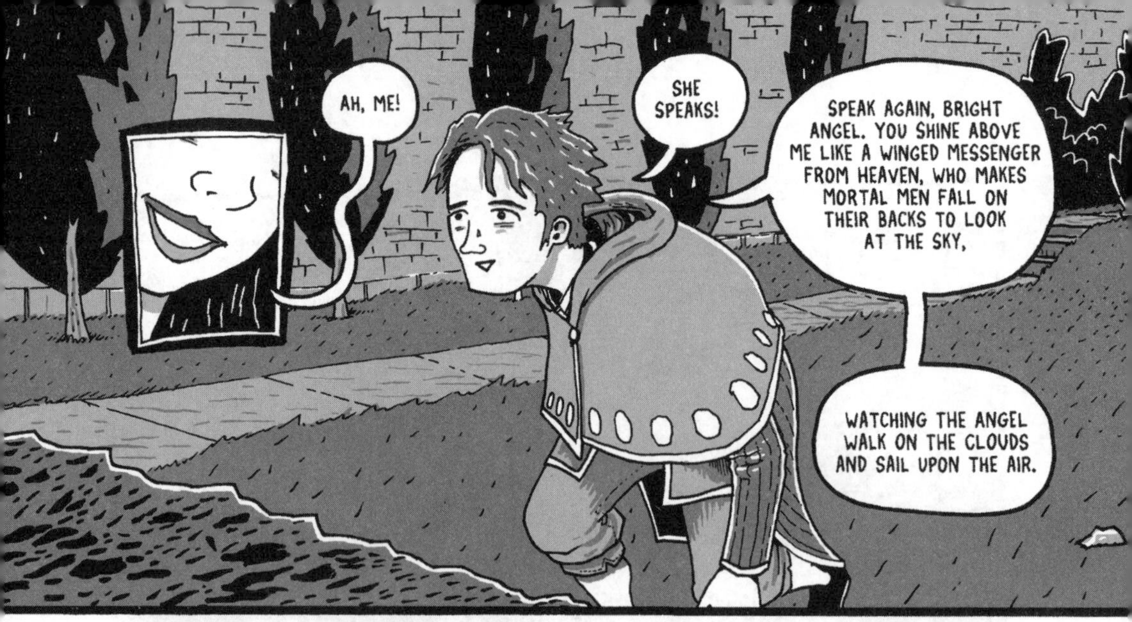
AH, ME!
SHE SPEAKS!
SPEAK AGAIN, BRIGHT ANGEL. YOU SHINE ABOVE ME LIKE A WINGED MESSENGER FROM HEAVEN, WHO MAKES MORTAL MEN FALL ON THEIR BACKS TO LOOK AT THE SKY,
WATCHING THE ANGEL WALK ON THE CLOUDS AND SAIL UPON THE AIR.

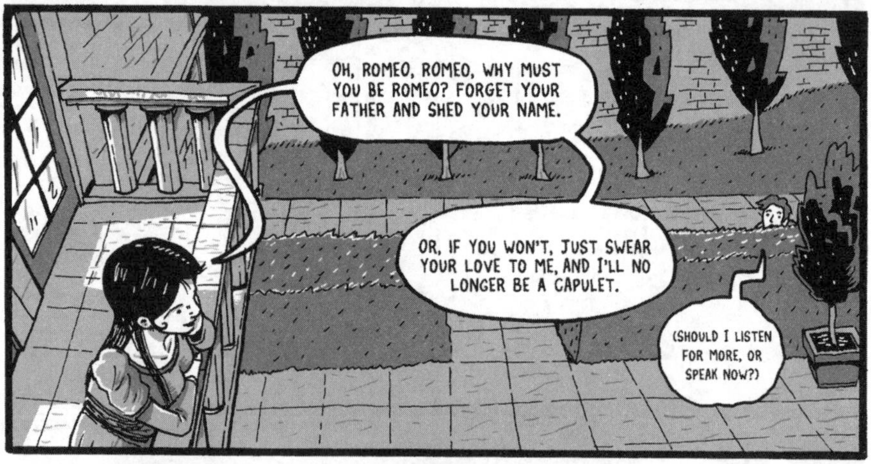
OH, ROMEO, ROMEO, WHY MUST YOU BE ROMEO? FORGET YOUR FATHER AND SHED YOUR NAME.
OR, IF YOU WON'T, JUST SWEAR YOUR LOVE TO ME, AND I'LL NO LONGER BE A CAPULET.
(SHOULD I LISTEN FOR MORE, OR SPEAK NOW?)

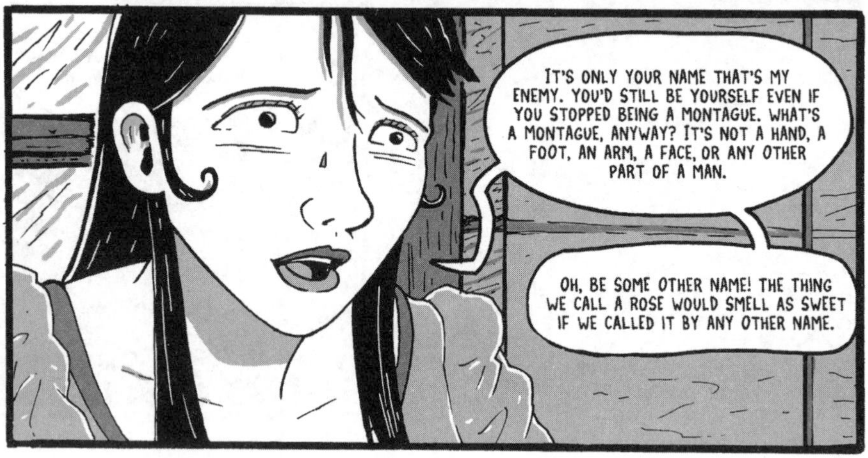
IT'S ONLY YOUR NAME THAT'S MY ENEMY. YOU'D STILL BE YOURSELF EVEN IF YOU STOPPED BEING A MONTAGUE. WHAT'S A MONTAGUE, ANYWAY? IT'S NOT A HAND, A FOOT, AN ARM, A FACE, OR ANY OTHER PART OF A MAN.
OH, BE SOME OTHER NAME! THE THING WE CALL A ROSE WOULD SMELL AS SWEET IF WE CALLED IT BY ANY OTHER NAME.

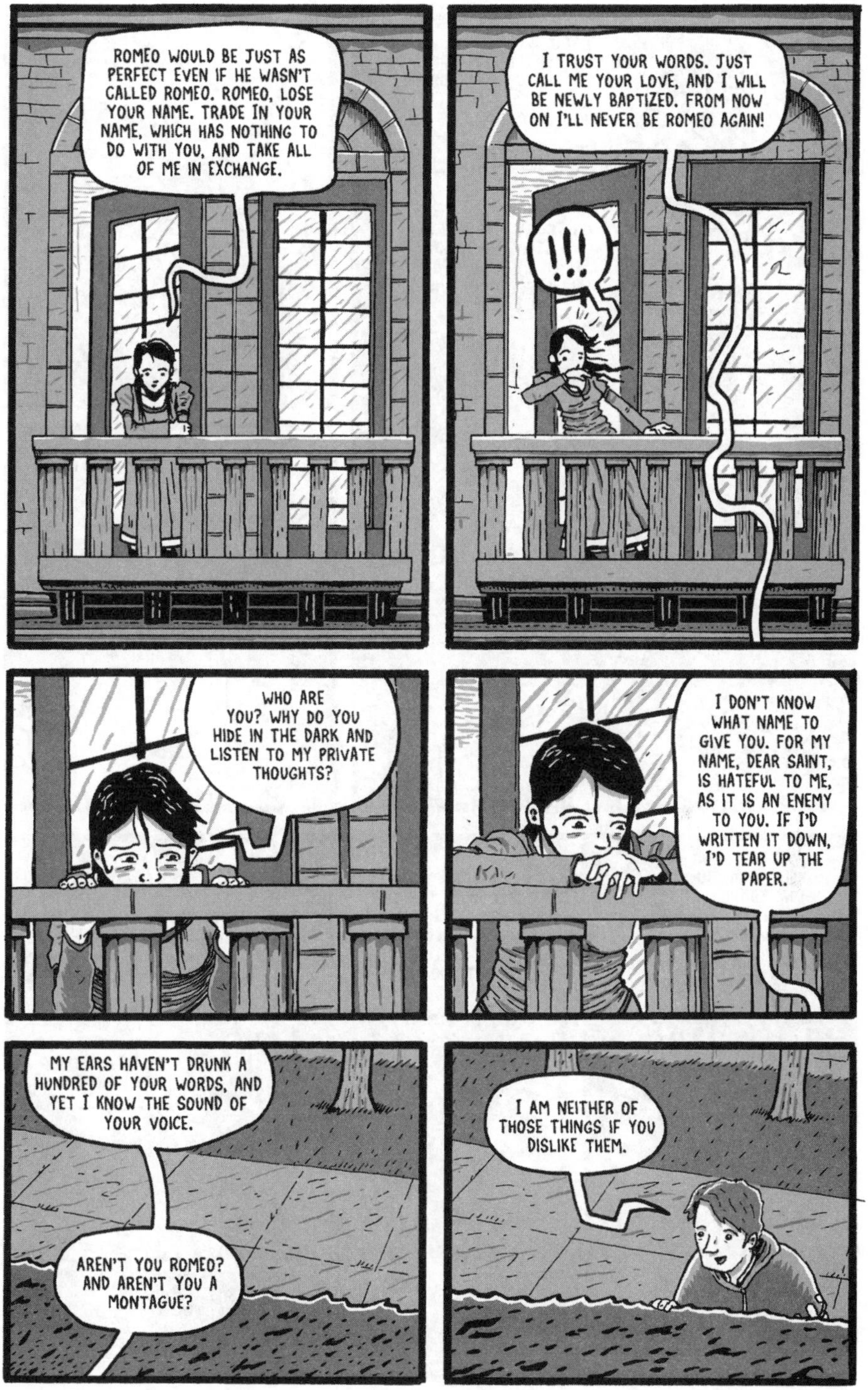
ROMEO WOULD BE JUST AS PERFECT EVEN IF HE WASN'T CALLED ROMEO. ROMEO, LOSE YOUR NAME. TRADE IN YOUR NAME, WHICH HAS NOTHING TO DO WITH YOU, AND TAKE ALL OF ME IN EXCHANGE.
I TRUST YOUR WORDS. JUST CALL ME YOUR LOVE, AND I WILL BE NEWLY BAPTIZED. FROM NOW ON I'LL NEVER BE ROMEO AGAIN!
!!!
WHO ARE YOU? WHY DO YOU HIDE IN THE DARK AND LISTEN TO MY PRIVATE THOUGHTS?
I DON'T KNOW WHAT NAME TO GIVE YOU. FOR MY NAME, DEAR SAINT, IS HATEFUL TO ME, AS IT IS AN ENEMY TO YOU. IF I'D WRITTEN IT DOWN, I'D TEAR UP THE PAPER.
MY EARS HAVEN'T DRUNK A HUNDRED OF YOUR WORDS, AND YET I KNOW THE SOUND OF YOUR VOICE.
AREN'T YOU ROMEO? AND AREN'T YOU A MONTAGUE?
I AM NEITHER OF THOSE THINGS IF YOU DISLIKE THEM.

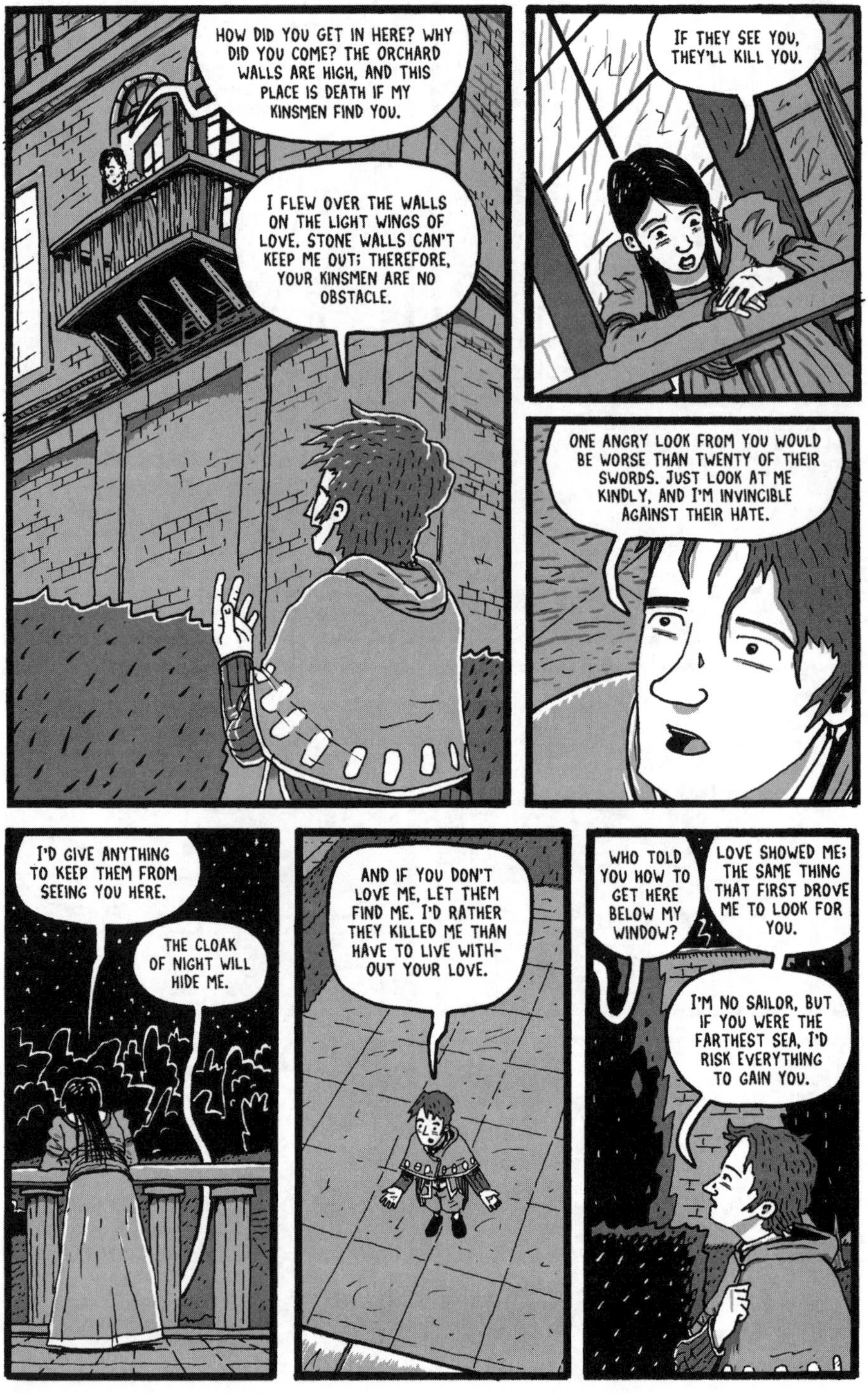
HOW DID YOU GET IN HERE? WHY DID YOU COME? THE ORCHARD WALLS ARE HIGH, AND THIS PLACE IS DEATH IF MY KINSMEN FIND YOU.
I FLEW OVER THE WALLS ON THE LIGHT WINGS OF LOVE. STONE WALLS CAN'T KEEP ME OUT; THEREFORE, YOUR KINSMEN ARE NO OBSTACLE.
IF THEY SEE YOU, THEY'LL KILL YOU.
ONE ANGRY LOOK FROM YOU WOULD BE WORSE THAN TWENTY OF THEIR SWORDS. JUST LOOK AT ME KINDLY, AND I'M INVINCIBLE AGAINST THEIR HATE.
I'D GIVE ANYTHING TO KEEP THEM FROM SEEING YOU HERE.
THE CLOAK OF NIGHT WILL HIDE ME.
AND IF YOU DON'T LOVE ME, LET THEM FIND ME. I'D RATHER THEY KILLED ME THAN HAVE TO LIVE WITHOUT YOUR LOVE.
WHO TOLD YOU HOW TO GET HERE BELOW MY WINDOW?
LOVE SHOWED ME; THE SAME THING THAT FIRST DROVE ME TO LOOK FOR YOU.
I'M NO SAILOR, BUT IF YOU WERE THE FARTHEST SEA, I'D RISK EVERYTHING TO GAIN YOU.

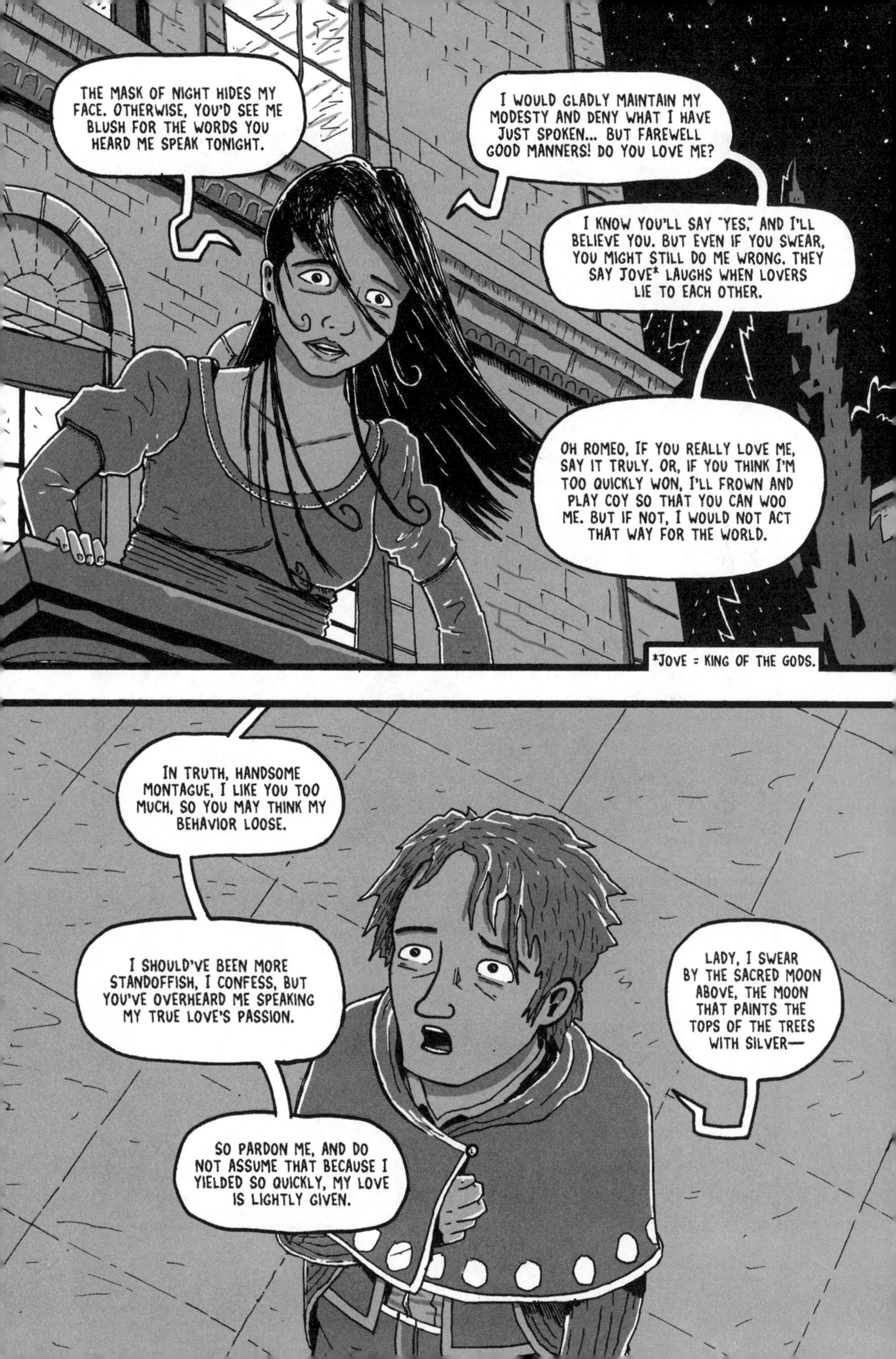
THE MASK OF NIGHT HIDES MY FACE. OTHERWISE, YOU'D SEE ME BLUSH FOR THE WORDS YOU HEARD ME SPEAK TONIGHT.
I WOULD GLADLY MAINTAIN MY MODESTY AND DENY WHAT I HAVE JUST SPOKEN... BUT FAREWELL GOOD MANNERS! DO YOU LOVE ME?
I KNOW YOU'LL SAY "YES," AND I'LL BELIEVE YOU. BUT EVEN IF YOU SWEAR, YOU MIGHT STILL DO ME WRONG. THEY SAY JOVE* LAUGHS WHEN LOVERS LIE TO EACH OTHER.
OH ROMEO, IF YOU REALLY LOVE ME, SAY IT TRULY. OR, IF YOU THINK I'M TOO QUICKLY WON, I'LL FROWN AND PLAY COY SO THAT YOU CAN WOO ME. BUT IF NOT, I WOULD NOT ACT THAT WAY FOR THE WORLD.
*JOVE = KING OF THE GODS.
IN TRUTH, HANDSOME MONTAGUE, I LIKE YOU TOO MUCH, SO YOU MAY THINK MY BEHAVIOR LOOSE.
I SHOULD'VE BEEN MORE STANDOFFISH, I CONFESS, BUT YOU'VE OVERHEARD ME SPEAKING MY TRUE LOVE'S PASSION.
SO PARDON ME, AND DO NOT ASSUME THAT BECAUSE I YIELDED SO QUICKLY, MY LOVE IS LIGHTLY GIVEN.
LADY, I SWEAR BY THE SACRED MOON ABOVE, THE MOON THAT PAINTS THE TOPS OF THE TREES WITH SILVER—

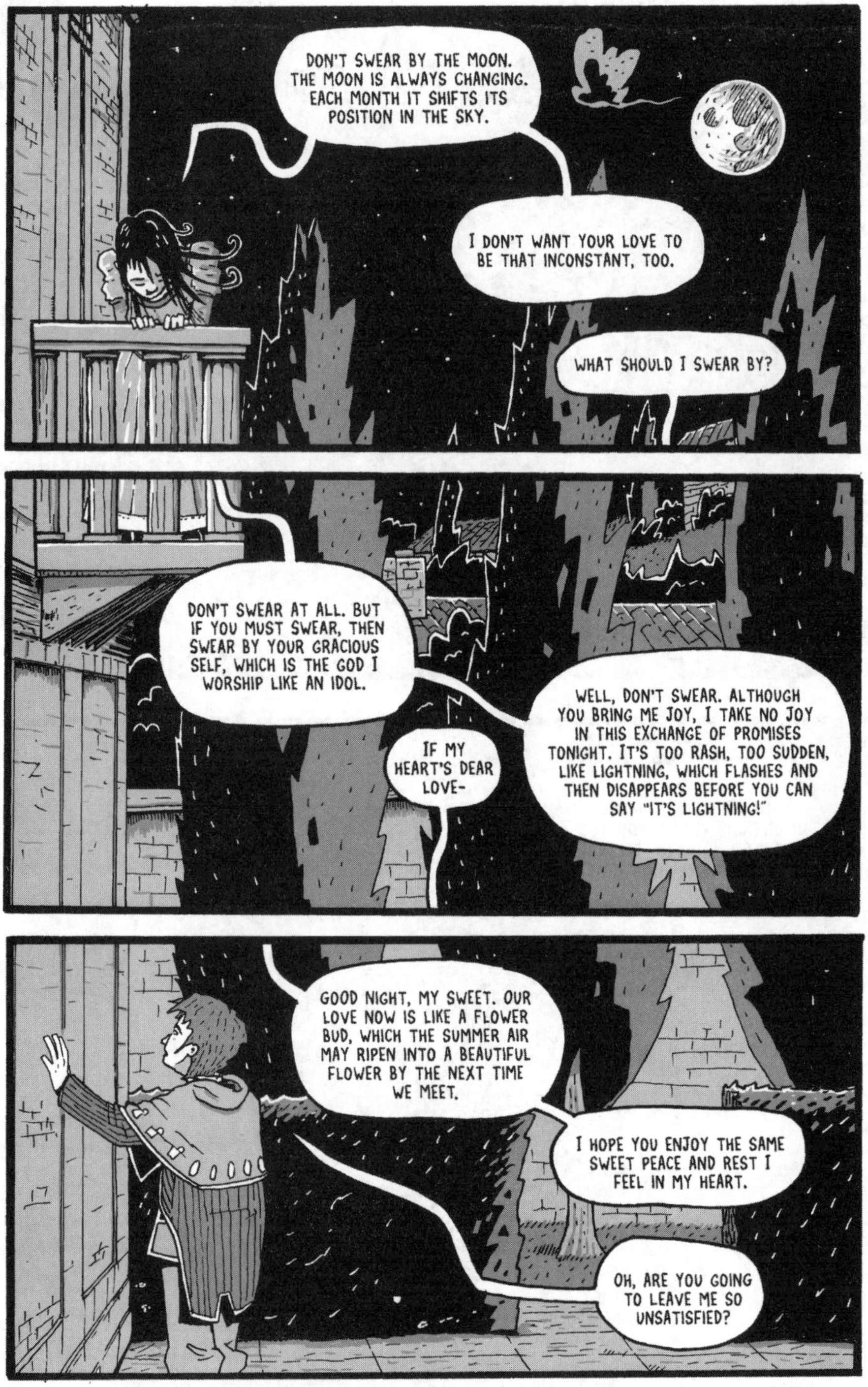
DON'T SWEAR BY THE MOON. THE MOON IS ALWAYS CHANGING. EACH MONTH IT SHIFTS ITS POSITION IN THE SKY.
I DON'T WANT YOUR LOVE TO BE THAT INCONSTANT, TOO.
WHAT SHOULD I SWEAR BY?
DON'T SWEAR AT ALL. BUT IF YOU MUST SWEAR, THEN SWEAR BY YOUR GRACIOUS SELF, WHICH IS THE GOD I WORSHIP LIKE AN IDOL.
IF MY HEART'S DEAR LOVE-
WELL, DON'T SWEAR. ALTHOUGH YOU BRING ME JOY, I TAKE NO JOY IN THIS EXCHANGE OF PROMISES TONIGHT. IT'S TOO RASH, TOO SUDDEN, LIKE LIGHTNING, WHICH FLASHES AND THEN DISAPPEARS BEFORE YOU CAN SAY "IT'S LIGHTNING!"
GOOD NIGHT, MY SWEET. OUR LOVE NOW IS LIKE A FLOWER BUD, WHICH THE SUMMER AIR MAY RIPEN INTO A BEAUTIFUL FLOWER BY THE NEXT TIME WE MEET.
I HOPE YOU ENJOY THE SAME SWEET PEACE AND REST I FEEL IN MY HEART.
OH, ARE YOU GOING TO LEAVE ME SO UNSATISFIED?

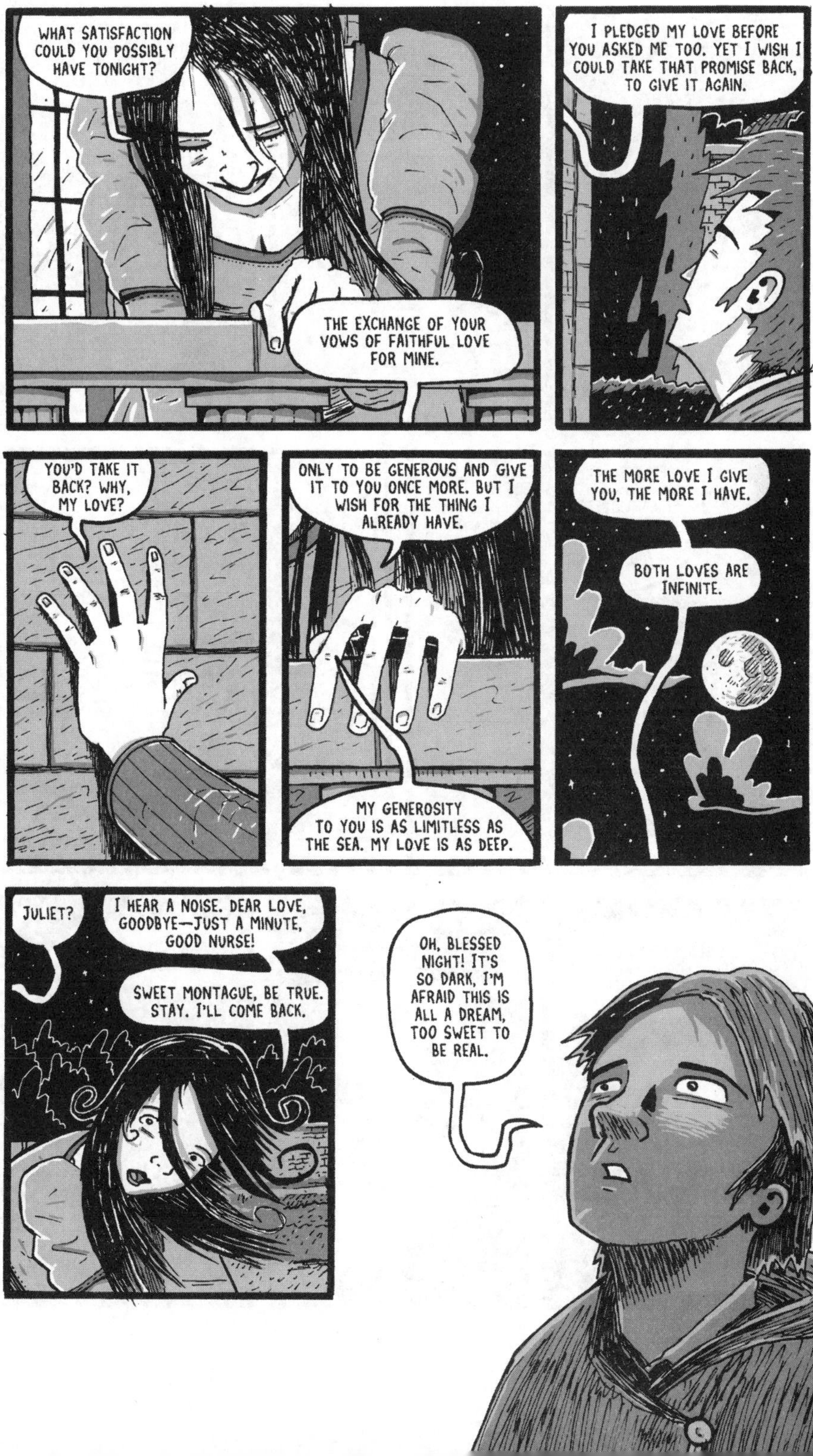
WHAT SATISFACTION COULD YOU POSSIBLY HAVE TONIGHT?
THE EXCHANGE OF YOUR VOWS OF FAITHFUL LOVE FOR MINE.
I PLEDGED MY LOVE BEFORE YOU ASKED ME TOO. YET I WISH I COULD TAKE THAT PROMISE BACK, TO GIVE IT AGAIN.
YOU'D TAKE IT BACK? WHY, MY LOVE?
ONLY TO BE GENEROUS AND GIVE IT TO YOU ONCE MORE. BUT I WISH FOR THE THING I ALREADY HAVE.
MY GENEROSITY TO YOU IS AS LIMITLESS AS THE SEA. MY LOVE IS AS DEEP.
THE MORE LOVE I GIVE YOU, THE MORE I HAVE.
BOTH LOVES ARE INFINITE.
JULIET?
I HEAR A NOISE. DEAR LOVE, GOODBYE—JUST A MINUTE, GOOD NURSE!
SWEET MONTAGUE, BE TRUE. STAY. I'LL COME BACK.
OH, BLESSED NIGHT! IT'S SO DARK, I'M AFRAID THIS IS ALL A DREAM, TOO SWEET TO BE REAL.

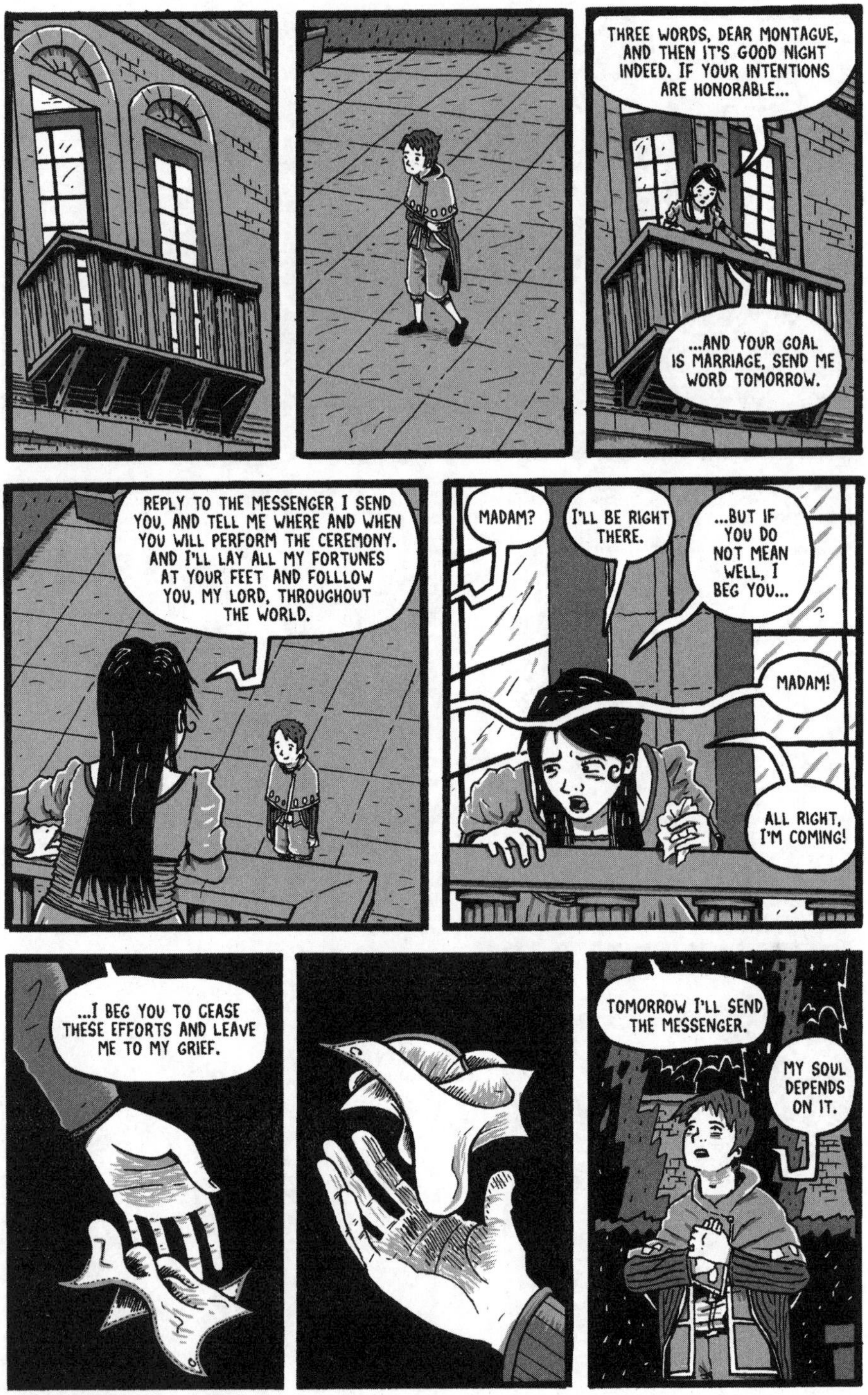
THREE WORDS, DEAR MONTAGUE, AND THEN IT'S GOOD NIGHT INDEED. IF YOUR INTENTIONS ARE HONORABLE...
...AND YOUR GOAL IS MARRIAGE, SEND ME WORD TOMORROW.
REPLY TO THE MESSENGER I SEND YOU, AND TELL ME WHERE AND WHEN YOU WILL PERFORM THE CEREMONY. AND I'LL LAY ALL MY FORTUNES AT YOUR FEET AND FOLLLOW YOU, MY LORD, THROUGHOUT THE WORLD.
MADAM?
I'LL BE RIGHT THERE.
...BUT IF YOU DO NOT MEAN WELL, I BEG YOU...
MADAM!
ALL RIGHT, I'M COMING!
...I BEG YOU TO CEASE THESE EFFORTS AND LEAVE ME TO MY GRIEF.
TOMORROW I'LL SEND THE MESSENGER.
MY SOUL DEPENDS ON IT.

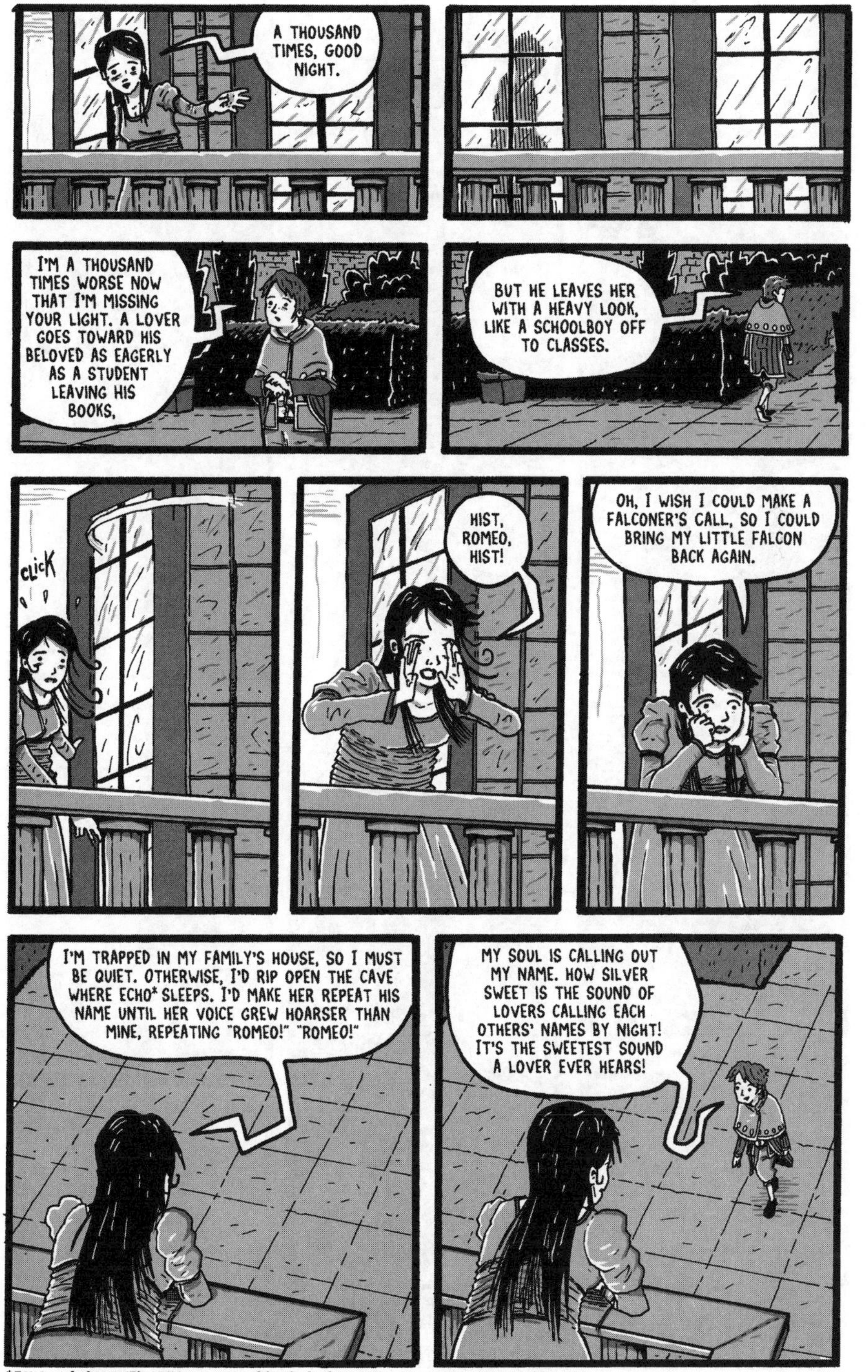
A THOUSAND TIMES, GOOD NIGHT.
I'M A THOUSAND TIMES WORSE NOW THAT I'M MISSING YOUR LIGHT. A LOVER GOES TOWARD HIS BELOVED AS EAGERLY AS A STUDENT LEAVING HIS BOOKS,
BUT HE LEAVES HER WITH A HEAVY LOOK, LIKE A SCHOOLBOY OFF TO CLASSES.
CLICK
HIST, ROMEO, HIST!
OH, I WISH I COULD MAKE A FALCONER'S CALL, SO I COULD BRING MY LITTLE FALCON BACK AGAIN.
I'M TRAPPED IN MY FAMILY'S HOUSE, SO I MUST BE QUIET. OTHERWISE, I'D RIP OPEN THE CAVE WHERE ECHO* SLEEPS. I'D MAKE HER REPEAT HIS NAME UNTIL HER VOICE GREW HOARSER THAN MINE, REPEATING "ROMEO!" "ROMEO!"
MY SOUL IS CALLING OUT MY NAME. HOW SILVER SWEET IS THE SOUND OF LOVERS CALLING EACH OTHERS' NAMES BY NIGHT! IT'S THE SWEETEST SOUND A LOVER EVER HEARS!

*ECHO = A SCORNED NYMPH WHO WASTED AWAY UNTIL ONLY HER VOICE WAS LEFT

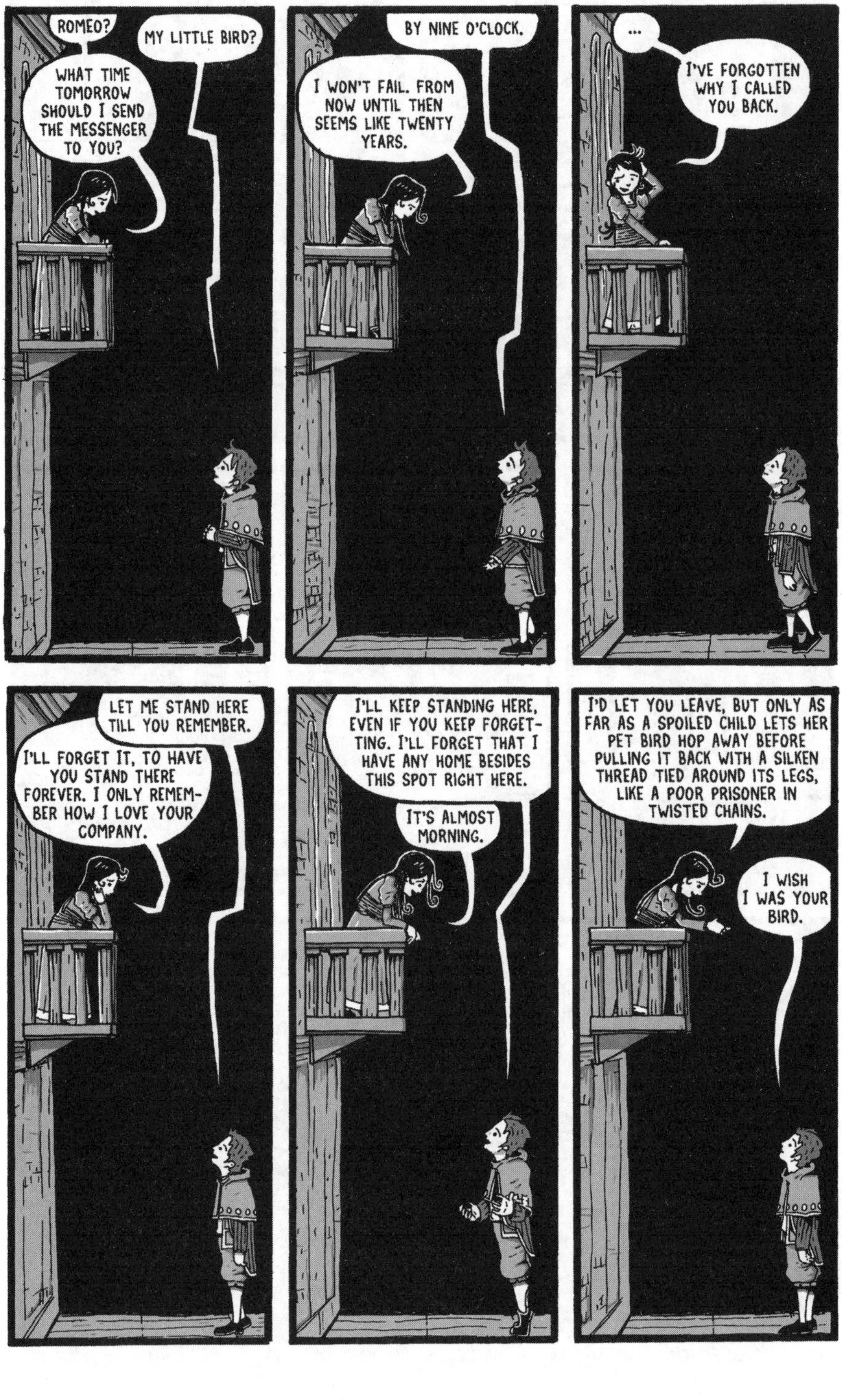
ROMEO?
MY LITTLE BIRD?
WHAT TIME TOMORROW SHOULD I SEND THE MESSENGER TO YOU?
BY NINE O'CLOCK.
I WON'T FAIL. FROM NOW UNTIL THEN SEEMS LIKE TWENTY YEARS.
...
I'VE FORGOTTEN WHY I CALLED YOU BACK.
LET ME STAND HERE TILL YOU REMEMBER.
I'LL FORGET IT, TO HAVE YOU STAND THERE FOREVER. I ONLY REMEMBER HOW I LOVE YOUR COMPANY.
I'LL KEEP STANDING HERE, EVEN IF YOU KEEP FORGETTING. I'LL FORGET THAT I HAVE ANY HOME BESIDES THIS SPOT RIGHT HERE.
IT'S ALMOST MORNING.
I'D LET YOU LEAVE, BUT ONLY AS FAR AS A SPOILED CHILD LETS HER PET BIRD HOP AWAY BEFORE PULLING IT BACK WITH A SILKEN THREAD TIED AROUND ITS LEGS, LIKE A POOR PRISONER IN TWISTED CHAINS.
I WISH I WAS YOUR BIRD.

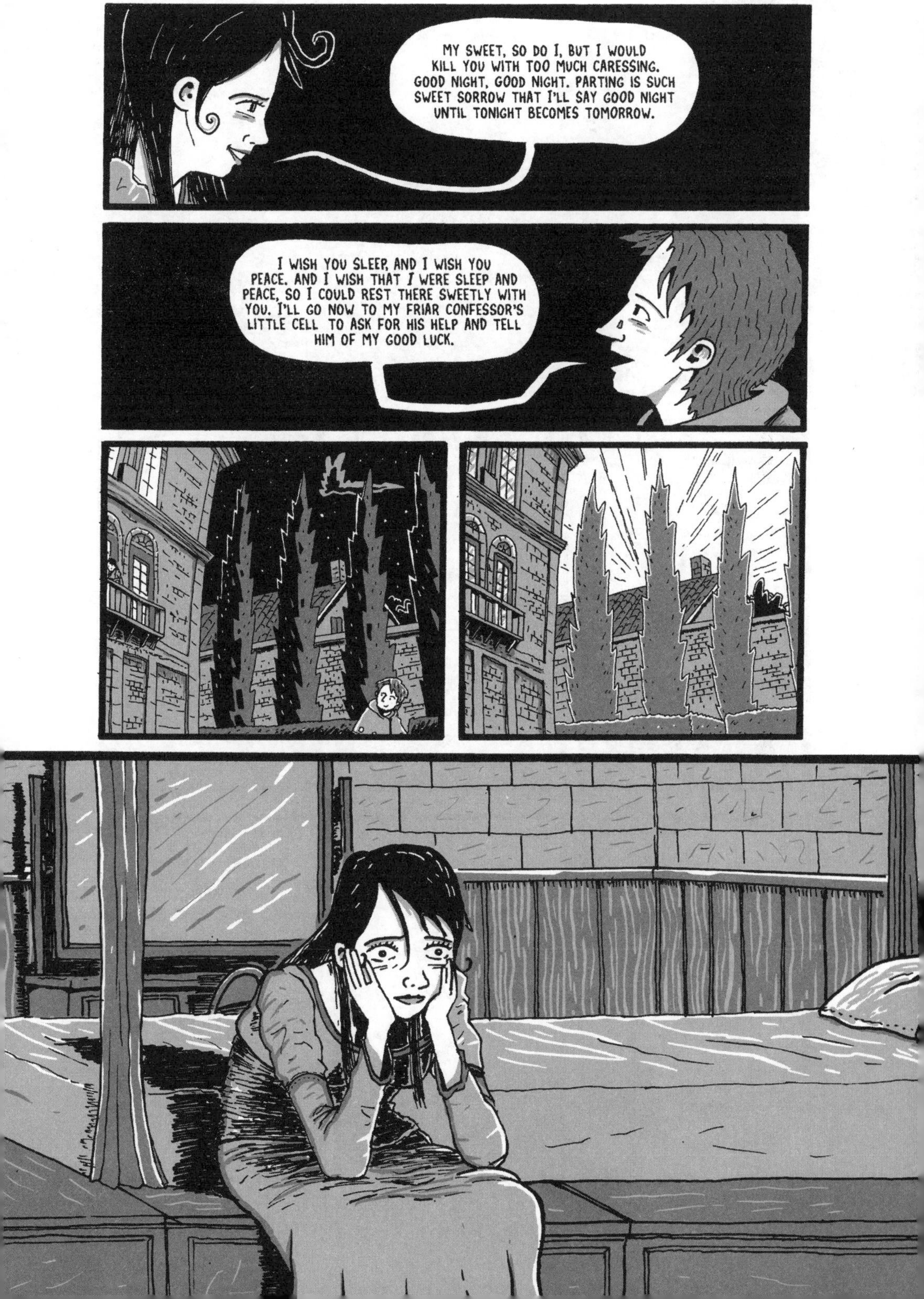
MY SWEET, SO DO I, BUT I WOULD KILL YOU WITH TOO MUCH CARESSING. GOOD NIGHT, GOOD NIGHT. PARTING IS SUCH SWEET SORROW THAT I'LL SAY GOOD NIGHT UNTIL TONIGHT BECOMES TOMORROW.
I WISH YOU SLEEP, AND I WISH YOU PEACE. AND I WISH THAT *I* WERE SLEEP AND PEACE, SO I COULD REST THERE SWEETLY WITH YOU. I'LL GO NOW TO MY FRIAR CONFESSOR'S LITTLE CELL TO ASK FOR HIS HELP AND TELL HIM OF MY GOOD LUCK.

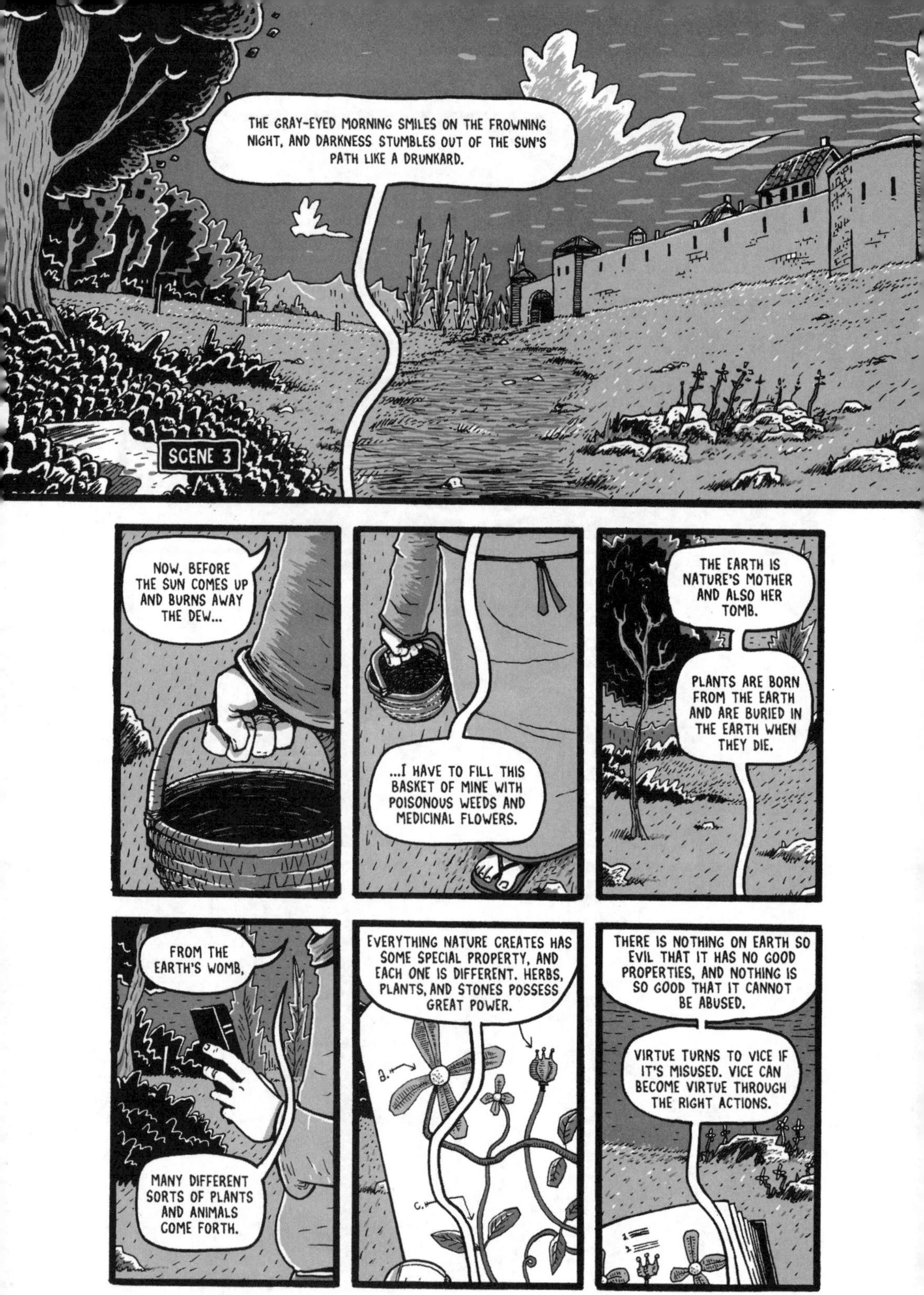
THE GRAY-EYED MORNING SMILES ON THE FROWNING NIGHT, AND DARKNESS STUMBLES OUT OF THE SUN'S PATH LIKE A DRUNKARD.
SCENE 3
NOW, BEFORE THE SUN COMES UP AND BURNS AWAY THE DEW...
...I HAVE TO FILL THIS BASKET OF MINE WITH POISONOUS WEEDS AND MEDICINAL FLOWERS.
THE EARTH IS NATURE'S MOTHER AND ALSO HER TOMB.
PLANTS ARE BORN FROM THE EARTH AND ARE BURIED IN THE EARTH WHEN THEY DIE.
FROM THE EARTH'S WOMB,
MANY DIFFERENT SORTS OF PLANTS AND ANIMALS COME FORTH.
EVERYTHING NATURE CREATES HAS SOME SPECIAL PROPERTY, AND EACH ONE IS DIFFERENT. HERBS, PLANTS, AND STONES POSSESS GREAT POWER.
THERE IS NOTHING ON EARTH SO EVIL THAT IT HAS NO GOOD PROPERTIES, AND NOTHING IS SO GOOD THAT IT CANNOT BE ABUSED.
VIRTUE TURNS TO VICE IF IT'S MISUSED. VICE CAN BECOME VIRTUE THROUGH THE RIGHT ACTIONS.

INSIDE THE RIND OF THIS WEAK FLOWER, THERE IS BOTH POISON AND POWERFUL MEDICINE.

IF YOU SMELL IT, IT CHEERS YOUR WHOLE BODY, BUT...

...IF YOU TASTE IT, IT STOPS YOUR HEART.

THERE ARE OPPOSITE ELEMENTS IN EVERYTHING, IN MEN AS WELL AS HERBS: HEAVENLY GRACE AND VIOLENT DESIRE.

GOOD MORNING, FATHER!

BENEDICTE. WHO GREETS ME SO EARLY IN THE MORNING?

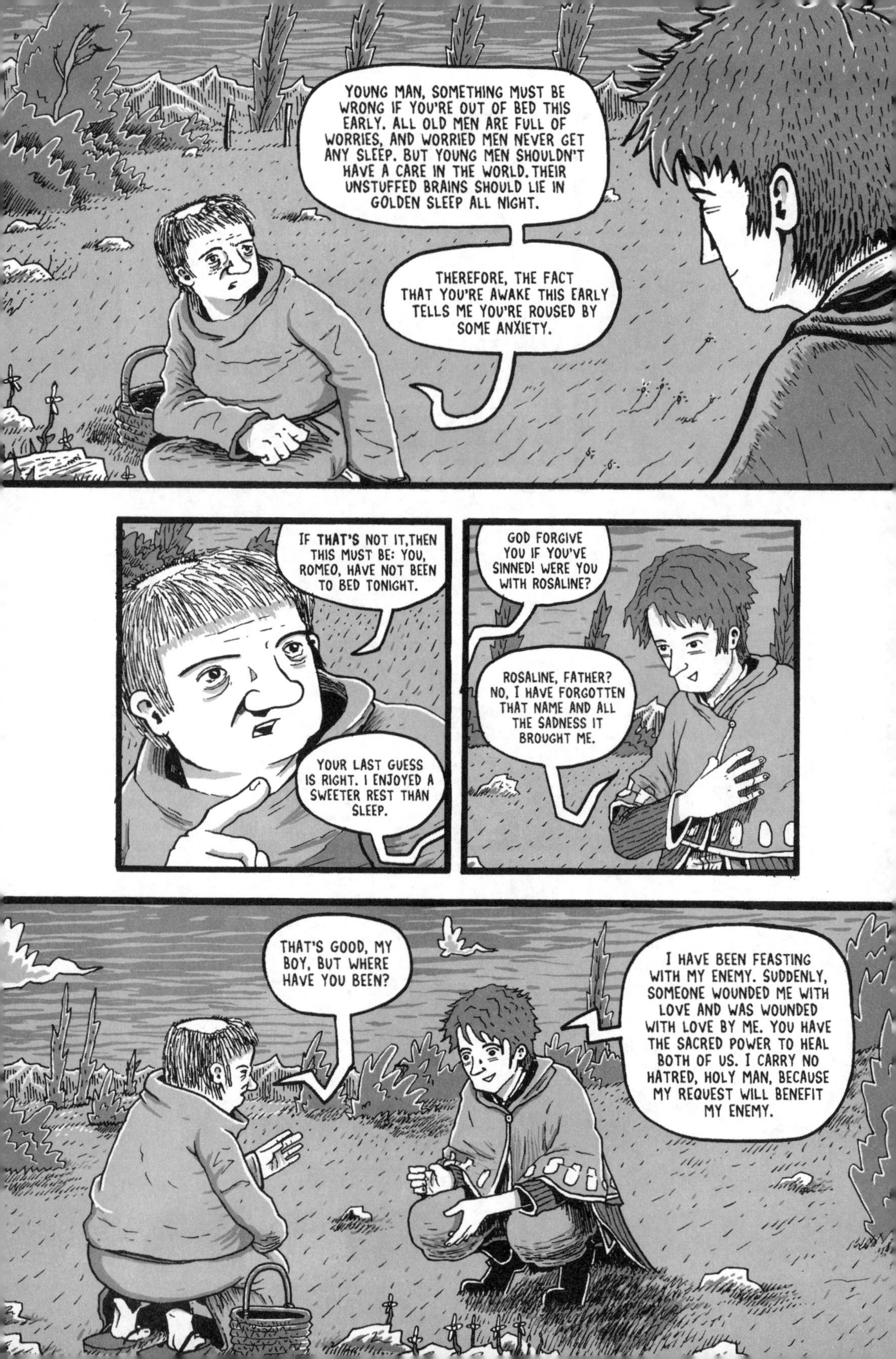
YOUNG MAN, SOMETHING MUST BE WRONG IF YOU'RE OUT OF BED THIS EARLY. ALL OLD MEN ARE FULL OF WORRIES, AND WORRIED MEN NEVER GET ANY SLEEP. BUT YOUNG MEN SHOULDN'T HAVE A CARE IN THE WORLD. THEIR UNSTUFFED BRAINS SHOULD LIE IN GOLDEN SLEEP ALL NIGHT.
THEREFORE, THE FACT THAT YOU'RE AWAKE THIS EARLY TELLS ME YOU'RE ROUSED BY SOME ANXIETY.
IF THAT'S NOT IT, THEN THIS MUST BE: YOU, ROMEO, HAVE NOT BEEN TO BED TONIGHT.
YOUR LAST GUESS IS RIGHT. I ENJOYED A SWEETER REST THAN SLEEP.
GOD FORGIVE YOU IF YOU'VE SINNED! WERE YOU WITH ROSALINE?
ROSALINE, FATHER? NO, I HAVE FORGOTTEN THAT NAME AND ALL THE SADNESS IT BROUGHT ME.
THAT'S GOOD, MY BOY, BUT WHERE HAVE YOU BEEN?
I HAVE BEEN FEASTING WITH MY ENEMY. SUDDENLY, SOMEONE WOUNDED ME WITH LOVE AND WAS WOUNDED WITH LOVE BY ME. YOU HAVE THE SACRED POWER TO HEAL BOTH OF US. I CARRY NO HATRED, HOLY MAN, BECAUSE MY REQUEST WILL BENEFIT MY ENEMY.

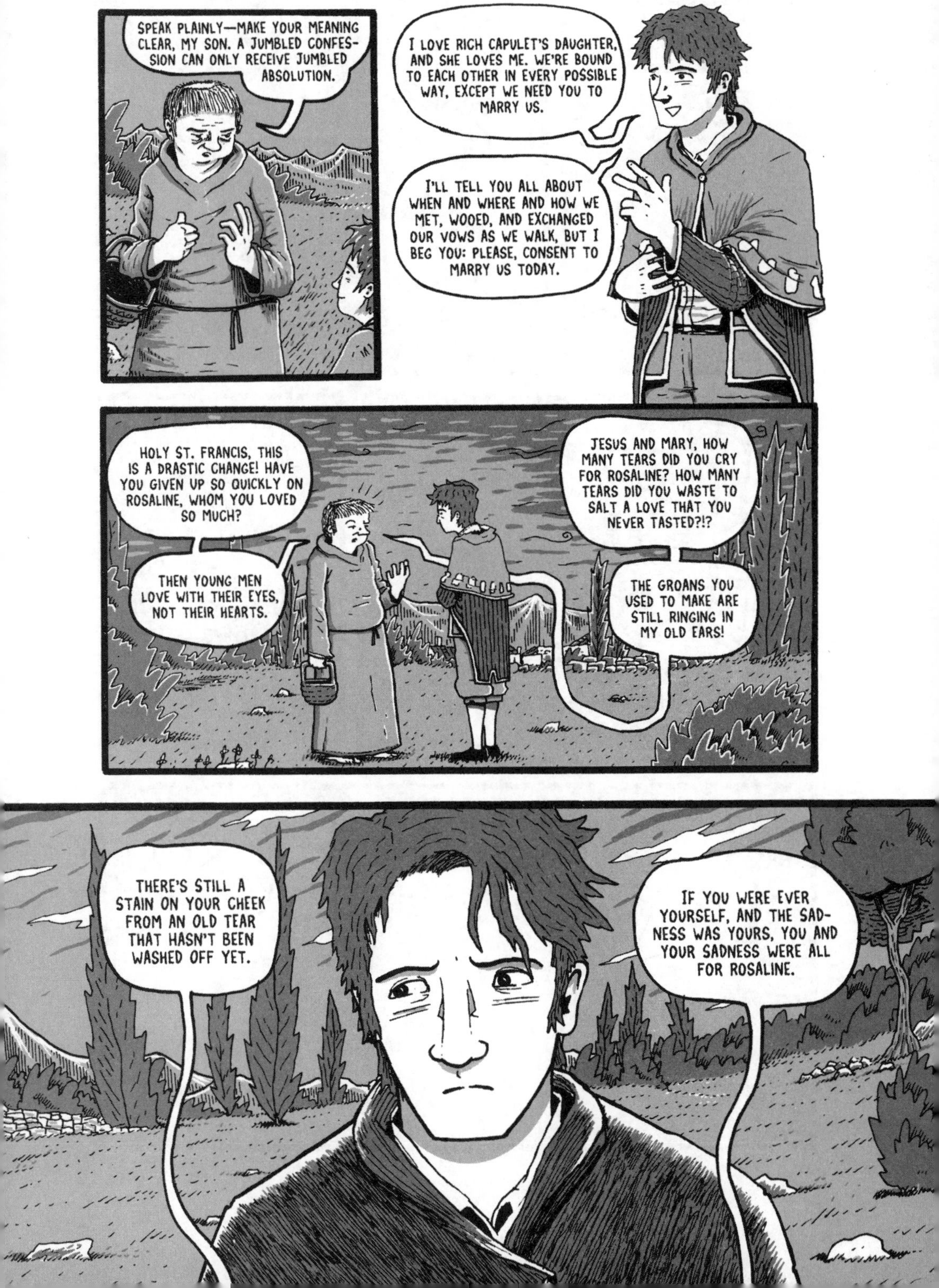
SPEAK PLAINLY—MAKE YOUR MEANING CLEAR, MY SON. A JUMBLED CONFESSION CAN ONLY RECEIVE JUMBLED ABSOLUTION.
I LOVE RICH CAPULET'S DAUGHTER, AND SHE LOVES ME. WE'RE BOUND TO EACH OTHER IN EVERY POSSIBLE WAY, EXCEPT WE NEED YOU TO MARRY US.
I'LL TELL YOU ALL ABOUT WHEN AND WHERE AND HOW WE MET, WOOED, AND EXCHANGED OUR VOWS AS WE WALK, BUT I BEG YOU: PLEASE, CONSENT TO MARRY US TODAY.
HOLY ST. FRANCIS, THIS IS A DRASTIC CHANGE! HAVE YOU GIVEN UP SO QUICKLY ON ROSALINE, WHOM YOU LOVED SO MUCH?
THEN YOUNG MEN LOVE WITH THEIR EYES, NOT THEIR HEARTS.
JESUS AND MARY, HOW MANY TEARS DID YOU CRY FOR ROSALINE? HOW MANY TEARS DID YOU WASTE TO SALT A LOVE THAT YOU NEVER TASTED?!?
THE GROANS YOU USED TO MAKE ARE STILL RINGING IN MY OLD EARS!
THERE'S STILL A STAIN ON YOUR CHEEK FROM AN OLD TEAR THAT HASN'T BEEN WASHED OFF YET.
IF YOU WERE EVER YOURSELF, AND THE SADNESS WAS YOURS, YOU AND YOUR SADNESS WERE ALL FOR ROSALINE.

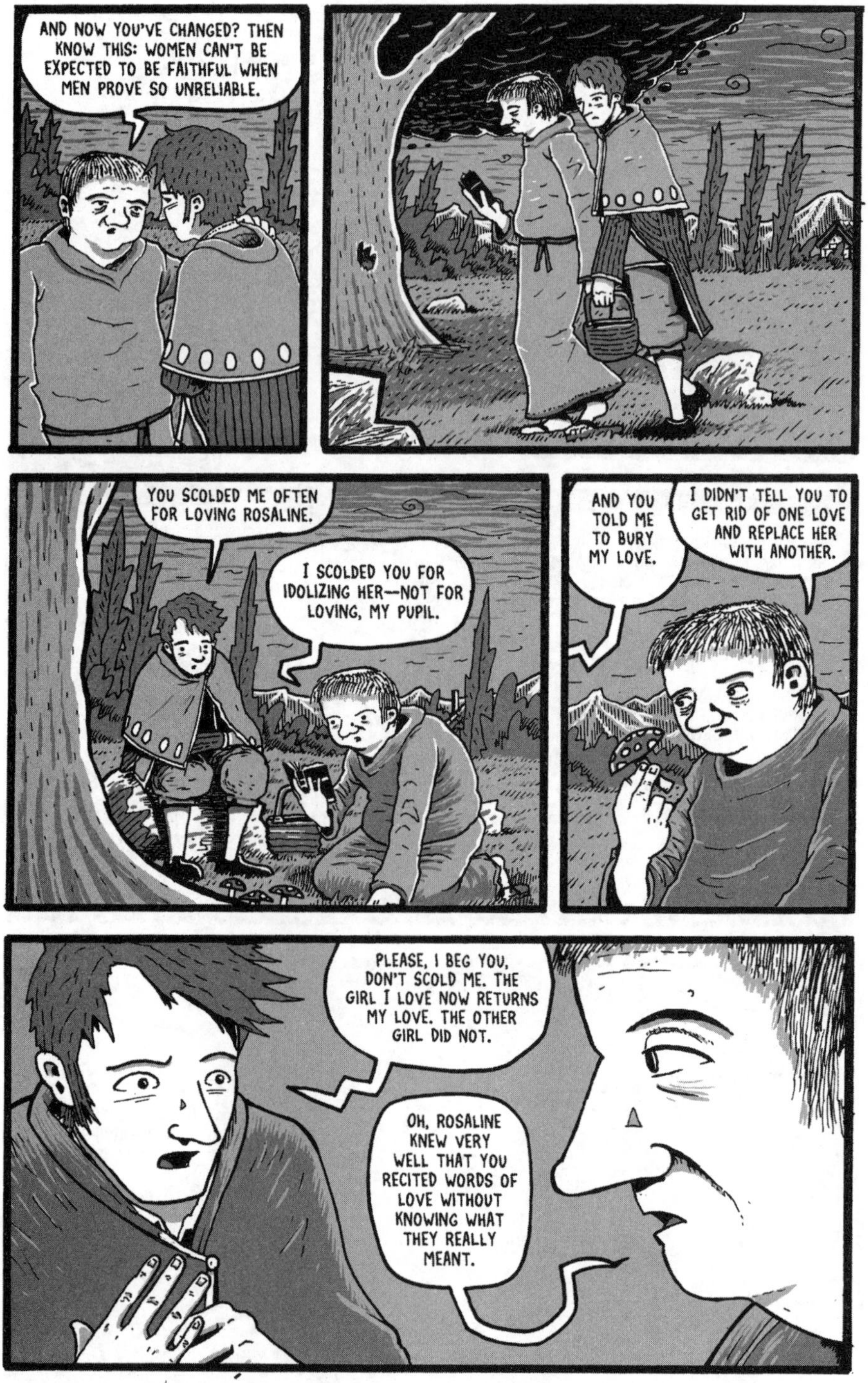
AND NOW YOU'VE CHANGED? THEN KNOW THIS: WOMEN CAN'T BE EXPECTED TO BE FAITHFUL WHEN MEN PROVE SO UNRELIABLE.
YOU SCOLDED ME OFTEN FOR LOVING ROSALINE.
I SCOLDED YOU FOR IDOLIZING HER--NOT FOR LOVING, MY PUPIL.
AND YOU TOLD ME TO BURY MY LOVE.
I DIDN'T TELL YOU TO GET RID OF ONE LOVE AND REPLACE HER WITH ANOTHER.
PLEASE, I BEG YOU, DON'T SCOLD ME. THE GIRL I LOVE NOW RETURNS MY LOVE. THE OTHER GIRL DID NOT.
OH, ROSALINE KNEW VERY WELL THAT YOU RECITED WORDS OF LOVE WITHOUT KNOWING WHAT THEY REALLY MEANT.

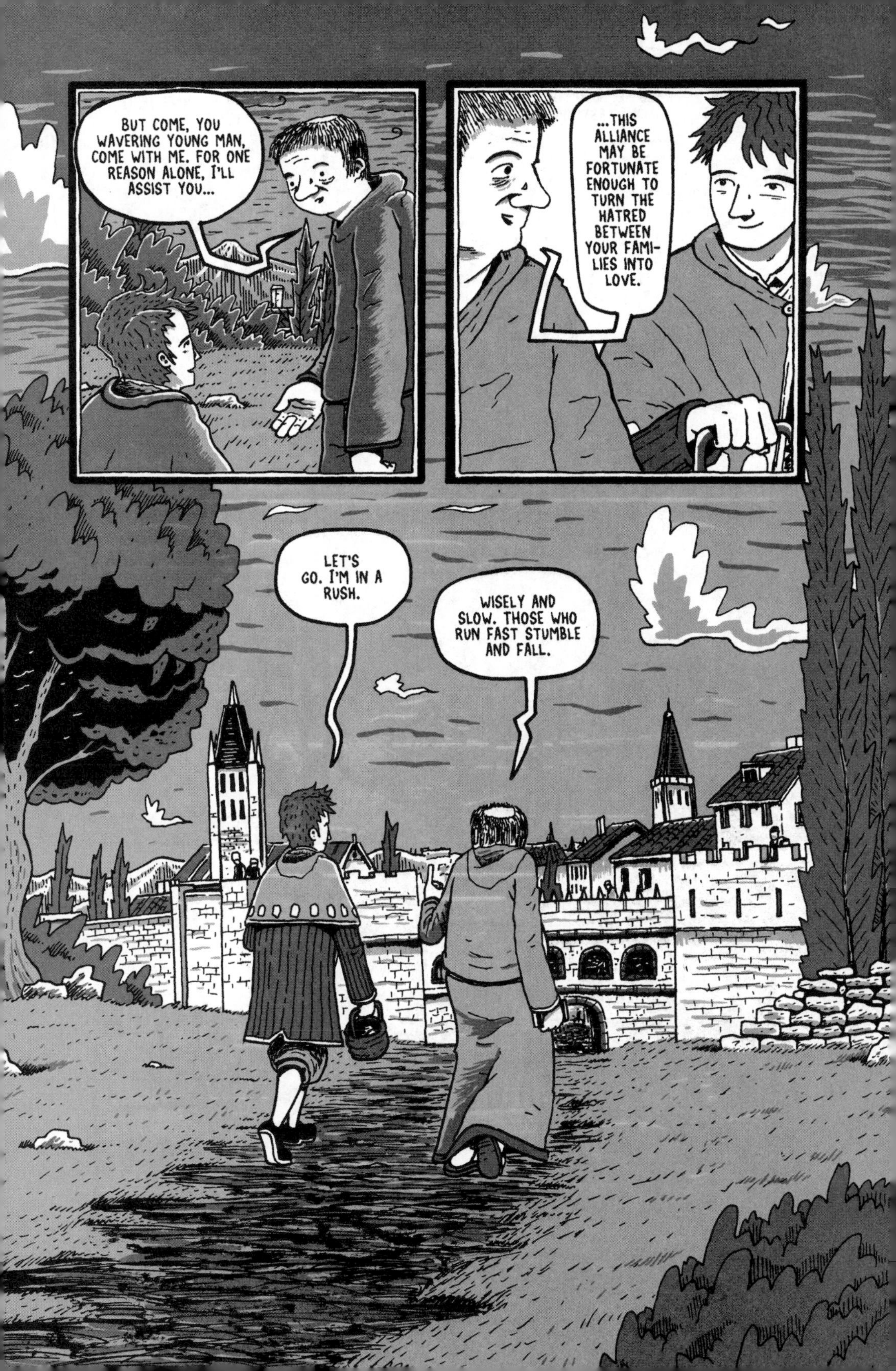
BUT COME, YOU WAVERING YOUNG MAN, COME WITH ME. FOR ONE REASON ALONE, I'LL ASSIST YOU...
...THIS ALLIANCE MAY BE FORTUNATE ENOUGH TO TURN THE HATRED BETWEEN YOUR FAMILIES INTO LOVE.
LET'S GO. I'M IN A RUSH.
WISELY AND SLOW. THOSE WHO RUN FAST STUMBLE AND FALL.

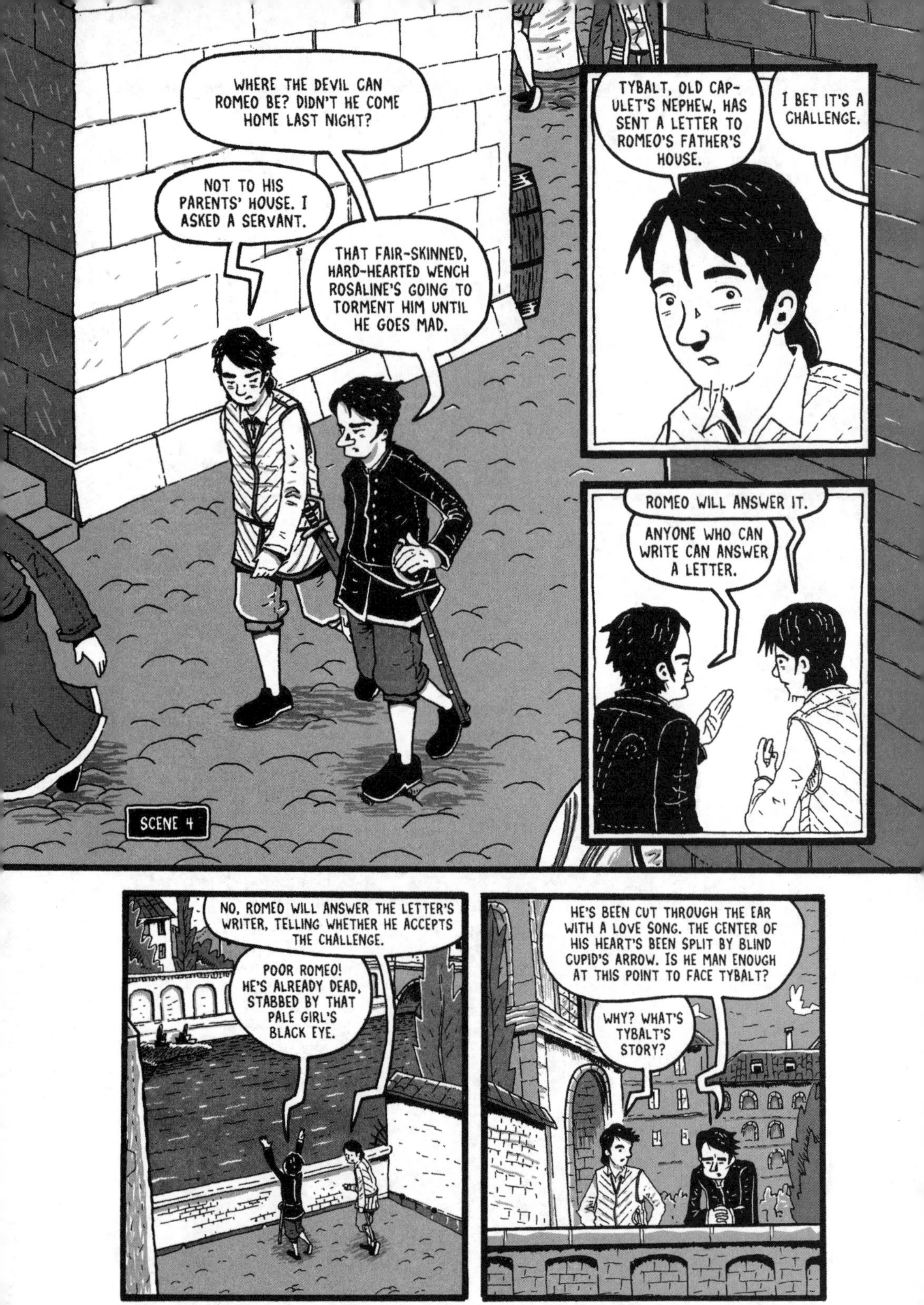
WHERE THE DEVIL CAN ROMEO BE? DIDN'T HE COME HOME LAST NIGHT?
NOT TO HIS PARENTS' HOUSE. I ASKED A SERVANT.
THAT FAIR-SKINNED, HARD-HEARTED WENCH ROSALINE'S GOING TO TORMENT HIM UNTIL HE GOES MAD.
SCENE 4
TYBALT, OLD CAP-ULET'S NEPHEW, HAS SENT A LETTER TO ROMEO'S FATHER'S HOUSE.
I BET IT'S A CHALLENGE.
ROMEO WILL ANSWER IT.
ANYONE WHO CAN WRITE CAN ANSWER A LETTER.
NO, ROMEO WILL ANSWER THE LETTER'S WRITER, TELLING WHETHER HE ACCEPTS THE CHALLENGE.
POOR ROMEO! HE'S ALREADY DEAD, STABBED BY THAT PALE GIRL'S BLACK EYE.
HE'S BEEN CUT THROUGH THE EAR WITH A LOVE SONG. THE CENTER OF HIS HEART'S BEEN SPLIT BY BLIND CUPID'S ARROW. IS HE MAN ENOUGH AT THIS POINT TO FACE TYBALT?
WHY? WHAT'S TYBALT'S STORY?

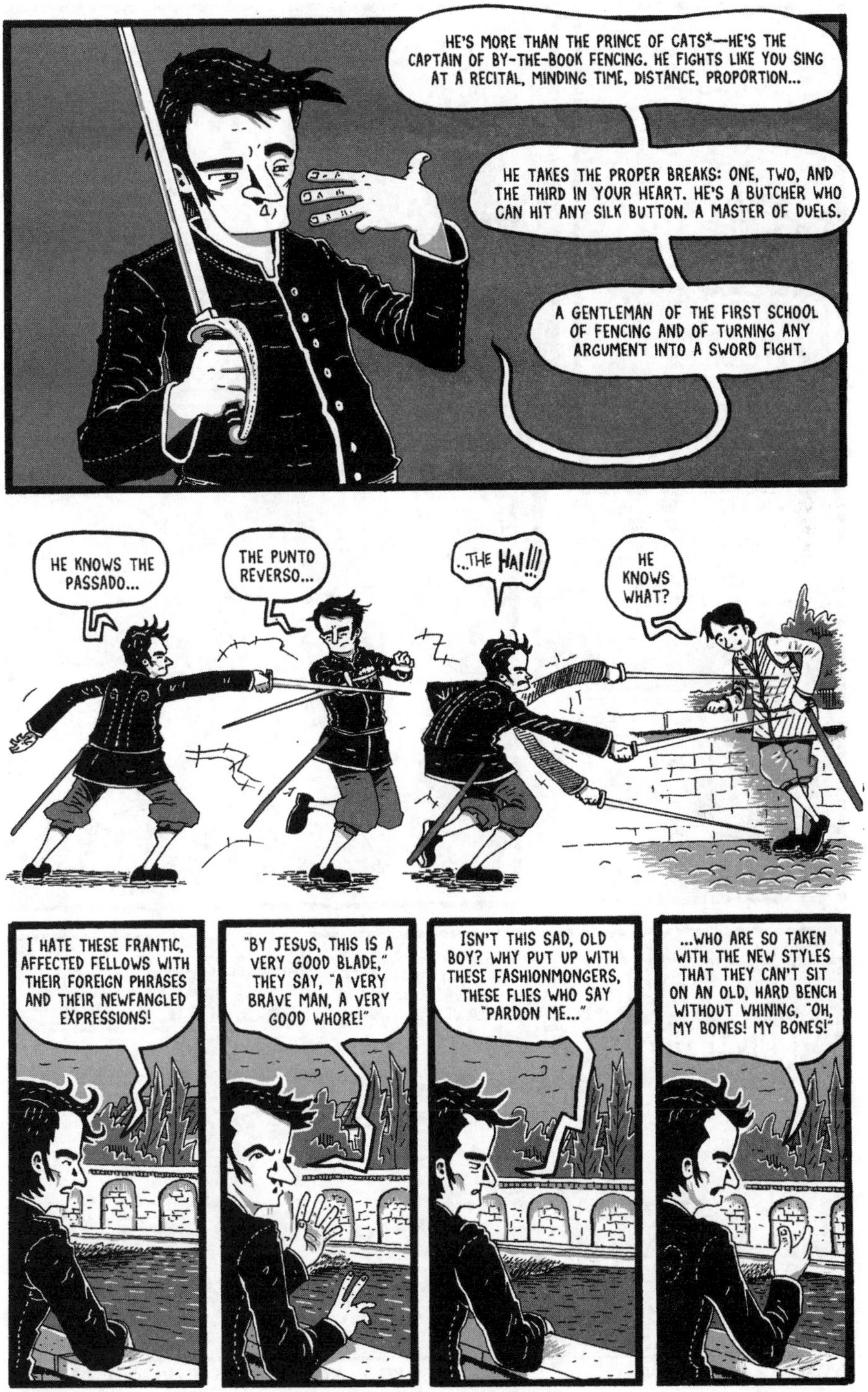
HE'S MORE THAN THE PRINCE OF CATS*—HE'S THE CAPTAIN OF BY-THE-BOOK FENCING. HE FIGHTS LIKE YOU SING AT A RECITAL, MINDING TIME, DISTANCE, PROPORTION...
HE TAKES THE PROPER BREAKS: ONE, TWO, AND THE THIRD IN YOUR HEART. HE'S A BUTCHER WHO CAN HIT ANY SILK BUTTON. A MASTER OF DUELS.
A GENTLEMAN OF THE FIRST SCHOOL OF FENCING AND OF TURNING ANY ARGUMENT INTO A SWORD FIGHT.
HE KNOWS THE PASSADO...
THE PUNTO REVERSO...
...THE HAI!!!
HE KNOWS WHAT?
I HATE THESE FRANTIC, AFFECTED FELLOWS WITH THEIR FOREIGN PHRASES AND THEIR NEWFANGLED EXPRESSIONS!
"BY JESUS, THIS IS A VERY GOOD BLADE," THEY SAY, "A VERY BRAVE MAN, A VERY GOOD WHORE!"
ISN'T THIS SAD, OLD BOY? WHY PUT UP WITH THESE FASHIONMONGERS, THESE FLIES WHO SAY "PARDON ME..."
...WHO ARE SO TAKEN WITH THE NEW STYLES THAT THEY CAN'T SIT ON AN OLD, HARD BENCH WITHOUT WHINING, "OH, MY BONES! MY BONES!"

*PRINCE OF CATS = A MEDEIVAL CHARACTER WHOSE NAME WAS ALSO TYBALT

HEY, HERE COMES ROMEO!

HE LOOKS LIKE A DRIED HERRING WITHOUT ITS EGGS, AND HE'S WITHOUT HIS GIRL.

OH, FLESH, FLESH, HOW YOU FISHIFY. NOW HE'S READY FOR PETRARCH.* COMPARED TO ROMEO'S GIRL, LAURA WAS A KITCHEN SLAVE. OF COURSE, SHE HAD A BETTER LOVE TO MAKE RHYMES FOR HER.

DIDO WAS SHABBILY DRESSED.†

CLEOPATRA WAS A GYPSY GIRL.

HELEN AND HERA WERE SLUTS AND HARLOTS.

THISBE MIGHT'VE HAD A BLUE EYE OR TWO, BUT IT DOESN'T MATTER.

SIGNOR ROMEO, *BONJOUR!* THERE'S A FRENCH GREETING FOR YOUR DROOPING FRENCH PANTS! YOU FAKED US OUT PRETTY WELL LAST NIGHT.

GOOD MORNING TO YOU BOTH. IN WHAT WAY DID I FAKE YOU OUT?

*PETRARCH = A FAMOUS LOVE POET   †DIDO, ETC. = MERCUTIO NAMES A SERIES OF FAMOUS FEMALE LOVERS

YOU GAVE US THE SLIP, SIR. THE **SLIP**. CAN YOU NOT CONCEIVE WHAT I'M SAYING?

PARDON ME, GOOD MERCUTIO. I HAD IMPORTANT BUSINESS-- SO IMPORTANT, I HAD TO FORGET COURTESY.

"IMPORTANT BUSINESS" THAT MADE YOU BEND AND THRUST, I'LL BET.

YOU MEAN DO A CURTSY?

YOU'VE HIT IT WELL.*

THAT'S A POLITE AND COURTEOUS EXPLANATION.

INDEED, I AM THE VERY PINK⁺ OF COURTESY.

"PINK" AS IN "FLOWER?"

RIGHT.

WELL THEN, MY SHOE IS WELL PINKED# WITH FLOWERS.

ALL RIGHT, MY WITTY FRIEND... FOLLOW ME ON THIS JOKE UNTIL YOU'VE WORN YOUR SHOE OUT.

WHEN ITS THIN SOLE IS WORN THROUGH, ONLY THE JOKE WILL REMAIN THERE, "SOLELY" SINGULAR.

O SINGLE-SOLED JOKE! SOLELY SINGLE FOR THE SINGLENESS.

*MERCUTIO'S BEING LEWD HERE.   ⁺PINK = PERFECT EXAMPLE   #PINKED = DECORATED

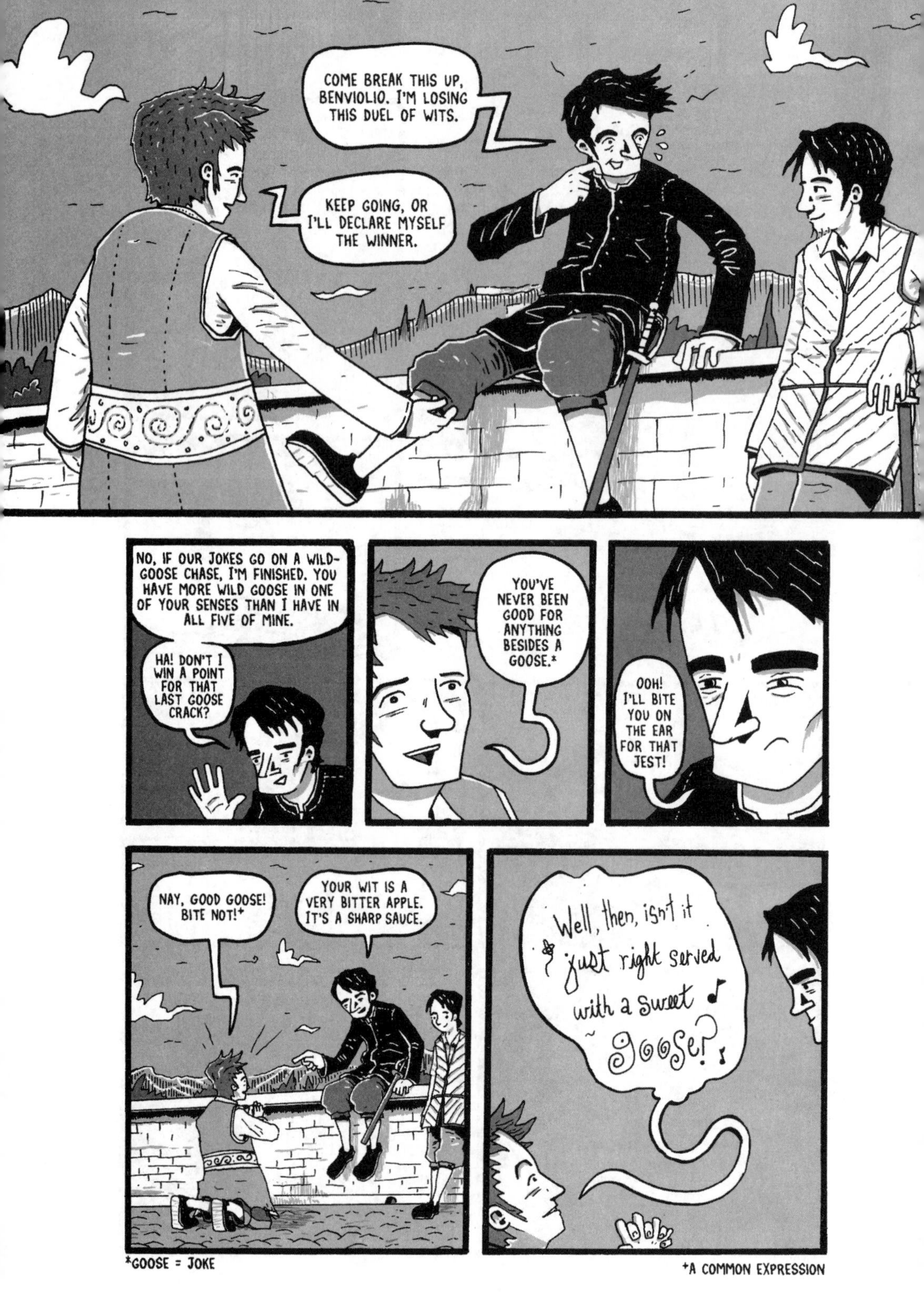
COME BREAK THIS UP, BENVIOLIO. I'M LOSING THIS DUEL OF WITS.
KEEP GOING, OR I'LL DECLARE MYSELF THE WINNER.
NO, IF OUR JOKES GO ON A WILD-GOOSE CHASE, I'M FINISHED. YOU HAVE MORE WILD GOOSE IN ONE OF YOUR SENSES THAN I HAVE IN ALL FIVE OF MINE.
HA! DON'T I WIN A POINT FOR THAT LAST GOOSE CRACK?
YOU'VE NEVER BEEN GOOD FOR ANYTHING BESIDES A GOOSE.*
OOH! I'LL BITE YOU ON THE EAR FOR THAT JEST!
NAY, GOOD GOOSE! BITE NOT!+
YOUR WIT IS A VERY BITTER APPLE. IT'S A SHARP SAUCE.
Well, then, isn't it just right served with a sweet goose?

*GOOSE = JOKE

+A COMMON EXPRESSION

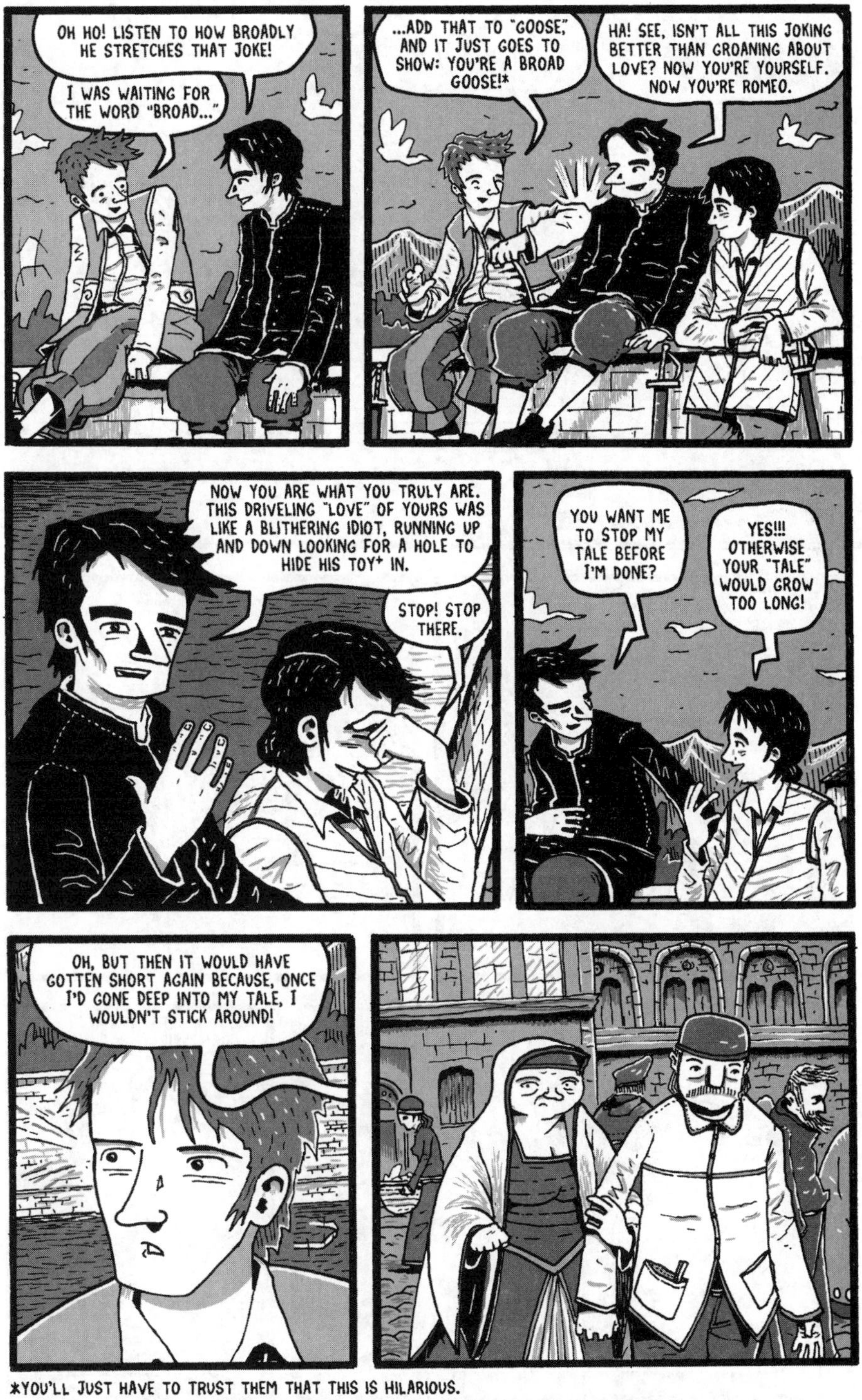
OH HO! LISTEN TO HOW BROADLY HE STRETCHES THAT JOKE!
I WAS WAITING FOR THE WORD "BROAD..."
...ADD THAT TO "GOOSE," AND IT JUST GOES TO SHOW: YOU'RE A BROAD GOOSE!*
HA! SEE, ISN'T ALL THIS JOKING BETTER THAN GROANING ABOUT LOVE? NOW YOU'RE YOURSELF. NOW YOU'RE ROMEO.
NOW YOU ARE WHAT YOU TRULY ARE. THIS DRIVELING "LOVE" OF YOURS WAS LIKE A BLITHERING IDIOT, RUNNING UP AND DOWN LOOKING FOR A HOLE TO HIDE HIS TOY+ IN.
STOP! STOP THERE.
YOU WANT ME TO STOP MY TALE BEFORE I'M DONE?
YES!!! OTHERWISE YOUR "TALE" WOULD GROW TOO LONG!
OH, BUT THEN IT WOULD HAVE GOTTEN SHORT AGAIN BECAUSE, ONCE I'D GONE DEEP INTO MY TALE, I WOULDN'T STICK AROUND!

*YOU'LL JUST HAVE TO TRUST THEM THAT THIS IS HILARIOUS.
+A STRING OF DIRTY JOKES FOLLOWS, PUNNING ON TALE AND TAIL (I.E., THE MALE GENITALS)

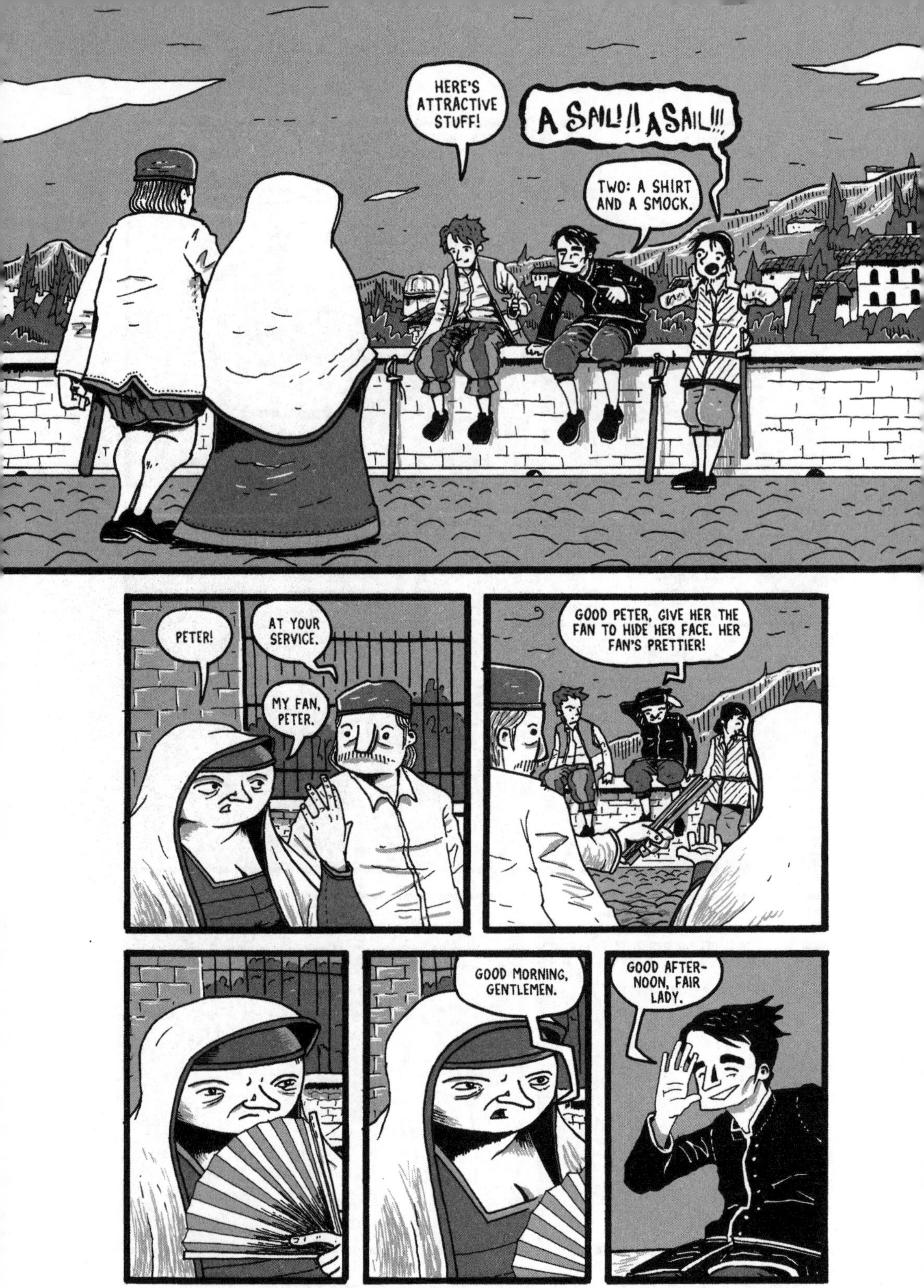
HERE'S ATTRACTIVE STUFF!
A SAIL!!! A SAIL!!!
TWO: A SHIRT AND A SMOCK.
PETER!
AT YOUR SERVICE.
MY FAN, PETER.
GOOD PETER, GIVE HER THE FAN TO HIDE HER FACE. HER FAN'S PRETTIER!
GOOD MORNING, GENTLEMEN.
GOOD AFTER-NOON, FAIR LADY.

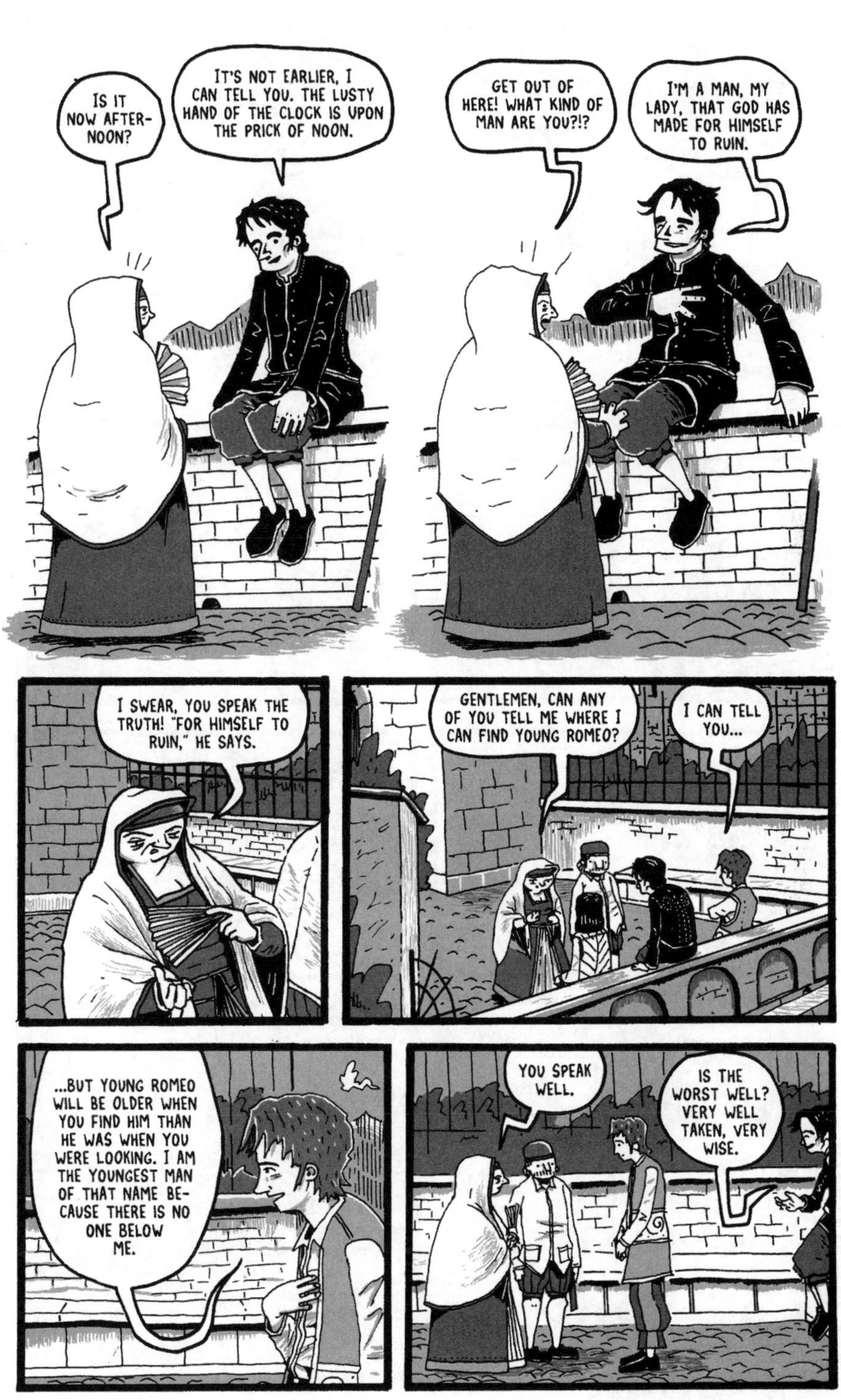
IS IT NOW AFTER-NOON?
IT'S NOT EARLIER, I CAN TELL YOU. THE LUSTY HAND OF THE CLOCK IS UPON THE PRICK OF NOON.
GET OUT OF HERE! WHAT KIND OF MAN ARE YOU?!?
I'M A MAN, MY LADY, THAT GOD HAS MADE FOR HIMSELF TO RUIN.
I SWEAR, YOU SPEAK THE TRUTH! "FOR HIMSELF TO RUIN," HE SAYS.
GENTLEMEN, CAN ANY OF YOU TELL ME WHERE I CAN FIND YOUNG ROMEO?
I CAN TELL YOU...
...BUT YOUNG ROMEO WILL BE OLDER WHEN YOU FIND HIM THAN HE WAS WHEN YOU WERE LOOKING. I AM THE YOUNGEST MAN OF THAT NAME BE-CAUSE THERE IS NO ONE BELOW ME.
YOU SPEAK WELL.
IS THE WORST WELL? VERY WELL TAKEN, VERY WISE.

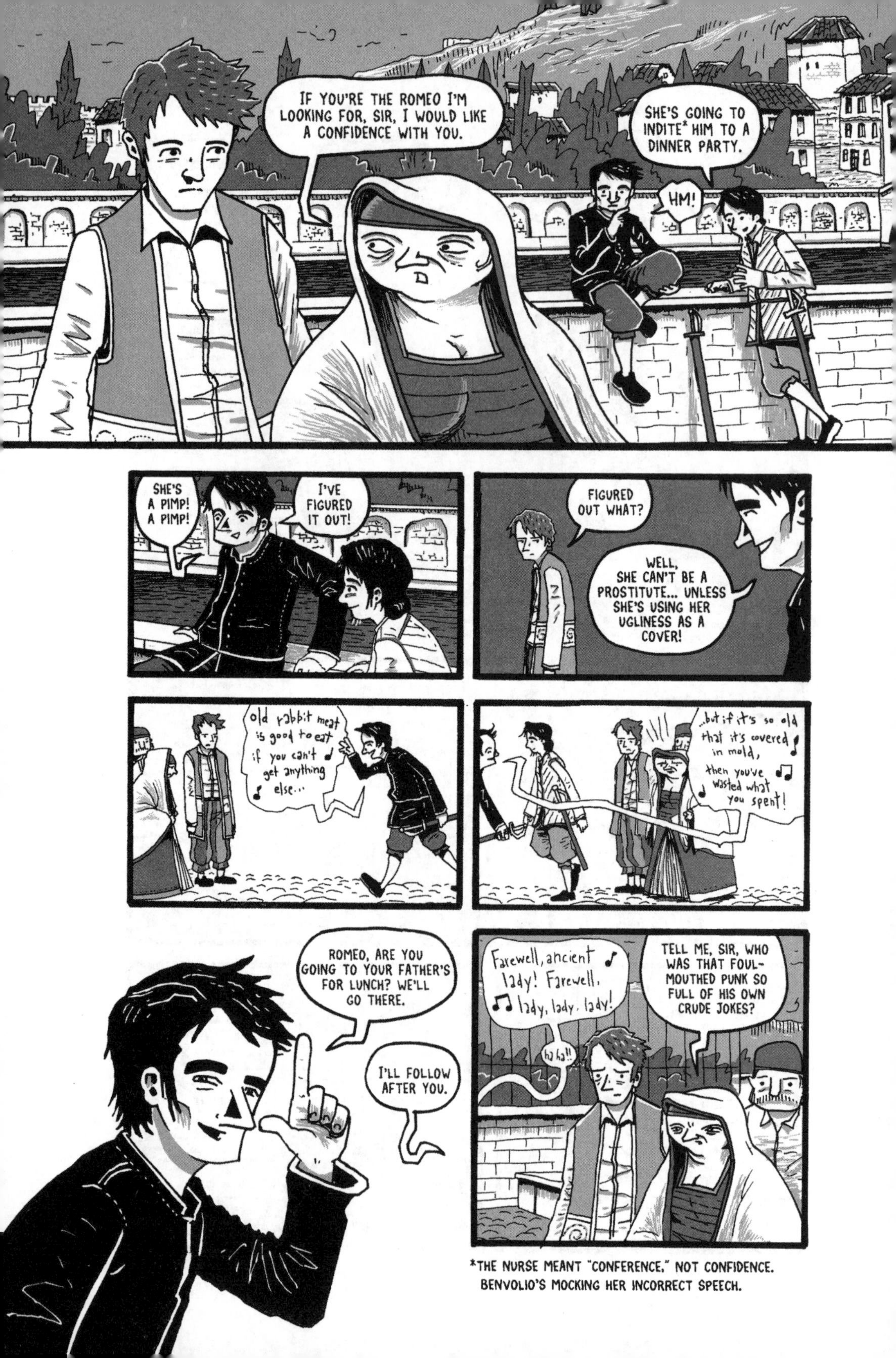
IF YOU'RE THE ROMEO I'M LOOKING FOR, SIR, I WOULD LIKE A CONFIDENCE WITH YOU.
SHE'S GOING TO INDITE* HIM TO A DINNER PARTY.
HM!
SHE'S A PIMP! A PIMP!
I'VE FIGURED IT OUT!
FIGURED OUT WHAT?
WELL, SHE CAN'T BE A PROSTITUTE... UNLESS SHE'S USING HER UGLINESS AS A COVER!
old rabbit meat is good to eat if you can't get anything else...
...but if it's so old that it's covered in mold, then you've wasted what you spent!
ROMEO, ARE YOU GOING TO YOUR FATHER'S FOR LUNCH? WE'LL GO THERE.
I'LL FOLLOW AFTER YOU.
Farewell, ancient lady! Farewell, lady, lady, lady!
ha ha!!
TELL ME, SIR, WHO WAS THAT FOUL-MOUTHED PUNK SO FULL OF HIS OWN CRUDE JOKES?

*THE NURSE MEANT "CONFERENCE," NOT CONFIDENCE. BENVOLIO'S MOCKING HER INCORRECT SPEECH.

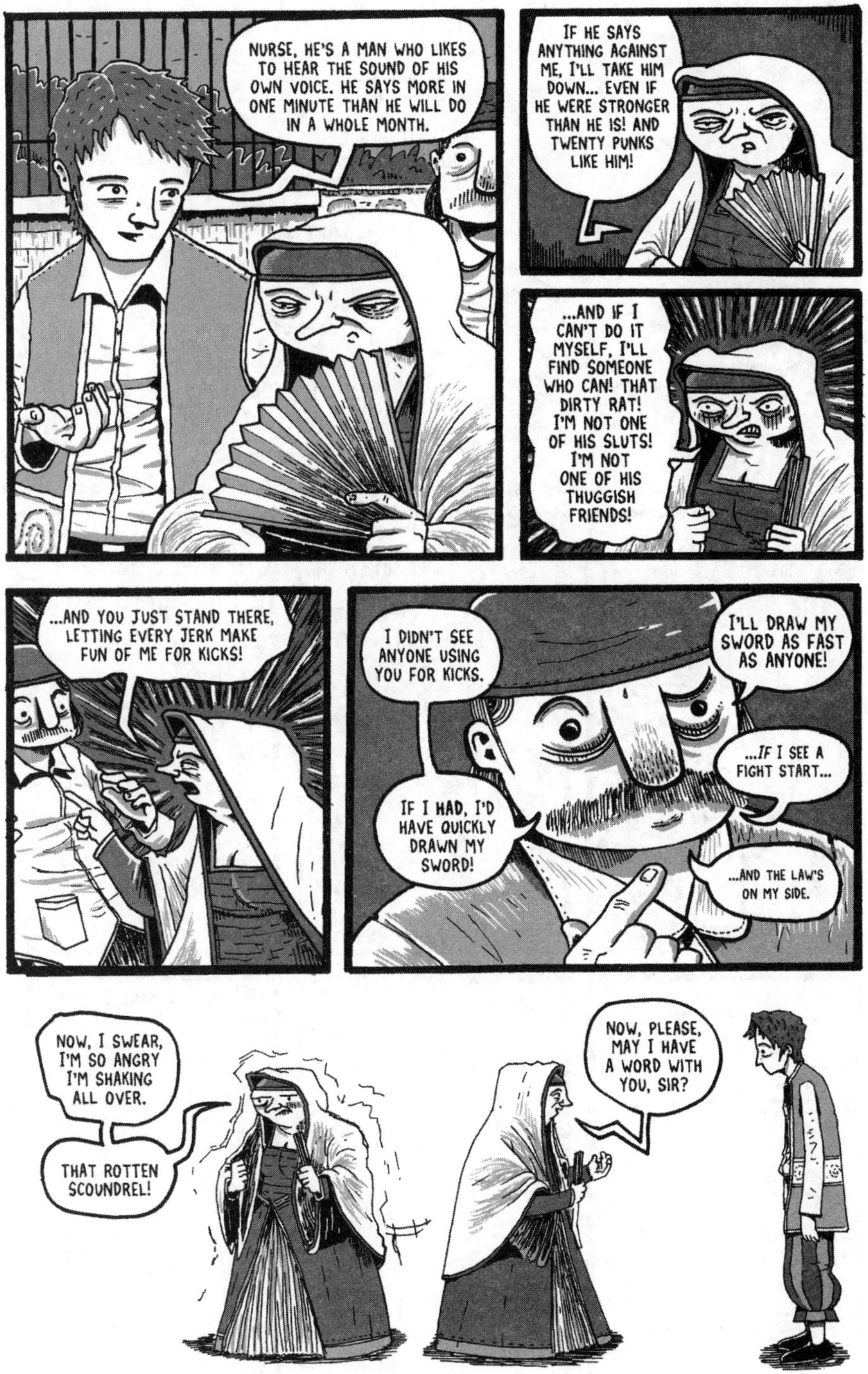
NURSE, HE'S A MAN WHO LIKES TO HEAR THE SOUND OF HIS OWN VOICE. HE SAYS MORE IN ONE MINUTE THAN HE WILL DO IN A WHOLE MONTH.
IF HE SAYS ANYTHING AGAINST ME, I'LL TAKE HIM DOWN... EVEN IF HE WERE STRONGER THAN HE IS! AND TWENTY PUNKS LIKE HIM!
...AND IF I CAN'T DO IT MYSELF, I'LL FIND SOMEONE WHO CAN! THAT DIRTY RAT! I'M NOT ONE OF HIS SLUTS! I'M NOT ONE OF HIS THUGGISH FRIENDS!
...AND YOU JUST STAND THERE, LETTING EVERY JERK MAKE FUN OF ME FOR KICKS!
I DIDN'T SEE ANYONE USING YOU FOR KICKS.
IF I HAD, I'D HAVE QUICKLY DRAWN MY SWORD!
I'LL DRAW MY SWORD AS FAST AS ANYONE!
...IF I SEE A FIGHT START...
...AND THE LAW'S ON MY SIDE.
NOW, I SWEAR, I'M SO ANGRY I'M SHAKING ALL OVER.
THAT ROTTEN SCOUNDREL!
NOW, PLEASE, MAY I HAVE A WORD WITH YOU, SIR?

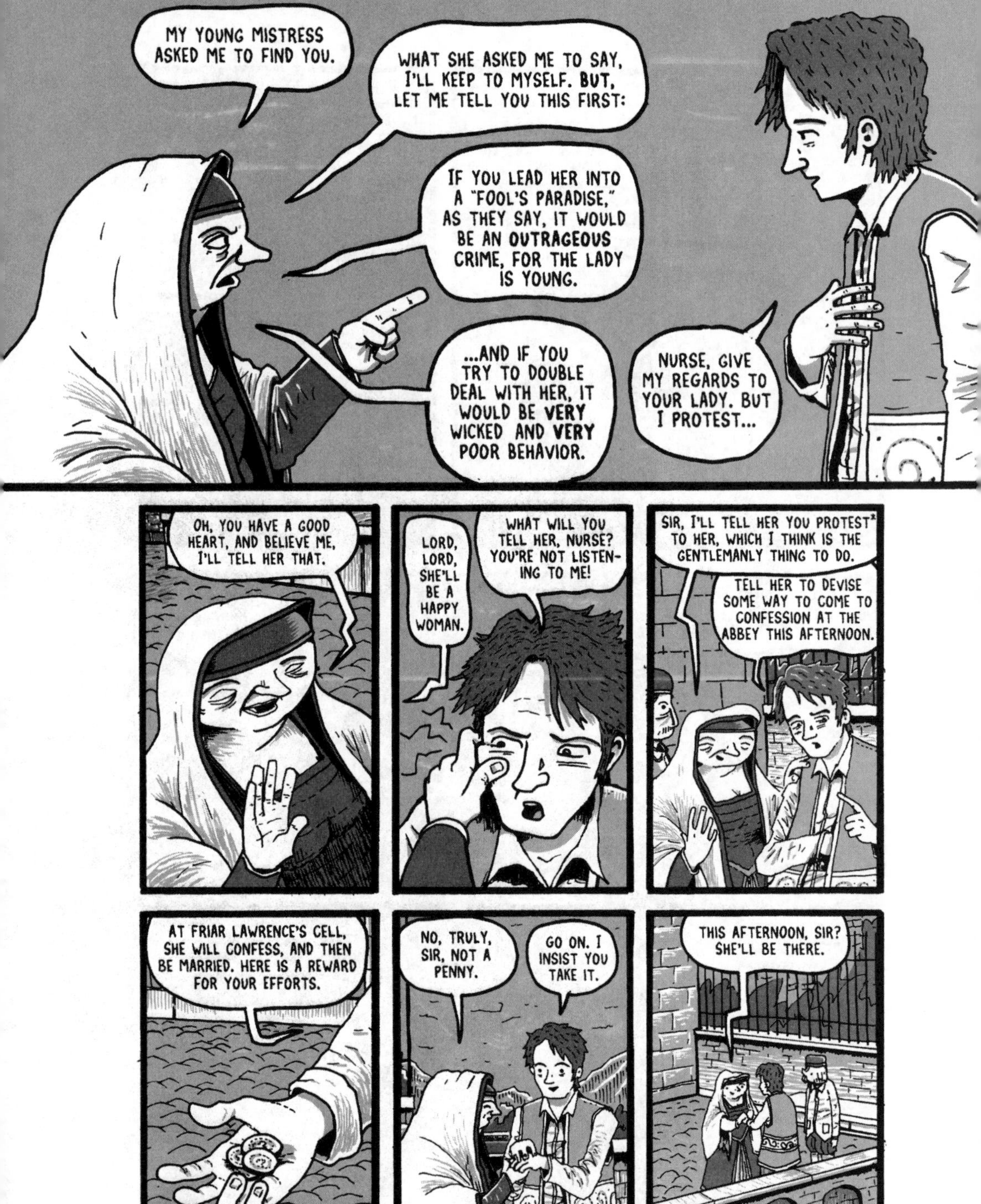
MY YOUNG MISTRESS ASKED ME TO FIND YOU.
WHAT SHE ASKED ME TO SAY, I'LL KEEP TO MYSELF. BUT, LET ME TELL YOU THIS FIRST:
IF YOU LEAD HER INTO A "FOOL'S PARADISE," AS THEY SAY, IT WOULD BE AN OUTRAGEOUS CRIME, FOR THE LADY IS YOUNG.
...AND IF YOU TRY TO DOUBLE DEAL WITH HER, IT WOULD BE VERY WICKED AND VERY POOR BEHAVIOR.
NURSE, GIVE MY REGARDS TO YOUR LADY. BUT I PROTEST...
OH, YOU HAVE A GOOD HEART, AND BELIEVE ME, I'LL TELL HER THAT.
LORD, LORD, SHE'LL BE A HAPPY WOMAN.
WHAT WILL YOU TELL HER, NURSE? YOU'RE NOT LISTENING TO ME!
SIR, I'LL TELL HER YOU PROTEST* TO HER, WHICH I THINK IS THE GENTLEMANLY THING TO DO.
TELL HER TO DEVISE SOME WAY TO COME TO CONFESSION AT THE ABBEY THIS AFTERNOON.
AT FRIAR LAWRENCE'S CELL, SHE WILL CONFESS, AND THEN BE MARRIED. HERE IS A REWARD FOR YOUR EFFORTS.
NO, TRULY, SIR, NOT A PENNY.
GO ON. I INSIST YOU TAKE IT.
THIS AFTERNOON, SIR? SHE'LL BE THERE.

*THE NURSE THINKS HE MEANS "PROPOSE."

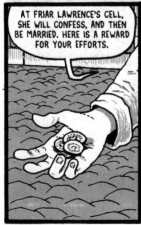

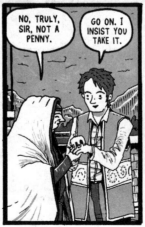

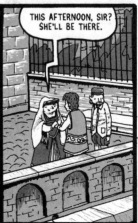

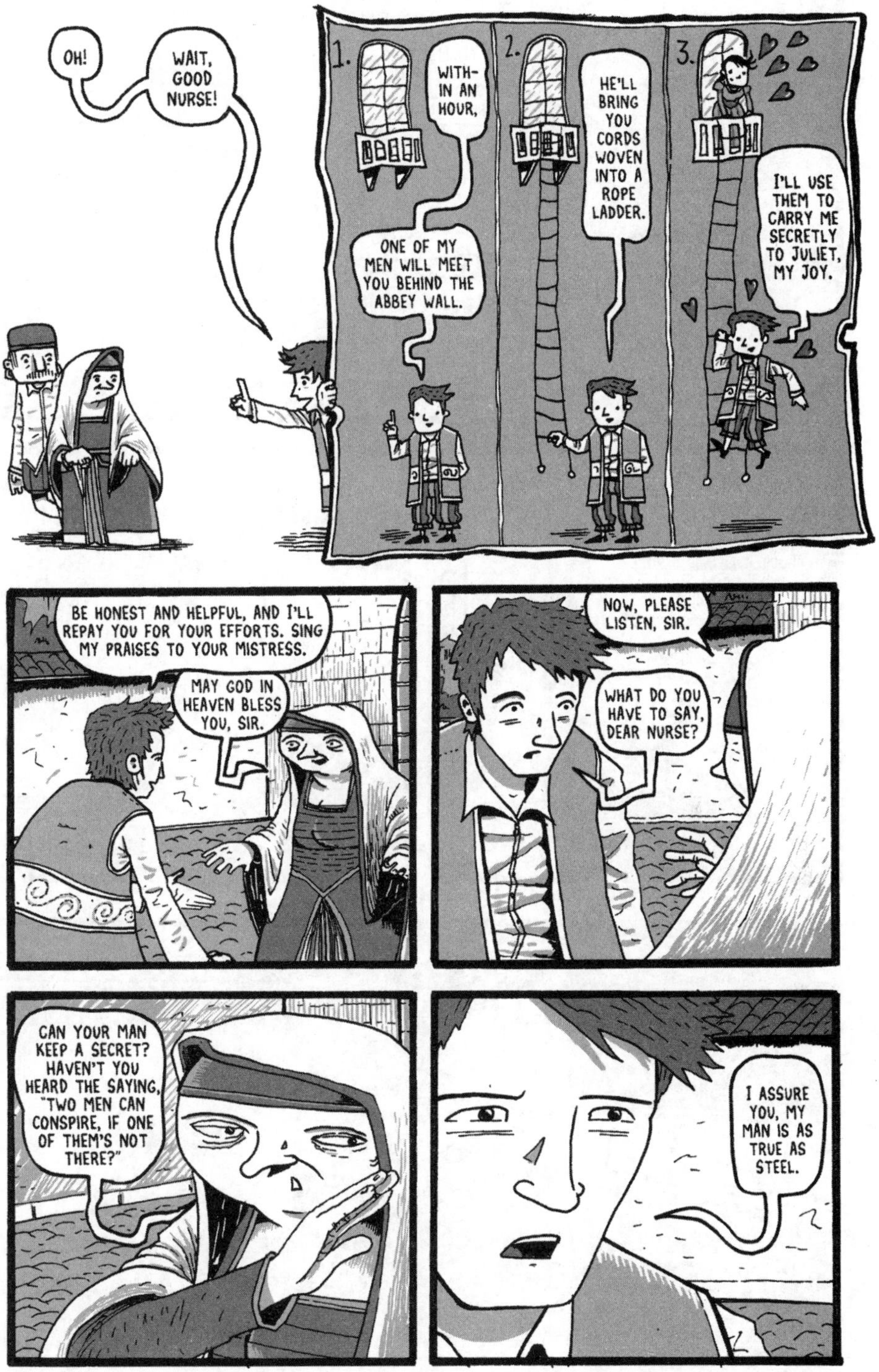
OH!
WAIT, GOOD NURSE!
1.
WITH-IN AN HOUR,
ONE OF MY MEN WILL MEET YOU BEHIND THE ABBEY WALL.
2.
HE'LL BRING YOU CORDS WOVEN INTO A ROPE LADDER.
3.
I'LL USE THEM TO CARRY ME SECRETLY TO JULIET, MY JOY.
BE HONEST AND HELPFUL, AND I'LL REPAY YOU FOR YOUR EFFORTS. SING MY PRAISES TO YOUR MISTRESS.
MAY GOD IN HEAVEN BLESS YOU, SIR.
NOW, PLEASE LISTEN, SIR.
WHAT DO YOU HAVE TO SAY, DEAR NURSE?
CAN YOUR MAN KEEP A SECRET? HAVEN'T YOU HEARD THE SAYING, "TWO MEN CAN CONSPIRE, IF ONE OF THEM'S NOT THERE?"
I ASSURE YOU, MY MAN IS AS TRUE AS STEEL.

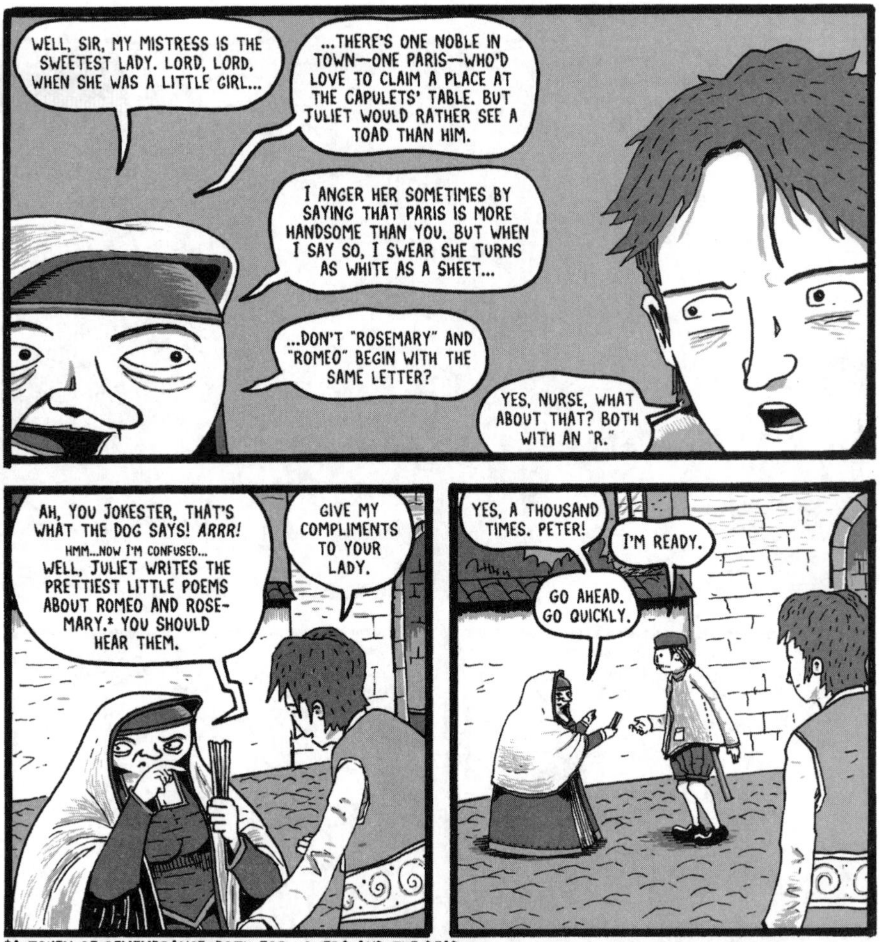
WELL, SIR, MY MISTRESS IS THE SWEETEST LADY. LORD, LORD, WHEN SHE WAS A LITTLE GIRL...
...THERE'S ONE NOBLE IN TOWN—ONE PARIS—WHO'D LOVE TO CLAIM A PLACE AT THE CAPULETS' TABLE. BUT JULIET WOULD RATHER SEE A TOAD THAN HIM.
I ANGER HER SOMETIMES BY SAYING THAT PARIS IS MORE HANDSOME THAN YOU. BUT WHEN I SAY SO, I SWEAR SHE TURNS AS WHITE AS A SHEET...
...DON'T "ROSEMARY" AND "ROMEO" BEGIN WITH THE SAME LETTER?
YES, NURSE, WHAT ABOUT THAT? BOTH WITH AN "R."
AH, YOU JOKESTER, THAT'S WHAT THE DOG SAYS! *ARRR!*
HMM...NOW I'M CONFUSED...
WELL, JULIET WRITES THE PRETTIEST LITTLE POEMS ABOUT ROMEO AND ROSEMARY.* YOU SHOULD HEAR THEM.
GIVE MY COMPLIMENTS TO YOUR LADY.
YES, A THOUSAND TIMES. PETER!
I'M READY.
GO AHEAD. GO QUICKLY.

*A TOKEN OF REMEMBRANCE, BOTH FOR LOVERS AND THE DEAD

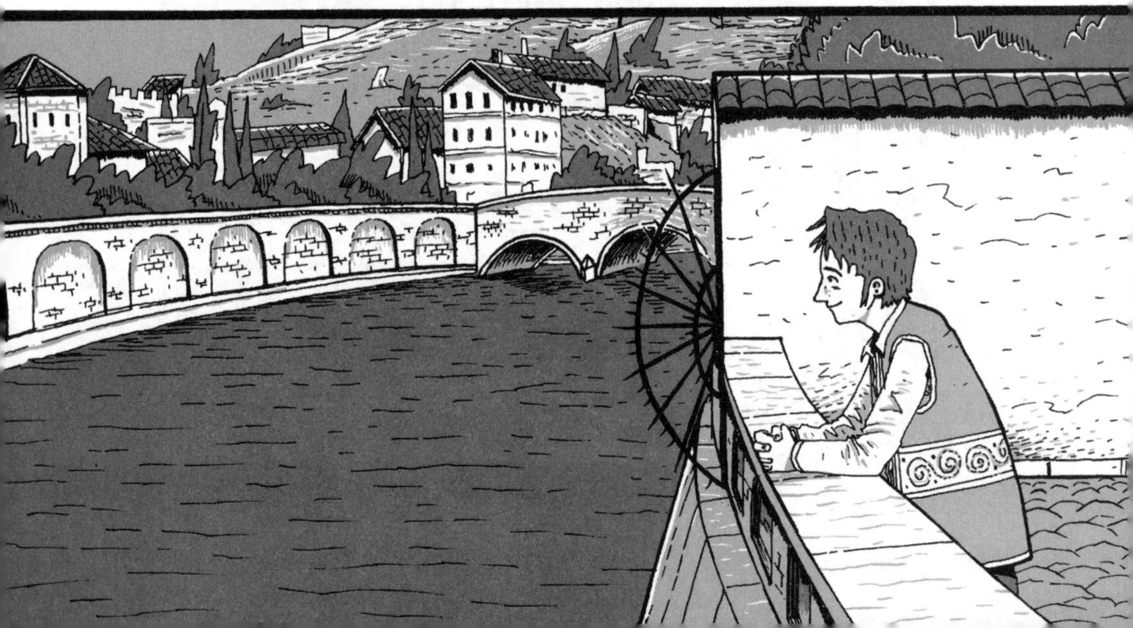

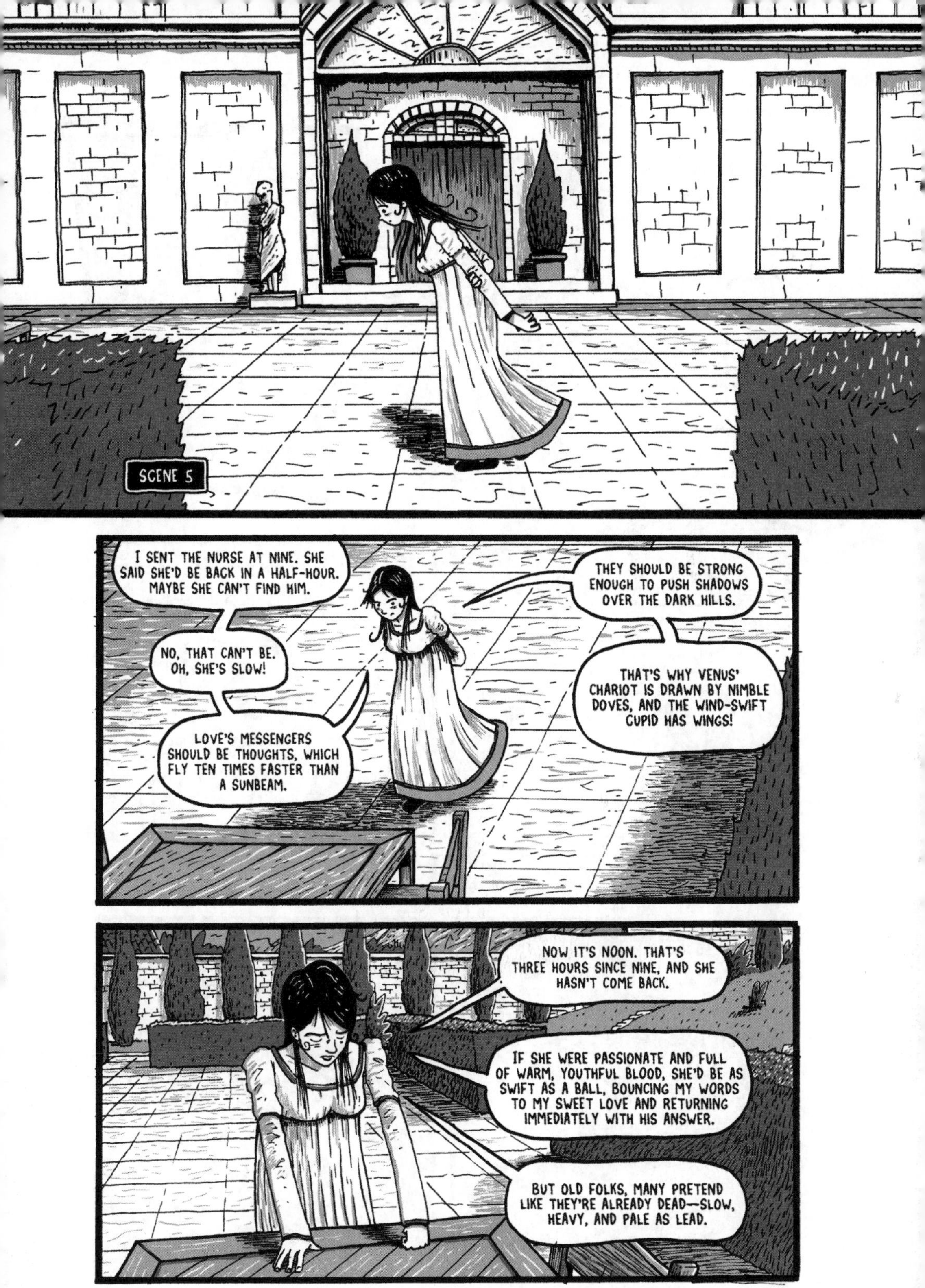
SCENE 5
I SENT THE NURSE AT NINE. SHE SAID SHE'D BE BACK IN A HALF-HOUR. MAYBE SHE CAN'T FIND HIM.
NO, THAT CAN'T BE. OH, SHE'S SLOW!
LOVE'S MESSENGERS SHOULD BE THOUGHTS, WHICH FLY TEN TIMES FASTER THAN A SUNBEAM.
THEY SHOULD BE STRONG ENOUGH TO PUSH SHADOWS OVER THE DARK HILLS.
THAT'S WHY VENUS' CHARIOT IS DRAWN BY NIMBLE DOVES, AND THE WIND-SWIFT CUPID HAS WINGS!
NOW IT'S NOON. THAT'S THREE HOURS SINCE NINE, AND SHE HASN'T COME BACK.
IF SHE WERE PASSIONATE AND FULL OF WARM, YOUTHFUL BLOOD, SHE'D BE AS SWIFT AS A BALL, BOUNCING MY WORDS TO MY SWEET LOVE AND RETURNING IMMEDIATELY WITH HIS ANSWER.
BUT OLD FOLKS, MANY PRETEND LIKE THEY'RE ALREADY DEAD—SLOW, HEAVY, AND PALE AS LEAD.

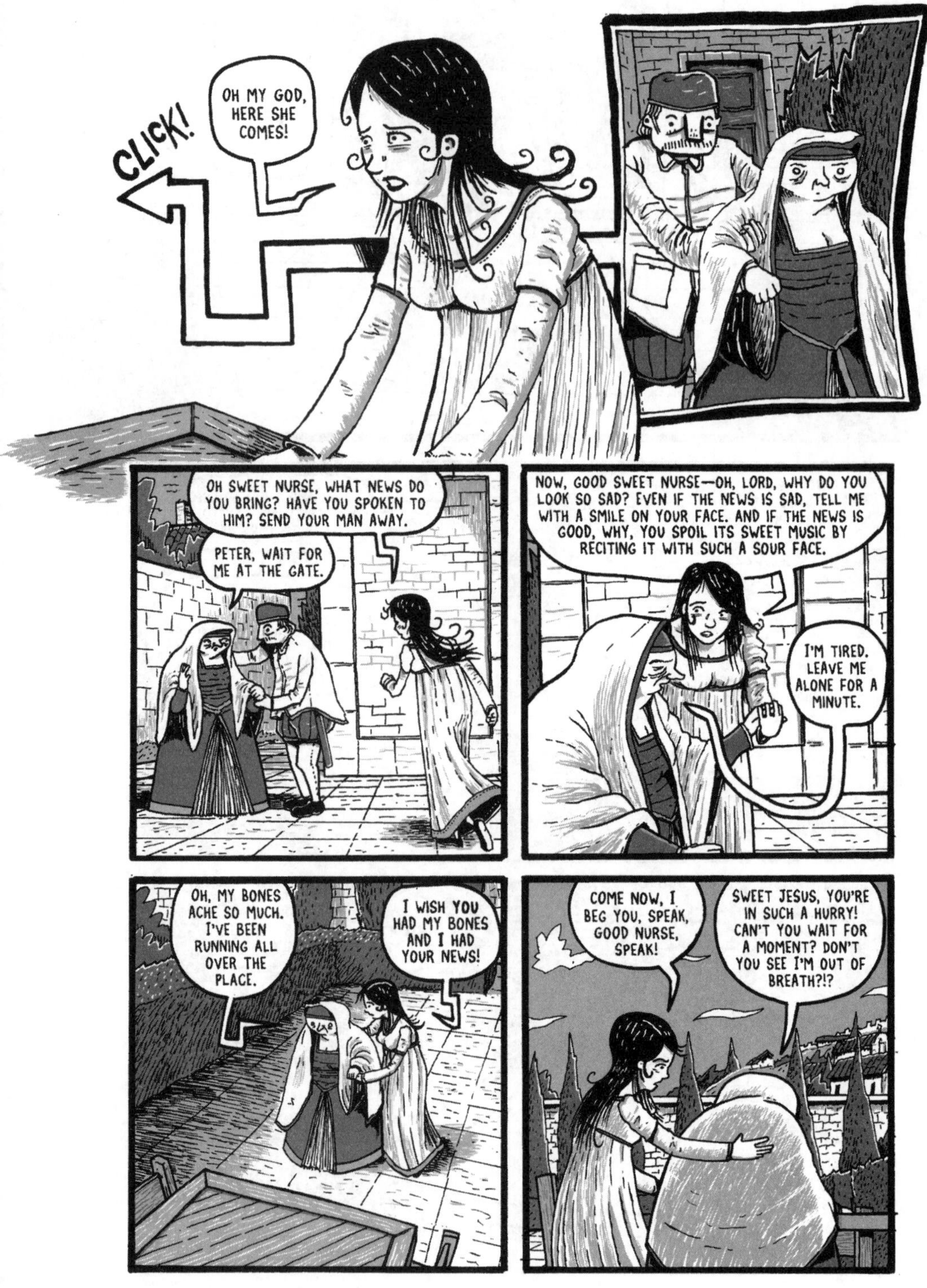
CLICK!
OH MY GOD, HERE SHE COMES!
OH SWEET NURSE, WHAT NEWS DO YOU BRING? HAVE YOU SPOKEN TO HIM? SEND YOUR MAN AWAY.
PETER, WAIT FOR ME AT THE GATE.
NOW, GOOD SWEET NURSE—OH, LORD, WHY DO YOU LOOK SO SAD? EVEN IF THE NEWS IS SAD, TELL ME WITH A SMILE ON YOUR FACE. AND IF THE NEWS IS GOOD, WHY, YOU SPOIL ITS SWEET MUSIC BY RECITING IT WITH SUCH A SOUR FACE.
I'M TIRED. LEAVE ME ALONE FOR A MINUTE.
OH, MY BONES ACHE SO MUCH. I'VE BEEN RUNNING ALL OVER THE PLACE.
I WISH YOU HAD MY BONES AND I HAD YOUR NEWS!
COME NOW, I BEG YOU, SPEAK, GOOD NURSE, SPEAK!
SWEET JESUS, YOU'RE IN SUCH A HURRY! CAN'T YOU WAIT FOR A MOMENT? DON'T YOU SEE I'M OUT OF BREATH?!?

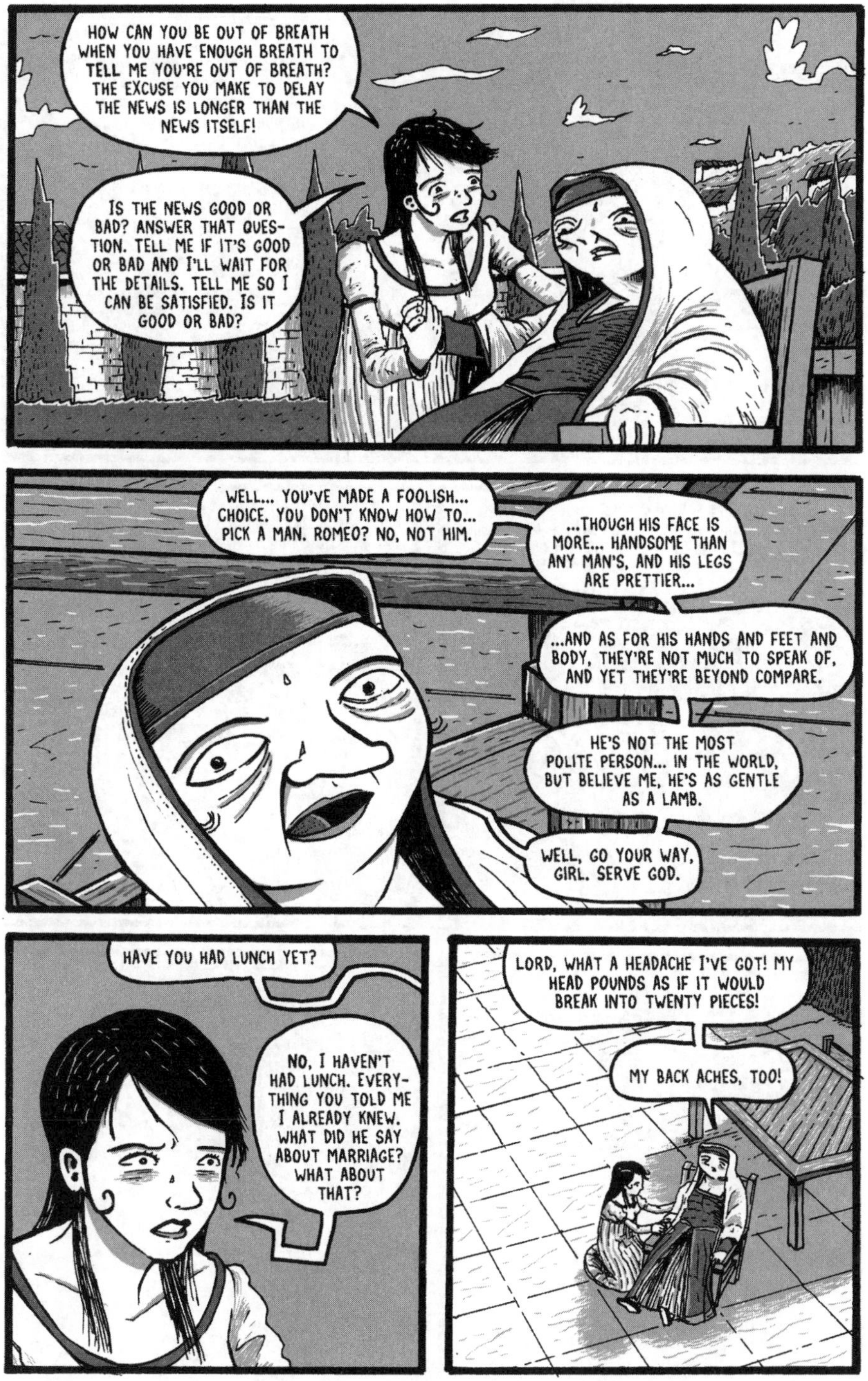
HOW CAN YOU BE OUT OF BREATH WHEN YOU HAVE ENOUGH BREATH TO TELL ME YOU'RE OUT OF BREATH? THE EXCUSE YOU MAKE TO DELAY THE NEWS IS LONGER THAN THE NEWS ITSELF!
IS THE NEWS GOOD OR BAD? ANSWER THAT QUESTION. TELL ME IF IT'S GOOD OR BAD AND I'LL WAIT FOR THE DETAILS. TELL ME SO I CAN BE SATISFIED. IS IT GOOD OR BAD?
WELL... YOU'VE MADE A FOOLISH... CHOICE. YOU DON'T KNOW HOW TO... PICK A MAN. ROMEO? NO, NOT HIM.
...THOUGH HIS FACE IS MORE... HANDSOME THAN ANY MAN'S, AND HIS LEGS ARE PRETTIER...
...AND AS FOR HIS HANDS AND FEET AND BODY, THEY'RE NOT MUCH TO SPEAK OF, AND YET THEY'RE BEYOND COMPARE.
HE'S NOT THE MOST POLITE PERSON... IN THE WORLD, BUT BELIEVE ME, HE'S AS GENTLE AS A LAMB.
WELL, GO YOUR WAY, GIRL. SERVE GOD.
HAVE YOU HAD LUNCH YET?
NO, I HAVEN'T HAD LUNCH. EVERYTHING YOU TOLD ME I ALREADY KNEW. WHAT DID HE SAY ABOUT MARRIAGE? WHAT ABOUT THAT?
LORD, WHAT A HEADACHE I'VE GOT! MY HEAD POUNDS AS IF IT WOULD BREAK INTO TWENTY PIECES!
MY BACK ACHES, TOO!

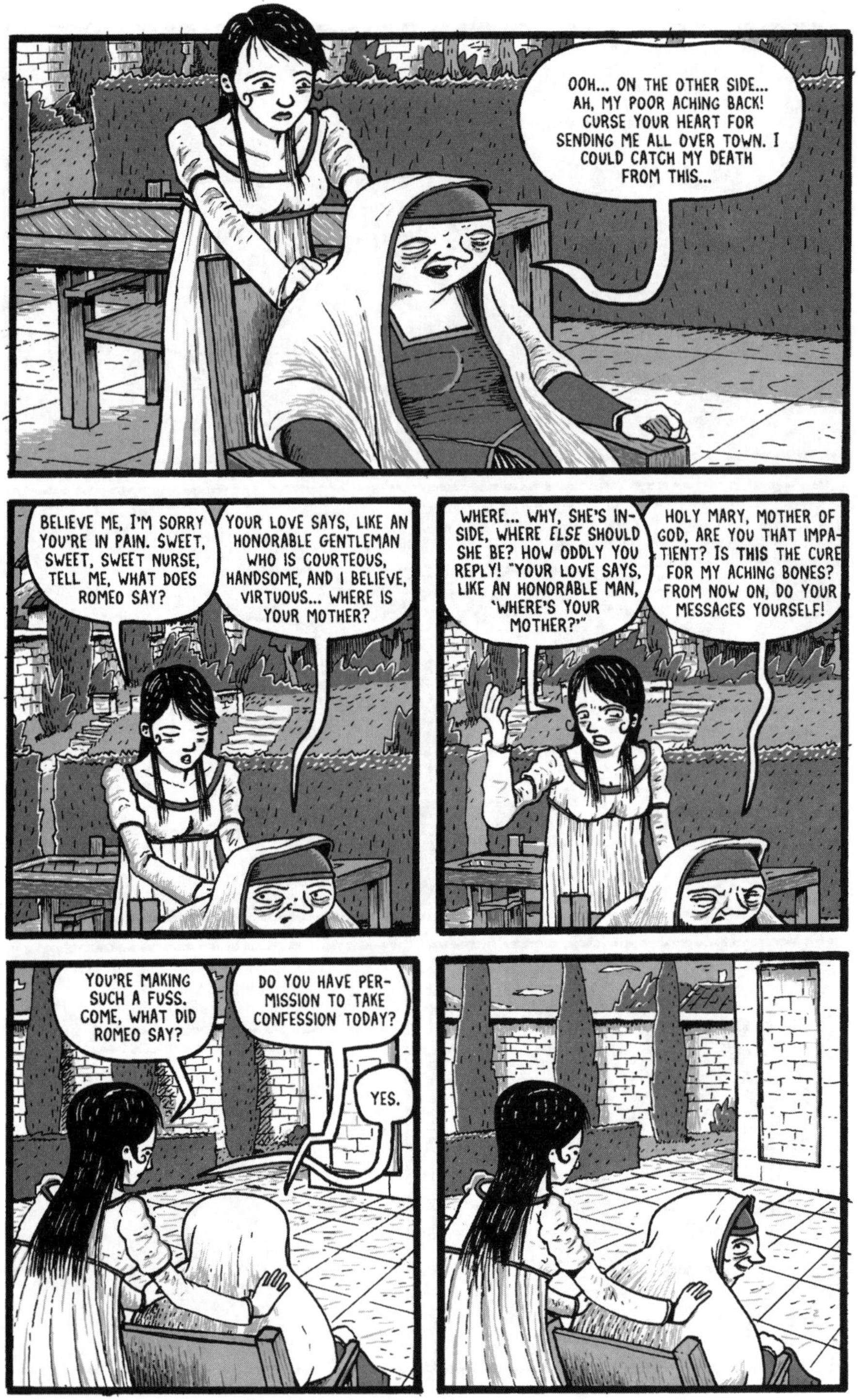
OOH... ON THE OTHER SIDE... AH, MY POOR ACHING BACK! CURSE YOUR HEART FOR SENDING ME ALL OVER TOWN. I COULD CATCH MY DEATH FROM THIS...
BELIEVE ME, I'M SORRY YOU'RE IN PAIN. SWEET, SWEET, SWEET NURSE, TELL ME, WHAT DOES ROMEO SAY?
YOUR LOVE SAYS, LIKE AN HONORABLE GENTLEMAN WHO IS COURTEOUS, HANDSOME, AND I BELIEVE, VIRTUOUS... WHERE IS YOUR MOTHER?
WHERE... WHY, SHE'S IN-SIDE, WHERE *ELSE* SHOULD SHE BE? HOW ODDLY YOU REPLY! "YOUR LOVE SAYS, LIKE AN HONORABLE MAN, 'WHERE'S YOUR MOTHER?'"
HOLY MARY, MOTHER OF GOD, ARE YOU THAT IMPA-TIENT? IS **THIS** THE CURE FOR MY ACHING BONES? FROM NOW ON, DO YOUR MESSAGES YOURSELF!
YOU'RE MAKING SUCH A FUSS. COME, WHAT DID ROMEO SAY?
DO YOU HAVE PER-MISSION TO TAKE CONFESSION TODAY?
YES.

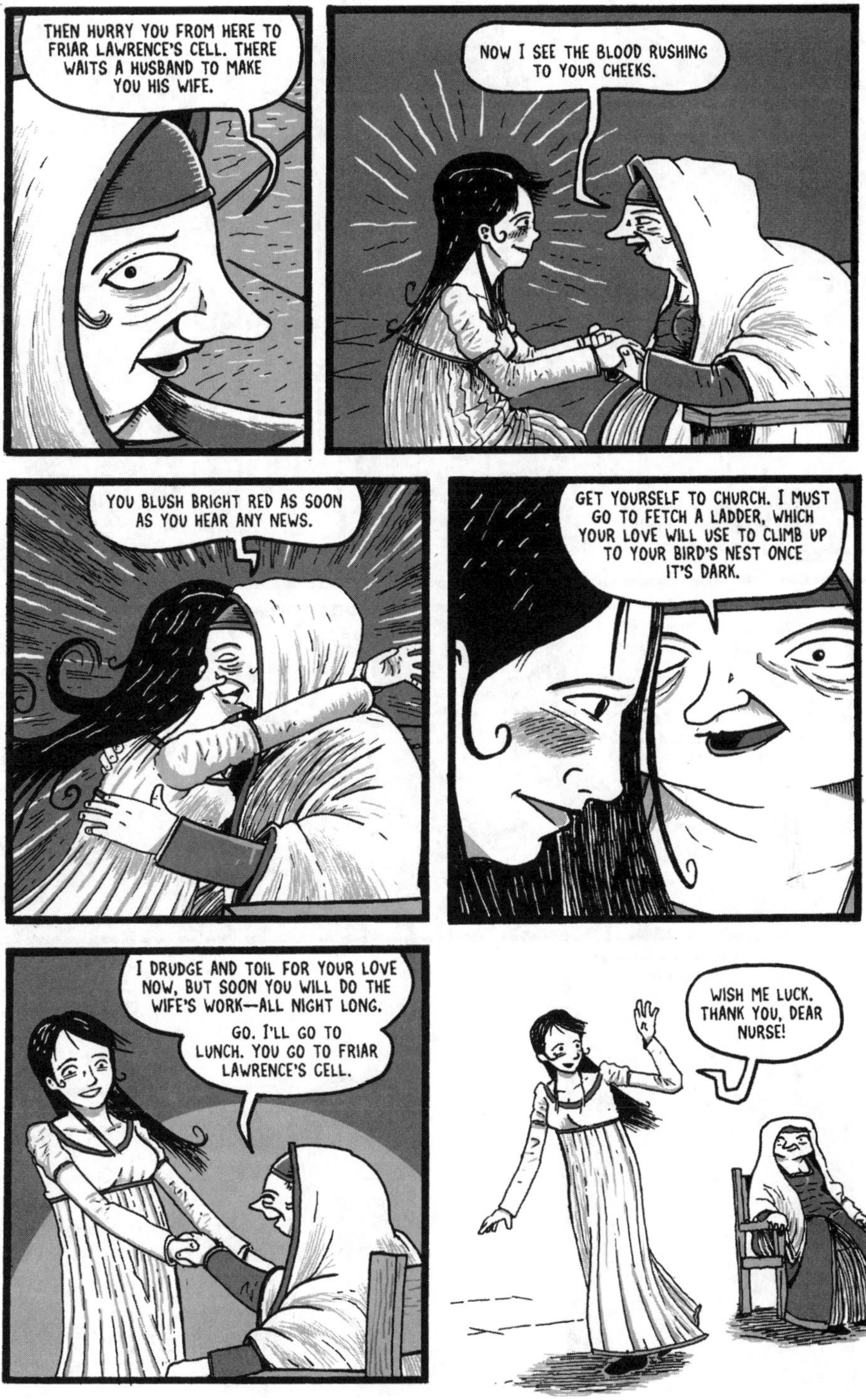
THEN HURRY YOU FROM HERE TO FRIAR LAWRENCE'S CELL. THERE WAITS A HUSBAND TO MAKE YOU HIS WIFE.
NOW I SEE THE BLOOD RUSHING TO YOUR CHEEKS.
YOU BLUSH BRIGHT RED AS SOON AS YOU HEAR ANY NEWS.
GET YOURSELF TO CHURCH. I MUST GO TO FETCH A LADDER, WHICH YOUR LOVE WILL USE TO CLIMB UP TO YOUR BIRD'S NEST ONCE IT'S DARK.
I DRUDGE AND TOIL FOR YOUR LOVE NOW, BUT SOON YOU WILL DO THE WIFE'S WORK—ALL NIGHT LONG.
GO. I'LL GO TO LUNCH. YOU GO TO FRIAR LAWRENCE'S CELL.
WISH ME LUCK. THANK YOU, DEAR NURSE!

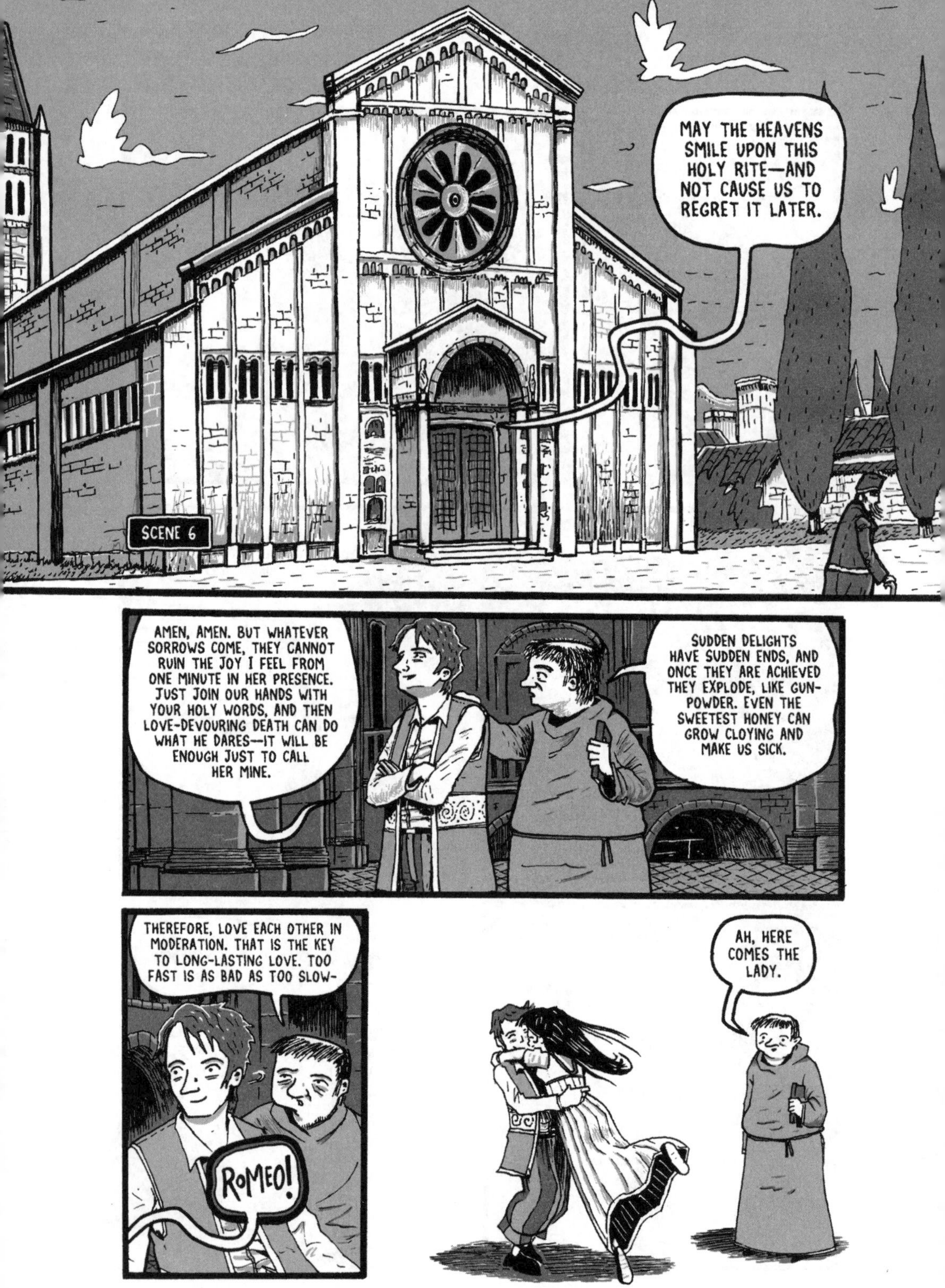
SCENE 6
MAY THE HEAVENS SMILE UPON THIS HOLY RITE—AND NOT CAUSE US TO REGRET IT LATER.
AMEN, AMEN. BUT WHATEVER SORROWS COME, THEY CANNOT RUIN THE JOY I FEEL FROM ONE MINUTE IN HER PRESENCE. JUST JOIN OUR HANDS WITH YOUR HOLY WORDS, AND THEN LOVE-DEVOURING DEATH CAN DO WHAT HE DARES--IT WILL BE ENOUGH JUST TO CALL HER MINE.
SUDDEN DELIGHTS HAVE SUDDEN ENDS, AND ONCE THEY ARE ACHIEVED THEY EXPLODE, LIKE GUN-POWDER. EVEN THE SWEETEST HONEY CAN GROW CLOYING AND MAKE US SICK.
THEREFORE, LOVE EACH OTHER IN MODERATION. THAT IS THE KEY TO LONG-LASTING LOVE. TOO FAST IS AS BAD AS TOO SLOW-
ROMEO!
AH, HERE COMES THE LADY.

OH, A FOOTSTEP AS LIGHT AS HERS WILL NEVER WEAR OUT THE STONY PATH OF LIFE. LOVERS MAY WALK ON SPIDERWEBS IDLING IN THE BREEZE—THAT'S HOW LIGHT AND UNREAL THEIR PLEASURE IS.

GOOD EVENING, MY SPIRITUAL CONFESSOR.

ROMEO WILL THANK YOU, MY GIRL, FOR BOTH OF US.

I'LL GIVE HIM EQUAL THANKS, SO WE'RE EVEN.

AH, JULIET, IF YOUR JOY IS AS GREAT AS MINE, AND YOUR ELOQUENCE GREATER, TELL ME ABOUT THE HAPPINESS YOU IMAGINE WE'LL HAVE.

MY FANTASIES ARE RICHER THAN MY WORDS. ONLY BEGGARS CAN COUNT HOW MUCH THEY HAVE. MY LOVE HAS GROWN TO SUCH EXCESS, I CANNOT COUNT EVEN HALF MY WEALTH.

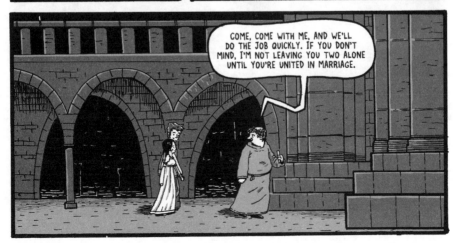

COME, COME WITH ME, AND WE'LL DO THE JOB QUICKLY. IF YOU DON'T MIND, I'M NOT LEAVING YOU TWO ALONE UNTIL YOU'RE UNITED IN MARRIAGE.

Act III

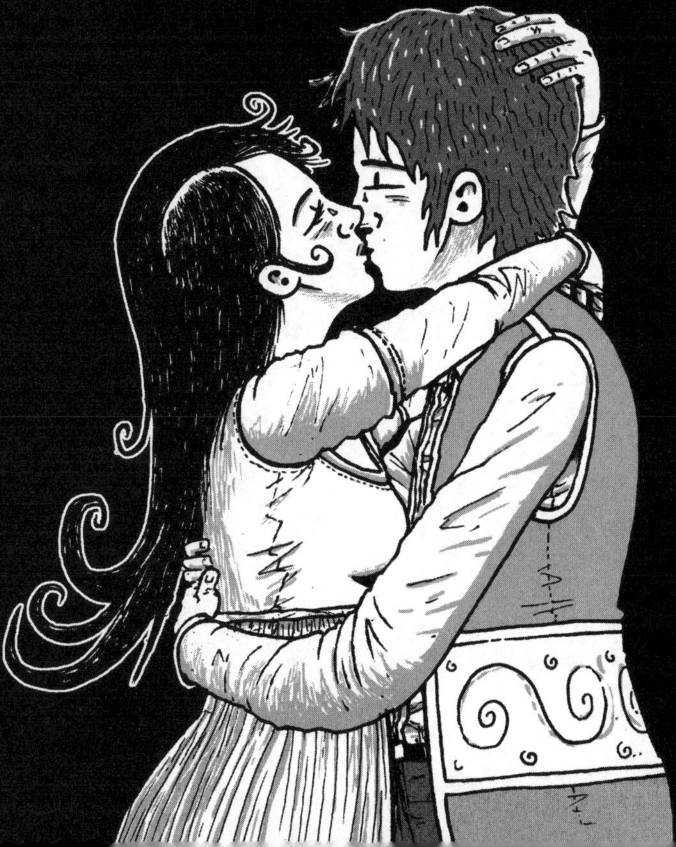

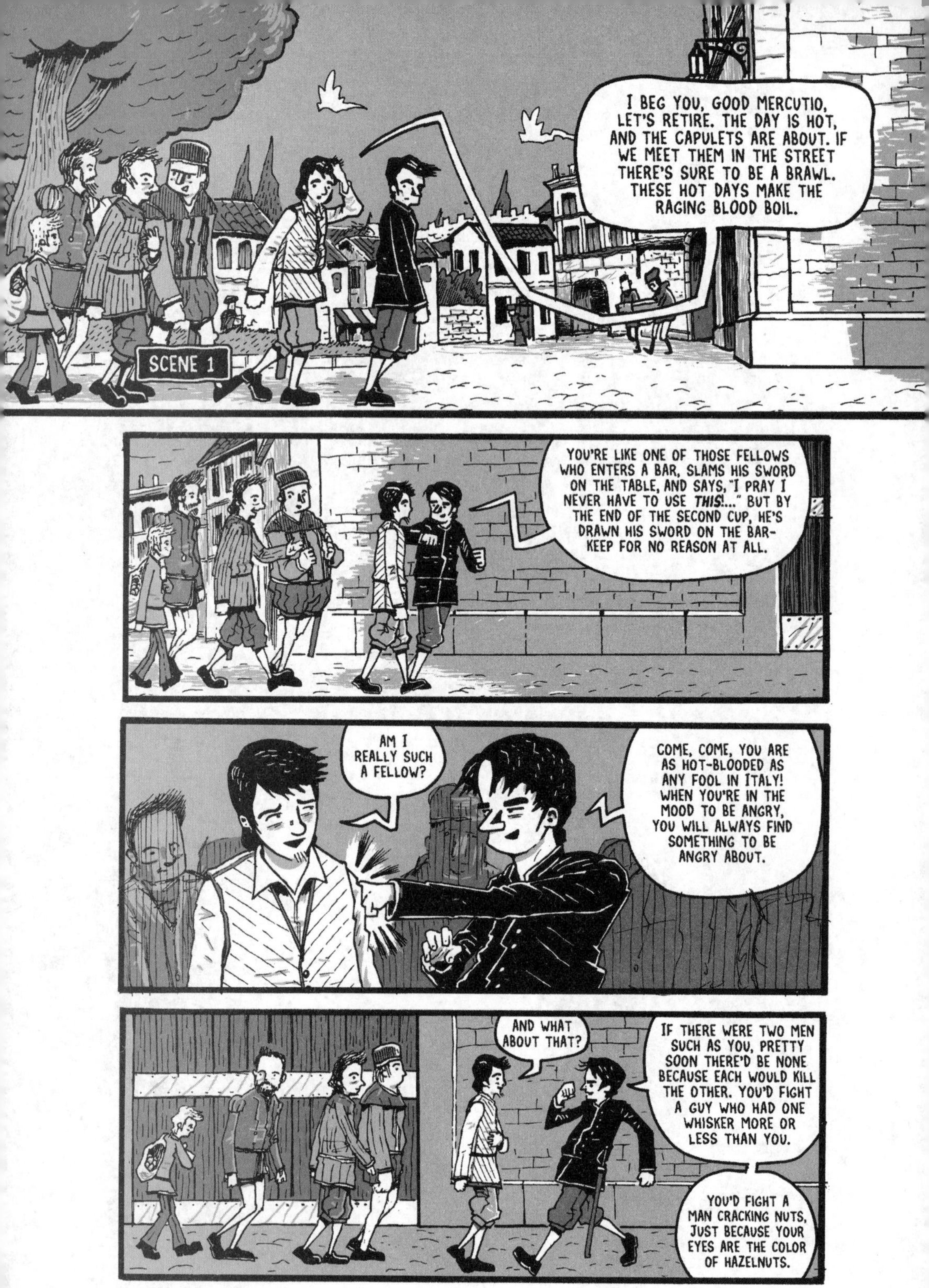
SCENE 1
I BEG YOU, GOOD MERCUTIO, LET'S RETIRE. THE DAY IS HOT, AND THE CAPULETS ARE ABOUT. IF WE MEET THEM IN THE STREET THERE'S SURE TO BE A BRAWL. THESE HOT DAYS MAKE THE RAGING BLOOD BOIL.
YOU'RE LIKE ONE OF THOSE FELLOWS WHO ENTERS A BAR, SLAMS HIS SWORD ON THE TABLE, AND SAYS, "I PRAY I NEVER HAVE TO USE *THIS*!..." BUT BY THE END OF THE SECOND CUP, HE'S DRAWN HIS SWORD ON THE BAR-KEEP FOR NO REASON AT ALL.
AM I REALLY SUCH A FELLOW?
COME, COME, YOU ARE AS HOT-BLOODED AS ANY FOOL IN ITALY! WHEN YOU'RE IN THE MOOD TO BE ANGRY, YOU WILL ALWAYS FIND SOMETHING TO BE ANGRY ABOUT.
AND WHAT ABOUT THAT?
IF THERE WERE TWO MEN SUCH AS YOU, PRETTY SOON THERE'D BE NONE BECAUSE EACH WOULD KILL THE OTHER. YOU'D FIGHT A GUY WHO HAD ONE WHISKER MORE OR LESS THAN YOU.
YOU'D FIGHT A MAN CRACKING NUTS, JUST BECAUSE YOUR EYES ARE THE COLOR OF HAZELNUTS.

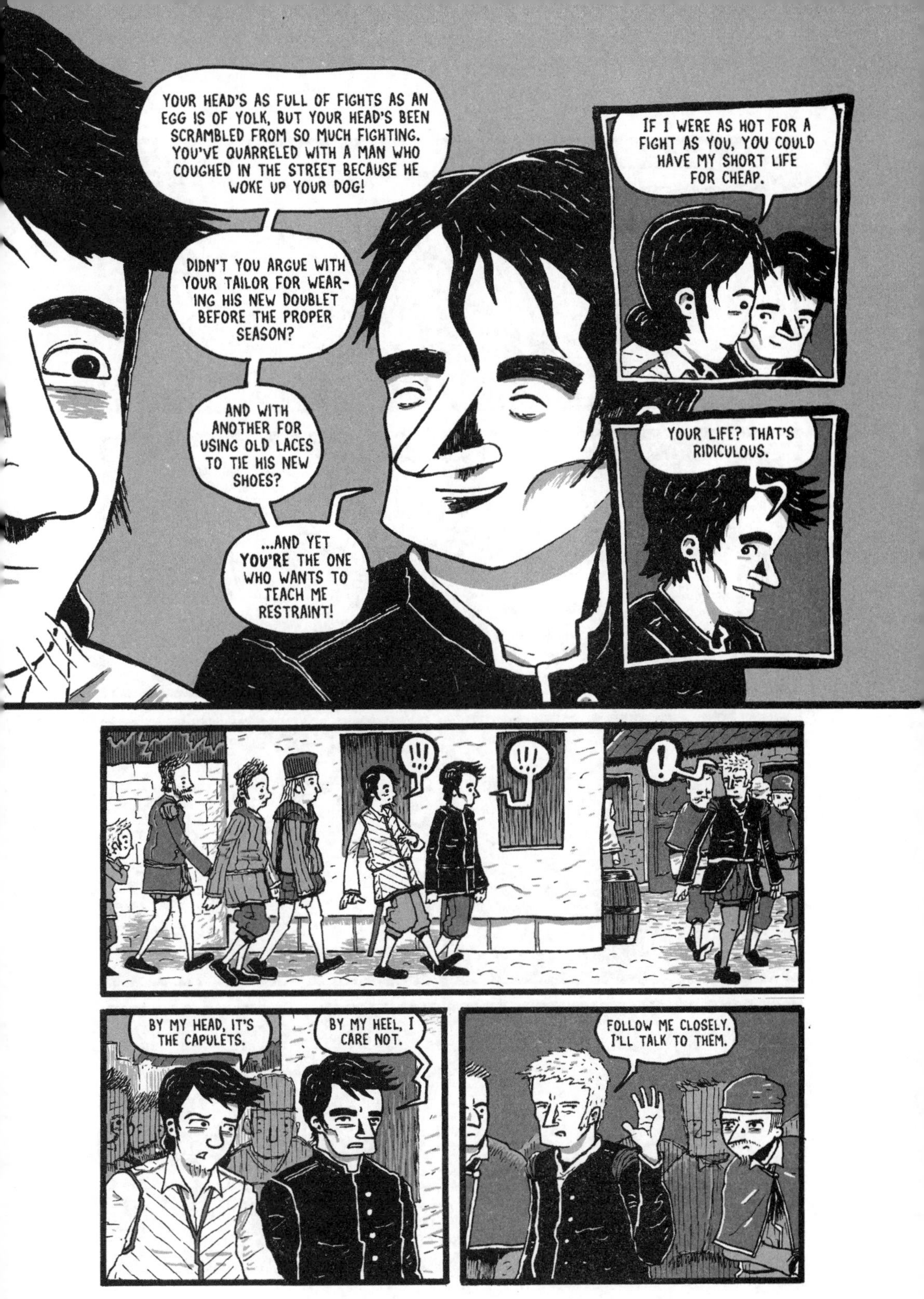
YOUR HEAD'S AS FULL OF FIGHTS AS AN EGG IS OF YOLK, BUT YOUR HEAD'S BEEN SCRAMBLED FROM SO MUCH FIGHTING. YOU'VE QUARRELED WITH A MAN WHO COUGHED IN THE STREET BECAUSE HE WOKE UP YOUR DOG!
DIDN'T YOU ARGUE WITH YOUR TAILOR FOR WEAR-ING HIS NEW DOUBLET BEFORE THE PROPER SEASON?
AND WITH ANOTHER FOR USING OLD LACES TO TIE HIS NEW SHOES?
...AND YET **YOU'RE** THE ONE WHO WANTS TO TEACH ME RESTRAINT!
IF I WERE AS HOT FOR A FIGHT AS YOU, YOU COULD HAVE MY SHORT LIFE FOR CHEAP.
YOUR LIFE? THAT'S RIDICULOUS.
!!!
!!!
!
BY MY HEAD, IT'S THE CAPULETS.
BY MY HEEL, I CARE NOT.
FOLLOW ME CLOSELY. I'LL TALK TO THEM.

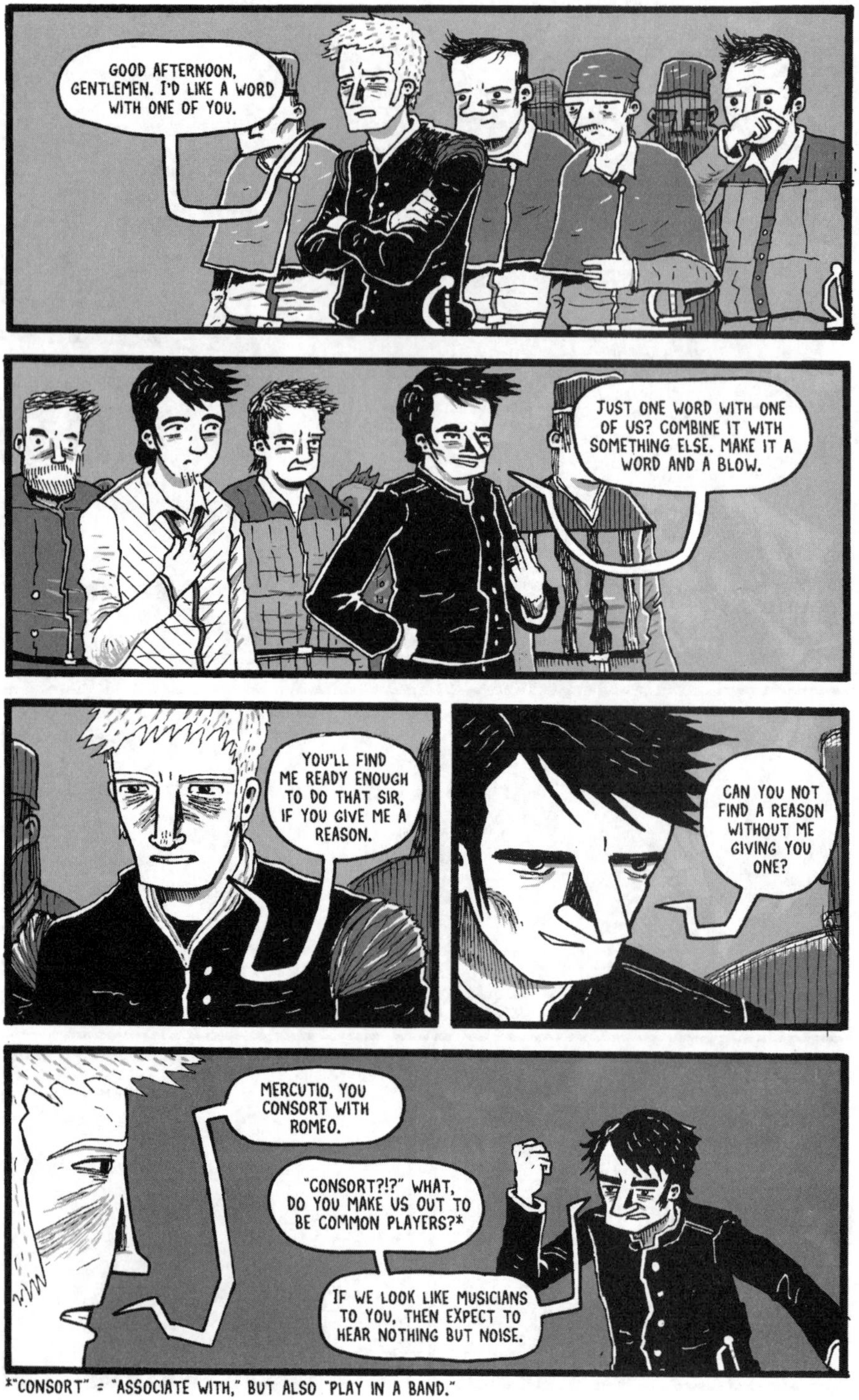
GOOD AFTERNOON, GENTLEMEN. I'D LIKE A WORD WITH ONE OF YOU.
JUST ONE WORD WITH ONE OF US? COMBINE IT WITH SOMETHING ELSE. MAKE IT A WORD AND A BLOW.
YOU'LL FIND ME READY ENOUGH TO DO THAT SIR, IF YOU GIVE ME A REASON.
CAN YOU NOT FIND A REASON WITHOUT ME GIVING YOU ONE?
MERCUTIO, YOU CONSORT WITH ROMEO.
"CONSORT?!?" WHAT, DO YOU MAKE US OUT TO BE COMMON PLAYERS?*
IF WE LOOK LIKE MUSICIANS TO YOU, THEN EXPECT TO HEAR NOTHING BUT NOISE.

*"CONSORT" = "ASSOCIATE WITH," BUT ALSO "PLAY IN A BAND."

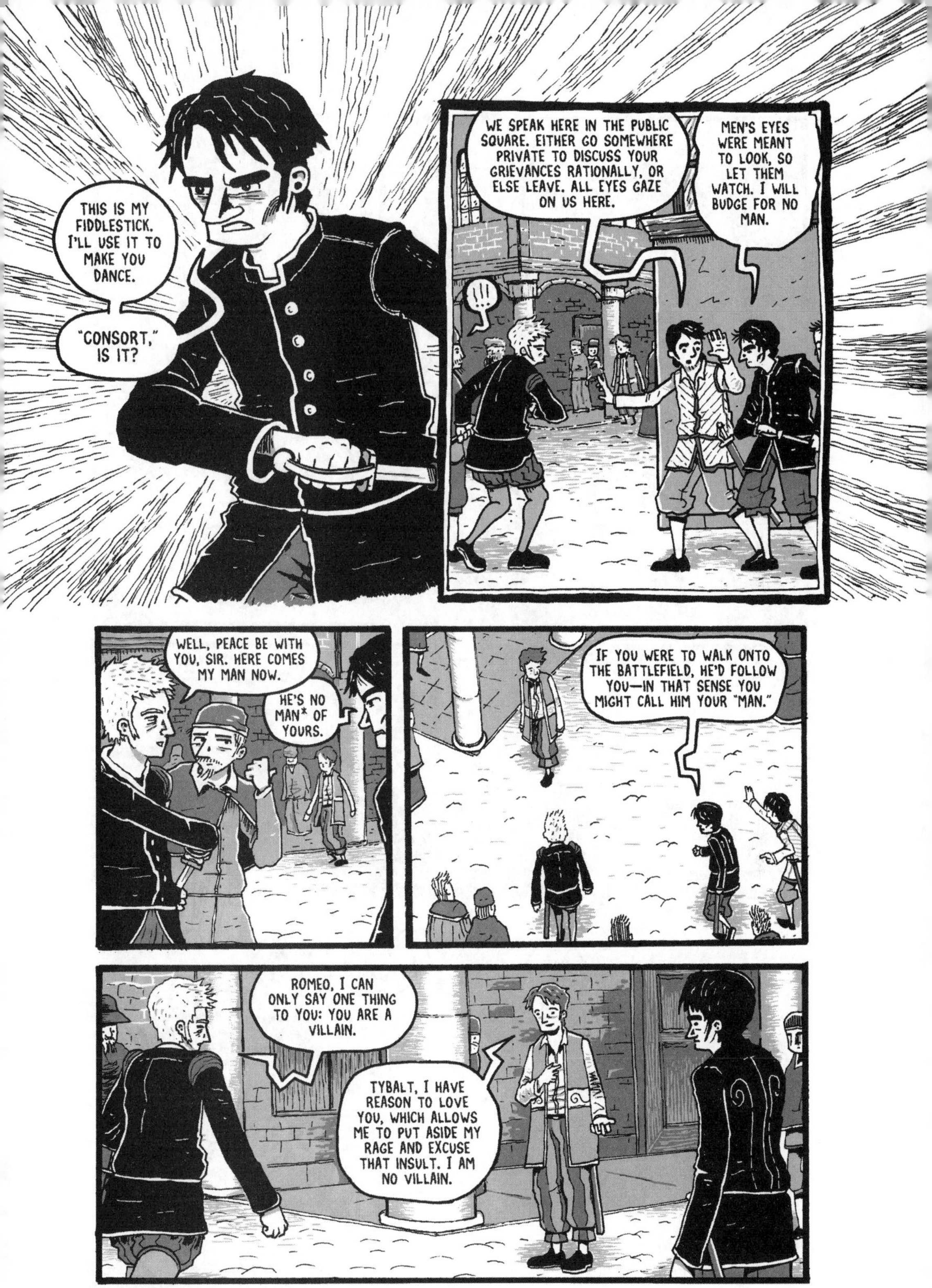
THIS IS MY FIDDLESTICK. I'LL USE IT TO MAKE YOU DANCE.
"CONSORT," IS IT?
WE SPEAK HERE IN THE PUBLIC SQUARE. EITHER GO SOMEWHERE PRIVATE TO DISCUSS YOUR GRIEVANCES RATIONALLY, OR ELSE LEAVE. ALL EYES GAZE ON US HERE.
MEN'S EYES WERE MEANT TO LOOK, SO LET THEM WATCH. I WILL BUDGE FOR NO MAN.
!!!
WELL, PEACE BE WITH YOU, SIR. HERE COMES MY MAN NOW.
HE'S NO MAN* OF YOURS.
IF YOU WERE TO WALK ONTO THE BATTLEFIELD, HE'D FOLLOW YOU—IN THAT SENSE YOU MIGHT CALL HIM YOUR "MAN."
ROMEO, I CAN ONLY SAY ONE THING TO YOU: YOU ARE A VILLAIN.
TYBALT, I HAVE REASON TO LOVE YOU, WHICH ALLOWS ME TO PUT ASIDE MY RAGE AND EXCUSE THAT INSULT. I AM NO VILLAIN.

*MAN = SERVANT

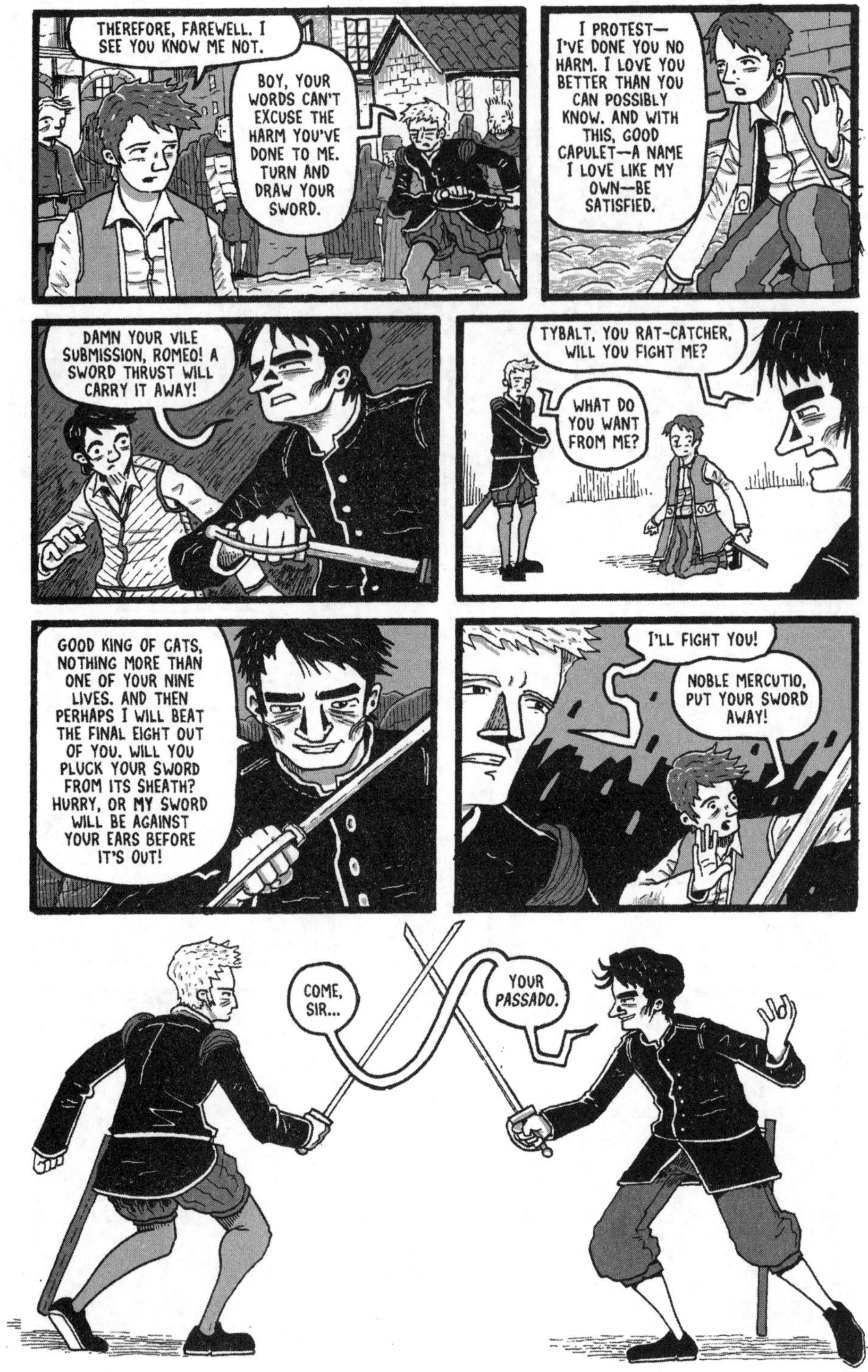
THEREFORE, FAREWELL. I SEE YOU KNOW ME NOT.
BOY, YOUR WORDS CAN'T EXCUSE THE HARM YOU'VE DONE TO ME. TURN AND DRAW YOUR SWORD.
I PROTEST— I'VE DONE YOU NO HARM. I LOVE YOU BETTER THAN YOU CAN POSSIBLY KNOW. AND WITH THIS, GOOD CAPULET—A NAME I LOVE LIKE MY OWN—BE SATISFIED.
DAMN YOUR VILE SUBMISSION, ROMEO! A SWORD THRUST WILL CARRY IT AWAY!
TYBALT, YOU RAT-CATCHER, WILL YOU FIGHT ME?
WHAT DO YOU WANT FROM ME?
GOOD KING OF CATS, NOTHING MORE THAN ONE OF YOUR NINE LIVES. AND THEN PERHAPS I WILL BEAT THE FINAL EIGHT OUT OF YOU. WILL YOU PLUCK YOUR SWORD FROM ITS SHEATH? HURRY, OR MY SWORD WILL BE AGAINST YOUR EARS BEFORE IT'S OUT!
I'LL FIGHT YOU!
NOBLE MERCUTIO, PUT YOUR SWORD AWAY!
COME, SIR...
YOUR PASSADO.

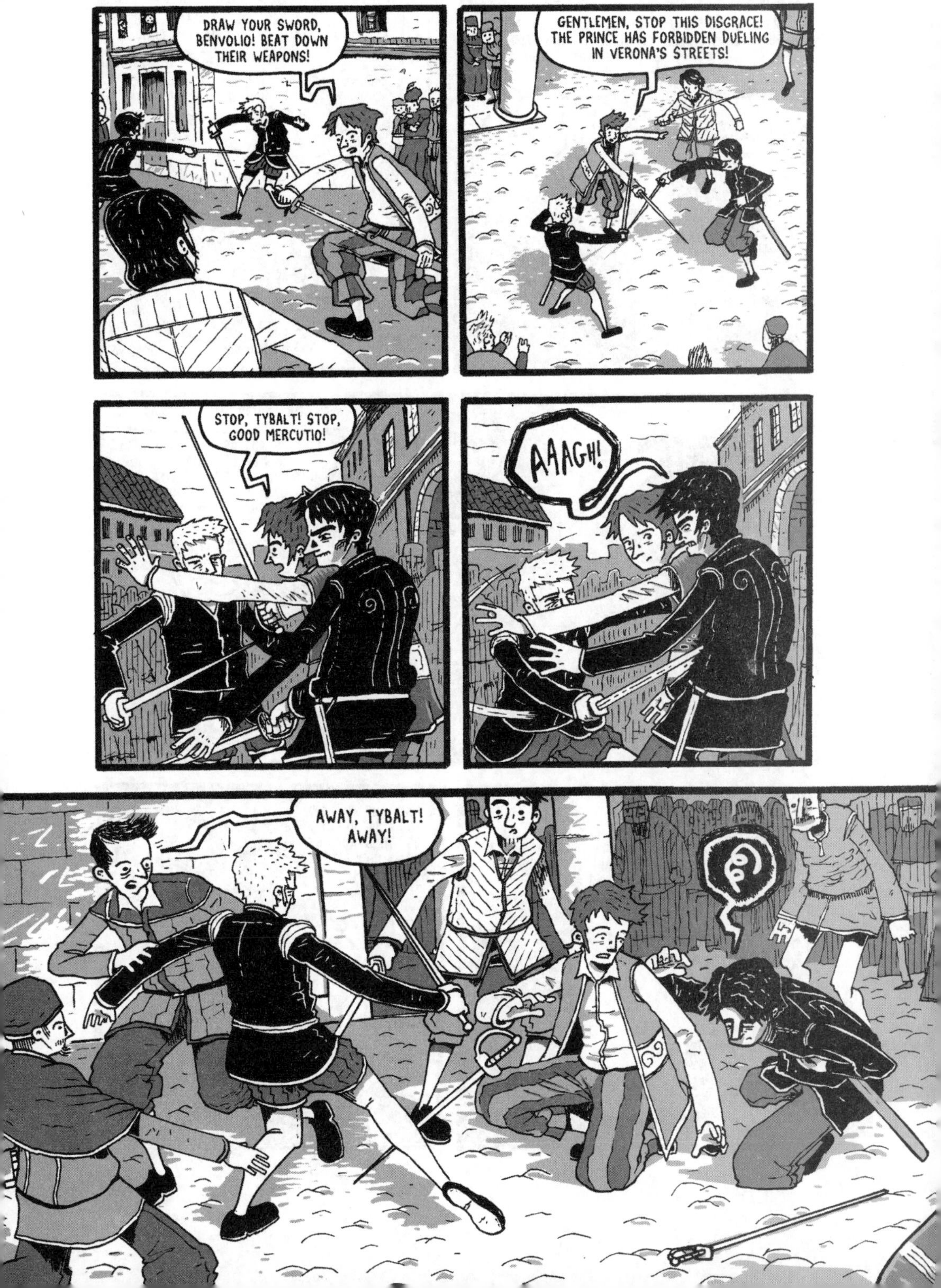
DRAW YOUR SWORD, BENVOLIO! BEAT DOWN THEIR WEAPONS!
GENTLEMEN, STOP THIS DISGRACE! THE PRINCE HAS FORBIDDEN DUELING IN VERONA'S STREETS!
STOP, TYBALT! STOP, GOOD MERCUTIO!
AAAGH!
AWAY, TYBALT! AWAY!

I'M HURT. MAY A PLAGUE CURSE BOTH YOUR FAMILIES! I'M FINISHED. DID HE GET AWAY CLEAN?
WHAT, YOU'RE HURT?
YES, IT'S A SCRATCH, JUST A SCRATCH, BUT IT'S ENOUGH.
WHERE'S MY PAGE? GO, BOY, GET ME A DOCTOR.
COURAGE, MAN, THE WOUND CAN'T BE THAT BAD.
NO, IT'S NOT AS DEEP AS A WELL OR AS WIDE AS A CHURCH DOOR, BUT IT'LL DO THE JOB. ASK FOR ME TOMORROW, AND YOU'LL FIND ME A GRAVE MAN. (HEH.) I'M DONE FOR IN THIS WORLD.
A PLAGUE ON BOTH YOUR HOUSES! GOD, THAT THAT DOG, THAT MOUSE, THAT CAT COULD SCRATCH ME TO DEATH! THAT BRAGGART! THAT VILLAIN WHO DUELS LIKE HE'S DOING ARITHMETIC!
WHY THE HELL DID YOU COME BETWEEN US? HE STRUCK ME FROM UNDER YOUR ARM.
I... THOUGHT IT WAS THE RIGHT THING TO DO...

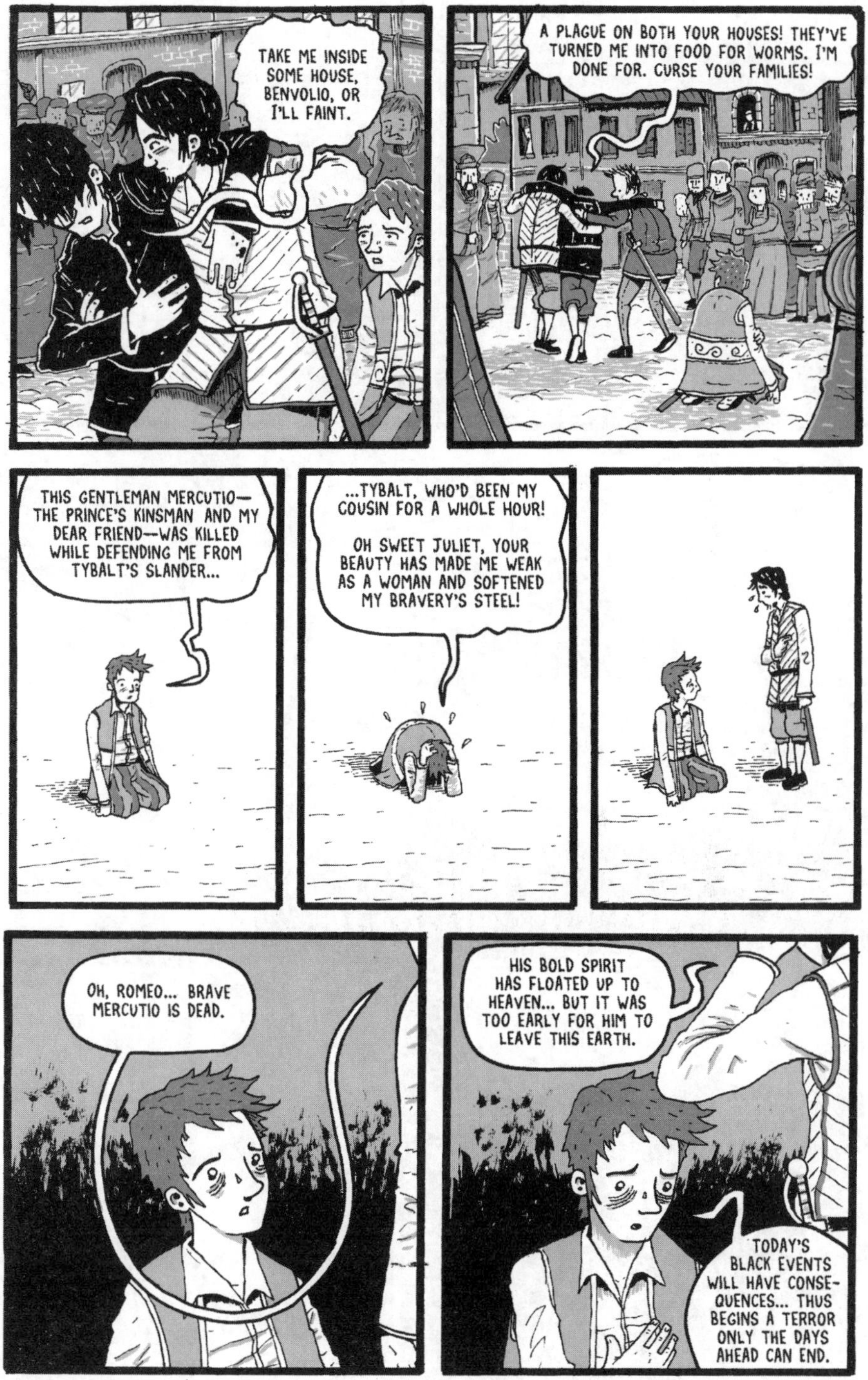
TAKE ME INSIDE SOME HOUSE, BENVOLIO, OR I'LL FAINT.
A PLAGUE ON BOTH YOUR HOUSES! THEY'VE TURNED ME INTO FOOD FOR WORMS. I'M DONE FOR. CURSE YOUR FAMILIES!
THIS GENTLEMAN MERCUTIO—THE PRINCE'S KINSMAN AND MY DEAR FRIEND--WAS KILLED WHILE DEFENDING ME FROM TYBALT'S SLANDER...
...TYBALT, WHO'D BEEN MY COUSIN FOR A WHOLE HOUR!
OH SWEET JULIET, YOUR BEAUTY HAS MADE ME WEAK AS A WOMAN AND SOFTENED MY BRAVERY'S STEEL!
OH, ROMEO... BRAVE MERCUTIO IS DEAD.
HIS BOLD SPIRIT HAS FLOATED UP TO HEAVEN... BUT IT WAS TOO EARLY FOR HIM TO LEAVE THIS EARTH.
TODAY'S BLACK EVENTS WILL HAVE CONSE-QUENCES... THUS BEGINS A TERROR ONLY THE DAYS AHEAD CAN END.

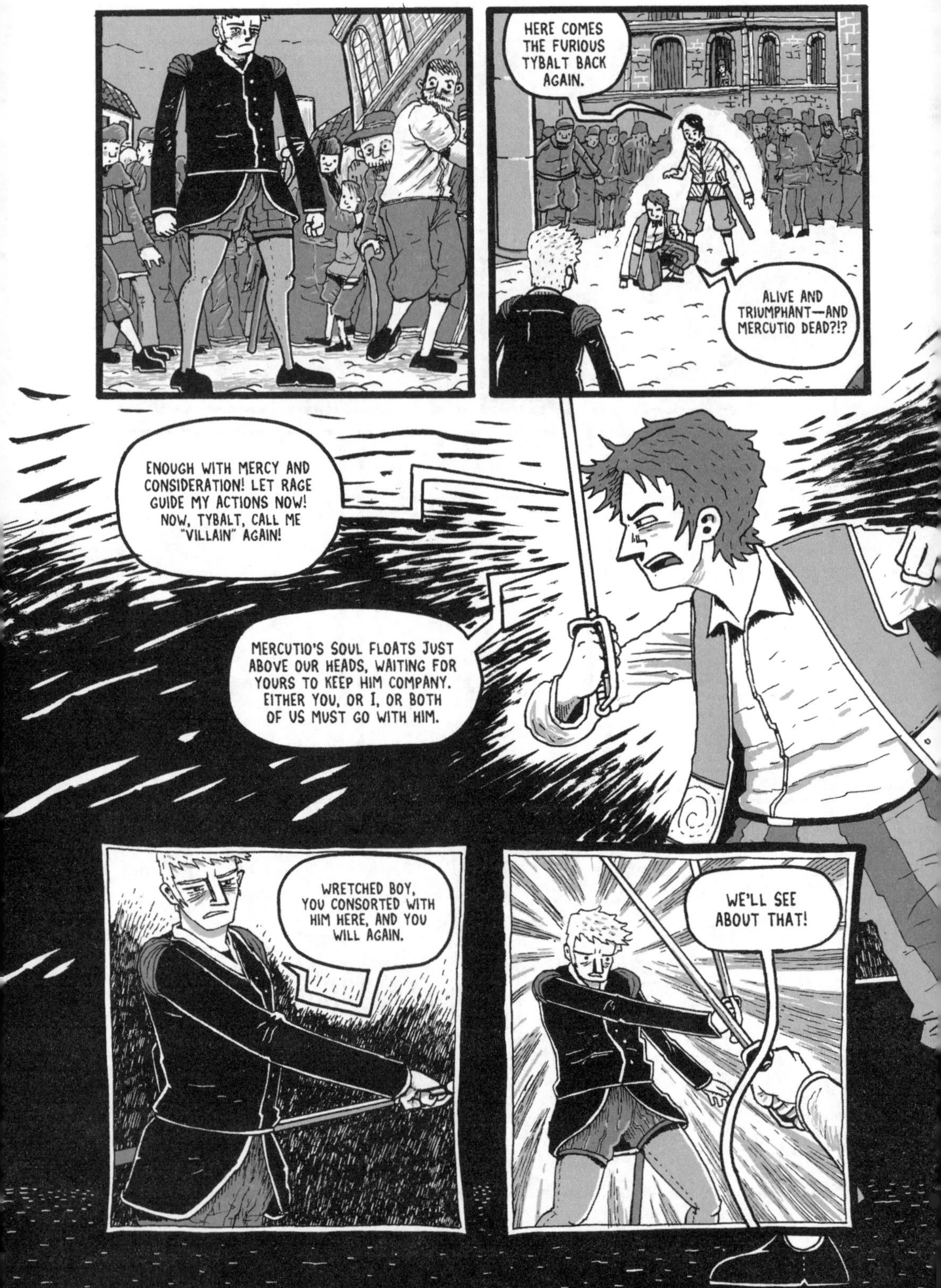
HERE COMES THE FURIOUS TYBALT BACK AGAIN.
ALIVE AND TRIUMPHANT—AND MERCUTIO DEAD?!?
ENOUGH WITH MERCY AND CONSIDERATION! LET RAGE GUIDE MY ACTIONS NOW! NOW, TYBALT, CALL ME "VILLAIN" AGAIN!
MERCUTIO'S SOUL FLOATS JUST ABOVE OUR HEADS, WAITING FOR YOURS TO KEEP HIM COMPANY. EITHER YOU, OR I, OR BOTH OF US MUST GO WITH HIM.
WRETCHED BOY, YOU CONSORTED WITH HIM HERE, AND YOU WILL AGAIN.
WE'LL SEE ABOUT THAT!

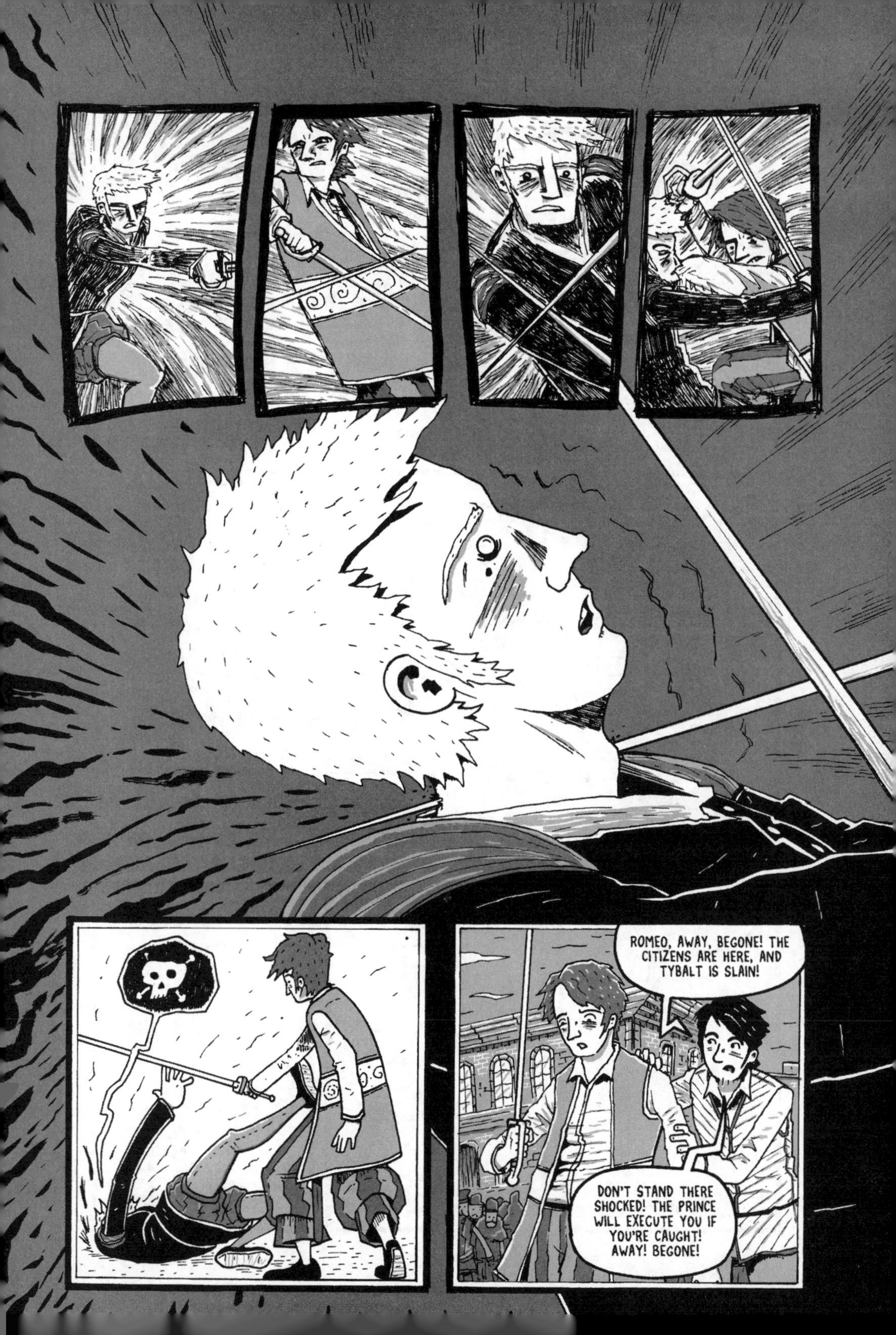
ROMEO, AWAY, BEGONE! THE CITIZENS ARE HERE, AND TYBALT IS SLAIN!
DON'T STAND THERE SHOCKED! THE PRINCE WILL EXECUTE YOU IF YOU'RE CAUGHT! AWAY! BEGONE!

OH, I AM FORTUNE'S FOOL!

WHY ARE YOU WAITING?

THE MAN WHO KILLED MERCUTIO, WHICH WAY DID HE GO?

TYBALT, THAT MURDERER, WHICH WAY DID HE RUN?

TYBALT LIES THERE.

GET UP, SIR, AND COME WITH ME.

I COMMAND YOU, BY AUTHORITY OF THE PRINCE, TO OBEY ME!

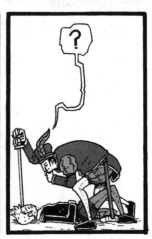

?

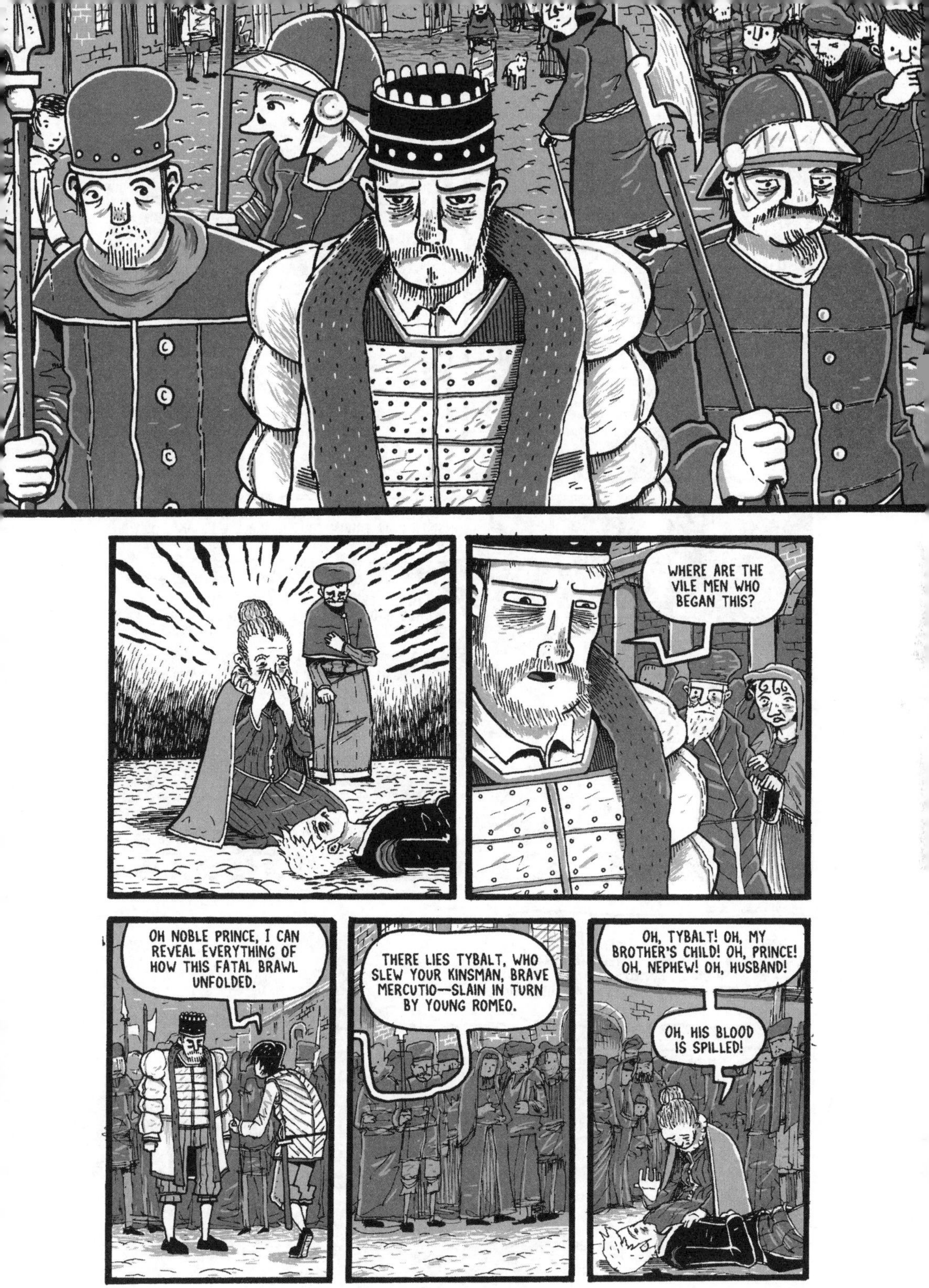
WHERE ARE THE VILE MEN WHO BEGAN THIS?
OH NOBLE PRINCE, I CAN REVEAL EVERYTHING OF HOW THIS FATAL BRAWL UNFOLDED.
THERE LIES TYBALT, WHO SLEW YOUR KINSMAN, BRAVE MERCUTIO--SLAIN IN TURN BY YOUNG ROMEO.
OH, TYBALT! OH, MY BROTHER'S CHILD! OH, PRINCE! OH, NEPHEW! OH, HUSBAND!
OH, HIS BLOOD IS SPILLED!

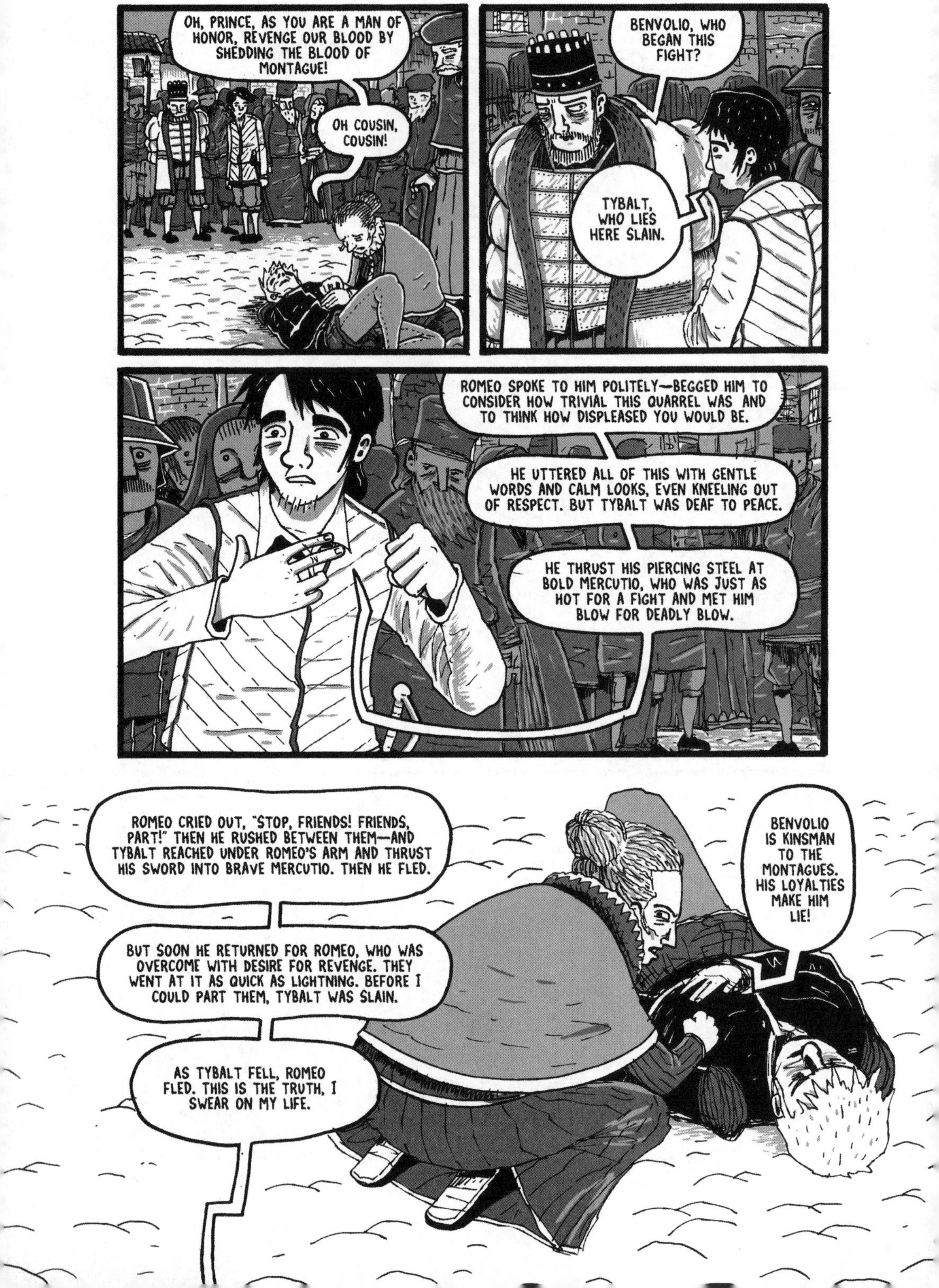
OH, PRINCE, AS YOU ARE A MAN OF HONOR, REVENGE OUR BLOOD BY SHEDDING THE BLOOD OF MONTAGUE!
OH COUSIN, COUSIN!
BENVOLIO, WHO BEGAN THIS FIGHT?
TYBALT, WHO LIES HERE SLAIN.
ROMEO SPOKE TO HIM POLITELY—BEGGED HIM TO CONSIDER HOW TRIVIAL THIS QUARREL WAS AND TO THINK HOW DISPLEASED YOU WOULD BE.
HE UTTERED ALL OF THIS WITH GENTLE WORDS AND CALM LOOKS, EVEN KNEELING OUT OF RESPECT. BUT TYBALT WAS DEAF TO PEACE.
HE THRUST HIS PIERCING STEEL AT BOLD MERCUTIO, WHO WAS JUST AS HOT FOR A FIGHT AND MET HIM BLOW FOR DEADLY BLOW.
ROMEO CRIED OUT, "STOP, FRIENDS! FRIENDS, PART!" THEN HE RUSHED BETWEEN THEM—AND TYBALT REACHED UNDER ROMEO'S ARM AND THRUST HIS SWORD INTO BRAVE MERCUTIO. THEN HE FLED.
BUT SOON HE RETURNED FOR ROMEO, WHO WAS OVERCOME WITH DESIRE FOR REVENGE. THEY WENT AT IT AS QUICK AS LIGHTNING. BEFORE I COULD PART THEM, TYBALT WAS SLAIN.
AS TYBALT FELL, ROMEO FLED. THIS IS THE TRUTH, I SWEAR ON MY LIFE.
BENVOLIO IS KINSMAN TO THE MONTAGUES. HIS LOYALTIES MAKE HIM LIE!

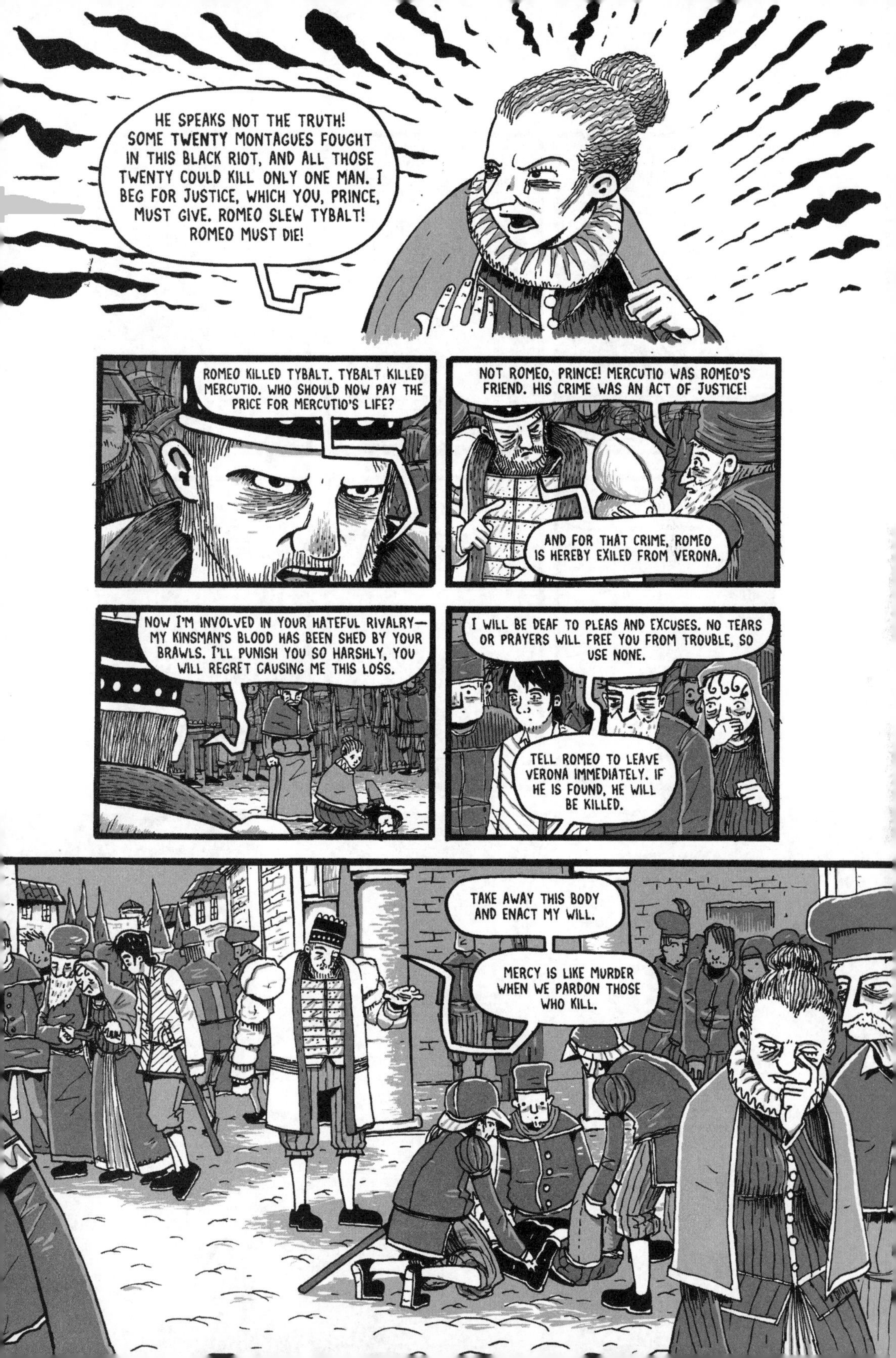
HE SPEAKS NOT THE TRUTH! SOME TWENTY MONTAGUES FOUGHT IN THIS BLACK RIOT, AND ALL THOSE TWENTY COULD KILL ONLY ONE MAN. I BEG FOR JUSTICE, WHICH YOU, PRINCE, MUST GIVE. ROMEO SLEW TYBALT! ROMEO MUST DIE!
ROMEO KILLED TYBALT. TYBALT KILLED MERCUTIO. WHO SHOULD NOW PAY THE PRICE FOR MERCUTIO'S LIFE?
NOT ROMEO, PRINCE! MERCUTIO WAS ROMEO'S FRIEND. HIS CRIME WAS AN ACT OF JUSTICE!
AND FOR THAT CRIME, ROMEO IS HEREBY EXILED FROM VERONA.
NOW I'M INVOLVED IN YOUR HATEFUL RIVALRY— MY KINSMAN'S BLOOD HAS BEEN SHED BY YOUR BRAWLS. I'LL PUNISH YOU SO HARSHLY, YOU WILL REGRET CAUSING ME THIS LOSS.
I WILL BE DEAF TO PLEAS AND EXCUSES. NO TEARS OR PRAYERS WILL FREE YOU FROM TROUBLE, SO USE NONE.
TELL ROMEO TO LEAVE VERONA IMMEDIATELY. IF HE IS FOUND, HE WILL BE KILLED.
TAKE AWAY THIS BODY AND ENACT MY WILL.
MERCY IS LIKE MURDER WHEN WE PARDON THOSE WHO KILL.

GALLOP, YOU FIERY STEEDS, AND PULL DOWN THE SUN'S CHARIOT!

SCENE 2

NIGHT, SPREAD YOUR DARK CURTAIN SO THAT ROMEO MAY COME TO ME AND LEAP INTO MY ARMS, UNSEEN.

IN THE DARKNESS, LOVERS CAN SEE BY THE LIGHT OF THEIR OWN BEAUTY.

OR, IF LOVE IS BLIND, THEN IT BELONGS TO THE DARKNESS.

COME, NIGHT—YOU SOLEMN WIDOW ALL IN BLACK.

CALM THE BLOOD THAT'S RUSHING TO MY CHEEKS AND TEACH THIS SHY, RESTLESS BIRD TO BE TAME. IN THE DARKNESS, SHOW ME HOW TO SURRENDER MY PURITY.

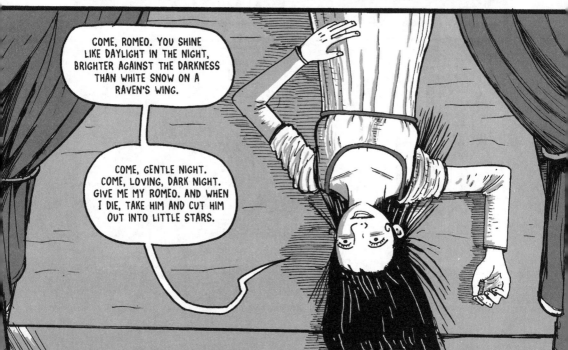

COME, ROMEO. YOU SHINE LIKE DAYLIGHT IN THE NIGHT, BRIGHTER AGAINST THE DARKNESS THAN WHITE SNOW ON A RAVEN'S WING.

COME, GENTLE NIGHT. COME, LOVING, DARK NIGHT. GIVE ME MY ROMEO. AND WHEN I DIE, TAKE HIM AND CUT HIM OUT INTO LITTLE STARS.

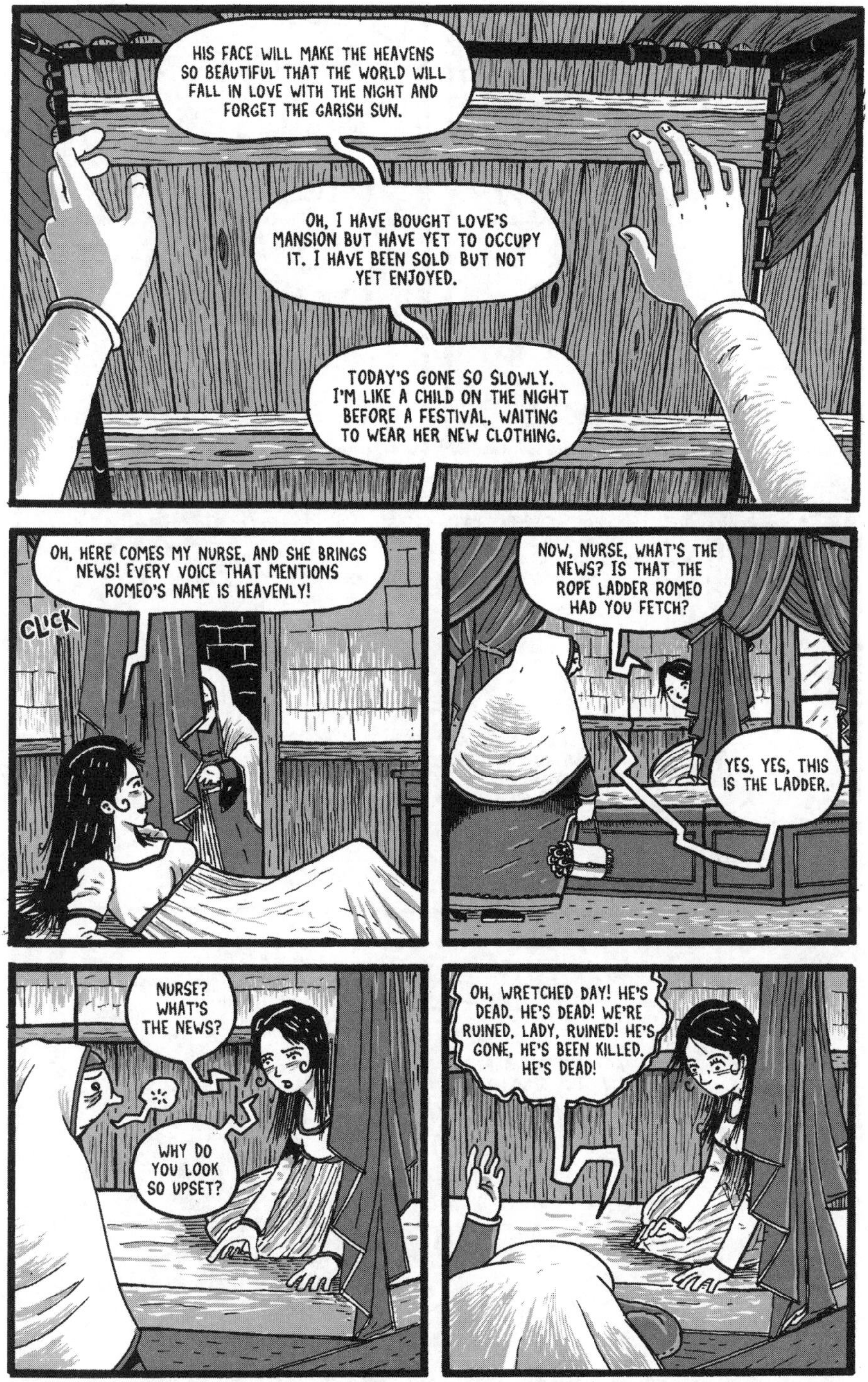
HIS FACE WILL MAKE THE HEAVENS SO BEAUTIFUL THAT THE WORLD WILL FALL IN LOVE WITH THE NIGHT AND FORGET THE GARISH SUN.
OH, I HAVE BOUGHT LOVE'S MANSION BUT HAVE YET TO OCCUPY IT. I HAVE BEEN SOLD BUT NOT YET ENJOYED.
TODAY'S GONE SO SLOWLY. I'M LIKE A CHILD ON THE NIGHT BEFORE A FESTIVAL, WAITING TO WEAR HER NEW CLOTHING.
OH, HERE COMES MY NURSE, AND SHE BRINGS NEWS! EVERY VOICE THAT MENTIONS ROMEO'S NAME IS HEAVENLY!
CLICK
NOW, NURSE, WHAT'S THE NEWS? IS THAT THE ROPE LADDER ROMEO HAD YOU FETCH?
YES, YES, THIS IS THE LADDER.
NURSE? WHAT'S THE NEWS?
WHY DO YOU LOOK SO UPSET?
OH, WRETCHED DAY! HE'S DEAD. HE'S DEAD! WE'RE RUINED, LADY, RUINED! HE'S GONE, HE'S BEEN KILLED. HE'S DEAD!

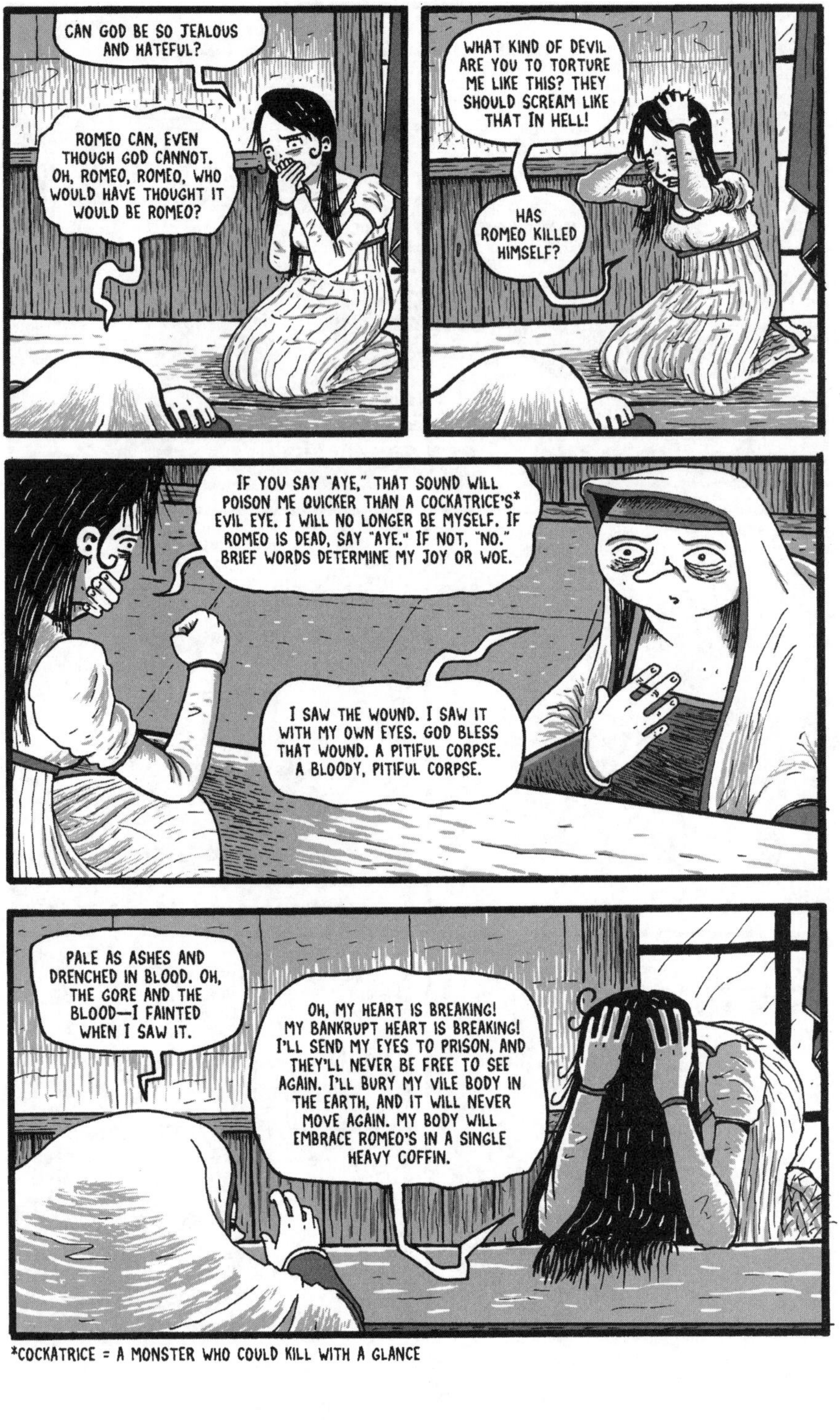
CAN GOD BE SO JEALOUS AND HATEFUL?
ROMEO CAN, EVEN THOUGH GOD CANNOT. OH, ROMEO, ROMEO, WHO WOULD HAVE THOUGHT IT WOULD BE ROMEO?
WHAT KIND OF DEVIL ARE YOU TO TORTURE ME LIKE THIS? THEY SHOULD SCREAM LIKE THAT IN HELL!
HAS ROMEO KILLED HIMSELF?
IF YOU SAY "AYE," THAT SOUND WILL POISON ME QUICKER THAN A COCKATRICE'S* EVIL EYE. I WILL NO LONGER BE MYSELF. IF ROMEO IS DEAD, SAY "AYE." IF NOT, "NO." BRIEF WORDS DETERMINE MY JOY OR WOE.
I SAW THE WOUND. I SAW IT WITH MY OWN EYES. GOD BLESS THAT WOUND. A PITIFUL CORPSE. A BLOODY, PITIFUL CORPSE.
PALE AS ASHES AND DRENCHED IN BLOOD. OH, THE GORE AND THE BLOOD—I FAINTED WHEN I SAW IT.
OH, MY HEART IS BREAKING! MY BANKRUPT HEART IS BREAKING! I'LL SEND MY EYES TO PRISON, AND THEY'LL NEVER BE FREE TO SEE AGAIN. I'LL BURY MY VILE BODY IN THE EARTH, AND IT WILL NEVER MOVE AGAIN. MY BODY WILL EMBRACE ROMEO'S IN A SINGLE HEAVY COFFIN.

*COCKATRICE = A MONSTER WHO COULD KILL WITH A GLANCE

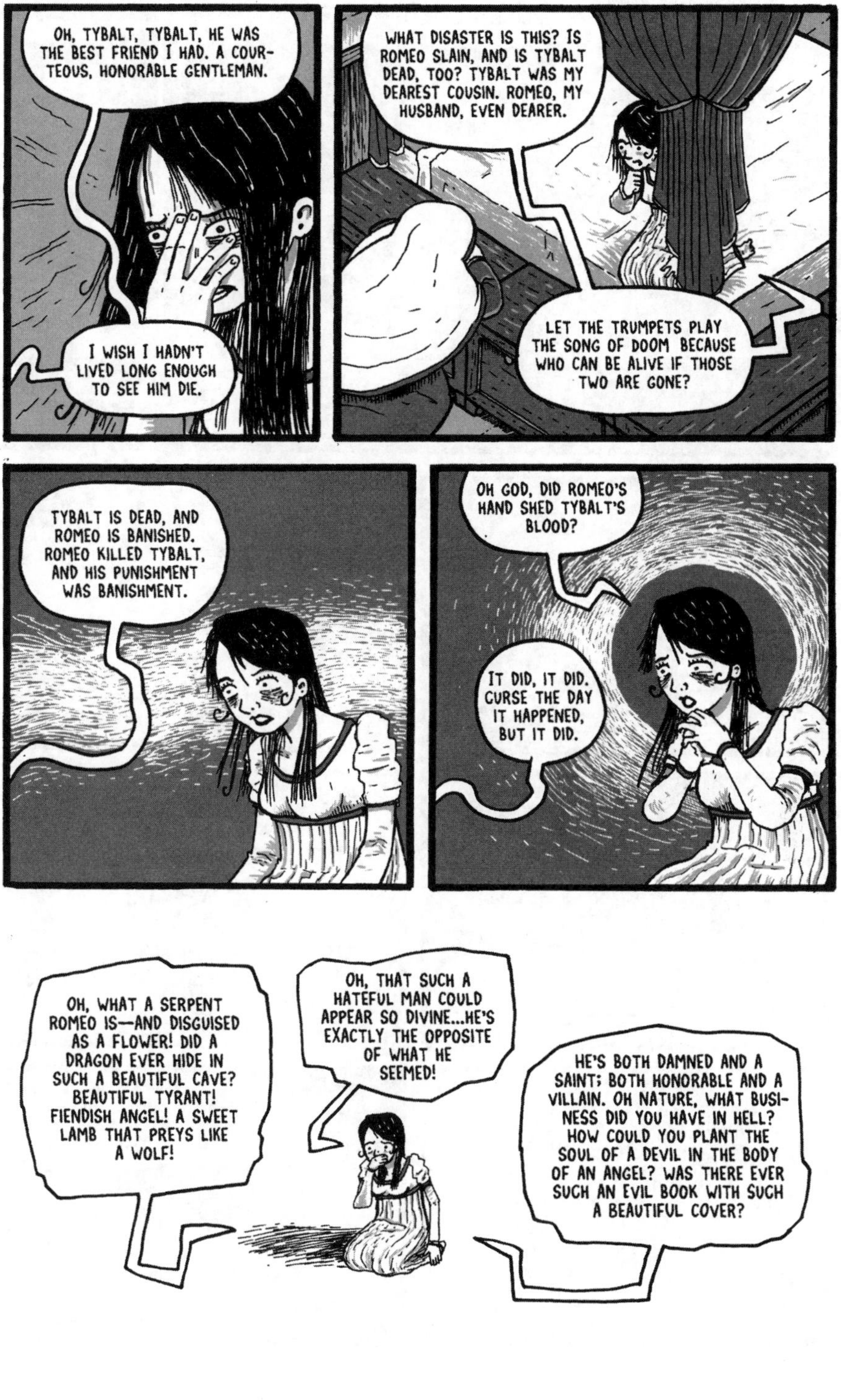
OH, TYBALT, TYBALT, HE WAS THE BEST FRIEND I HAD. A COURTEOUS, HONORABLE GENTLEMAN.
I WISH I HADN'T LIVED LONG ENOUGH TO SEE HIM DIE.
WHAT DISASTER IS THIS? IS ROMEO SLAIN, AND IS TYBALT DEAD, TOO? TYBALT WAS MY DEAREST COUSIN. ROMEO, MY HUSBAND, EVEN DEARER.
LET THE TRUMPETS PLAY THE SONG OF DOOM BECAUSE WHO CAN BE ALIVE IF THOSE TWO ARE GONE?
TYBALT IS DEAD, AND ROMEO IS BANISHED. ROMEO KILLED TYBALT, AND HIS PUNISHMENT WAS BANISHMENT.
OH GOD, DID ROMEO'S HAND SHED TYBALT'S BLOOD?
IT DID, IT DID. CURSE THE DAY IT HAPPENED, BUT IT DID.
OH, WHAT A SERPENT ROMEO IS—AND DISGUISED AS A FLOWER! DID A DRAGON EVER HIDE IN SUCH A BEAUTIFUL CAVE? BEAUTIFUL TYRANT! FIENDISH ANGEL! A SWEET LAMB THAT PREYS LIKE A WOLF!
OH, THAT SUCH A HATEFUL MAN COULD APPEAR SO DIVINE...HE'S EXACTLY THE OPPOSITE OF WHAT HE SEEMED!
HE'S BOTH DAMNED AND A SAINT; BOTH HONORABLE AND A VILLAIN. OH NATURE, WHAT BUSINESS DID YOU HAVE IN HELL? HOW COULD YOU PLANT THE SOUL OF A DEVIL IN THE BODY OF AN ANGEL? WAS THERE EVER SUCH AN EVIL BOOK WITH SUCH A BEAUTIFUL COVER?

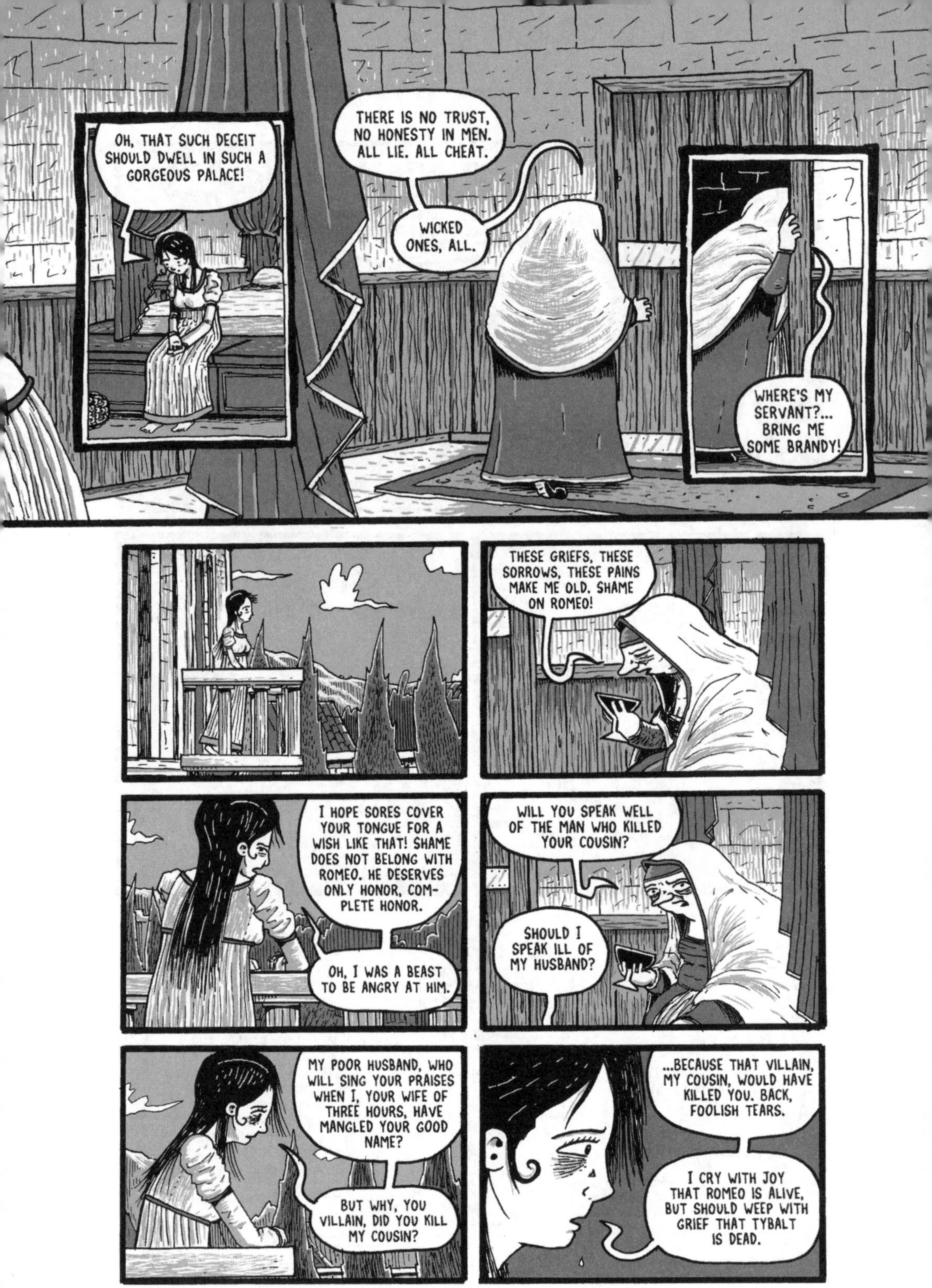

OH, THAT SUCH DECEIT SHOULD DWELL IN SUCH A GORGEOUS PALACE!
THERE IS NO TRUST, NO HONESTY IN MEN. ALL LIE. ALL CHEAT.
WICKED ONES, ALL.
WHERE'S MY SERVANT?... BRING ME SOME BRANDY!
THESE GRIEFS, THESE SORROWS, THESE PAINS MAKE ME OLD. SHAME ON ROMEO!
I HOPE SORES COVER YOUR TONGUE FOR A WISH LIKE THAT! SHAME DOES NOT BELONG WITH ROMEO. HE DESERVES ONLY HONOR, COMPLETE HONOR.
OH, I WAS A BEAST TO BE ANGRY AT HIM.
WILL YOU SPEAK WELL OF THE MAN WHO KILLED YOUR COUSIN?
SHOULD I SPEAK ILL OF MY HUSBAND?
MY POOR HUSBAND, WHO WILL SING YOUR PRAISES WHEN I, YOUR WIFE OF THREE HOURS, HAVE MANGLED YOUR GOOD NAME?
BUT WHY, YOU VILLAIN, DID YOU KILL MY COUSIN?
...BECAUSE THAT VILLAIN, MY COUSIN, WOULD HAVE KILLED YOU. BACK, FOOLISH TEARS.
I CRY WITH JOY THAT ROMEO IS ALIVE, BUT SHOULD WEEP WITH GRIEF THAT TYBALT IS DEAD.

MY HUSBAND, WHOM TYBALT WISHED TO KILL, IS ALIVE. TYBALT, WHO WISHED TO KILL MY HUSBAND, IS DEAD. ALL THIS IS COMFORTING NEWS. WHY, THEN, SHOULD I CRY?
BUT THERE WAS A WORD, WORSE THAN THE NEWS OF TYBALT'S DEATH... A WORD THAT MADE ME WANT TO DIE. I WOULD GLADLY FORGET IT, BUT IT WEIGHS ON MY MEMORY LIKE GUILT ON THE MIND OF A SINNER.
"TYBALT IS DEAD, AND ROMEO IS BANISHED." THAT "BANISHED" IS WORSE THAN THE MURDER OF TEN THOUSAND TYBALTS. TYBALT'S DEATH WOULD BE BAD ENOUGH, IF THAT WAS ALL.
OR PERHAPS MISERY LOVES COMPANY AND INSISTS THAT PAIN BE FOLLOWED BY MORE PAIN. IF ONLY THE NURSE HAD FOLLOWED "TYBALT'S DEAD" BY TELLING ME THAT MY MOTHER, OR FATHER, OR BOTH, WERE GONE—I COULD HAVE TOLERATED IT.
...BUT TO FOLLOW THAT WITH THE WORDS "ROMEO IS BANISHED" IS LIKE SAYING THAT MY FATHER, MY MOTHER, TYBALT, ROMEO, AND JULIET ARE ALL SLAIN, ALL DEAD.
"ROMEO IS BANISHED." THAT IS AN ENDLESS DEATH. NO WORDS CAN EXPRESS THAT PAIN.

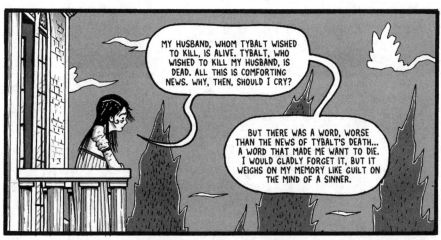

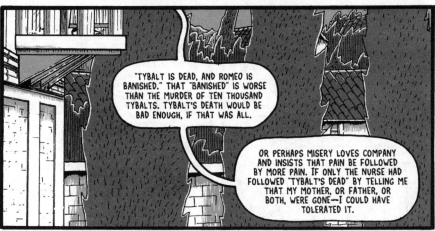

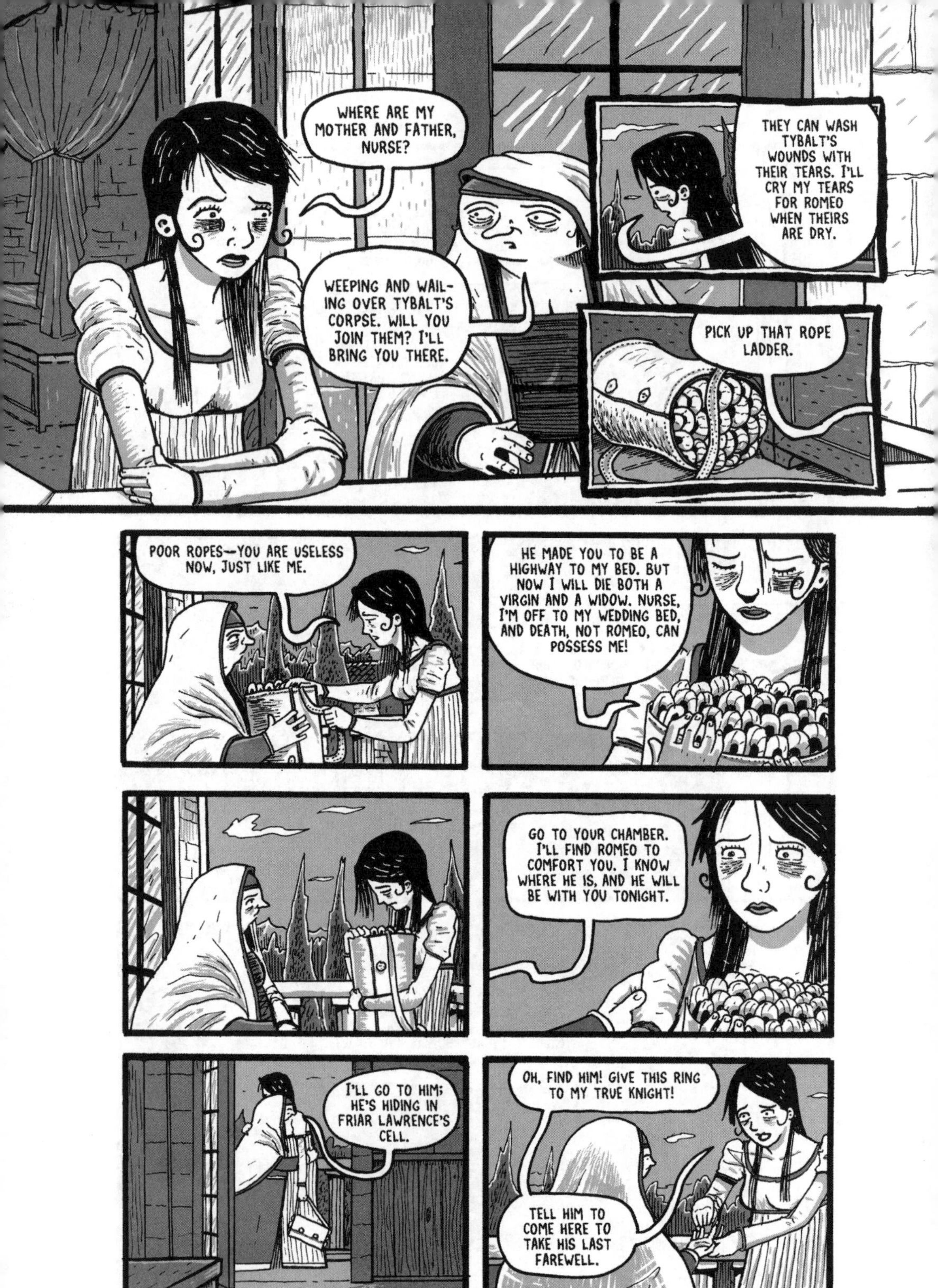
WHERE ARE MY MOTHER AND FATHER, NURSE?
WEEPING AND WAILING OVER TYBALT'S CORPSE. WILL YOU JOIN THEM? I'LL BRING YOU THERE.
THEY CAN WASH TYBALT'S WOUNDS WITH THEIR TEARS. I'LL CRY MY TEARS FOR ROMEO WHEN THEIRS ARE DRY.
PICK UP THAT ROPE LADDER.
POOR ROPES—YOU ARE USELESS NOW, JUST LIKE ME.
HE MADE YOU TO BE A HIGHWAY TO MY BED. BUT NOW I WILL DIE BOTH A VIRGIN AND A WIDOW. NURSE, I'M OFF TO MY WEDDING BED, AND DEATH, NOT ROMEO, CAN POSSESS ME!
GO TO YOUR CHAMBER. I'LL FIND ROMEO TO COMFORT YOU. I KNOW WHERE HE IS, AND HE WILL BE WITH YOU TONIGHT.
I'LL GO TO HIM; HE'S HIDING IN FRIAR LAWRENCE'S CELL.
OH, FIND HIM! GIVE THIS RING TO MY TRUE KNIGHT!
TELL HIM TO COME HERE TO TAKE HIS LAST FAREWELL.

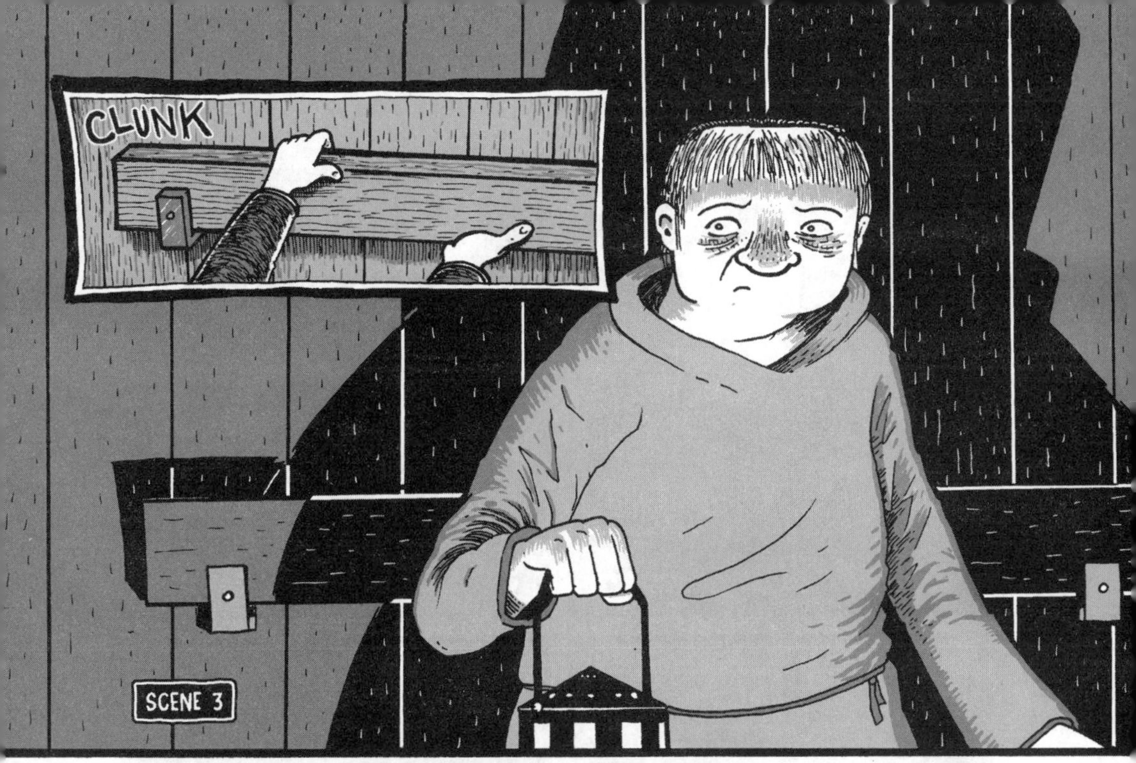
CLUNK
SCENE 3

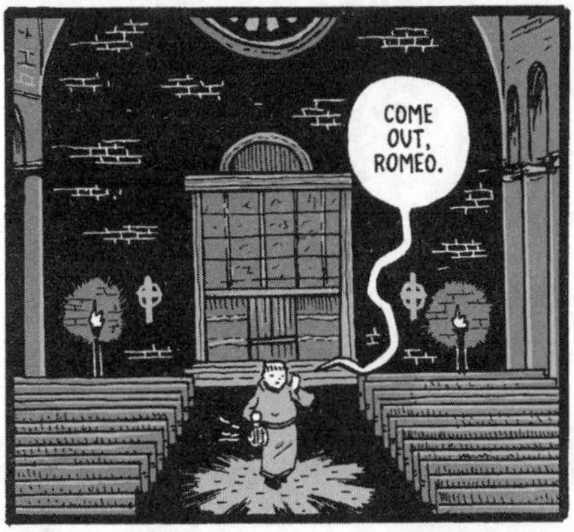
COME OUT, ROMEO.

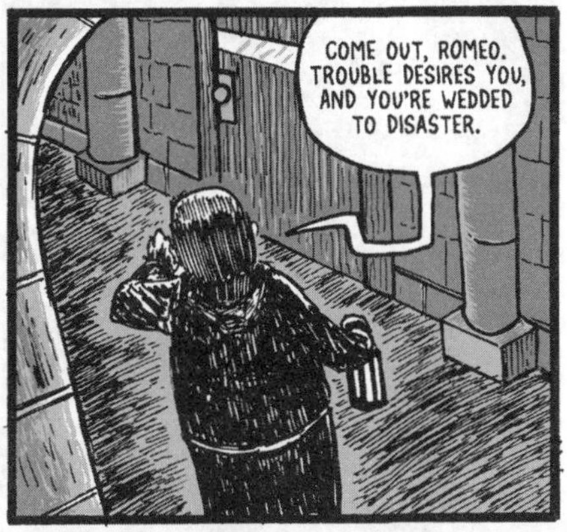
COME OUT, ROMEO. TROUBLE DESIRES YOU, AND YOU'RE WEDDED TO DISASTER.

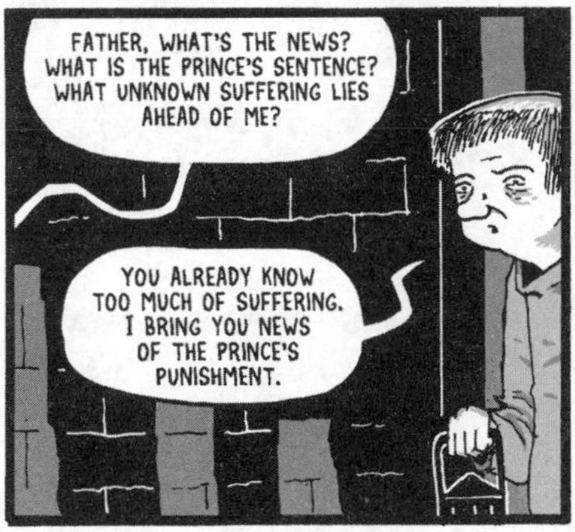
FATHER, WHAT'S THE NEWS? WHAT IS THE PRINCE'S SENTENCE? WHAT UNKNOWN SUFFERING LIES AHEAD OF ME?
YOU ALREADY KNOW TOO MUCH OF SUFFERING. I BRING YOU NEWS OF THE PRINCE'S PUNISHMENT.

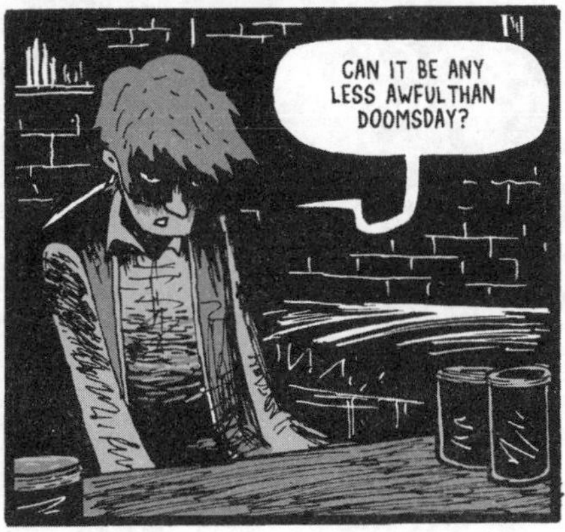
CAN IT BE ANY LESS AWFULTHAN DOOMSDAY?

HE MADE A GENTLER DECISION. YOU WON'T DIE, BUT YOU'LL BE BANISHED.

BANISHMENT?

BE MERCIFUL AND SAY "DEATH." EXILE IS MUCH WORSE THAN DEATH. DON'T SAY "BANISHMENT."

FROM NOW ON, YOU ARE BANISHED FROM VERONA.

BE PATIENT AND ENDURE, FOR THE WORLD IS BROAD AND WIDE.

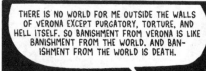

THERE IS NO WORLD FOR ME OUTSIDE THE WALLS OF VERONA EXCEPT PURGATORY, TORTURE, AND HELL ITSELF. SO BANISHMENT FROM VERONA IS LIKE BANISHMENT FROM THE WORLD. AND BANISHMENT FROM THE WORLD IS DEATH.

BANISHMENT IS DEATH BY THE WRONG NAME. CALLING DEATH BANISHMENT IS LIKE CUTTING OFF MY HEAD WITH A GOLDEN AX AND SMILING AS I'M MURDERED.

OH RUDE AND UNTHANKFUL BOY! THE LAW CALLS FOR YOUR DEATH, BUT THE KIND PRINCE HAS TAKEN SYMPATHY ON YOU AND TURNS THAT DEATH TO BANISHMENT. THIS IS KIND MERCY, AND YOU DON'T REALIZE IT.

IT'S TORTURE, NOT MERCY.

HEAVEN IS HERE, WHERE JULIET LIVES! EVERY CAT AND DOG AND LITTLE MOUSE, EVERY UNWORTHY BEAST LIVES HERE AND MAY SEE HER, BUT ROMEO CANNOT!

RANCID FLIES LIVE IN MORE HEALTH, HONOR, AND LOVE THAN ROMEO.

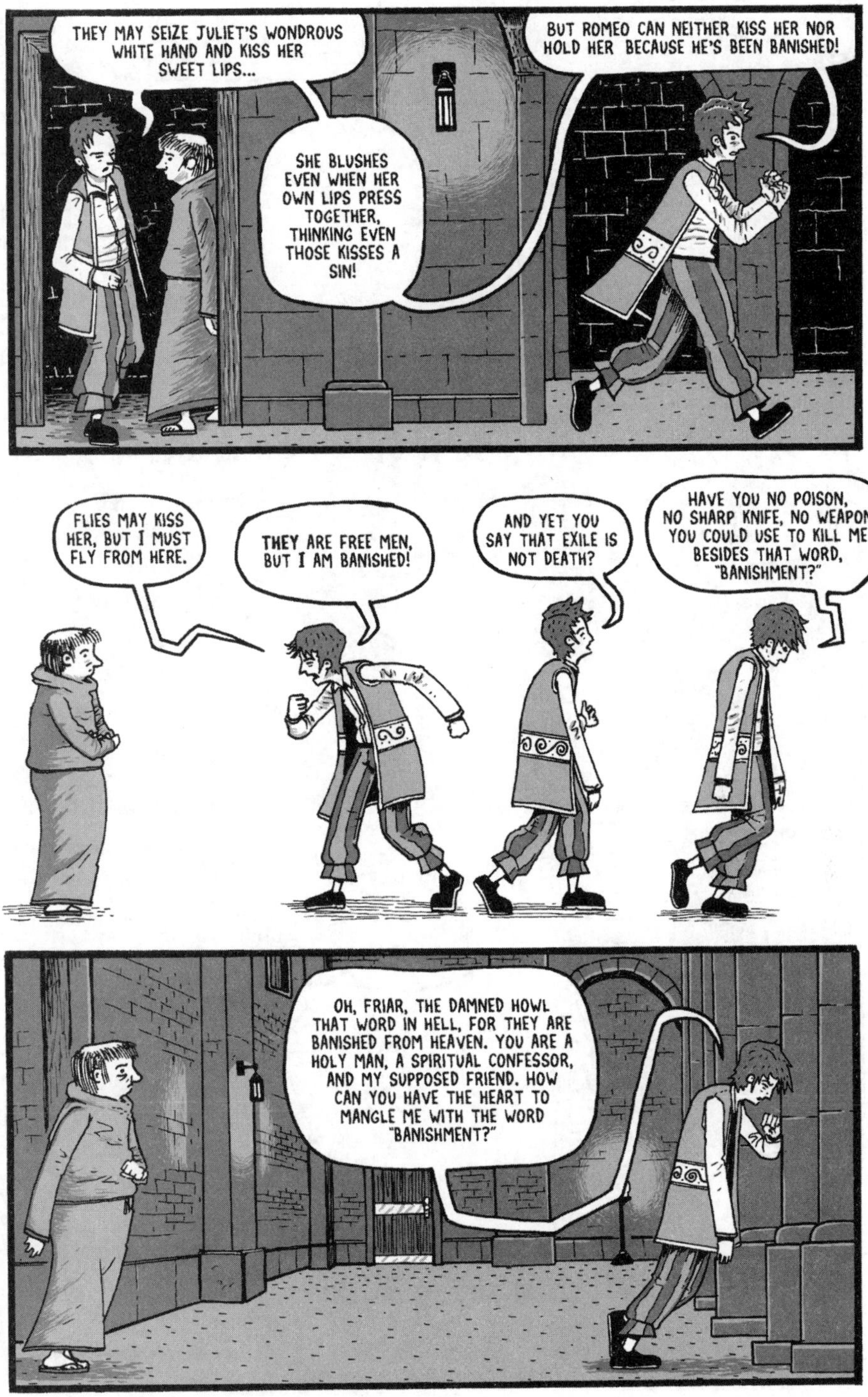
THEY MAY SEIZE JULIET'S WONDROUS WHITE HAND AND KISS HER SWEET LIPS...
SHE BLUSHES EVEN WHEN HER OWN LIPS PRESS TOGETHER, THINKING EVEN THOSE KISSES A SIN!
BUT ROMEO CAN NEITHER KISS HER NOR HOLD HER BECAUSE HE'S BEEN BANISHED!
FLIES MAY KISS HER, BUT I MUST FLY FROM HERE.
THEY ARE FREE MEN, BUT I AM BANISHED!
AND YET YOU SAY THAT EXILE IS NOT DEATH?
HAVE YOU NO POISON, NO SHARP KNIFE, NO WEAPON YOU COULD USE TO KILL ME BESIDES THAT WORD, "BANISHMENT?"
OH, FRIAR, THE DAMNED HOWL THAT WORD IN HELL, FOR THEY ARE BANISHED FROM HEAVEN. YOU ARE A HOLY MAN, A SPIRITUAL CONFESSOR, AND MY SUPPOSED FRIEND. HOW CAN YOU HAVE THE HEART TO MANGLE ME WITH THE WORD "BANISHMENT?"

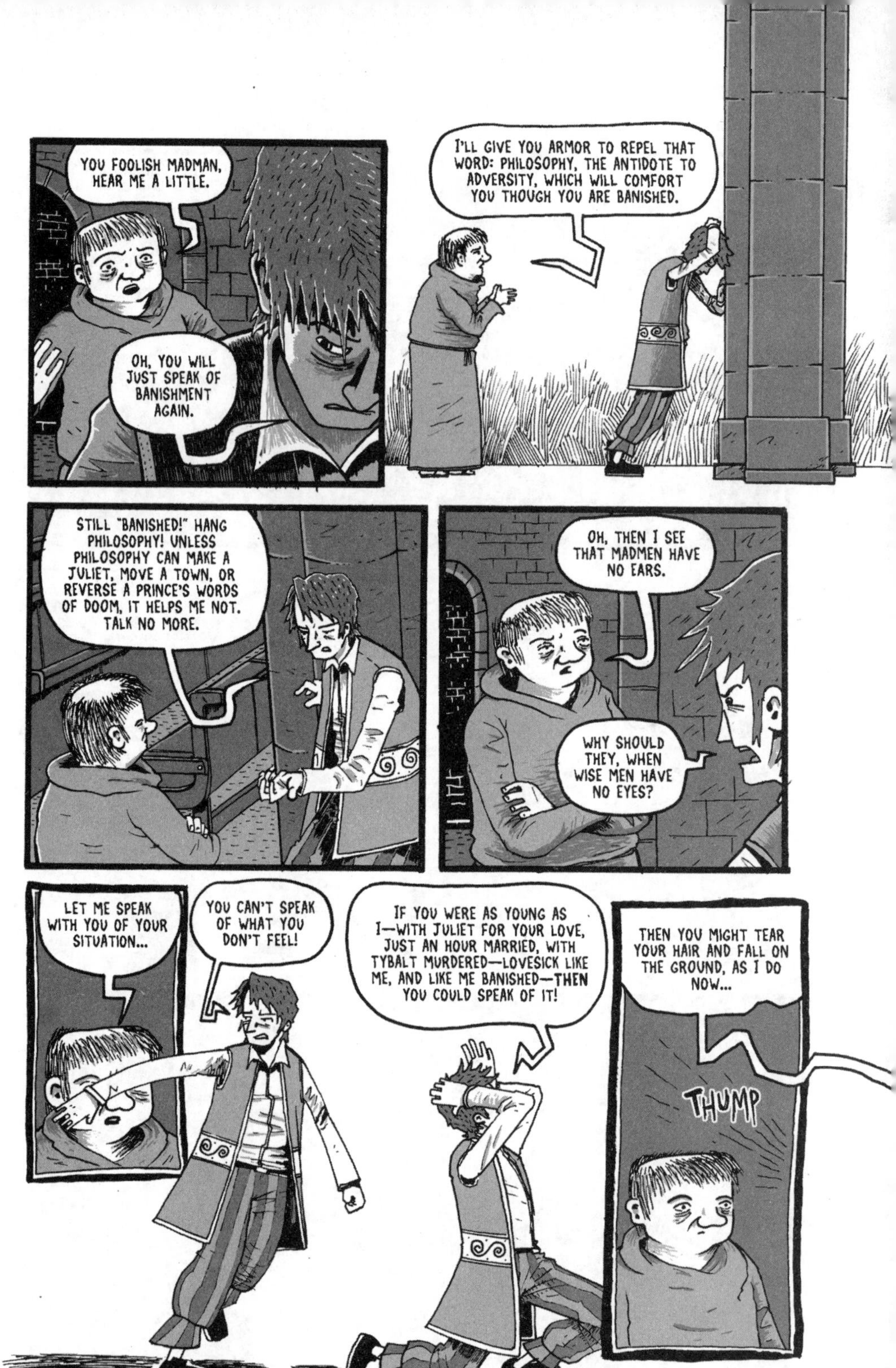
YOU FOOLISH MADMAN, HEAR ME A LITTLE.
OH, YOU WILL JUST SPEAK OF BANISHMENT AGAIN.
I'LL GIVE YOU ARMOR TO REPEL THAT WORD: PHILOSOPHY, THE ANTIDOTE TO ADVERSITY, WHICH WILL COMFORT YOU THOUGH YOU ARE BANISHED.
STILL "BANISHED!" HANG PHILOSOPHY! UNLESS PHILOSOPHY CAN MAKE A JULIET, MOVE A TOWN, OR REVERSE A PRINCE'S WORDS OF DOOM, IT HELPS ME NOT. TALK NO MORE.
OH, THEN I SEE THAT MADMEN HAVE NO EARS.
WHY SHOULD THEY, WHEN WISE MEN HAVE NO EYES?
LET ME SPEAK WITH YOU OF YOUR SITUATION...
YOU CAN'T SPEAK OF WHAT YOU DON'T FEEL!
IF YOU WERE AS YOUNG AS I—WITH JULIET FOR YOUR LOVE, JUST AN HOUR MARRIED, WITH TYBALT MURDERED—LOVESICK LIKE ME, AND LIKE ME BANISHED—THEN YOU COULD SPEAK OF IT!
THEN YOU MIGHT TEAR YOUR HAIR AND FALL ON THE GROUND, AS I DO NOW...
THUMP

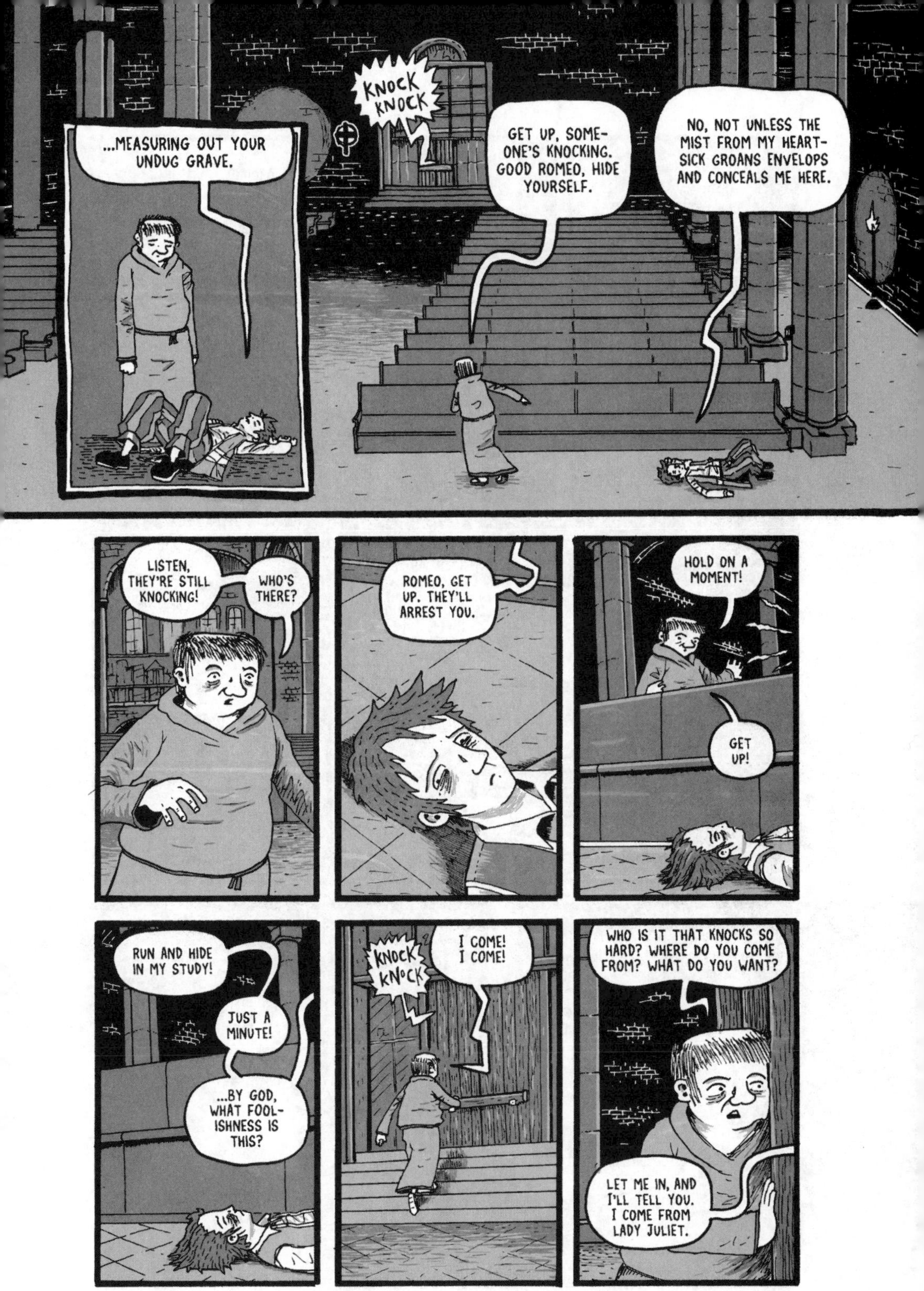
...MEASURING OUT YOUR UNDUG GRAVE.
KNOCK KNOCK
GET UP, SOME-ONE'S KNOCKING. GOOD ROMEO, HIDE YOURSELF.
NO, NOT UNLESS THE MIST FROM MY HEART-SICK GROANS ENVELOPS AND CONCEALS ME HERE.
LISTEN, THEY'RE STILL KNOCKING!
WHO'S THERE?
ROMEO, GET UP. THEY'LL ARREST YOU.
HOLD ON A MOMENT!
GET UP!
RUN AND HIDE IN MY STUDY!
JUST A MINUTE!
...BY GOD, WHAT FOOL-ISHNESS IS THIS?
KNOCK KNOCK
I COME! I COME!
WHO IS IT THAT KNOCKS SO HARD? WHERE DO YOU COME FROM? WHAT DO YOU WANT?
LET ME IN, AND I'LL TELL YOU. I COME FROM LADY JULIET.

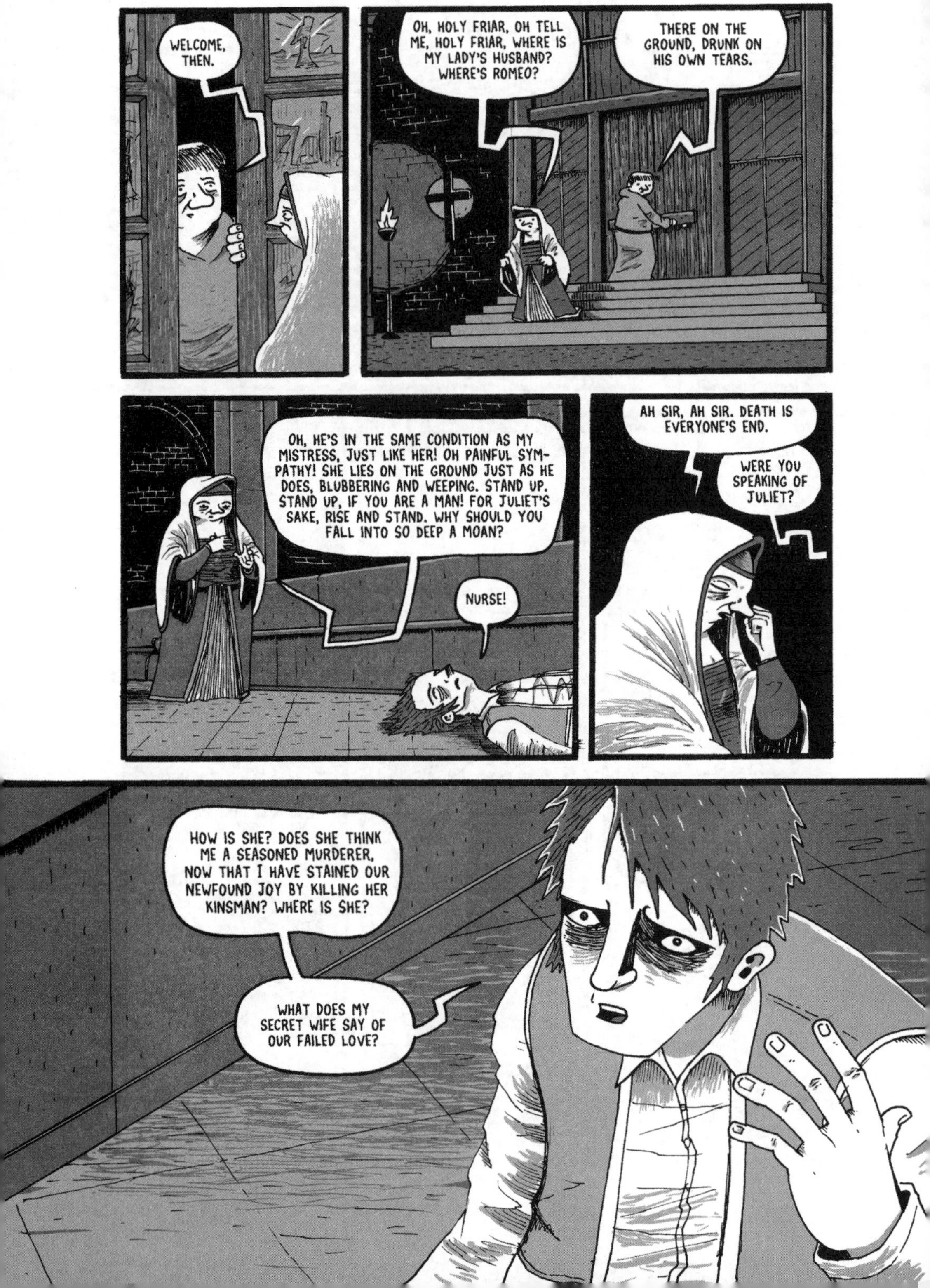
WELCOME, THEN.
OH, HOLY FRIAR, OH TELL ME, HOLY FRIAR, WHERE IS MY LADY'S HUSBAND? WHERE'S ROMEO?
THERE ON THE GROUND, DRUNK ON HIS OWN TEARS.
OH, HE'S IN THE SAME CONDITION AS MY MISTRESS, JUST LIKE HER! OH PAINFUL SYMPATHY! SHE LIES ON THE GROUND JUST AS HE DOES, BLUBBERING AND WEEPING. STAND UP. STAND UP, IF YOU ARE A MAN! FOR JULIET'S SAKE, RISE AND STAND. WHY SHOULD YOU FALL INTO SO DEEP A MOAN?
NURSE!
AH SIR, AH SIR. DEATH IS EVERYONE'S END.
WERE YOU SPEAKING OF JULIET?
HOW IS SHE? DOES SHE THINK ME A SEASONED MURDERER, NOW THAT I HAVE STAINED OUR NEWFOUND JOY BY KILLING HER KINSMAN? WHERE IS SHE?
WHAT DOES MY SECRET WIFE SAY OF OUR FAILED LOVE?

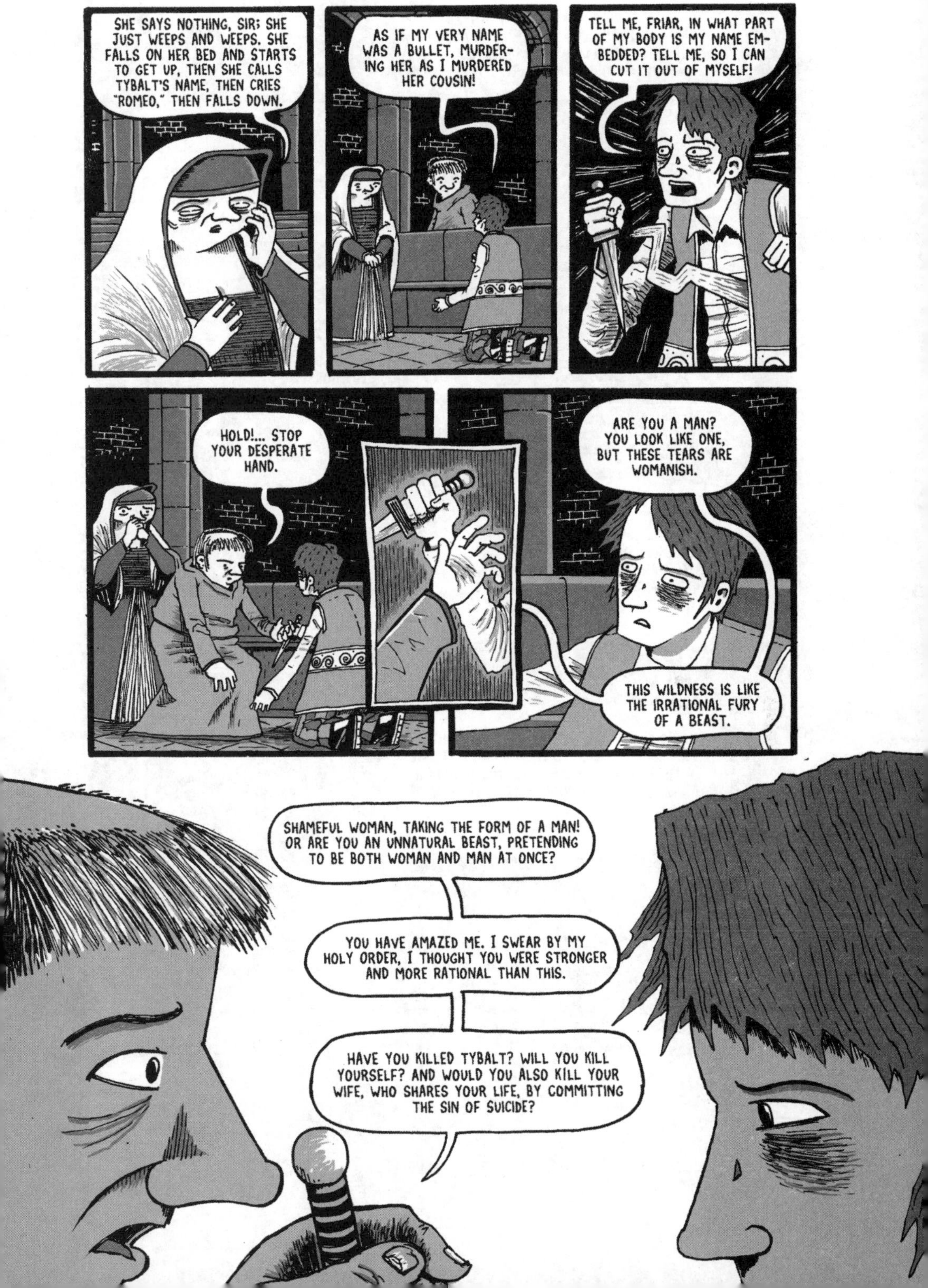
SHE SAYS NOTHING, SIR; SHE JUST WEEPS AND WEEPS. SHE FALLS ON HER BED AND STARTS TO GET UP, THEN SHE CALLS TYBALT'S NAME, THEN CRIES "ROMEO," THEN FALLS DOWN.
AS IF MY VERY NAME WAS A BULLET, MURDERING HER AS I MURDERED HER COUSIN!
TELL ME, FRIAR, IN WHAT PART OF MY BODY IS MY NAME EMBEDDED? TELL ME, SO I CAN CUT IT OUT OF MYSELF!
HOLD!... STOP YOUR DESPERATE HAND.
ARE YOU A MAN? YOU LOOK LIKE ONE, BUT THESE TEARS ARE WOMANISH.
THIS WILDNESS IS LIKE THE IRRATIONAL FURY OF A BEAST.
SHAMEFUL WOMAN, TAKING THE FORM OF A MAN! OR ARE YOU AN UNNATURAL BEAST, PRETENDING TO BE BOTH WOMAN AND MAN AT ONCE?
YOU HAVE AMAZED ME. I SWEAR BY MY HOLY ORDER, I THOUGHT YOU WERE STRONGER AND MORE RATIONAL THAN THIS.
HAVE YOU KILLED TYBALT? WILL YOU KILL YOURSELF? AND WOULD YOU ALSO KILL YOUR WIFE, WHO SHARES YOUR LIFE, BY COMMITTING THE SIN OF SUICIDE?

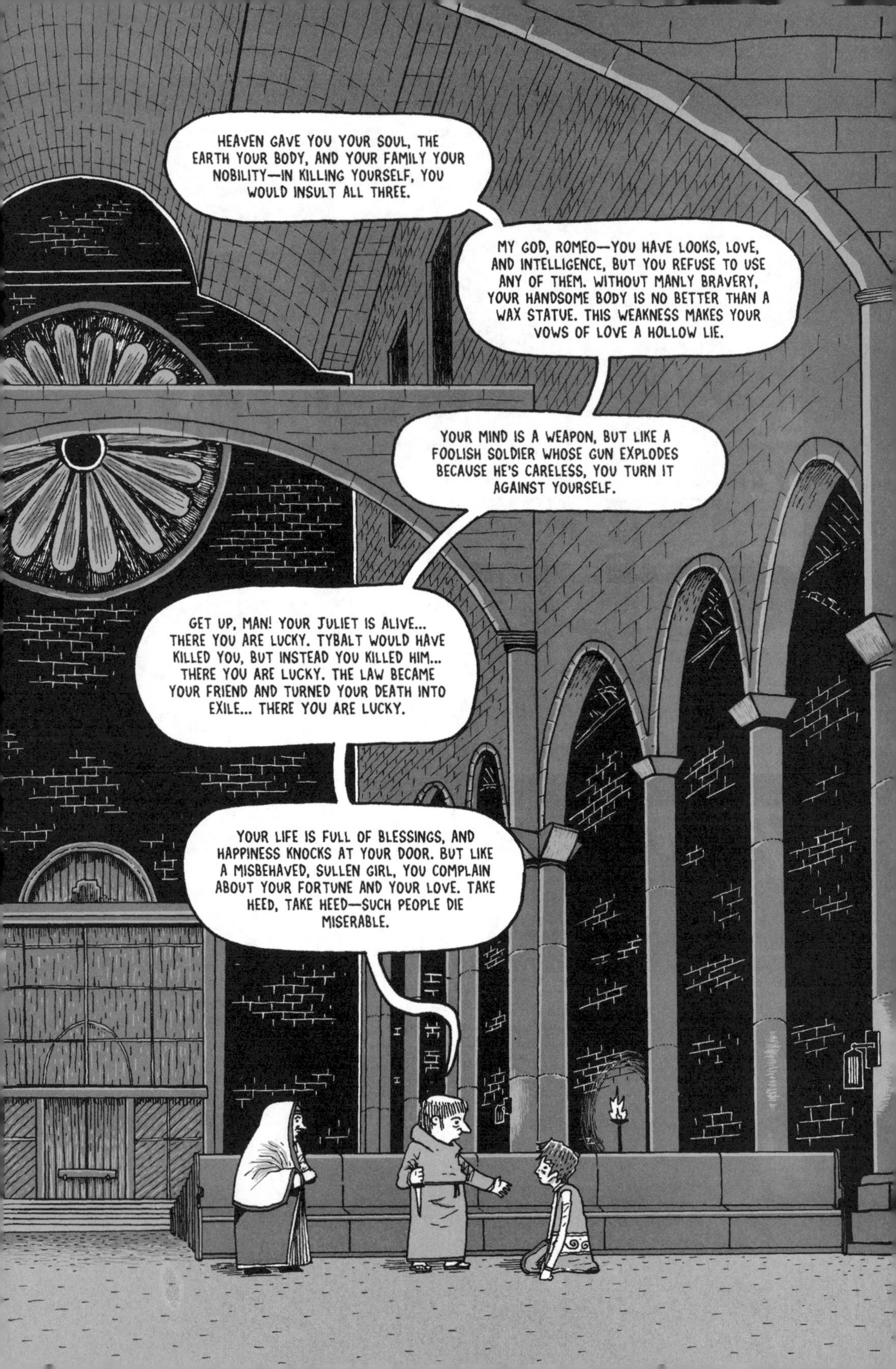
HEAVEN GAVE YOU YOUR SOUL, THE EARTH YOUR BODY, AND YOUR FAMILY YOUR NOBILITY—IN KILLING YOURSELF, YOU WOULD INSULT ALL THREE.
MY GOD, ROMEO—YOU HAVE LOOKS, LOVE, AND INTELLIGENCE, BUT YOU REFUSE TO USE ANY OF THEM. WITHOUT MANLY BRAVERY, YOUR HANDSOME BODY IS NO BETTER THAN A WAX STATUE. THIS WEAKNESS MAKES YOUR VOWS OF LOVE A HOLLOW LIE.
YOUR MIND IS A WEAPON, BUT LIKE A FOOLISH SOLDIER WHOSE GUN EXPLODES BECAUSE HE'S CARELESS, YOU TURN IT AGAINST YOURSELF.
GET UP, MAN! YOUR JULIET IS ALIVE... THERE YOU ARE LUCKY. TYBALT WOULD HAVE KILLED YOU, BUT INSTEAD YOU KILLED HIM... THERE YOU ARE LUCKY. THE LAW BECAME YOUR FRIEND AND TURNED YOUR DEATH INTO EXILE... THERE YOU ARE LUCKY.
YOUR LIFE IS FULL OF BLESSINGS, AND HAPPINESS KNOCKS AT YOUR DOOR. BUT LIKE A MISBEHAVED, SULLEN GIRL, YOU COMPLAIN ABOUT YOUR FORTUNE AND YOUR LOVE. TAKE HEED, TAKE HEED—SUCH PEOPLE DIE MISERABLE.

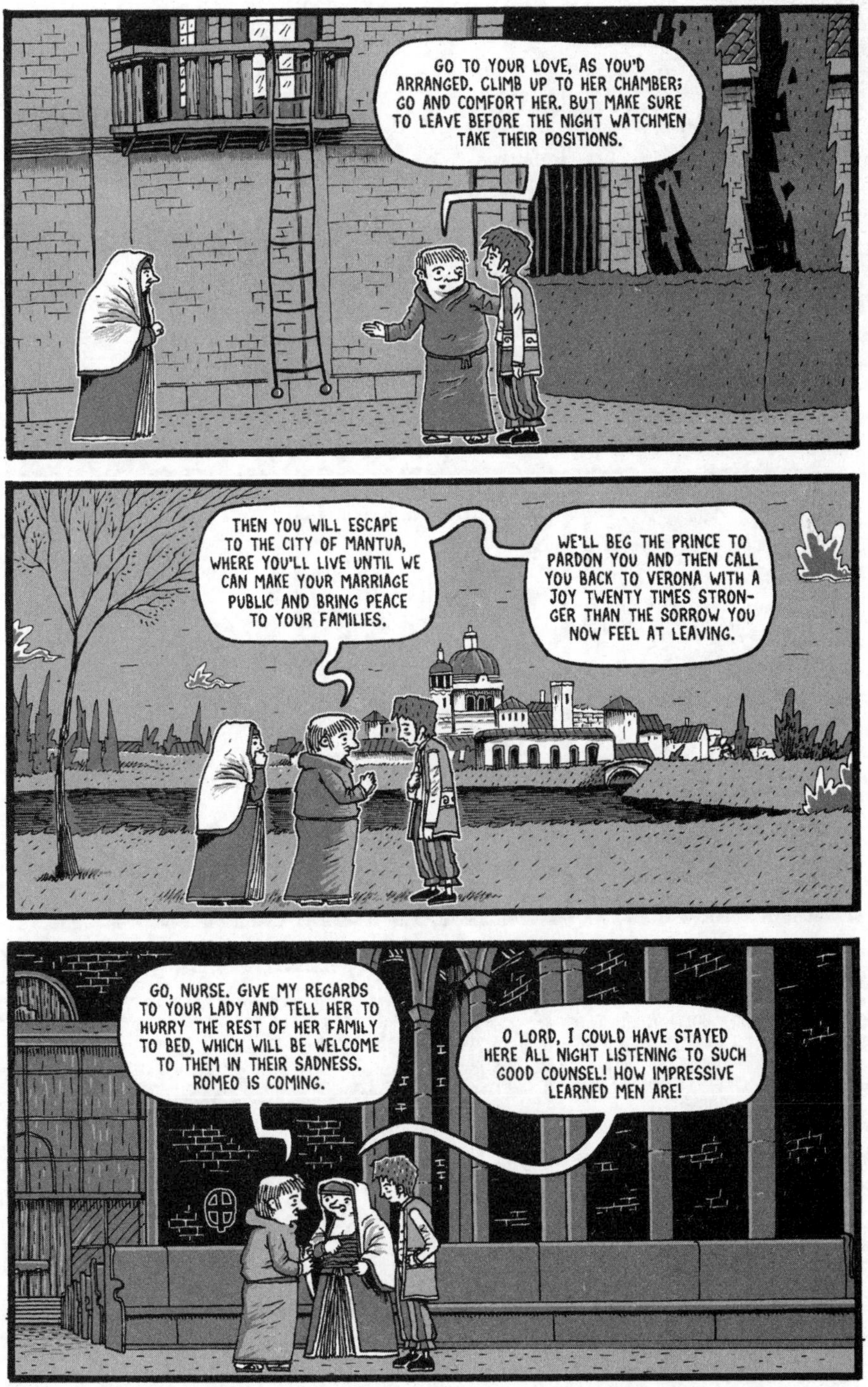
GO TO YOUR LOVE, AS YOU'D ARRANGED. CLIMB UP TO HER CHAMBER; GO AND COMFORT HER. BUT MAKE SURE TO LEAVE BEFORE THE NIGHT WATCHMEN TAKE THEIR POSITIONS.
THEN YOU WILL ESCAPE TO THE CITY OF MANTUA, WHERE YOU'LL LIVE UNTIL WE CAN MAKE YOUR MARRIAGE PUBLIC AND BRING PEACE TO YOUR FAMILIES.
WE'LL BEG THE PRINCE TO PARDON YOU AND THEN CALL YOU BACK TO VERONA WITH A JOY TWENTY TIMES STRONGER THAN THE SORROW YOU NOW FEEL AT LEAVING.
GO, NURSE. GIVE MY REGARDS TO YOUR LADY AND TELL HER TO HURRY THE REST OF HER FAMILY TO BED, WHICH WILL BE WELCOME TO THEM IN THEIR SADNESS. ROMEO IS COMING.
O LORD, I COULD HAVE STAYED HERE ALL NIGHT LISTENING TO SUCH GOOD COUNSEL! HOW IMPRESSIVE LEARNED MEN ARE!

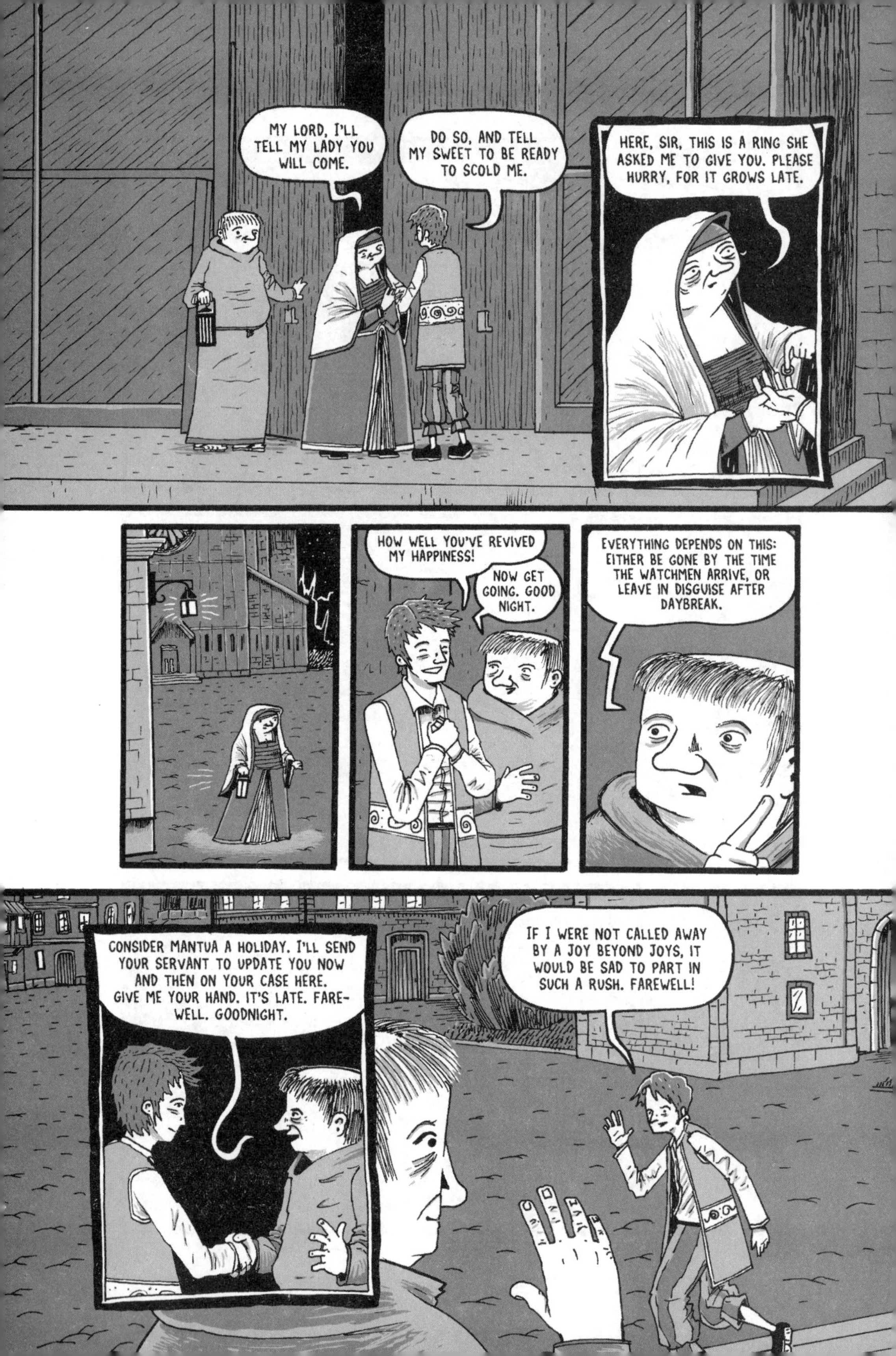
MY LORD, I'LL TELL MY LADY YOU WILL COME.
DO SO, AND TELL MY SWEET TO BE READY TO SCOLD ME.
HERE, SIR, THIS IS A RING SHE ASKED ME TO GIVE YOU. PLEASE HURRY, FOR IT GROWS LATE.
HOW WELL YOU'VE REVIVED MY HAPPINESS!
NOW GET GOING. GOOD NIGHT.
EVERYTHING DEPENDS ON THIS: EITHER BE GONE BY THE TIME THE WATCHMEN ARRIVE, OR LEAVE IN DISGUISE AFTER DAYBREAK.
CONSIDER MANTUA A HOLIDAY. I'LL SEND YOUR SERVANT TO UPDATE YOU NOW AND THEN ON YOUR CASE HERE. GIVE ME YOUR HAND. IT'S LATE. FAREWELL. GOODNIGHT.
IF I WERE NOT CALLED AWAY BY A JOY BEYOND JOYS, IT WOULD BE SAD TO PART IN SUCH A RUSH. FAREWELL!

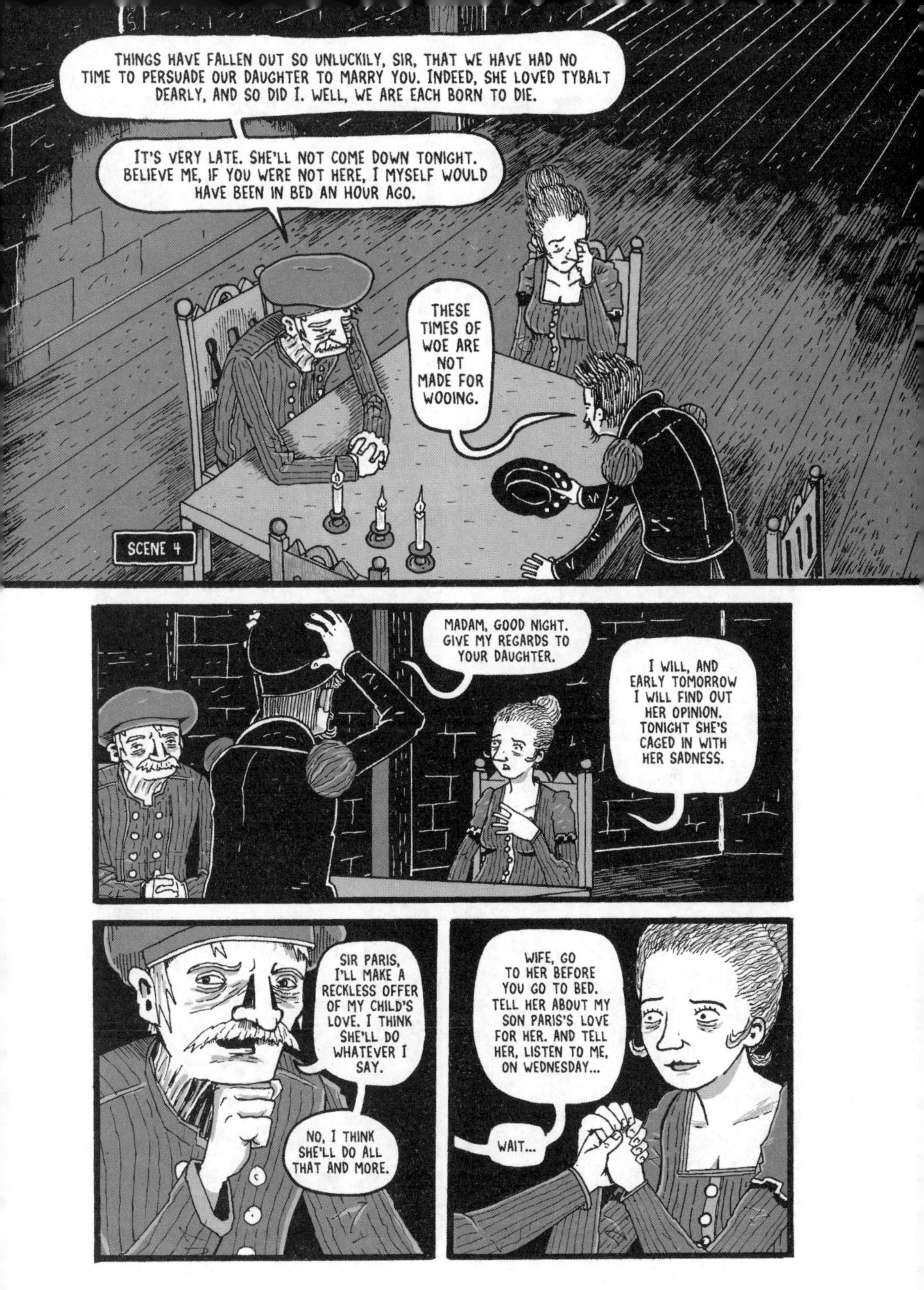
THINGS HAVE FALLEN OUT SO UNLUCKILY, SIR, THAT WE HAVE HAD NO TIME TO PERSUADE OUR DAUGHTER TO MARRY YOU. INDEED, SHE LOVED TYBALT DEARLY, AND SO DID I. WELL, WE ARE EACH BORN TO DIE.
IT'S VERY LATE. SHE'LL NOT COME DOWN TONIGHT. BELIEVE ME, IF YOU WERE NOT HERE, I MYSELF WOULD HAVE BEEN IN BED AN HOUR AGO.
THESE TIMES OF WOE ARE NOT MADE FOR WOOING.
SCENE 4
MADAM, GOOD NIGHT. GIVE MY REGARDS TO YOUR DAUGHTER.
I WILL, AND EARLY TOMORROW I WILL FIND OUT HER OPINION. TONIGHT SHE'S CAGED IN WITH HER SADNESS.
SIR PARIS, I'LL MAKE A RECKLESS OFFER OF MY CHILD'S LOVE. I THINK SHE'LL DO WHATEVER I SAY.
NO, I THINK SHE'LL DO ALL THAT AND MORE.
WIFE, GO TO HER BEFORE YOU GO TO BED. TELL HER ABOUT MY SON PARIS'S LOVE FOR HER. AND TELL HER, LISTEN TO ME, ON WEDNESDAY...
WAIT...

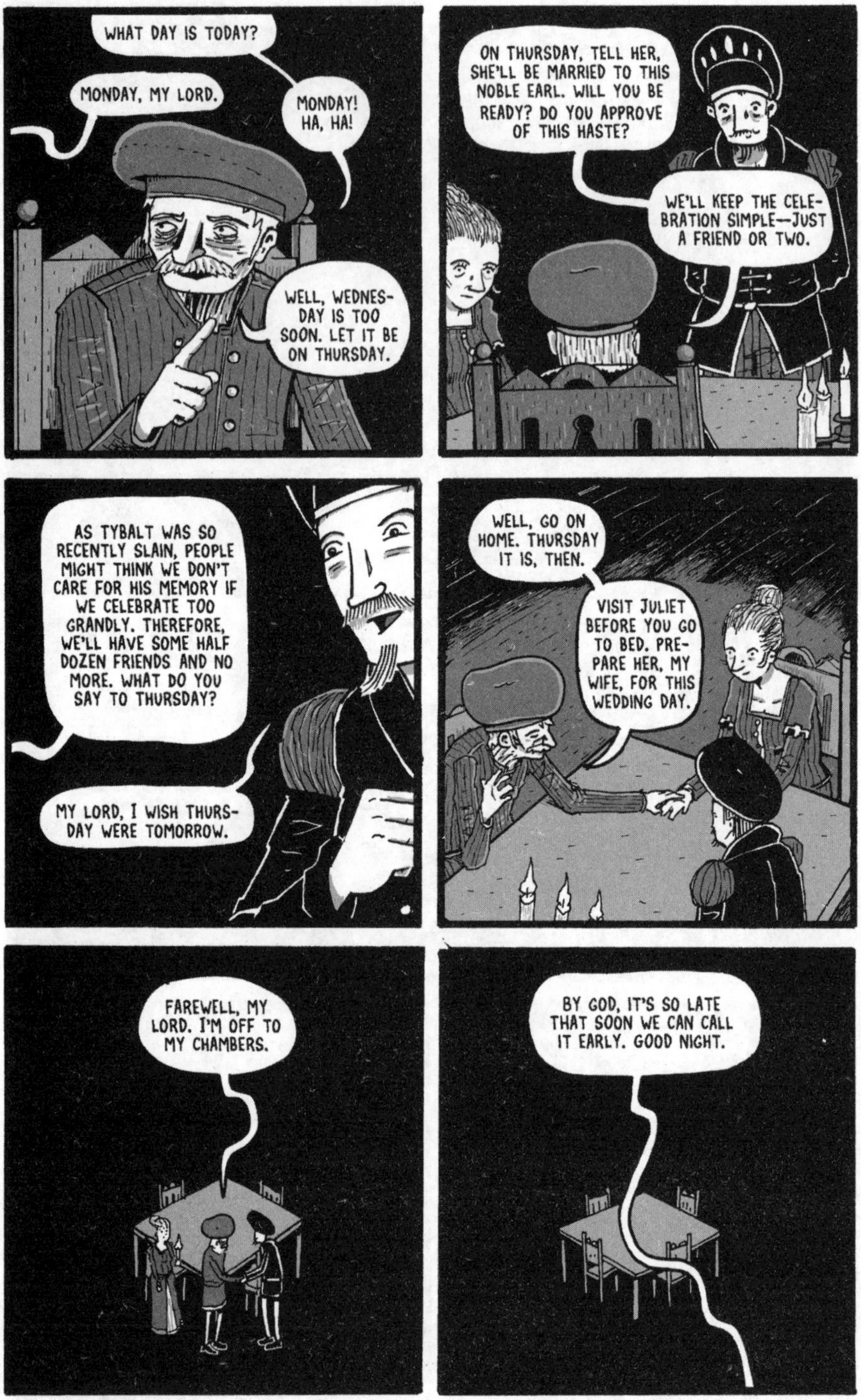
WHAT DAY IS TODAY?
MONDAY, MY LORD.
MONDAY! HA, HA!
WELL, WEDNESDAY IS TOO SOON. LET IT BE ON THURSDAY.
ON THURSDAY, TELL HER, SHE'LL BE MARRIED TO THIS NOBLE EARL. WILL YOU BE READY? DO YOU APPROVE OF THIS HASTE?
WE'LL KEEP THE CELEBRATION SIMPLE—JUST A FRIEND OR TWO.
AS TYBALT WAS SO RECENTLY SLAIN, PEOPLE MIGHT THINK WE DON'T CARE FOR HIS MEMORY IF WE CELEBRATE TOO GRANDLY. THEREFORE, WE'LL HAVE SOME HALF DOZEN FRIENDS AND NO MORE. WHAT DO YOU SAY TO THURSDAY?
MY LORD, I WISH THURSDAY WERE TOMORROW.
WELL, GO ON HOME. THURSDAY IT IS, THEN.
VISIT JULIET BEFORE YOU GO TO BED. PREPARE HER, MY WIFE, FOR THIS WEDDING DAY.
FAREWELL, MY LORD. I'M OFF TO MY CHAMBERS.
BY GOD, IT'S SO LATE THAT SOON WE CAN CALL IT EARLY. GOOD NIGHT.

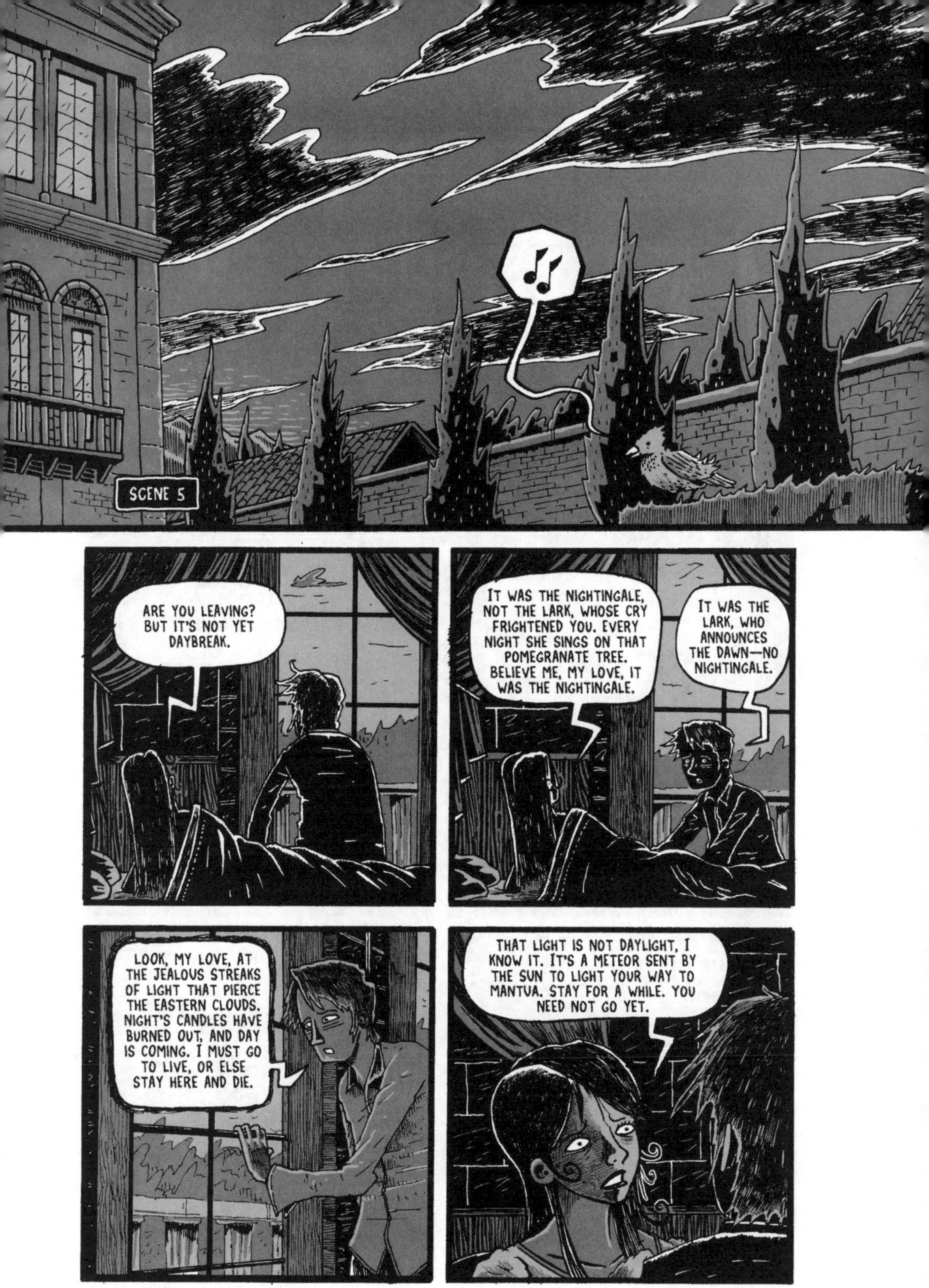
SCENE 5
ARE YOU LEAVING? BUT IT'S NOT YET DAYBREAK.
IT WAS THE NIGHTINGALE, NOT THE LARK, WHOSE CRY FRIGHTENED YOU. EVERY NIGHT SHE SINGS ON THAT POMEGRANATE TREE. BELIEVE ME, MY LOVE, IT WAS THE NIGHTINGALE.
IT WAS THE LARK, WHO ANNOUNCES THE DAWN—NO NIGHTINGALE.
LOOK, MY LOVE, AT THE JEALOUS STREAKS OF LIGHT THAT PIERCE THE EASTERN CLOUDS. NIGHT'S CANDLES HAVE BURNED OUT, AND DAY IS COMING. I MUST GO TO LIVE, OR ELSE STAY HERE AND DIE.
THAT LIGHT IS NOT DAYLIGHT, I KNOW IT. IT'S A METEOR SENT BY THE SUN TO LIGHT YOUR WAY TO MANTUA. STAY FOR A WHILE. YOU NEED NOT GO YET.

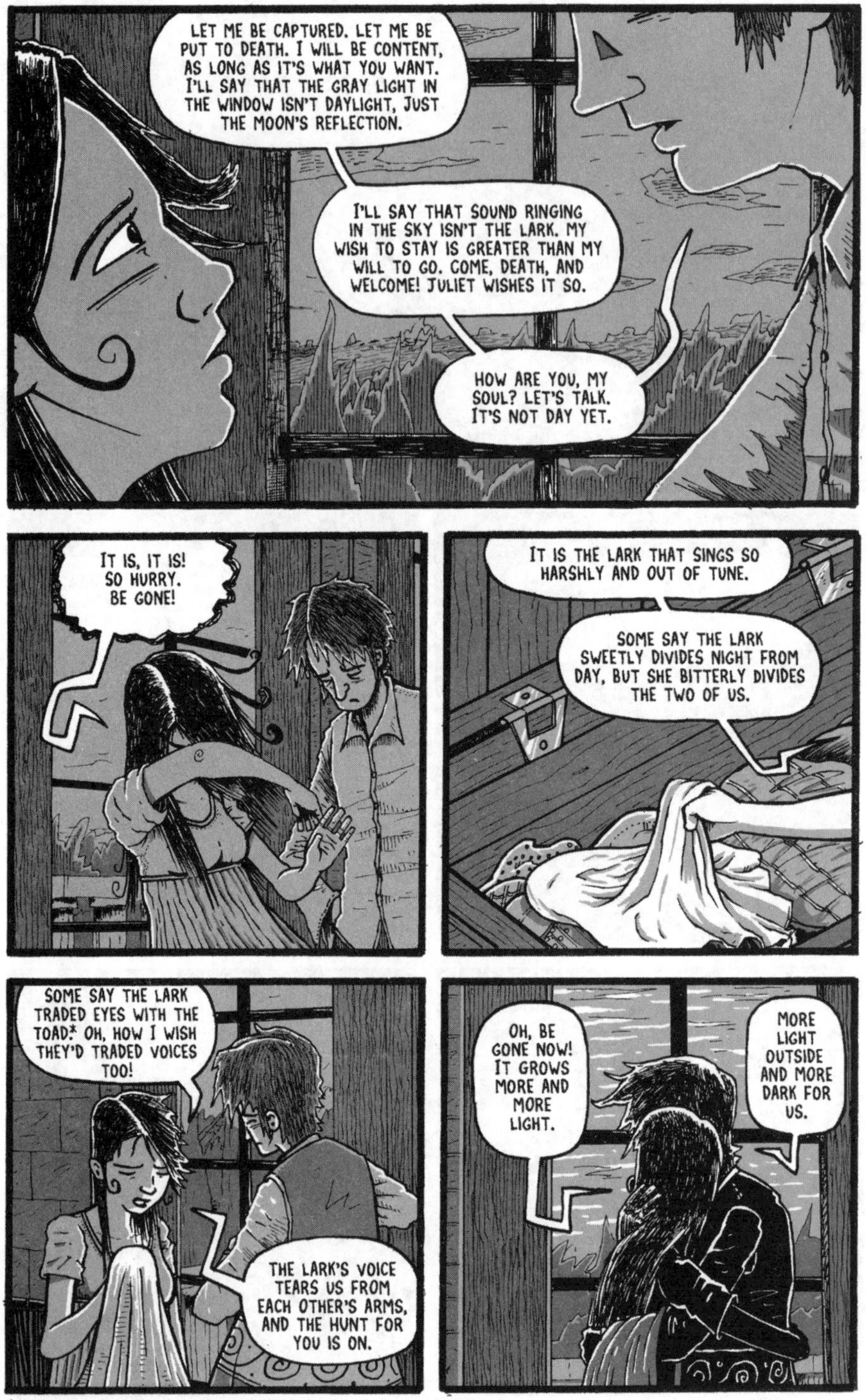
LET ME BE CAPTURED. LET ME BE PUT TO DEATH. I WILL BE CONTENT, AS LONG AS IT'S WHAT YOU WANT. I'LL SAY THAT THE GRAY LIGHT IN THE WINDOW ISN'T DAYLIGHT, JUST THE MOON'S REFLECTION.
I'LL SAY THAT SOUND RINGING IN THE SKY ISN'T THE LARK. MY WISH TO STAY IS GREATER THAN MY WILL TO GO. COME, DEATH, AND WELCOME! JULIET WISHES IT SO.
HOW ARE YOU, MY SOUL? LET'S TALK. IT'S NOT DAY YET.
IT IS, IT IS! SO HURRY. BE GONE!
IT IS THE LARK THAT SINGS SO HARSHLY AND OUT OF TUNE.
SOME SAY THE LARK SWEETLY DIVIDES NIGHT FROM DAY, BUT SHE BITTERLY DIVIDES THE TWO OF US.
SOME SAY THE LARK TRADED EYES WITH THE TOAD.* OH, HOW I WISH THEY'D TRADED VOICES TOO!
THE LARK'S VOICE TEARS US FROM EACH OTHER'S ARMS, AND THE HUNT FOR YOU IS ON.
OH, BE GONE NOW! IT GROWS MORE AND MORE LIGHT.
MORE LIGHT OUTSIDE AND MORE DARK FOR US.

*BECAUSE THE TOAD HAS PRETTY EYES AND THE LARK UGLY ONES.

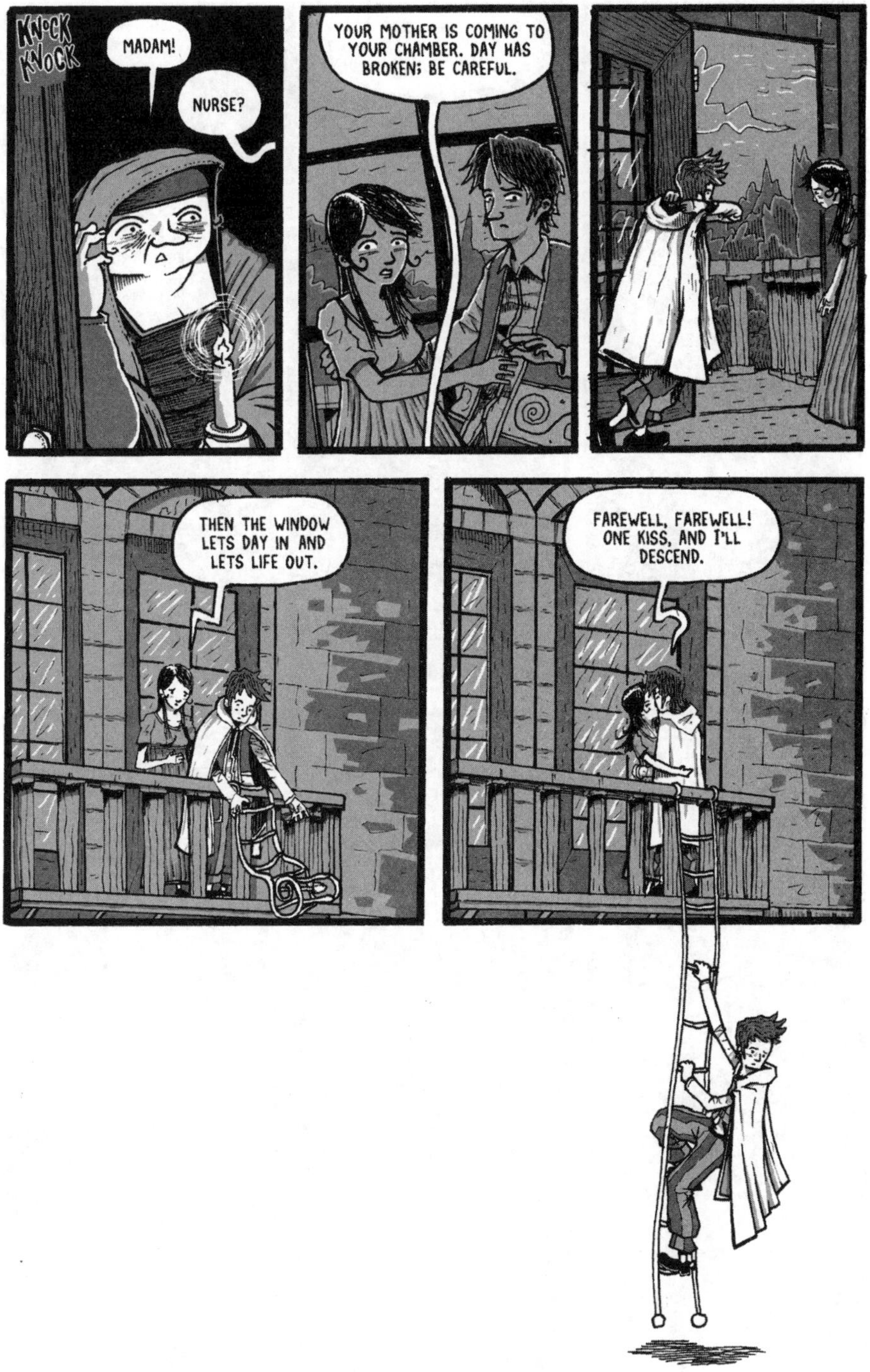
KNOCK KNOCK
MADAM!
NURSE?
YOUR MOTHER IS COMING TO YOUR CHAMBER. DAY HAS BROKEN; BE CAREFUL.
THEN THE WINDOW LETS DAY IN AND LETS LIFE OUT.
FAREWELL, FAREWELL! ONE KISS, AND I'LL DESCEND.

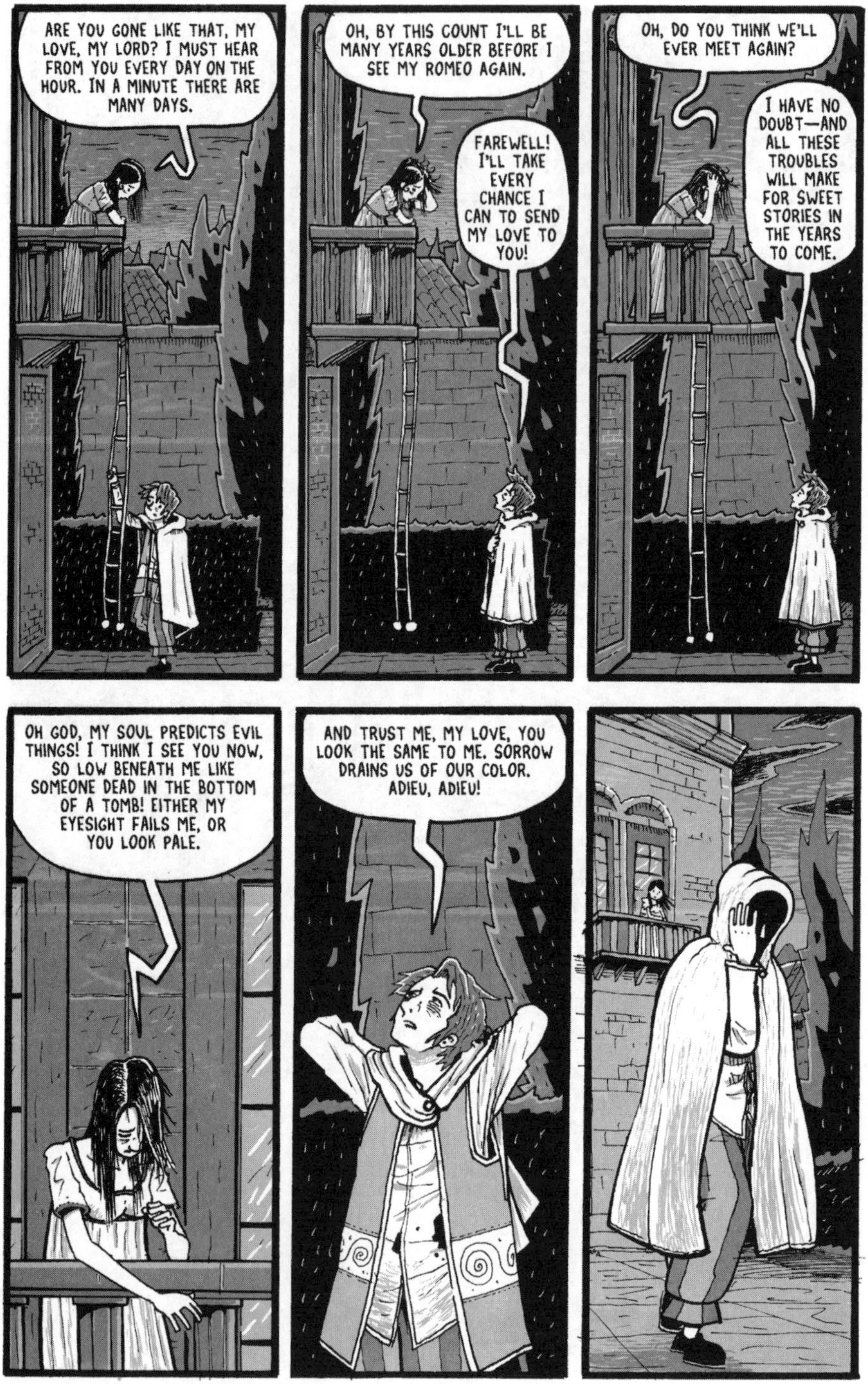
ARE YOU GONE LIKE THAT, MY LOVE, MY LORD? I MUST HEAR FROM YOU EVERY DAY ON THE HOUR. IN A MINUTE THERE ARE MANY DAYS.
OH, BY THIS COUNT I'LL BE MANY YEARS OLDER BEFORE I SEE MY ROMEO AGAIN.
FAREWELL! I'LL TAKE EVERY CHANCE I CAN TO SEND MY LOVE TO YOU!
OH, DO YOU THINK WE'LL EVER MEET AGAIN?
I HAVE NO DOUBT—AND ALL THESE TROUBLES WILL MAKE FOR SWEET STORIES IN THE YEARS TO COME.
OH GOD, MY SOUL PREDICTS EVIL THINGS! I THINK I SEE YOU NOW, SO LOW BENEATH ME LIKE SOMEONE DEAD IN THE BOTTOM OF A TOMB! EITHER MY EYESIGHT FAILS ME, OR YOU LOOK PALE.
AND TRUST ME, MY LOVE, YOU LOOK THE SAME TO ME. SORROW DRAINS US OF OUR COLOR. ADIEU, ADIEU!

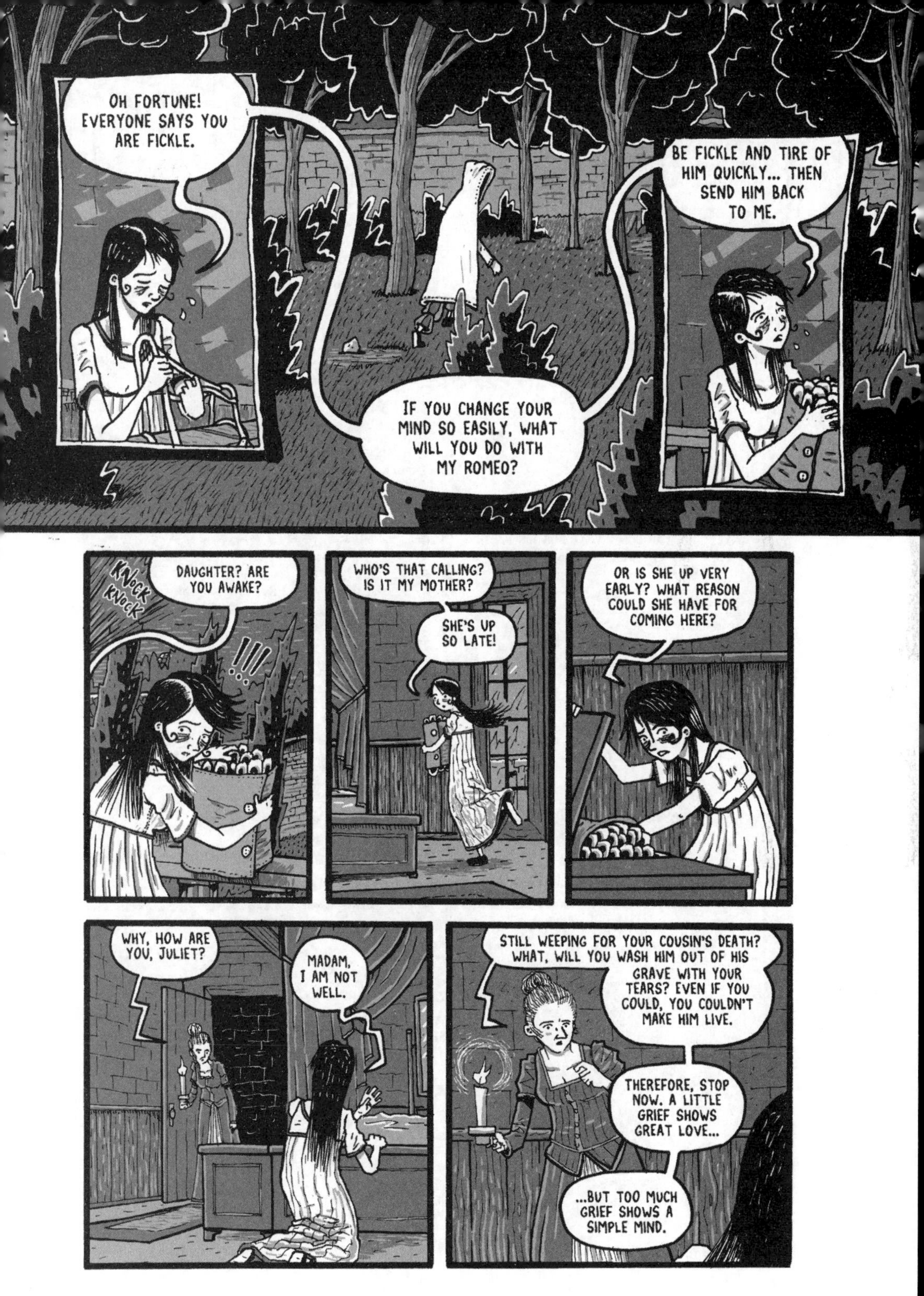
OH FORTUNE! EVERYONE SAYS YOU ARE FICKLE.
IF YOU CHANGE YOUR MIND SO EASILY, WHAT WILL YOU DO WITH MY ROMEO?
BE FICKLE AND TIRE OF HIM QUICKLY... THEN SEND HIM BACK TO ME.
KNOCK KNOCK
DAUGHTER? ARE YOU AWAKE?
!!!
WHO'S THAT CALLING? IS IT MY MOTHER?
SHE'S UP SO LATE!
OR IS SHE UP VERY EARLY? WHAT REASON COULD SHE HAVE FOR COMING HERE?
WHY, HOW ARE YOU, JULIET?
MADAM, I AM NOT WELL.
STILL WEEPING FOR YOUR COUSIN'S DEATH? WHAT, WILL YOU WASH HIM OUT OF HIS GRAVE WITH YOUR TEARS? EVEN IF YOU COULD, YOU COULDN'T MAKE HIM LIVE.
THEREFORE, STOP NOW. A LITTLE GRIEF SHOWS GREAT LOVE...
...BUT TOO MUCH GRIEF SHOWS A SIMPLE MIND.

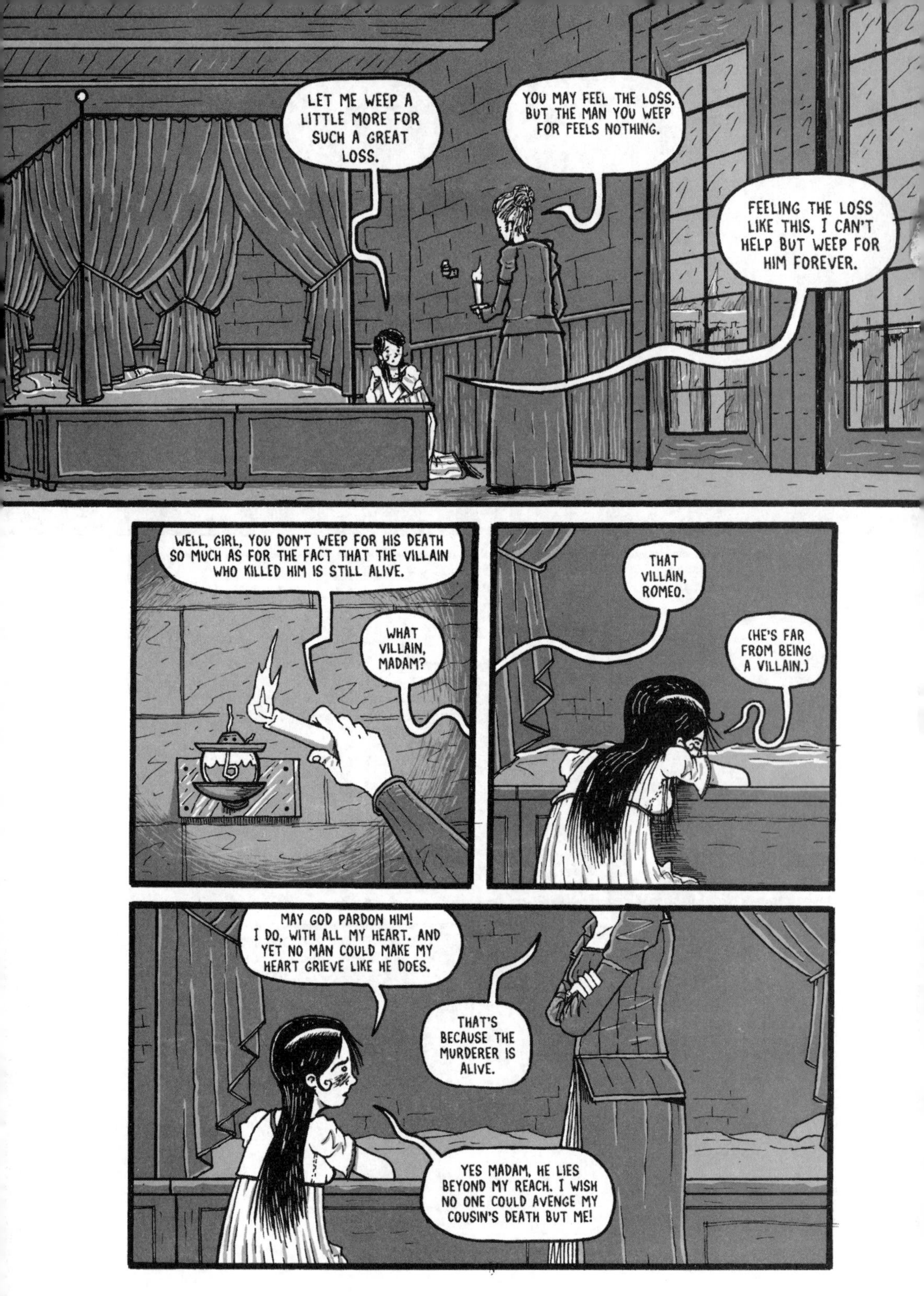
LET ME WEEP A LITTLE MORE FOR SUCH A GREAT LOSS.
YOU MAY FEEL THE LOSS, BUT THE MAN YOU WEEP FOR FEELS NOTHING.
FEELING THE LOSS LIKE THIS, I CAN'T HELP BUT WEEP FOR HIM FOREVER.
WELL, GIRL, YOU DON'T WEEP FOR HIS DEATH SO MUCH AS FOR THE FACT THAT THE VILLAIN WHO KILLED HIM IS STILL ALIVE.
WHAT VILLAIN, MADAM?
THAT VILLAIN, ROMEO.
(HE'S FAR FROM BEING A VILLAIN.)
MAY GOD PARDON HIM! I DO, WITH ALL MY HEART. AND YET NO MAN COULD MAKE MY HEART GRIEVE LIKE HE DOES.
THAT'S BECAUSE THE MURDERER IS ALIVE.
YES MADAM, HE LIES BEYOND MY REACH. I WISH NO ONE COULD AVENGE MY COUSIN'S DEATH BUT ME!

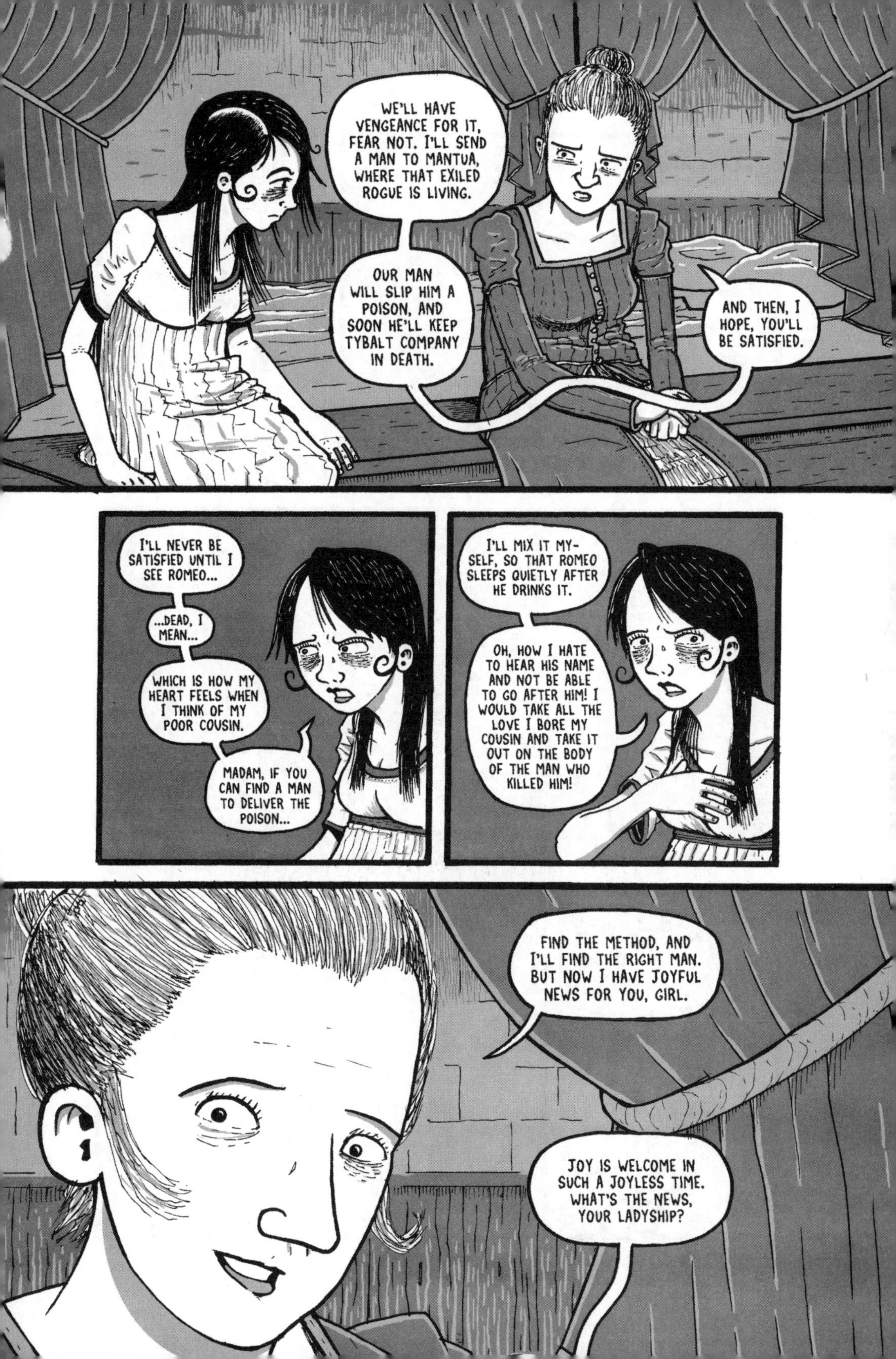
WE'LL HAVE VENGEANCE FOR IT, FEAR NOT. I'LL SEND A MAN TO MANTUA, WHERE THAT EXILED ROGUE IS LIVING.
OUR MAN WILL SLIP HIM A POISON, AND SOON HE'LL KEEP TYBALT COMPANY IN DEATH.
AND THEN, I HOPE, YOU'LL BE SATISFIED.
I'LL NEVER BE SATISFIED UNTIL I SEE ROMEO...
...DEAD, I MEAN...
WHICH IS HOW MY HEART FEELS WHEN I THINK OF MY POOR COUSIN.
MADAM, IF YOU CAN FIND A MAN TO DELIVER THE POISON...
I'LL MIX IT MY-SELF, SO THAT ROMEO SLEEPS QUIETLY AFTER HE DRINKS IT.
OH, HOW I HATE TO HEAR HIS NAME AND NOT BE ABLE TO GO AFTER HIM! I WOULD TAKE ALL THE LOVE I BORE MY COUSIN AND TAKE IT OUT ON THE BODY OF THE MAN WHO KILLED HIM!
FIND THE METHOD, AND I'LL FIND THE RIGHT MAN. BUT NOW I HAVE JOYFUL NEWS FOR YOU, GIRL.
JOY IS WELCOME IN SUCH A JOYLESS TIME. WHAT'S THE NEWS, YOUR LADYSHIP?

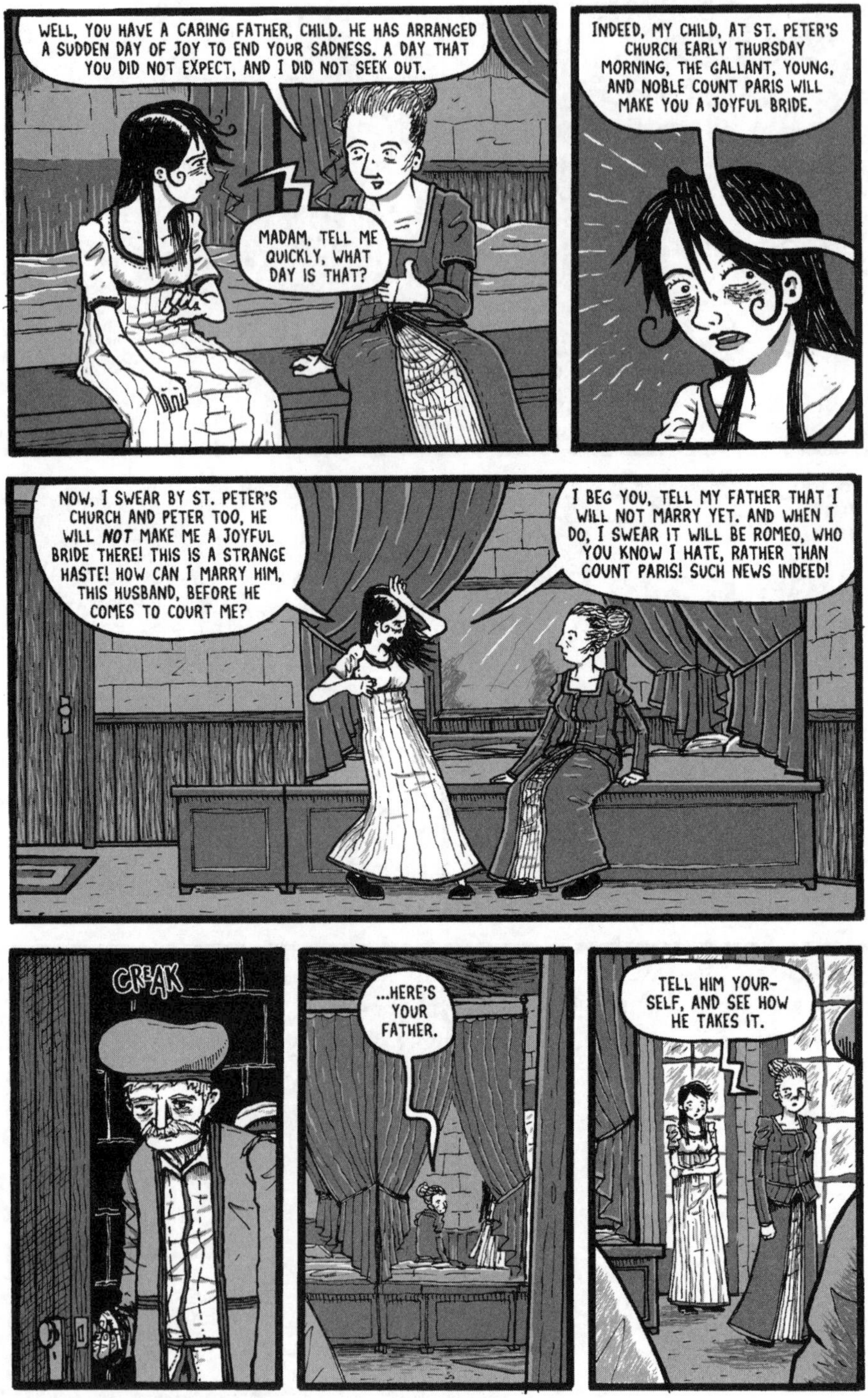
WELL, YOU HAVE A CARING FATHER, CHILD. HE HAS ARRANGED A SUDDEN DAY OF JOY TO END YOUR SADNESS. A DAY THAT YOU DID NOT EXPECT, AND I DID NOT SEEK OUT.
MADAM, TELL ME QUICKLY, WHAT DAY IS THAT?
INDEED, MY CHILD, AT ST. PETER'S CHURCH EARLY THURSDAY MORNING, THE GALLANT, YOUNG, AND NOBLE COUNT PARIS WILL MAKE YOU A JOYFUL BRIDE.
NOW, I SWEAR BY ST. PETER'S CHURCH AND PETER TOO, HE WILL *NOT* MAKE ME A JOYFUL BRIDE THERE! THIS IS A STRANGE HASTE! HOW CAN I MARRY HIM, THIS HUSBAND, BEFORE HE COMES TO COURT ME?
I BEG YOU, TELL MY FATHER THAT I WILL NOT MARRY YET. AND WHEN I DO, I SWEAR IT WILL BE ROMEO, WHO YOU KNOW I HATE, RATHER THAN COUNT PARIS! SUCH NEWS INDEED!
CREAK
...HERE'S YOUR FATHER.
TELL HIM YOUR-SELF, AND SEE HOW HE TAKES IT.

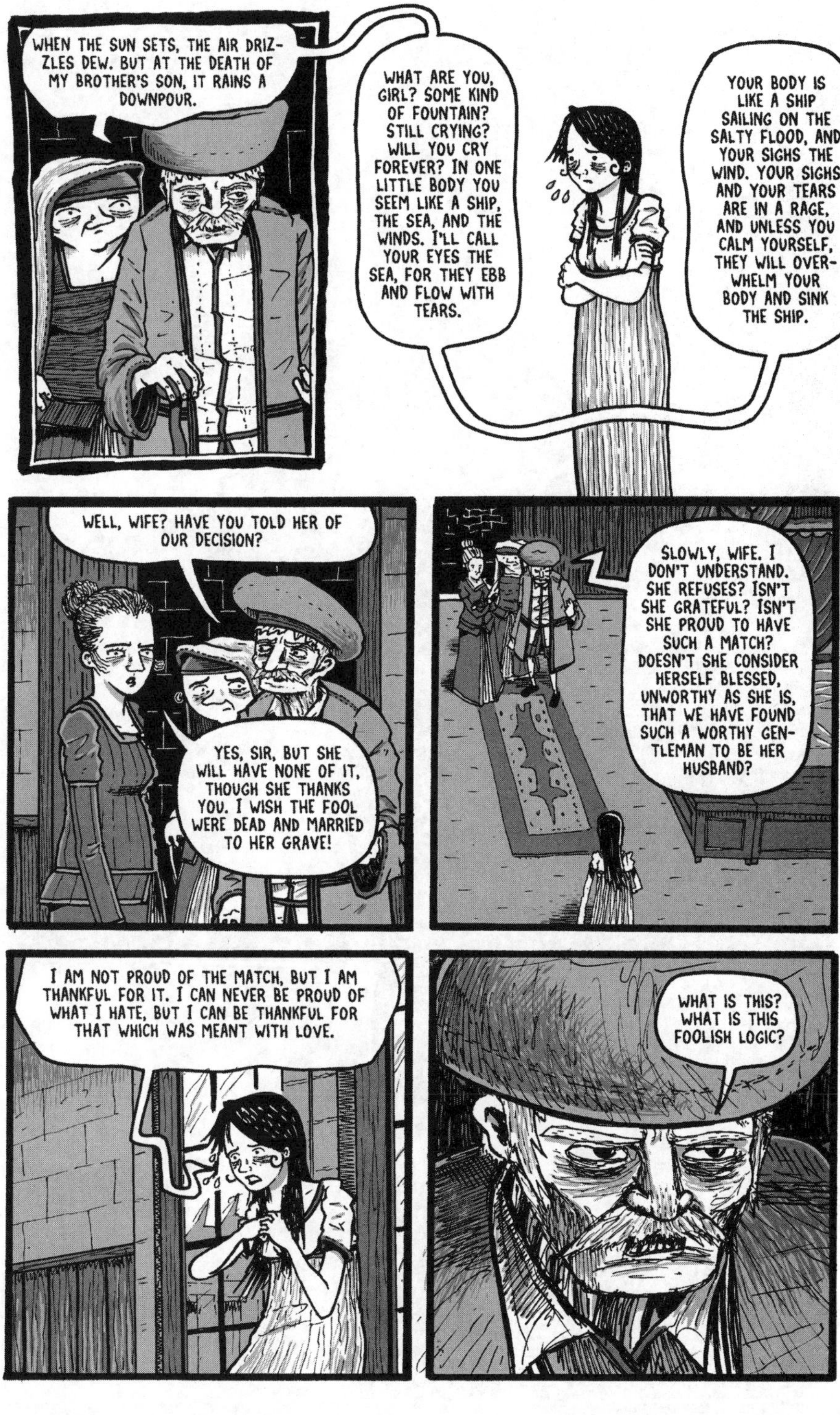
WHEN THE SUN SETS, THE AIR DRIZZLES DEW. BUT AT THE DEATH OF MY BROTHER'S SON, IT RAINS A DOWNPOUR.
WHAT ARE YOU, GIRL? SOME KIND OF FOUNTAIN? STILL CRYING? WILL YOU CRY FOREVER? IN ONE LITTLE BODY YOU SEEM LIKE A SHIP, THE SEA, AND THE WINDS. I'LL CALL YOUR EYES THE SEA, FOR THEY EBB AND FLOW WITH TEARS.
YOUR BODY IS LIKE A SHIP SAILING ON THE SALTY FLOOD, AND YOUR SIGHS THE WIND. YOUR SIGHS AND YOUR TEARS ARE IN A RAGE, AND UNLESS YOU CALM YOURSELF, THEY WILL OVERWHELM YOUR BODY AND SINK THE SHIP.
WELL, WIFE? HAVE YOU TOLD HER OF OUR DECISION?
YES, SIR, BUT SHE WILL HAVE NONE OF IT, THOUGH SHE THANKS YOU. I WISH THE FOOL WERE DEAD AND MARRIED TO HER GRAVE!
SLOWLY, WIFE. I DON'T UNDERSTAND. SHE REFUSES? ISN'T SHE GRATEFUL? ISN'T SHE PROUD TO HAVE SUCH A MATCH? DOESN'T SHE CONSIDER HERSELF BLESSED, UNWORTHY AS SHE IS, THAT WE HAVE FOUND SUCH A WORTHY GENTLEMAN TO BE HER HUSBAND?
I AM NOT PROUD OF THE MATCH, BUT I AM THANKFUL FOR IT. I CAN NEVER BE PROUD OF WHAT I HATE, BUT I CAN BE THANKFUL FOR THAT WHICH WAS MEANT WITH LOVE.
WHAT IS THIS? WHAT IS THIS FOOLISH LOGIC?

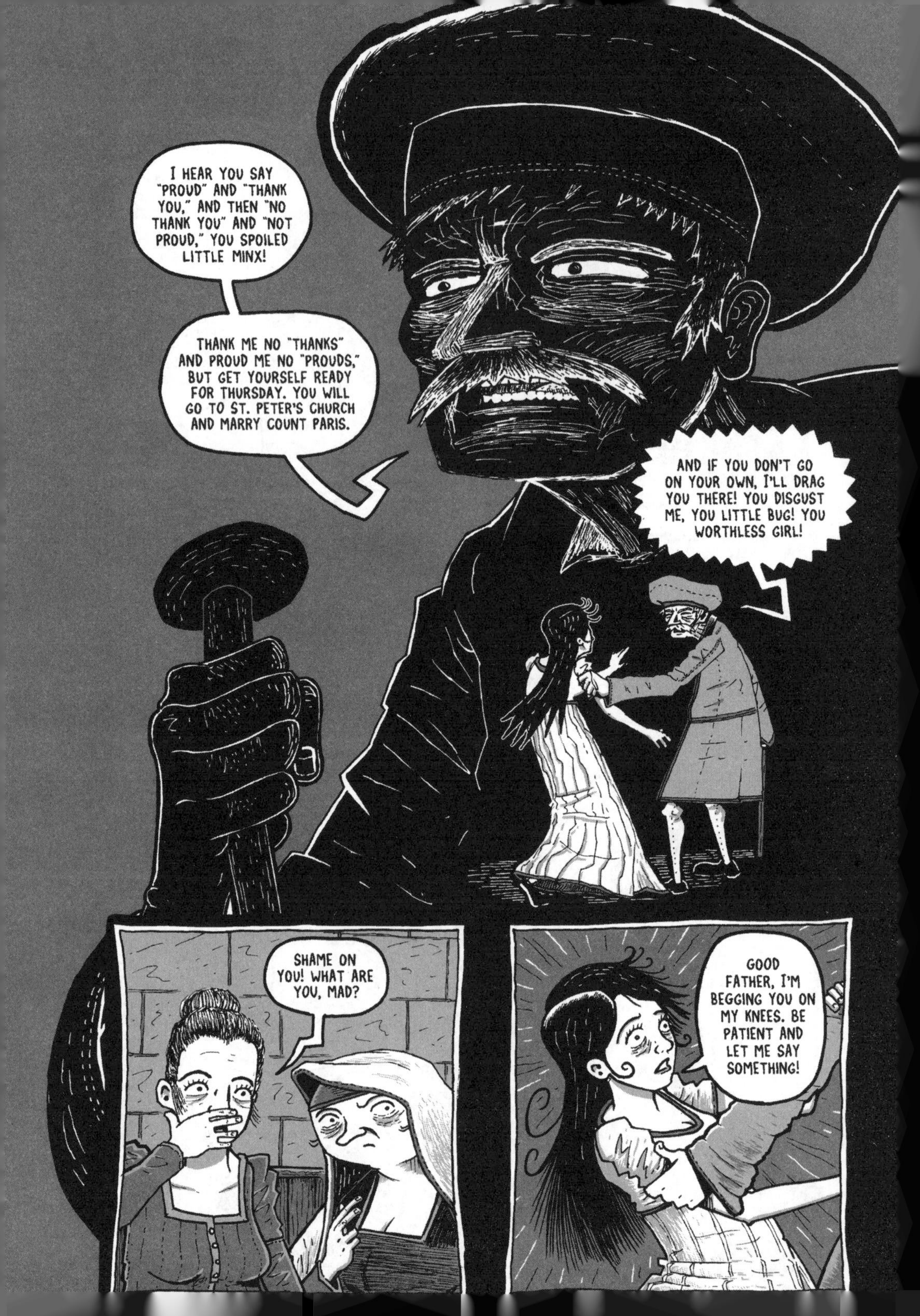
I HEAR YOU SAY "PROUD" AND "THANK YOU," AND THEN "NO THANK YOU" AND "NOT PROUD," YOU SPOILED LITTLE MINX!
THANK ME NO "THANKS" AND PROUD ME NO "PROUDS," BUT GET YOURSELF READY FOR THURSDAY. YOU WILL GO TO ST. PETER'S CHURCH AND MARRY COUNT PARIS.
AND IF YOU DON'T GO ON YOUR OWN, I'LL DRAG YOU THERE! YOU DISGUST ME, YOU LITTLE BUG! YOU WORTHLESS GIRL!
SHAME ON YOU! WHAT ARE YOU, MAD?
GOOD FATHER, I'M BEGGING YOU ON MY KNEES. BE PATIENT AND LET ME SAY SOMETHING!

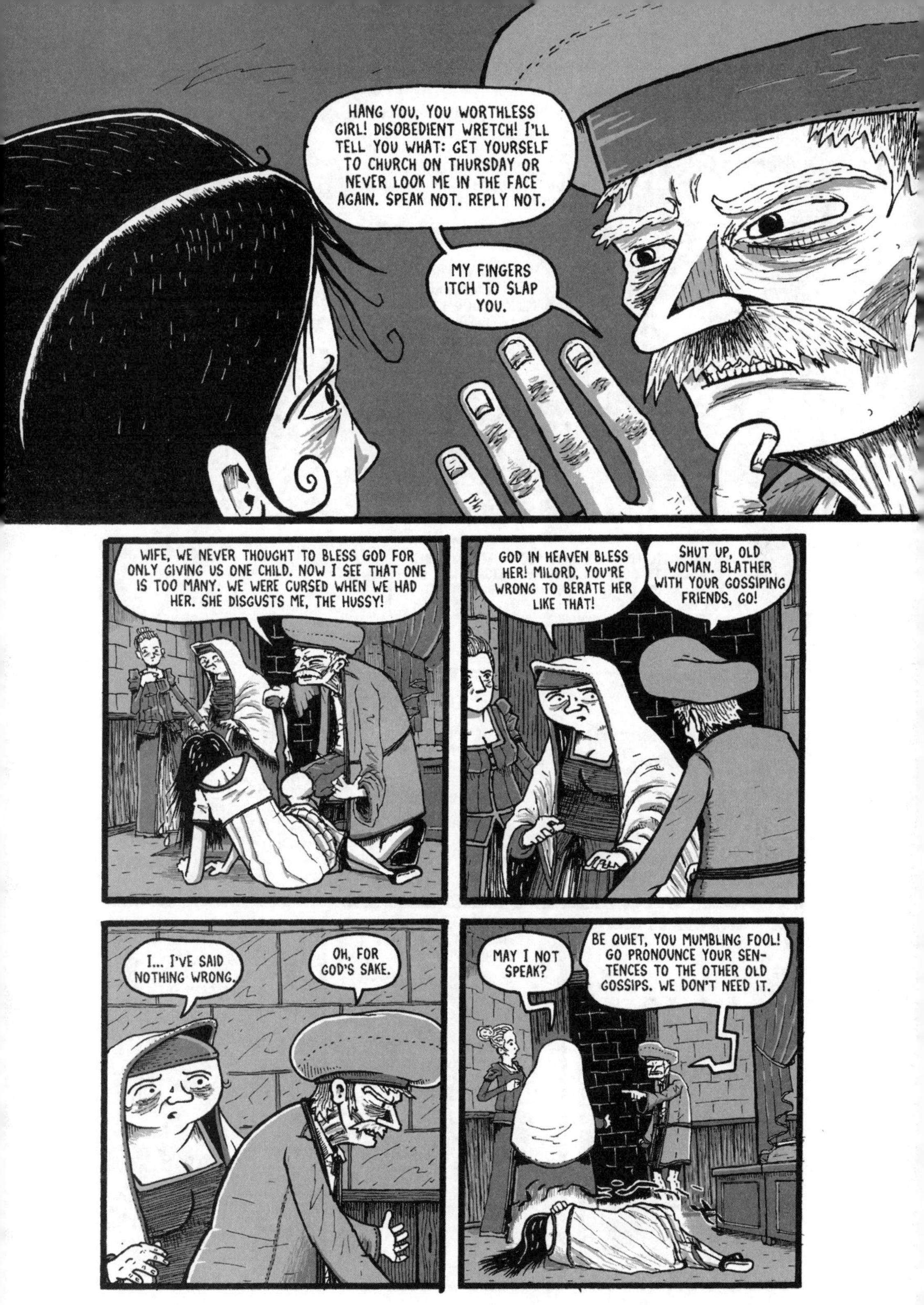
HANG YOU, YOU WORTHLESS GIRL! DISOBEDIENT WRETCH! I'LL TELL YOU WHAT: GET YOURSELF TO CHURCH ON THURSDAY OR NEVER LOOK ME IN THE FACE AGAIN. SPEAK NOT. REPLY NOT.
MY FINGERS ITCH TO SLAP YOU.
WIFE, WE NEVER THOUGHT TO BLESS GOD FOR ONLY GIVING US ONE CHILD. NOW I SEE THAT ONE IS TOO MANY. WE WERE CURSED WHEN WE HAD HER. SHE DISGUSTS ME, THE HUSSY!
GOD IN HEAVEN BLESS HER! MILORD, YOU'RE WRONG TO BERATE HER LIKE THAT!
SHUT UP, OLD WOMAN. BLATHER WITH YOUR GOSSIPING FRIENDS, GO!
I... I'VE SAID NOTHING WRONG.
OH, FOR GOD'S SAKE.
MAY I NOT SPEAK?
BE QUIET, YOU MUMBLING FOOL! GO PRONOUNCE YOUR SEN-TENCES TO THE OTHER OLD GOSSIPS. WE DON'T NEED IT.

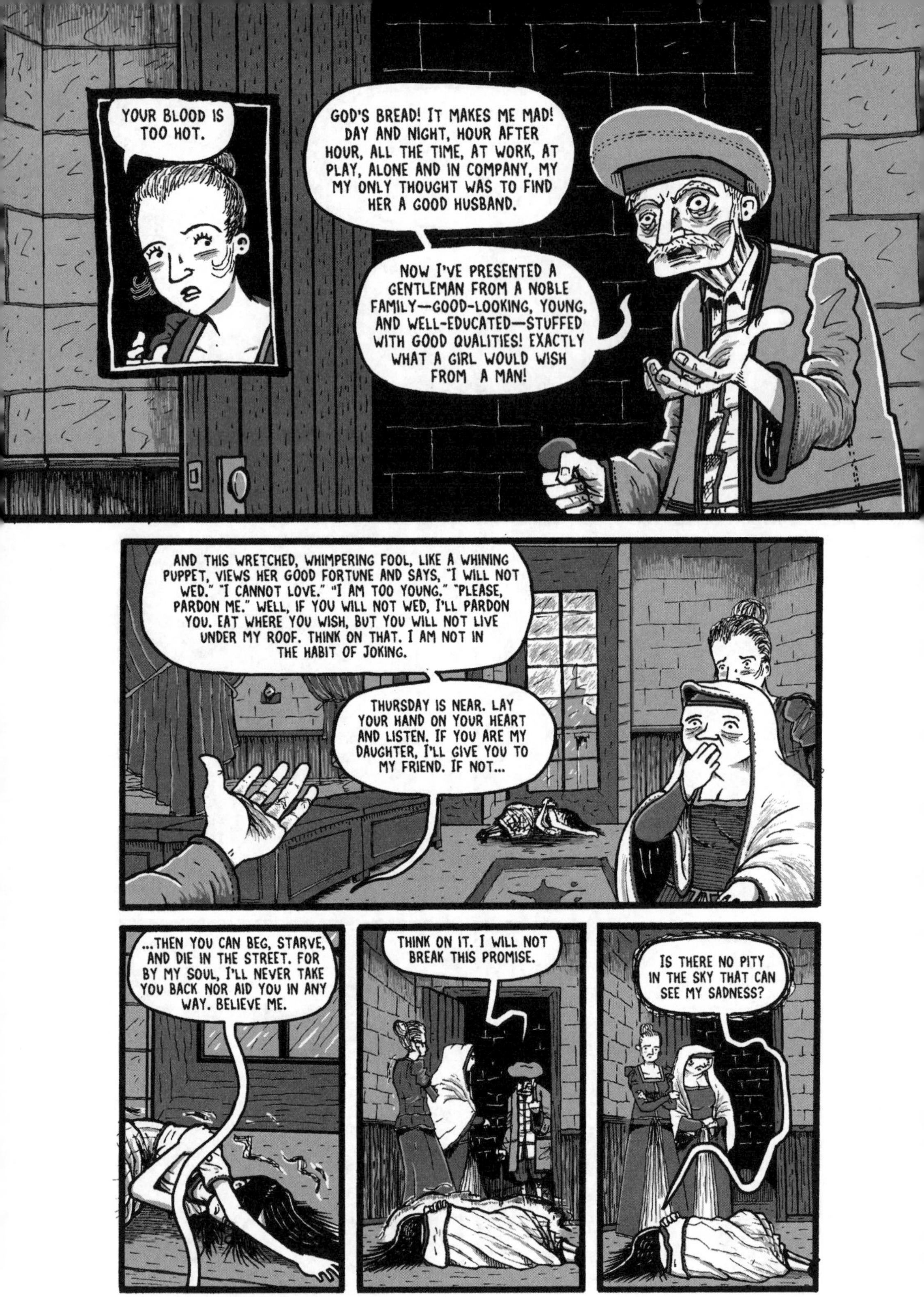
YOUR BLOOD IS TOO HOT.
GOD'S BREAD! IT MAKES ME MAD! DAY AND NIGHT, HOUR AFTER HOUR, ALL THE TIME, AT WORK, AT PLAY, ALONE AND IN COMPANY, MY MY ONLY THOUGHT WAS TO FIND HER A GOOD HUSBAND.
NOW I'VE PRESENTED A GENTLEMAN FROM A NOBLE FAMILY—GOOD-LOOKING, YOUNG, AND WELL-EDUCATED—STUFFED WITH GOOD QUALITIES! EXACTLY WHAT A GIRL WOULD WISH FROM A MAN!
AND THIS WRETCHED, WHIMPERING FOOL, LIKE A WHINING PUPPET, VIEWS HER GOOD FORTUNE AND SAYS, "I WILL NOT WED." "I CANNOT LOVE." "I AM TOO YOUNG." "PLEASE, PARDON ME." WELL, IF YOU WILL NOT WED, I'LL PARDON YOU. EAT WHERE YOU WISH, BUT YOU WILL NOT LIVE UNDER MY ROOF. THINK ON THAT. I AM NOT IN THE HABIT OF JOKING.
THURSDAY IS NEAR. LAY YOUR HAND ON YOUR HEART AND LISTEN. IF YOU ARE MY DAUGHTER, I'LL GIVE YOU TO MY FRIEND. IF NOT...
...THEN YOU CAN BEG, STARVE, AND DIE IN THE STREET. FOR BY MY SOUL, I'LL NEVER TAKE YOU BACK NOR AID YOU IN ANY WAY. BELIEVE ME.
THINK ON IT. I WILL NOT BREAK THIS PROMISE.
IS THERE NO PITY IN THE SKY THAT CAN SEE MY SADNESS?

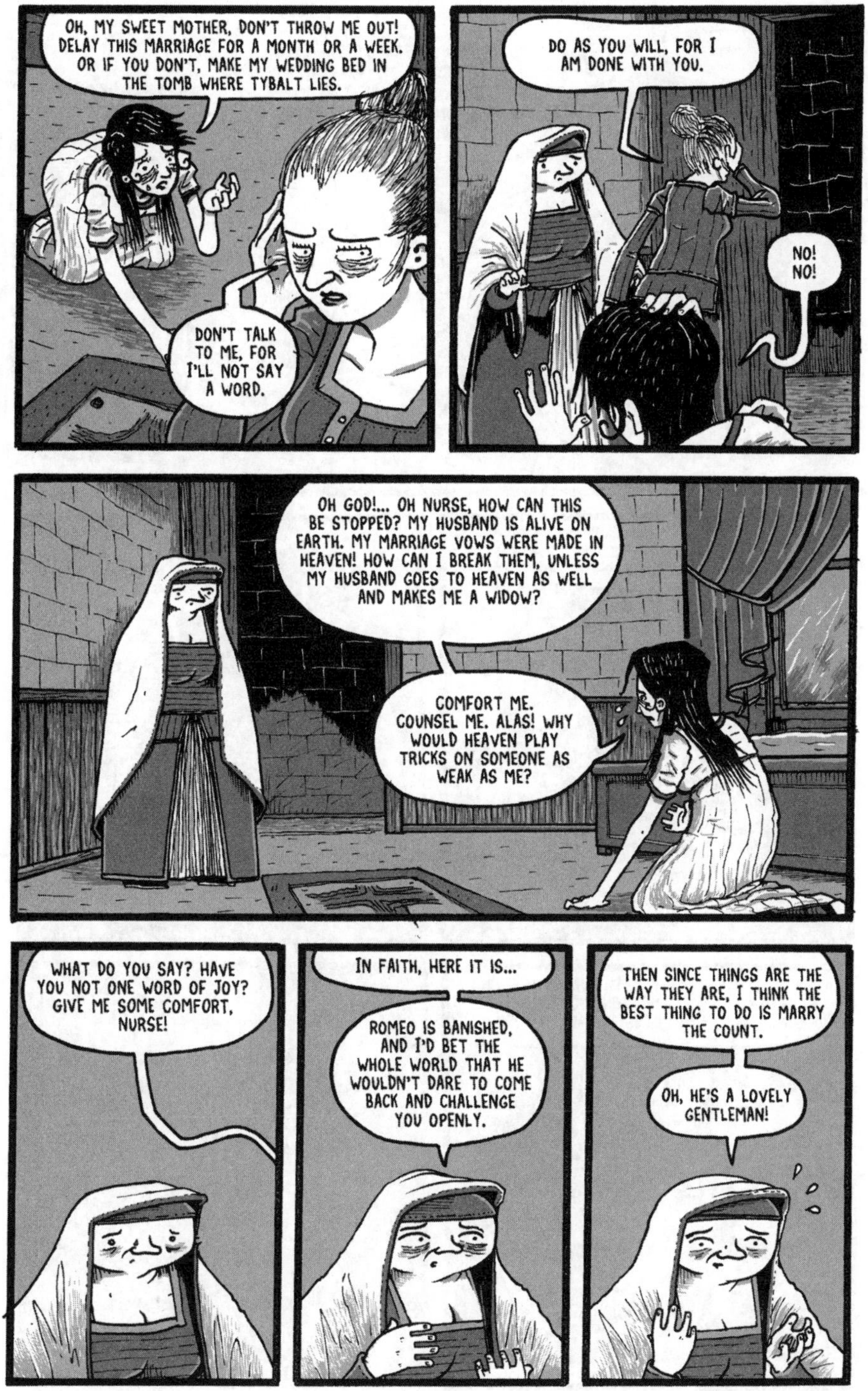

OH, MY SWEET MOTHER, DON'T THROW ME OUT! DELAY THIS MARRIAGE FOR A MONTH OR A WEEK. OR IF YOU DON'T, MAKE MY WEDDING BED IN THE TOMB WHERE TYBALT LIES.
DON'T TALK TO ME, FOR I'LL NOT SAY A WORD.
DO AS YOU WILL, FOR I AM DONE WITH YOU.
NO! NO!
OH GOD!... OH NURSE, HOW CAN THIS BE STOPPED? MY HUSBAND IS ALIVE ON EARTH. MY MARRIAGE VOWS WERE MADE IN HEAVEN! HOW CAN I BREAK THEM, UNLESS MY HUSBAND GOES TO HEAVEN AS WELL AND MAKES ME A WIDOW?
COMFORT ME. COUNSEL ME. ALAS! WHY WOULD HEAVEN PLAY TRICKS ON SOMEONE AS WEAK AS ME?
WHAT DO YOU SAY? HAVE YOU NOT ONE WORD OF JOY? GIVE ME SOME COMFORT, NURSE!
IN FAITH, HERE IT IS...
ROMEO IS BANISHED, AND I'D BET THE WHOLE WORLD THAT HE WOULDN'T DARE TO COME BACK AND CHALLENGE YOU OPENLY.
THEN SINCE THINGS ARE THE WAY THEY ARE, I THINK THE BEST THING TO DO IS MARRY THE COUNT.
OH, HE'S A LOVELY GENTLEMAN!

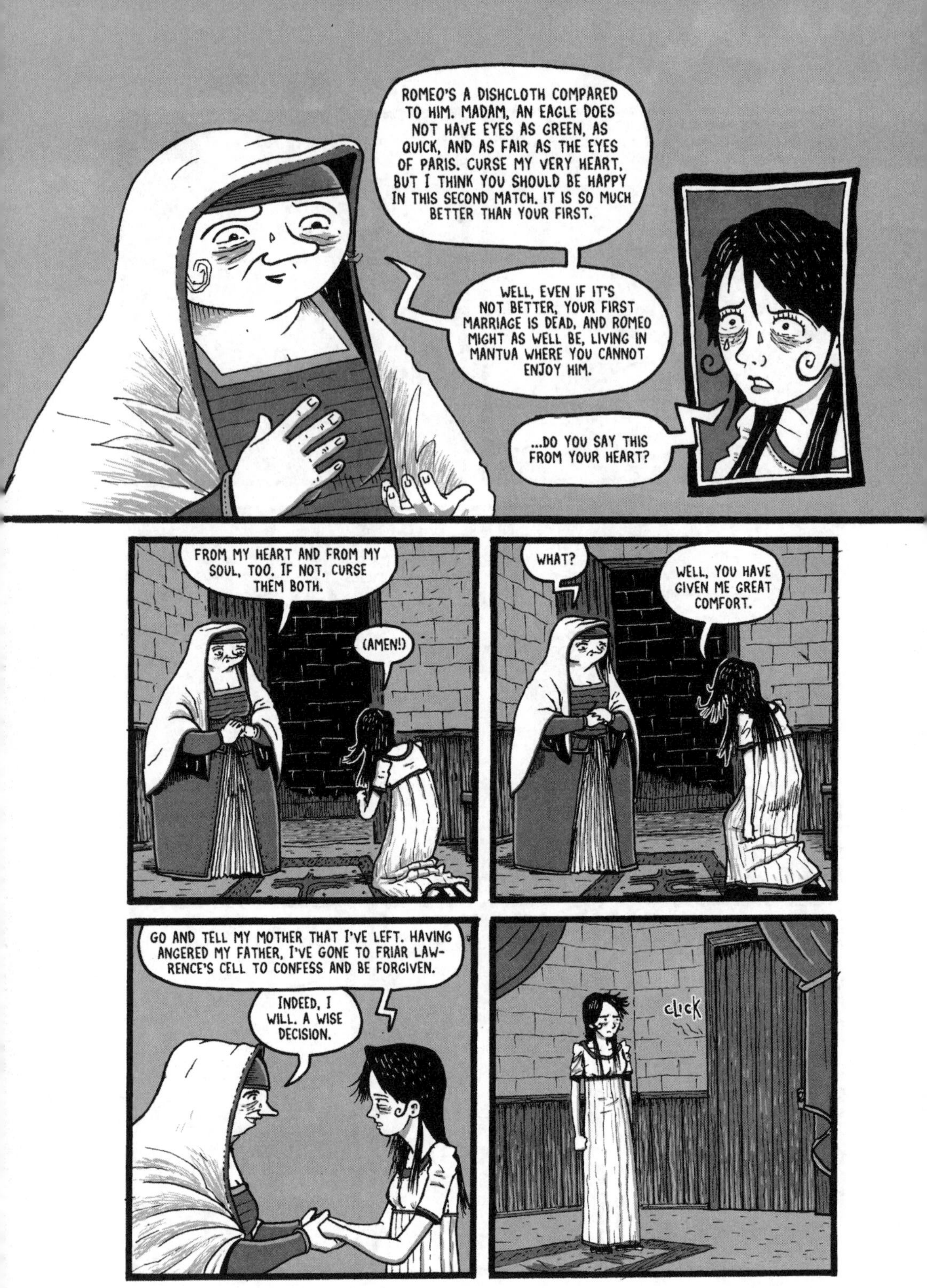
ROMEO'S A DISHCLOTH COMPARED TO HIM. MADAM, AN EAGLE DOES NOT HAVE EYES AS GREEN, AS QUICK, AND AS FAIR AS THE EYES OF PARIS. CURSE MY VERY HEART, BUT I THINK YOU SHOULD BE HAPPY IN THIS SECOND MATCH. IT IS SO MUCH BETTER THAN YOUR FIRST.
WELL, EVEN IF IT'S NOT BETTER, YOUR FIRST MARRIAGE IS DEAD, AND ROMEO MIGHT AS WELL BE, LIVING IN MANTUA WHERE YOU CANNOT ENJOY HIM.
...DO YOU SAY THIS FROM YOUR HEART?
FROM MY HEART AND FROM MY SOUL, TOO. IF NOT, CURSE THEM BOTH.
(AMEN!)
WHAT?
WELL, YOU HAVE GIVEN ME GREAT COMFORT.
GO AND TELL MY MOTHER THAT I'VE LEFT. HAVING ANGERED MY FATHER, I'VE GONE TO FRIAR LAWRENCE'S CELL TO CONFESS AND BE FORGIVEN.
INDEED, I WILL. A WISE DECISION.
CLICK

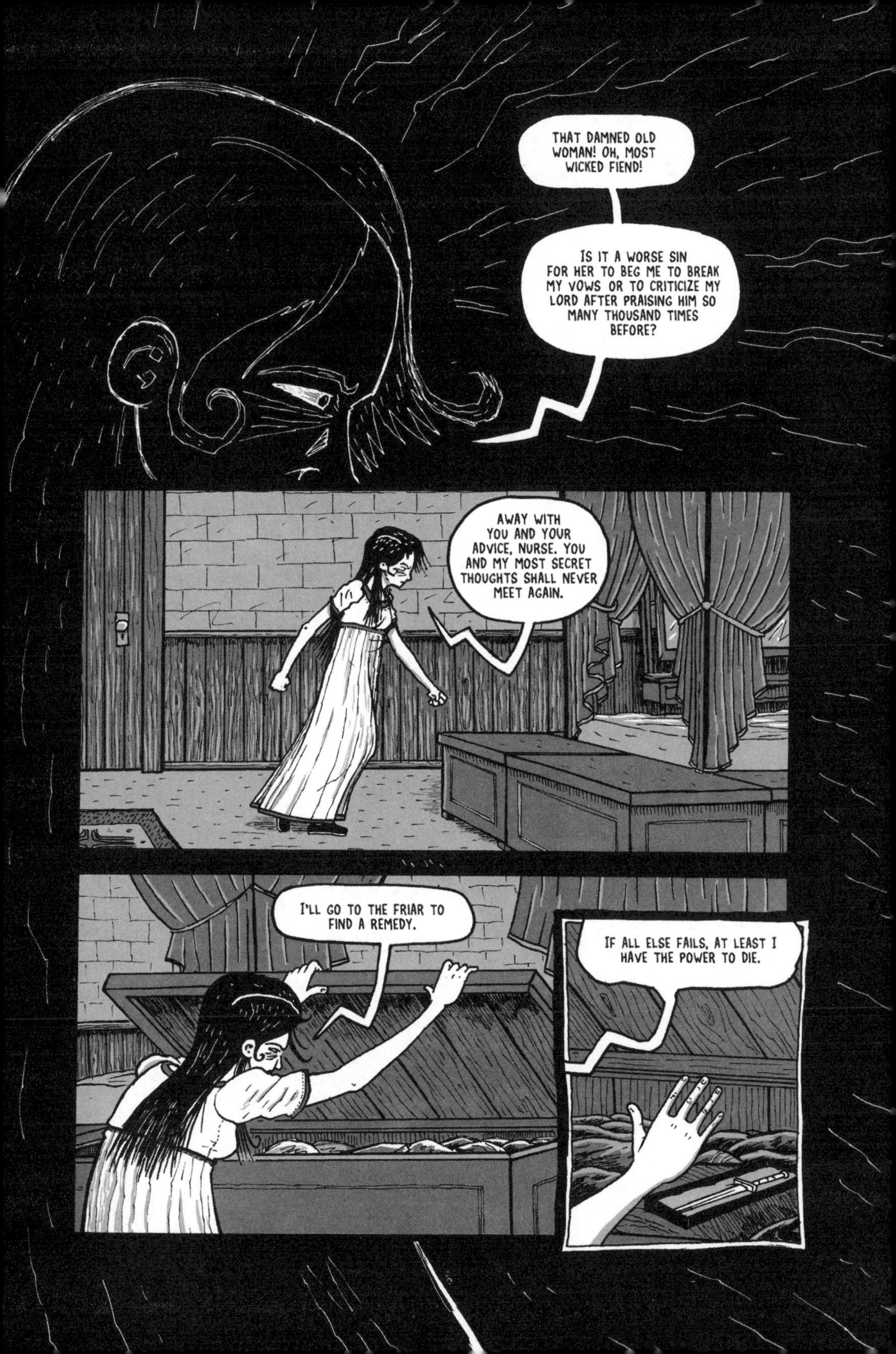
THAT DAMNED OLD WOMAN! OH, MOST WICKED FIEND!
IS IT A WORSE SIN FOR HER TO BEG ME TO BREAK MY VOWS OR TO CRITICIZE MY LORD AFTER PRAISING HIM SO MANY THOUSAND TIMES BEFORE?
AWAY WITH YOU AND YOUR ADVICE, NURSE. YOU AND MY MOST SECRET THOUGHTS SHALL NEVER MEET AGAIN.
I'LL GO TO THE FRIAR TO FIND A REMEDY.
IF ALL ELSE FAILS, AT LEAST I HAVE THE POWER TO DIE.

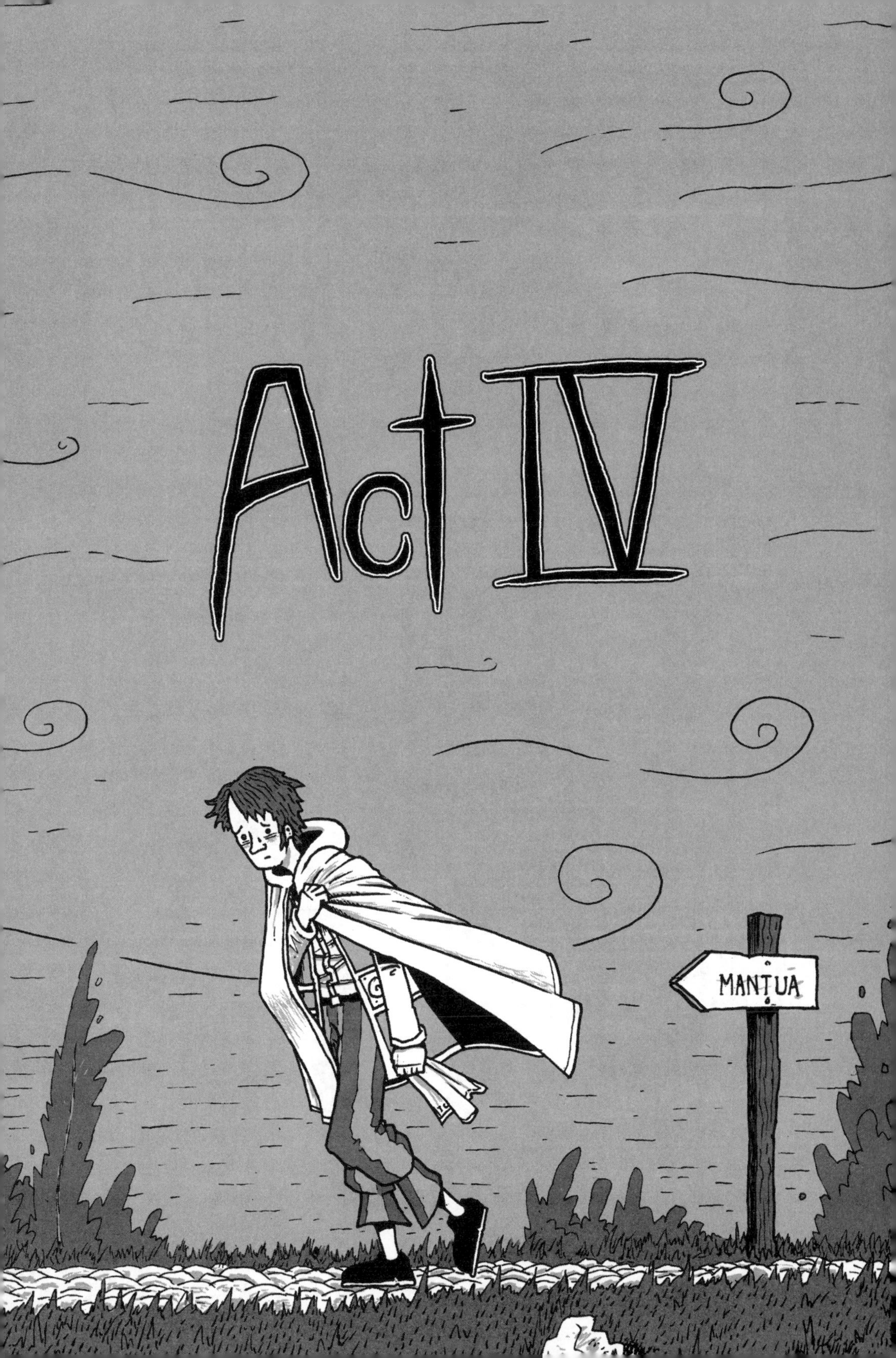
Act IV
MANTUA

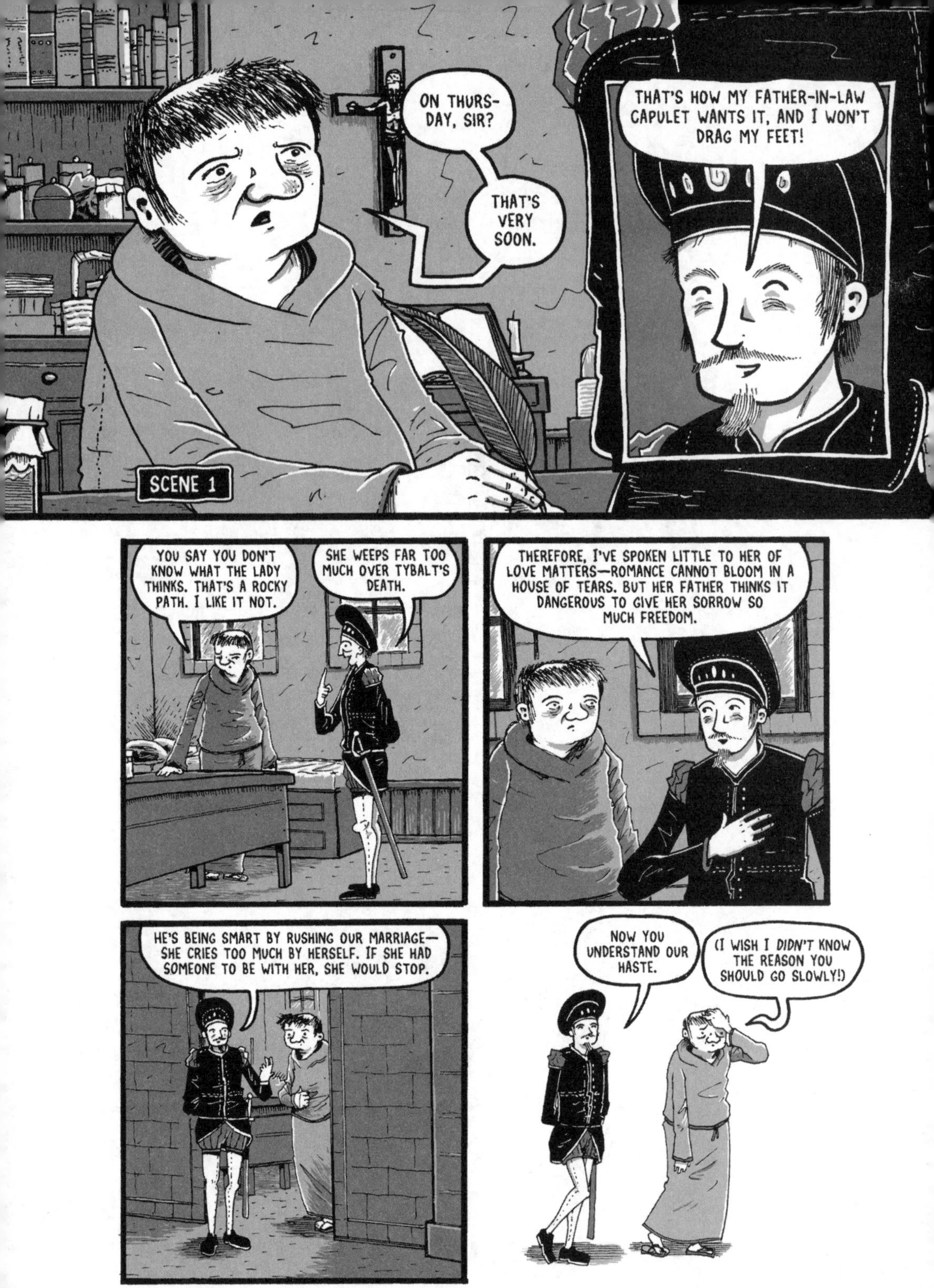
ON THURS-DAY, SIR?
THAT'S VERY SOON.
THAT'S HOW MY FATHER-IN-LAW CAPULET WANTS IT, AND I WON'T DRAG MY FEET!
SCENE 1
YOU SAY YOU DON'T KNOW WHAT THE LADY THINKS. THAT'S A ROCKY PATH. I LIKE IT NOT.
SHE WEEPS FAR TOO MUCH OVER TYBALT'S DEATH.
THEREFORE, I'VE SPOKEN LITTLE TO HER OF LOVE MATTERS—ROMANCE CANNOT BLOOM IN A HOUSE OF TEARS. BUT HER FATHER THINKS IT DANGEROUS TO GIVE HER SORROW SO MUCH FREEDOM.
HE'S BEING SMART BY RUSHING OUR MARRIAGE—SHE CRIES TOO MUCH BY HERSELF. IF SHE HAD SOMEONE TO BE WITH HER, SHE WOULD STOP.
NOW YOU UNDERSTAND OUR HASTE.
(I WISH I *DIDN'T* KNOW THE REASON YOU SHOULD GO SLOWLY!)

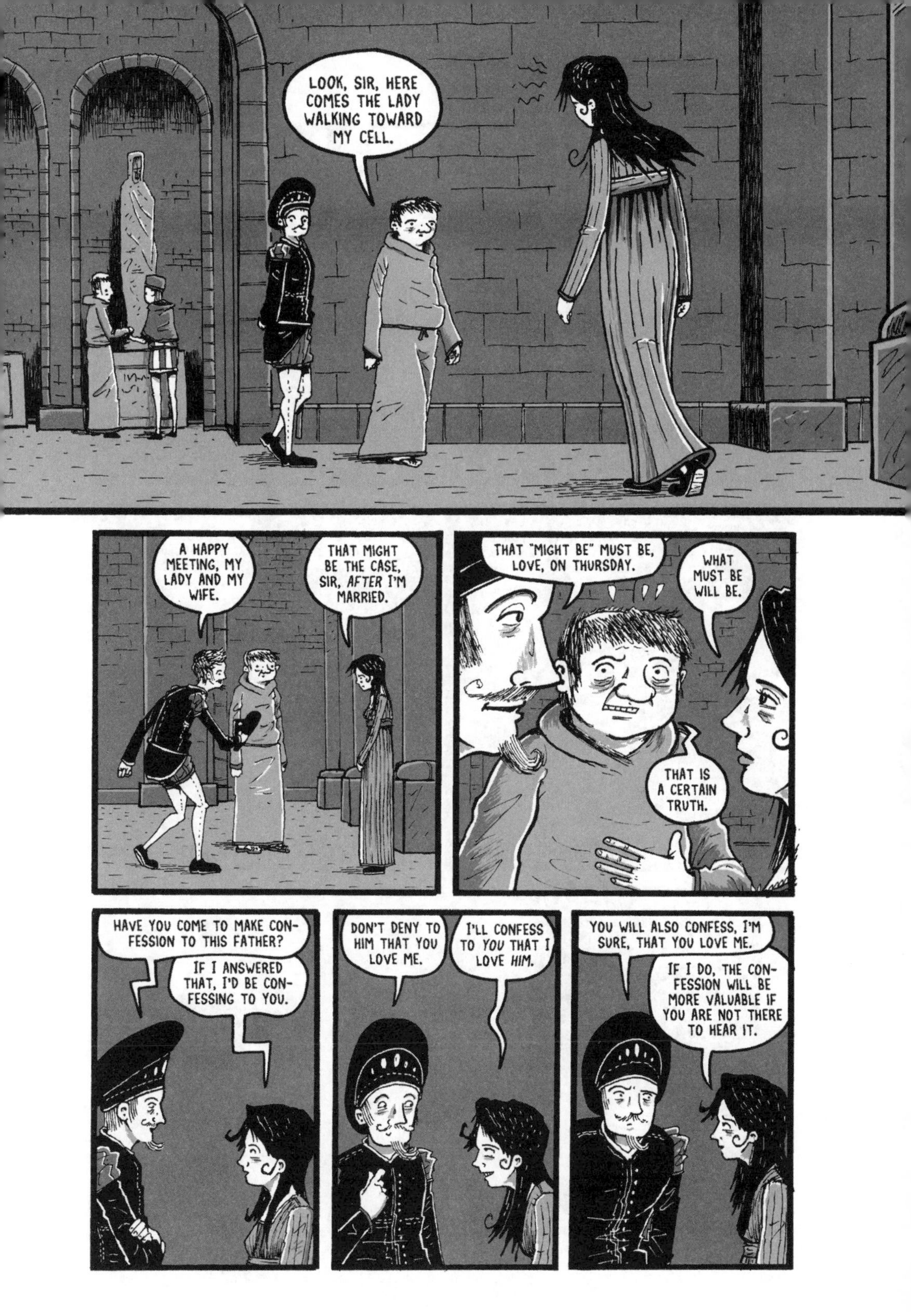
LOOK, SIR, HERE COMES THE LADY WALKING TOWARD MY CELL.
A HAPPY MEETING, MY LADY AND MY WIFE.
THAT MIGHT BE THE CASE, SIR, *AFTER* I'M MARRIED.
THAT "MIGHT BE" MUST BE, LOVE, ON THURSDAY.
WHAT MUST BE WILL BE.
THAT IS A CERTAIN TRUTH.
HAVE YOU COME TO MAKE CONFESSION TO THIS FATHER?
IF I ANSWERED THAT, I'D BE CONFESSING TO YOU.
DON'T DENY TO HIM THAT YOU LOVE ME.
I'LL CONFESS TO *YOU* THAT I LOVE *HIM*.
YOU WILL ALSO CONFESS, I'M SURE, THAT YOU LOVE ME.
IF I DO, THE CONFESSION WILL BE MORE VALUABLE IF YOU ARE NOT THERE TO HEAR IT.

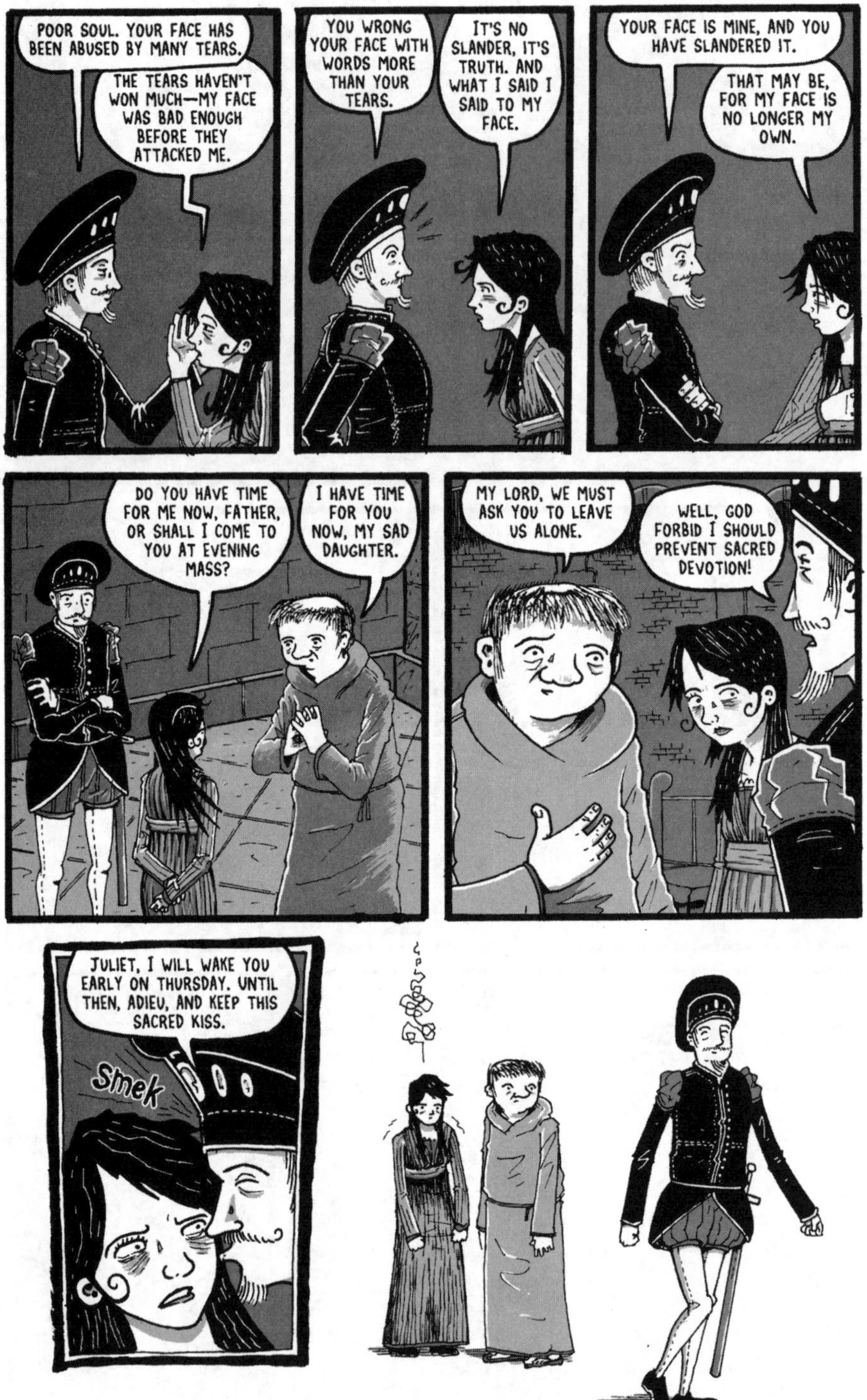
POOR SOUL. YOUR FACE HAS BEEN ABUSED BY MANY TEARS.
THE TEARS HAVEN'T WON MUCH—MY FACE WAS BAD ENOUGH BEFORE THEY ATTACKED ME.
YOU WRONG YOUR FACE WITH WORDS MORE THAN YOUR TEARS.
IT'S NO SLANDER, IT'S TRUTH. AND WHAT I SAID I SAID TO MY FACE.
YOUR FACE IS MINE, AND YOU HAVE SLANDERED IT.
THAT MAY BE, FOR MY FACE IS NO LONGER MY OWN.
DO YOU HAVE TIME FOR ME NOW, FATHER, OR SHALL I COME TO YOU AT EVENING MASS?
I HAVE TIME FOR YOU NOW, MY SAD DAUGHTER.
MY LORD, WE MUST ASK YOU TO LEAVE US ALONE.
WELL, GOD FORBID I SHOULD PREVENT SACRED DEVOTION!
JULIET, I WILL WAKE YOU EARLY ON THURSDAY. UNTIL THEN, ADIEU, AND KEEP THIS SACRED KISS.
Smek

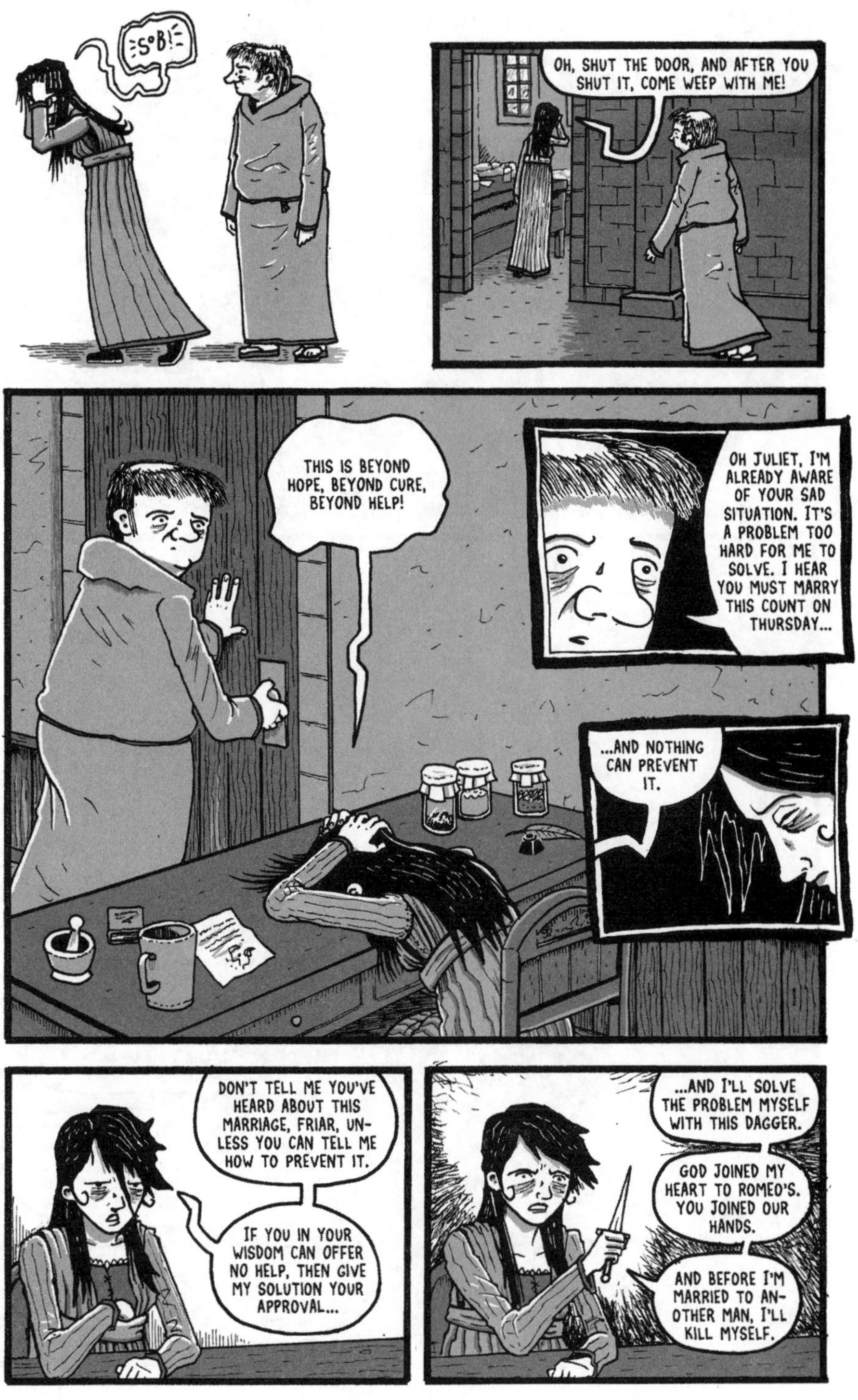
SOB!
OH, SHUT THE DOOR, AND AFTER YOU SHUT IT, COME WEEP WITH ME!
THIS IS BEYOND HOPE, BEYOND CURE, BEYOND HELP!
OH JULIET, I'M ALREADY AWARE OF YOUR SAD SITUATION. IT'S A PROBLEM TOO HARD FOR ME TO SOLVE. I HEAR YOU MUST MARRY THIS COUNT ON THURSDAY...
...AND NOTHING CAN PREVENT IT.
DON'T TELL ME YOU'VE HEARD ABOUT THIS MARRIAGE, FRIAR, UNLESS YOU CAN TELL ME HOW TO PREVENT IT.
IF YOU IN YOUR WISDOM CAN OFFER NO HELP, THEN GIVE MY SOLUTION YOUR APPROVAL...
...AND I'LL SOLVE THE PROBLEM MYSELF WITH THIS DAGGER.
GOD JOINED MY HEART TO ROMEO'S. YOU JOINED OUR HANDS.
AND BEFORE I'M MARRIED TO ANOTHER MAN, I'LL KILL MYSELF.

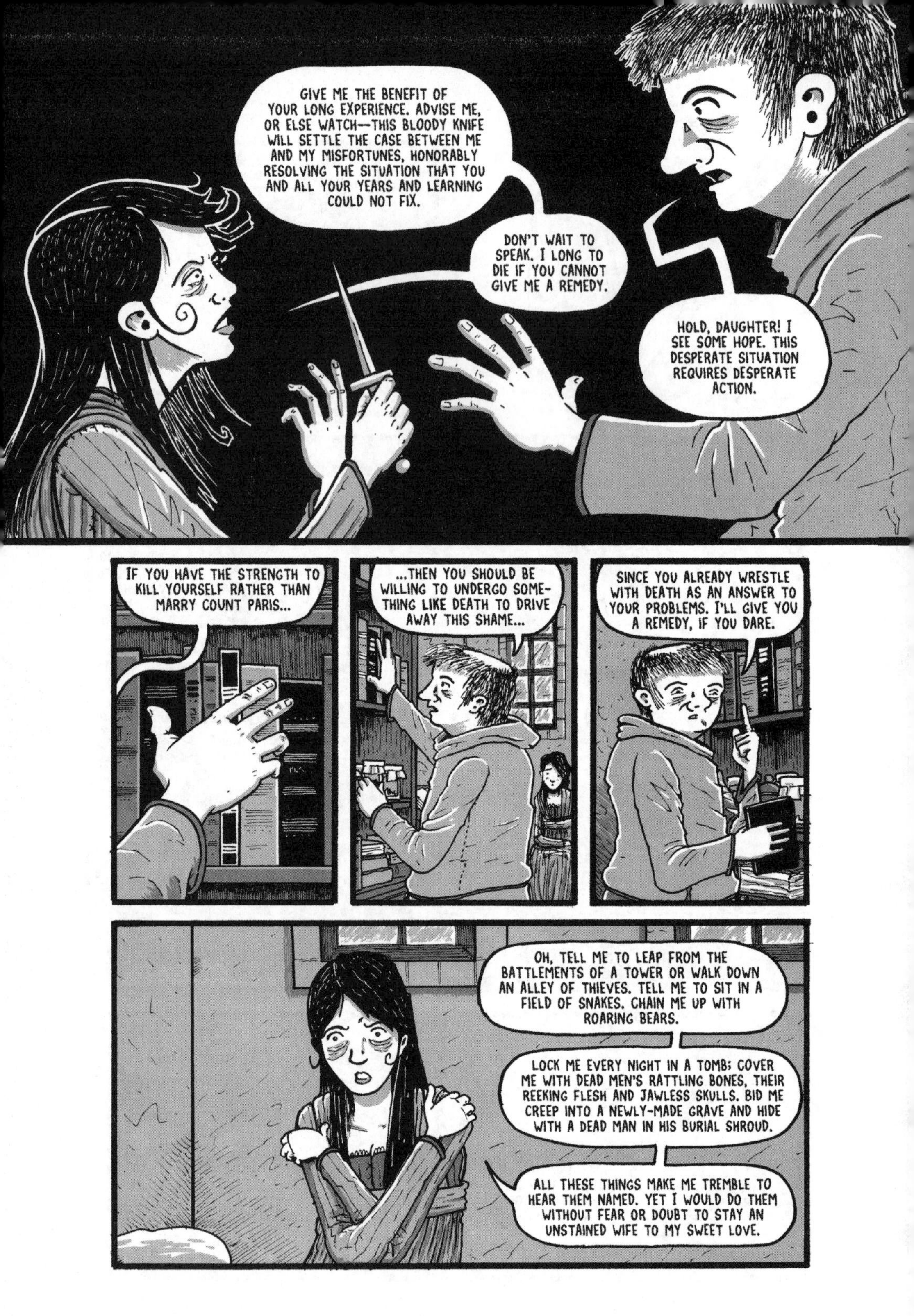
GIVE ME THE BENEFIT OF YOUR LONG EXPERIENCE. ADVISE ME, OR ELSE WATCH—THIS BLOODY KNIFE WILL SETTLE THE CASE BETWEEN ME AND MY MISFORTUNES, HONORABLY RESOLVING THE SITUATION THAT YOU AND ALL YOUR YEARS AND LEARNING COULD NOT FIX.
DON'T WAIT TO SPEAK. I LONG TO DIE IF YOU CANNOT GIVE ME A REMEDY.
HOLD, DAUGHTER! I SEE SOME HOPE. THIS DESPERATE SITUATION REQUIRES DESPERATE ACTION.
IF YOU HAVE THE STRENGTH TO KILL YOURSELF RATHER THAN MARRY COUNT PARIS...
...THEN YOU SHOULD BE WILLING TO UNDERGO SOMETHING LIKE DEATH TO DRIVE AWAY THIS SHAME...
SINCE YOU ALREADY WRESTLE WITH DEATH AS AN ANSWER TO YOUR PROBLEMS. I'LL GIVE YOU A REMEDY, IF YOU DARE.
OH, TELL ME TO LEAP FROM THE BATTLEMENTS OF A TOWER OR WALK DOWN AN ALLEY OF THIEVES. TELL ME TO SIT IN A FIELD OF SNAKES. CHAIN ME UP WITH ROARING BEARS.
LOCK ME EVERY NIGHT IN A TOMB; COVER ME WITH DEAD MEN'S RATTLING BONES, THEIR REEKING FLESH AND JAWLESS SKULLS. BID ME CREEP INTO A NEWLY-MADE GRAVE AND HIDE WITH A DEAD MAN IN HIS BURIAL SHROUD.
ALL THESE THINGS MAKE ME TREMBLE TO HEAR THEM NAMED. YET I WOULD DO THEM WITHOUT FEAR OR DOUBT TO STAY AN UNSTAINED WIFE TO MY SWEET LOVE.

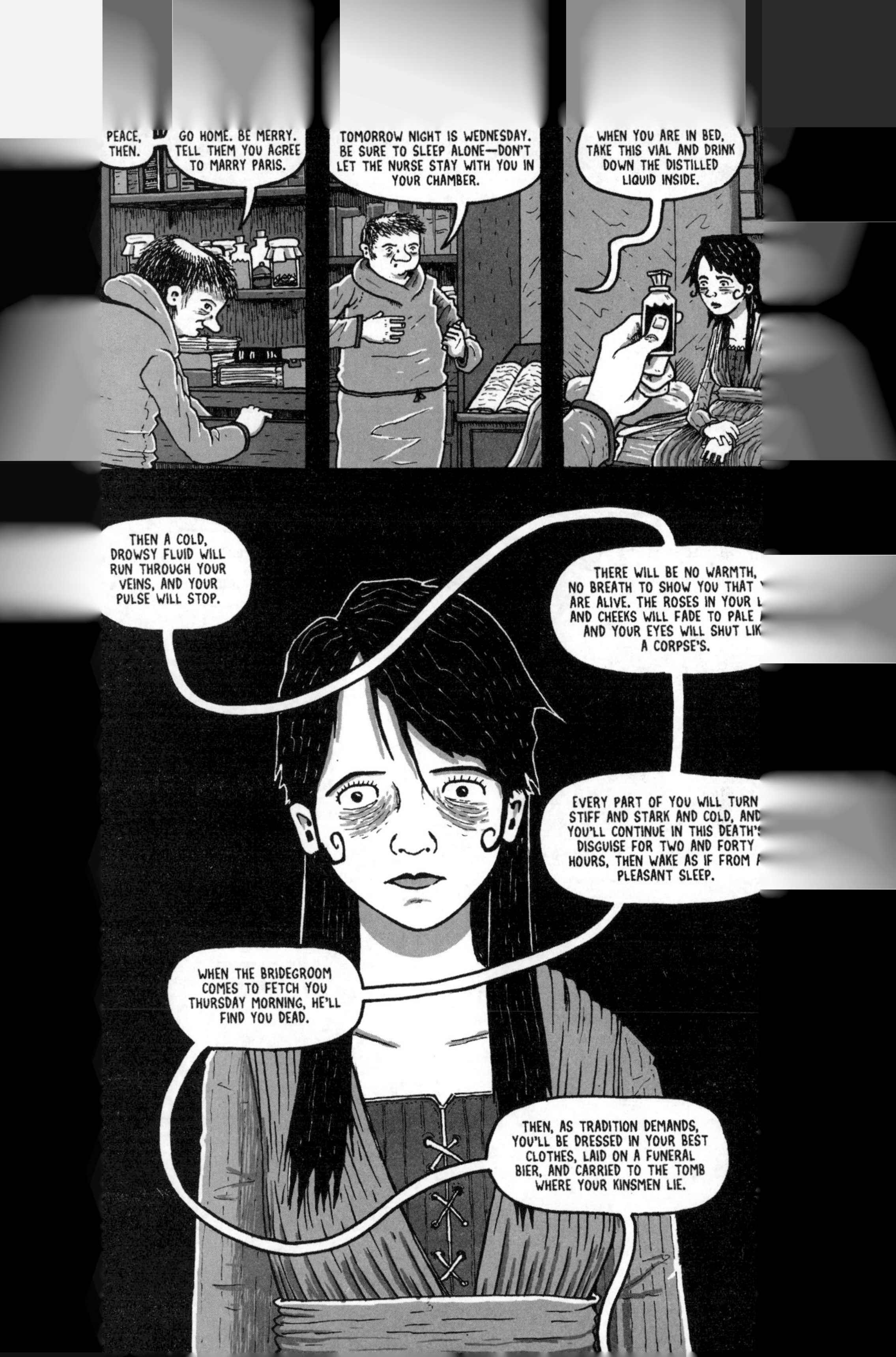

PEACE, THEN.
GO HOME. BE MERRY. TELL THEM YOU AGREE TO MARRY PARIS.
TOMORROW NIGHT IS WEDNESDAY. BE SURE TO SLEEP ALONE—DON'T LET THE NURSE STAY WITH YOU IN YOUR CHAMBER.
WHEN YOU ARE IN BED, TAKE THIS VIAL AND DRINK DOWN THE DISTILLED LIQUID INSIDE.
THEN A COLD, DROWSY FLUID WILL RUN THROUGH YOUR VEINS, AND YOUR PULSE WILL STOP.
THERE WILL BE NO WARMTH, NO BREATH TO SHOW YOU THAT ARE ALIVE. THE ROSES IN YOUR AND CHEEKS WILL FADE TO PALE AND YOUR EYES WILL SHUT A CORPSE'S.
EVERY PART OF YOU WILL TURN STIFF AND STARK AND COLD, AND YOU'LL CONTINUE IN THIS DISGUISE FOR TWO AND FORTY HOURS, THEN WAKE AS IF FROM PLEASANT SLEEP.
WHEN THE BRIDEGROOM COMES TO FETCH YOU THURSDAY MORNING, HE'LL FIND YOU DEAD.
THEN, AS TRADITION DEMANDS, YOU'LL BE DRESSED IN YOUR BEST CLOTHES, LAID ON A FUNERAL BIER, AND CARRIED TO THE TOMB WHERE YOUR KINSMEN LIE.

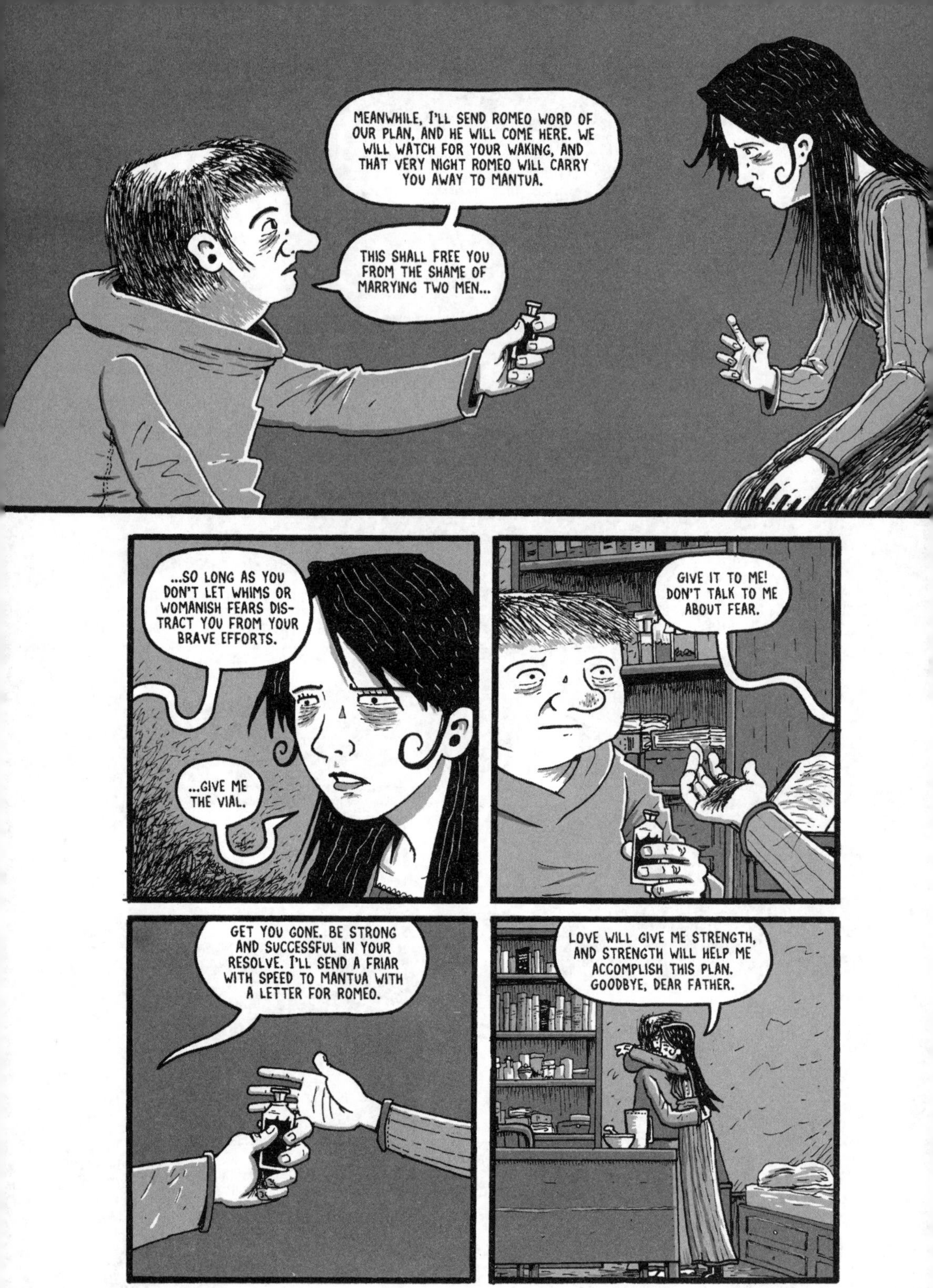
MEANWHILE, I'LL SEND ROMEO WORD OF OUR PLAN, AND HE WILL COME HERE. WE WILL WATCH FOR YOUR WAKING, AND THAT VERY NIGHT ROMEO WILL CARRY YOU AWAY TO MANTUA.
THIS SHALL FREE YOU FROM THE SHAME OF MARRYING TWO MEN...
...SO LONG AS YOU DON'T LET WHIMS OR WOMANISH FEARS DISTRACT YOU FROM YOUR BRAVE EFFORTS.
...GIVE ME THE VIAL.
GIVE IT TO ME! DON'T TALK TO ME ABOUT FEAR.
GET YOU GONE. BE STRONG AND SUCCESSFUL IN YOUR RESOLVE. I'LL SEND A FRIAR WITH SPEED TO MANTUA WITH A LETTER FOR ROMEO.
LOVE WILL GIVE ME STRENGTH, AND STRENGTH WILL HELP ME ACCOMPLISH THIS PLAN. GOODBYE, DEAR FATHER.

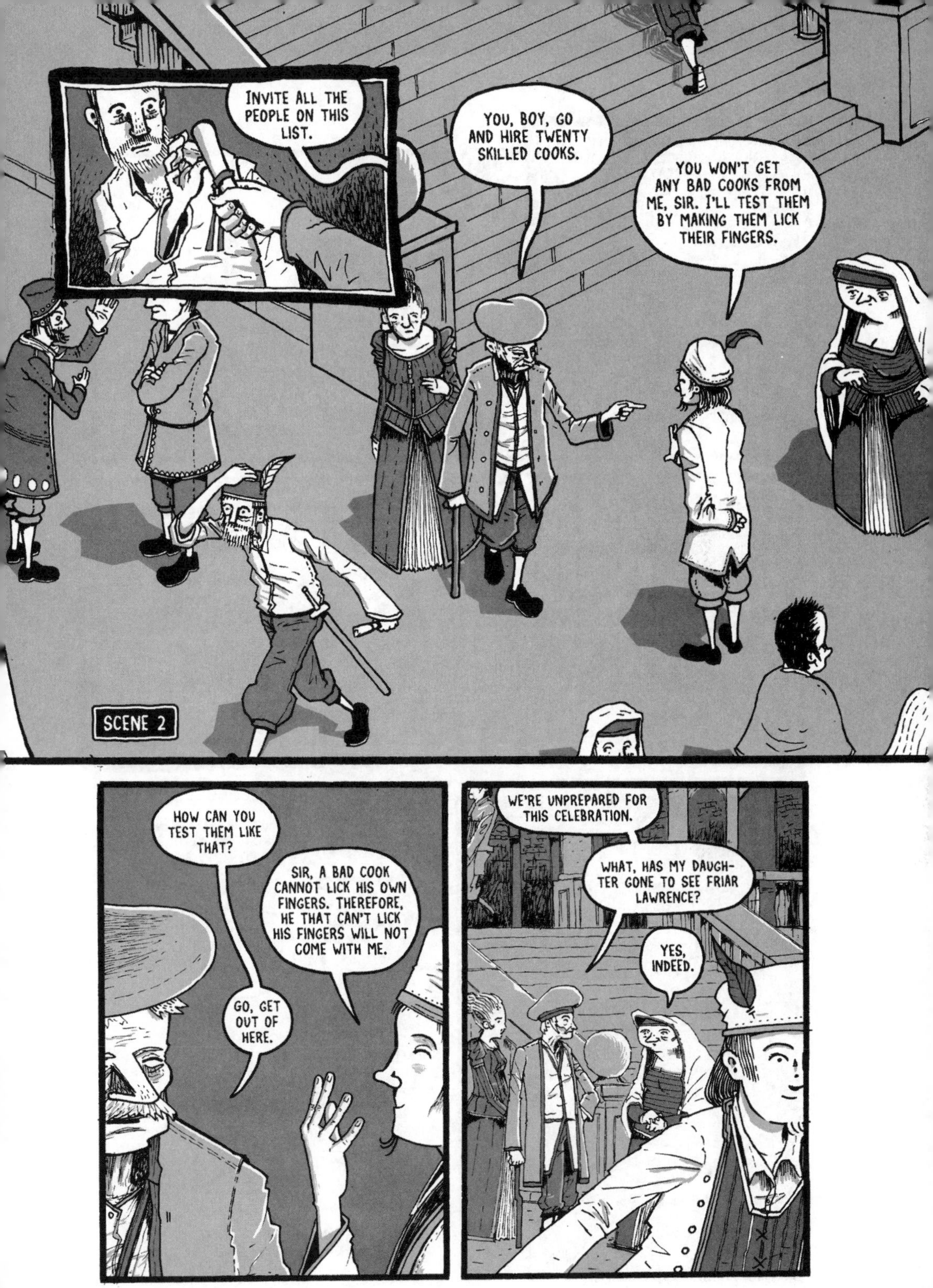
SCENE 2
INVITE ALL THE PEOPLE ON THIS LIST.
YOU, BOY, GO AND HIRE TWENTY SKILLED COOKS.
YOU WON'T GET ANY BAD COOKS FROM ME, SIR. I'LL TEST THEM BY MAKING THEM LICK THEIR FINGERS.
HOW CAN YOU TEST THEM LIKE THAT?
SIR, A BAD COOK CANNOT LICK HIS OWN FINGERS. THEREFORE, HE THAT CAN'T LICK HIS FINGERS WILL NOT COME WITH ME.
GO, GET OUT OF HERE.
WE'RE UNPREPARED FOR THIS CELEBRATION.
WHAT, HAS MY DAUGHTER GONE TO SEE FRIAR LAWRENCE?
YES, INDEED.

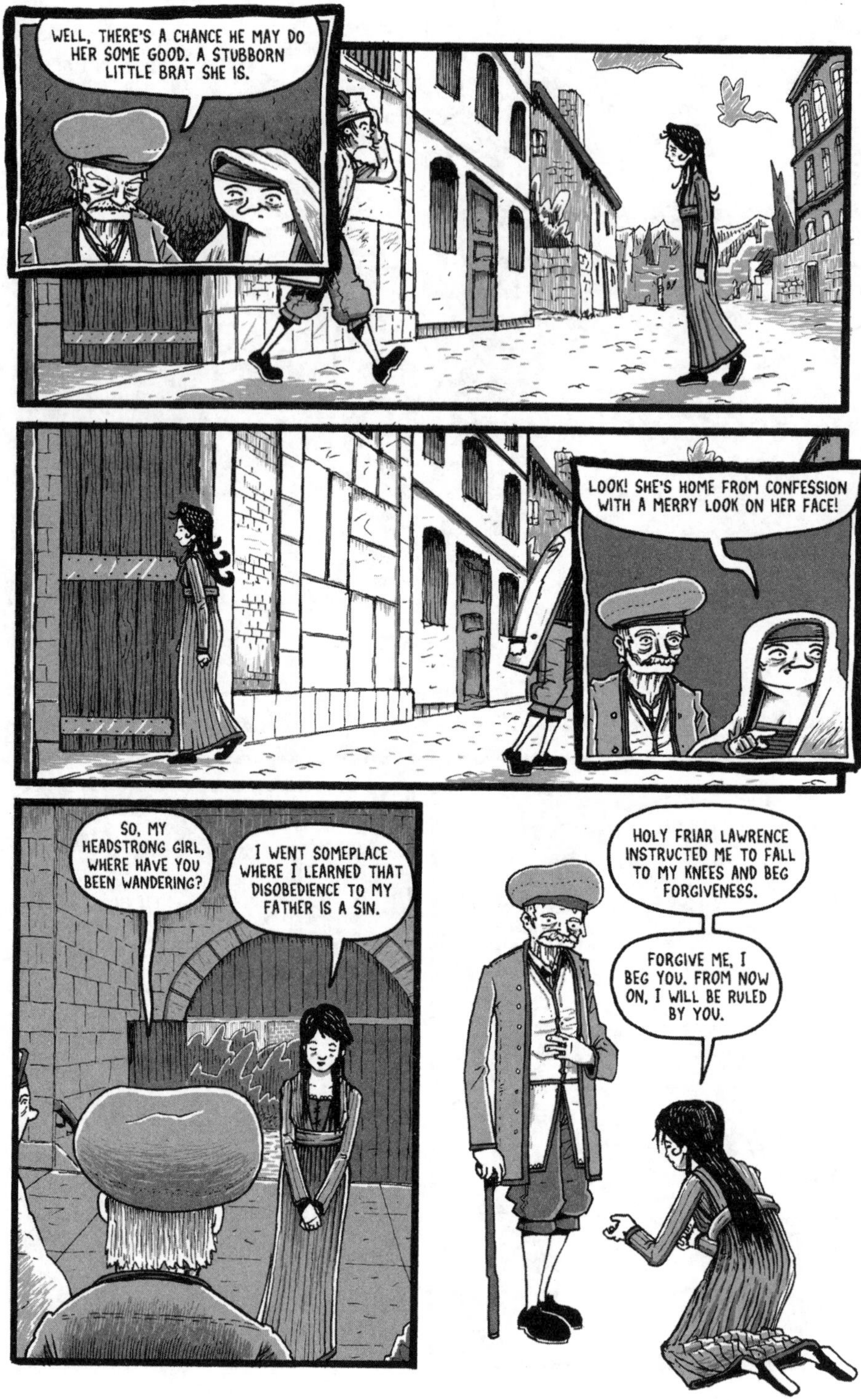
WELL, THERE'S A CHANCE HE MAY DO HER SOME GOOD. A STUBBORN LITTLE BRAT SHE IS.
LOOK! SHE'S HOME FROM CONFESSION WITH A MERRY LOOK ON HER FACE!
SO, MY HEADSTRONG GIRL, WHERE HAVE YOU BEEN WANDERING?
I WENT SOMEPLACE WHERE I LEARNED THAT DISOBEDIENCE TO MY FATHER IS A SIN.
HOLY FRIAR LAWRENCE INSTRUCTED ME TO FALL TO MY KNEES AND BEG FORGIVENESS.
FORGIVE ME, I BEG YOU. FROM NOW ON, I WILL BE RULED BY YOU.

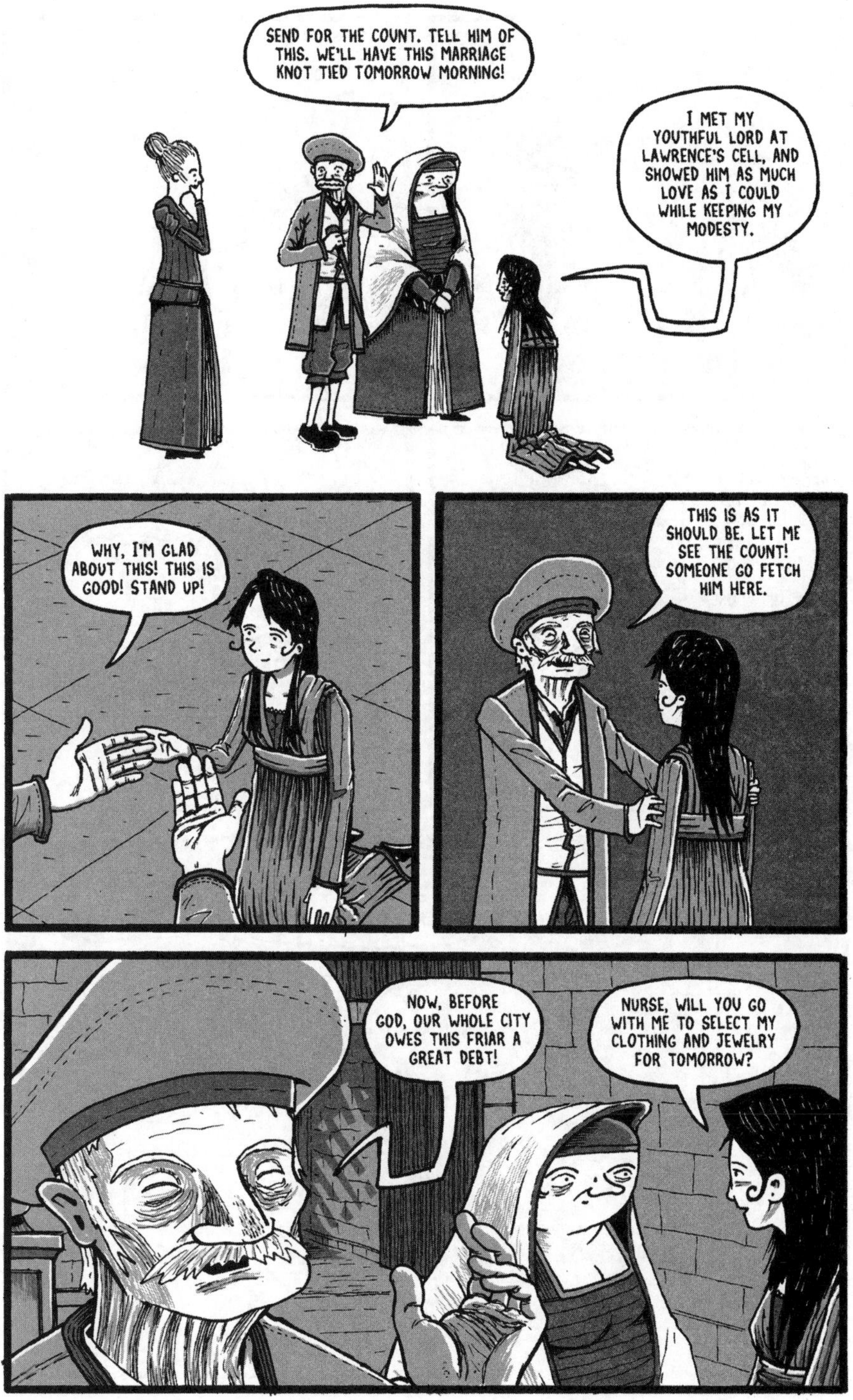
SEND FOR THE COUNT. TELL HIM OF THIS. WE'LL HAVE THIS MARRIAGE KNOT TIED TOMORROW MORNING!
I MET MY YOUTHFUL LORD AT LAWRENCE'S CELL, AND SHOWED HIM AS MUCH LOVE AS I COULD WHILE KEEPING MY MODESTY.
WHY, I'M GLAD ABOUT THIS! THIS IS GOOD! STAND UP!
THIS IS AS IT SHOULD BE. LET ME SEE THE COUNT! SOMEONE GO FETCH HIM HERE.
NOW, BEFORE GOD, OUR WHOLE CITY OWES THIS FRIAR A GREAT DEBT!
NURSE, WILL YOU GO WITH ME TO SELECT MY CLOTHING AND JEWELRY FOR TOMORROW?

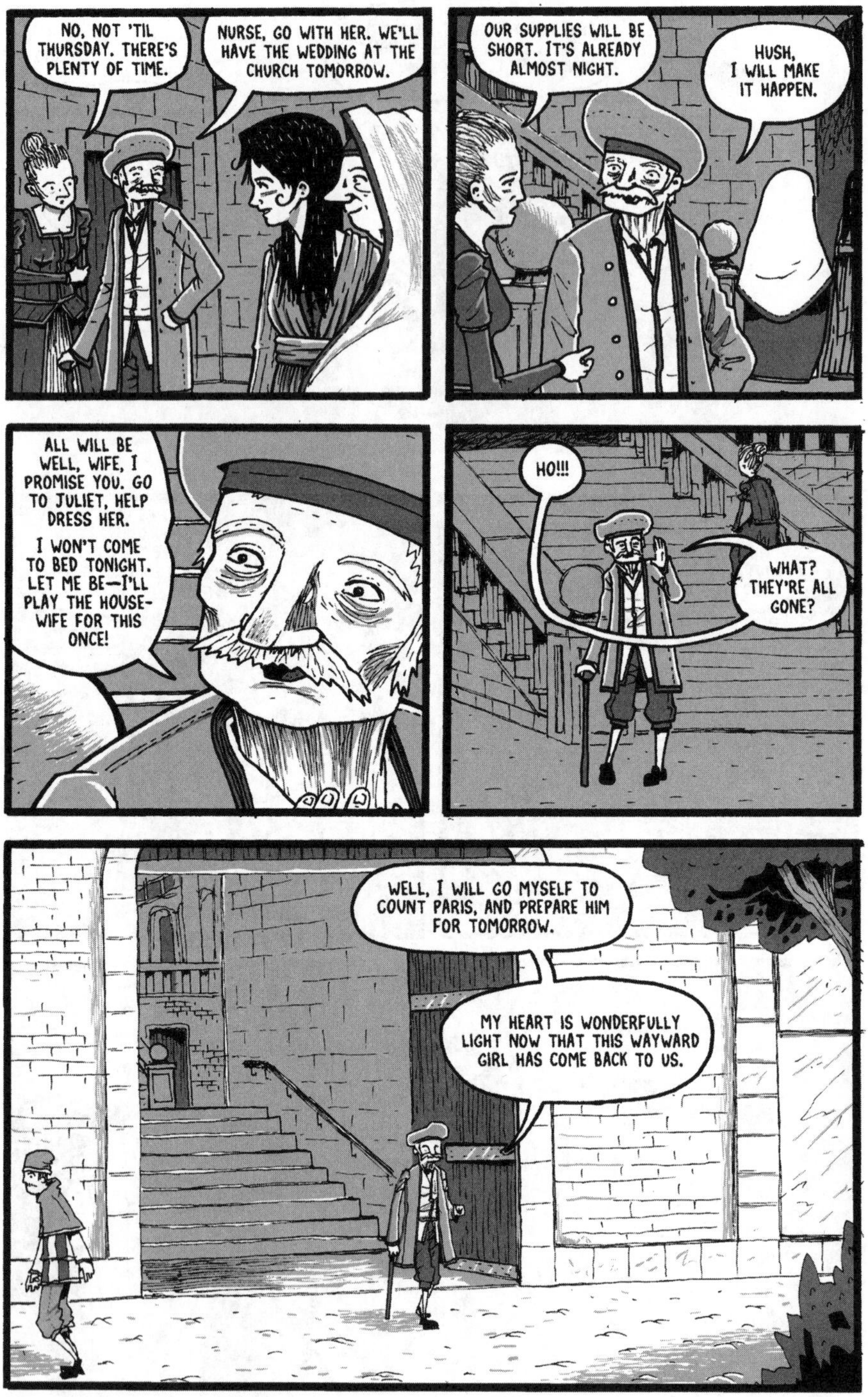

NO, NOT 'TIL THURSDAY. THERE'S PLENTY OF TIME.
NURSE, GO WITH HER. WE'LL HAVE THE WEDDING AT THE CHURCH TOMORROW.
OUR SUPPLIES WILL BE SHORT. IT'S ALREADY ALMOST NIGHT.
HUSH, I WILL MAKE IT HAPPEN.
ALL WILL BE WELL, WIFE, I PROMISE YOU. GO TO JULIET, HELP DRESS HER.
I WON'T COME TO BED TONIGHT. LET ME BE—I'LL PLAY THE HOUSE-WIFE FOR THIS ONCE!
HO!!!
WHAT? THEY'RE ALL GONE?
WELL, I WILL GO MYSELF TO COUNT PARIS, AND PREPARE HIM FOR TOMORROW.
MY HEART IS WONDERFULLY LIGHT NOW THAT THIS WAYWARD GIRL HAS COME BACK TO US.

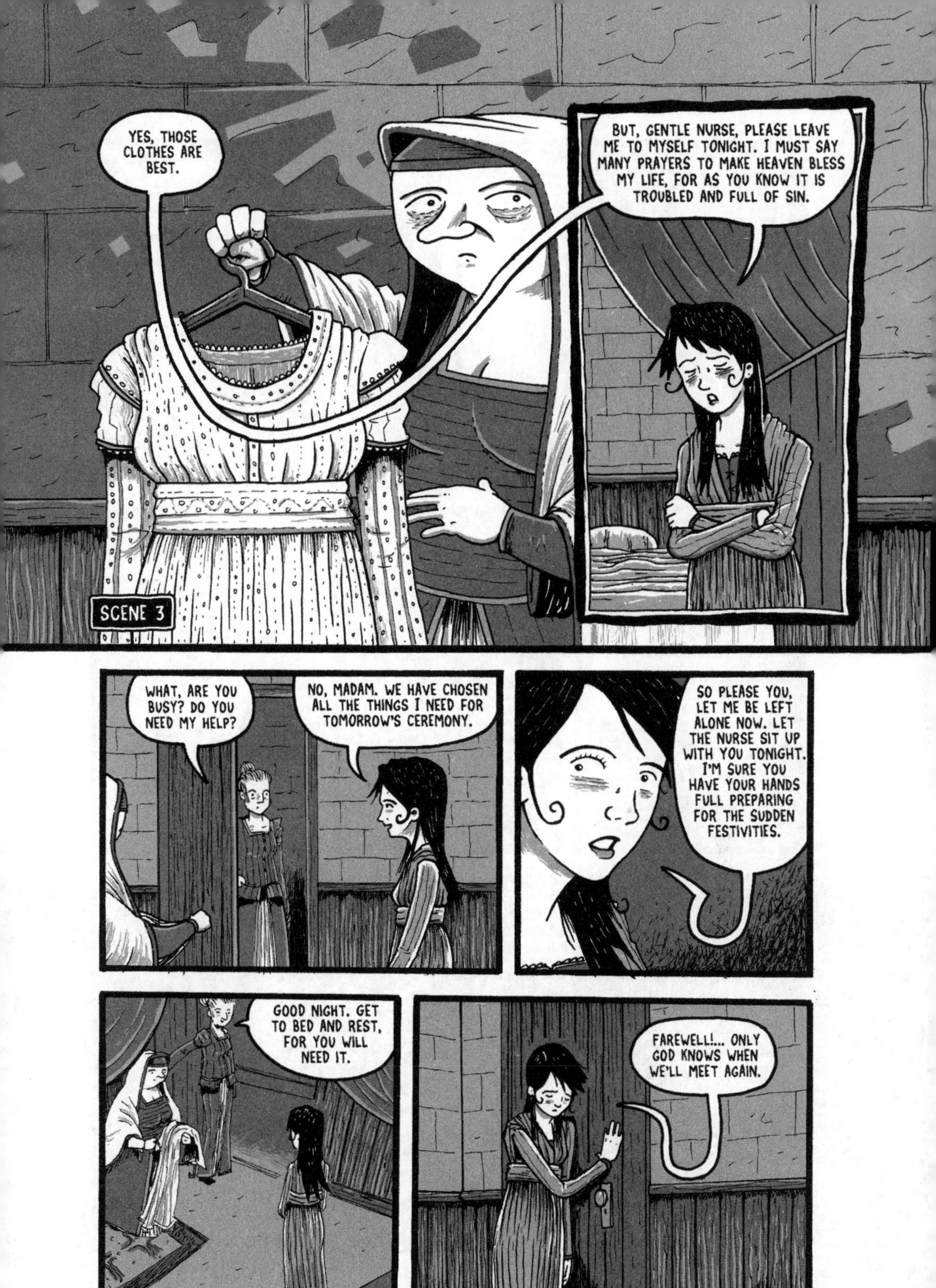
YES, THOSE CLOTHES ARE BEST.
BUT, GENTLE NURSE, PLEASE LEAVE ME TO MYSELF TONIGHT. I MUST SAY MANY PRAYERS TO MAKE HEAVEN BLESS MY LIFE, FOR AS YOU KNOW IT IS TROUBLED AND FULL OF SIN.
SCENE 3
WHAT, ARE YOU BUSY? DO YOU NEED MY HELP?
NO, MADAM. WE HAVE CHOSEN ALL THE THINGS I NEED FOR TOMORROW'S CEREMONY.
SO PLEASE YOU, LET ME BE LEFT ALONE NOW. LET THE NURSE SIT UP WITH YOU TONIGHT. I'M SURE YOU HAVE YOUR HANDS FULL PREPARING FOR THE SUDDEN FESTIVITIES.
GOOD NIGHT. GET TO BED AND REST, FOR YOU WILL NEED IT.
FAREWELL!... ONLY GOD KNOWS WHEN WE'LL MEET AGAIN.

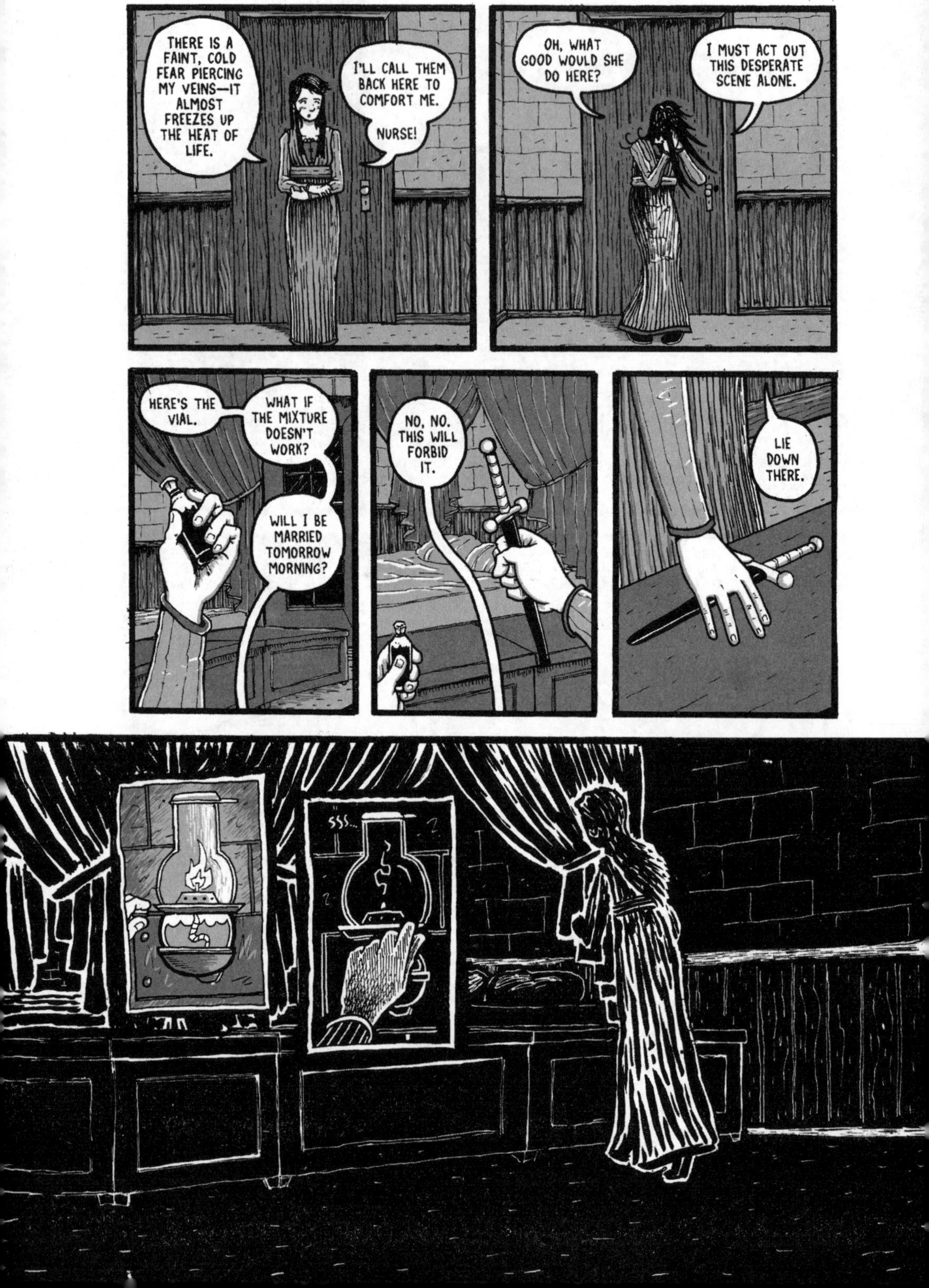
THERE IS A FAINT, COLD FEAR PIERCING MY VEINS—IT ALMOST FREEZES UP THE HEAT OF LIFE.
I'LL CALL THEM BACK HERE TO COMFORT ME.
NURSE!
OH, WHAT GOOD WOULD SHE DO HERE?
I MUST ACT OUT THIS DESPERATE SCENE ALONE.
HERE'S THE VIAL.
WHAT IF THE MIXTURE DOESN'T WORK?
WILL I BE MARRIED TOMORROW MORNING?
NO, NO. THIS WILL FORBID IT.
LIE DOWN THERE.
SSS...

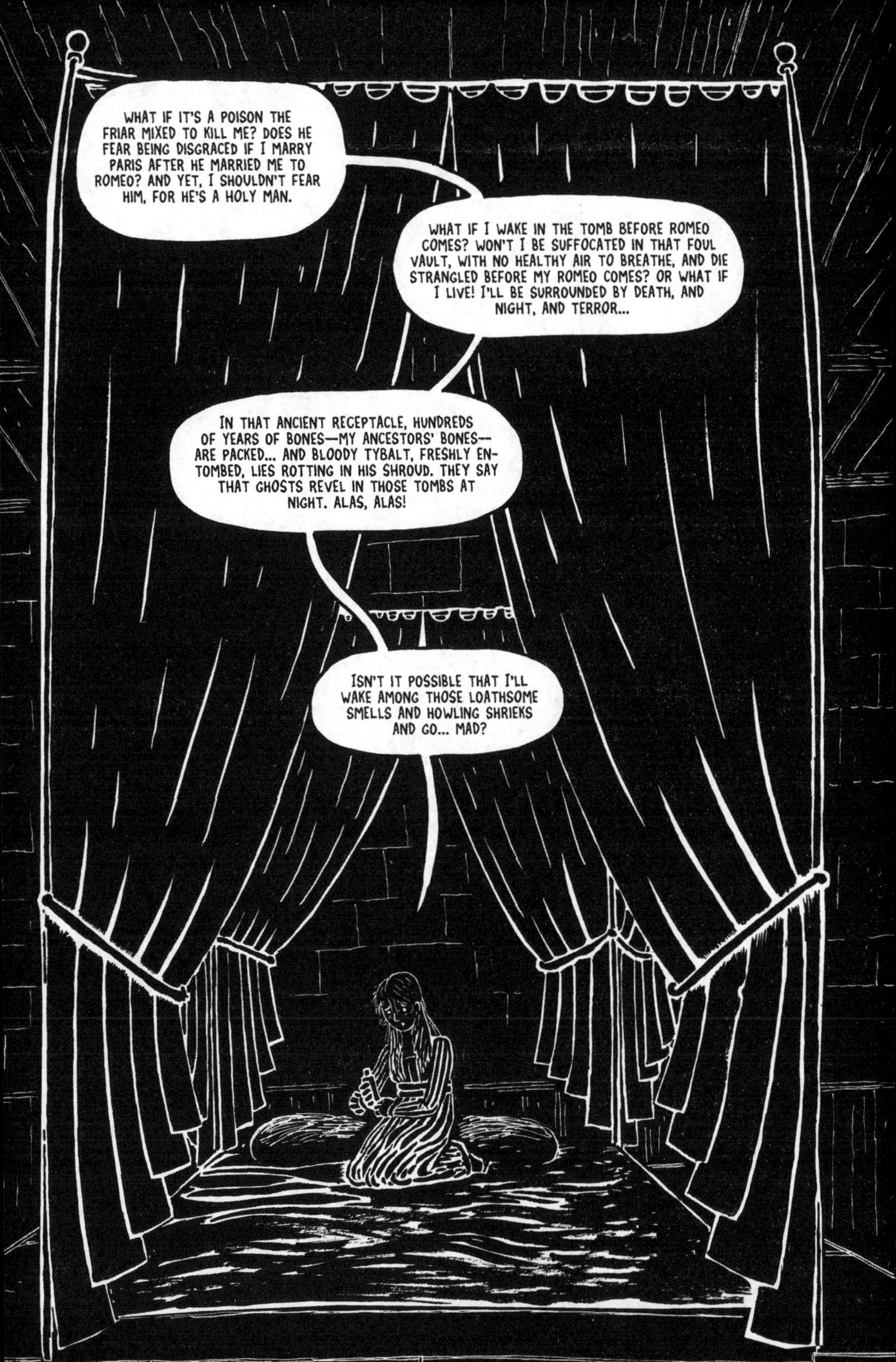
WHAT IF IT'S A POISON THE FRIAR MIXED TO KILL ME? DOES HE FEAR BEING DISGRACED IF I MARRY PARIS AFTER HE MARRIED ME TO ROMEO? AND YET, I SHOULDN'T FEAR HIM, FOR HE'S A HOLY MAN.
WHAT IF I WAKE IN THE TOMB BEFORE ROMEO COMES? WON'T I BE SUFFOCATED IN THAT FOUL VAULT, WITH NO HEALTHY AIR TO BREATHE, AND DIE STRANGLED BEFORE MY ROMEO COMES? OR WHAT IF I LIVE! I'LL BE SURROUNDED BY DEATH, AND NIGHT, AND TERROR...
IN THAT ANCIENT RECEPTACLE, HUNDREDS OF YEARS OF BONES—MY ANCESTORS' BONES—ARE PACKED... AND BLOODY TYBALT, FRESHLY ENTOMBED, LIES ROTTING IN HIS SHROUD. THEY SAY THAT GHOSTS REVEL IN THOSE TOMBS AT NIGHT. ALAS, ALAS!
ISN'T IT POSSIBLE THAT I'LL WAKE AMONG THOSE LOATHSOME SMELLS AND HOWLING SHRIEKS AND GO... MAD?

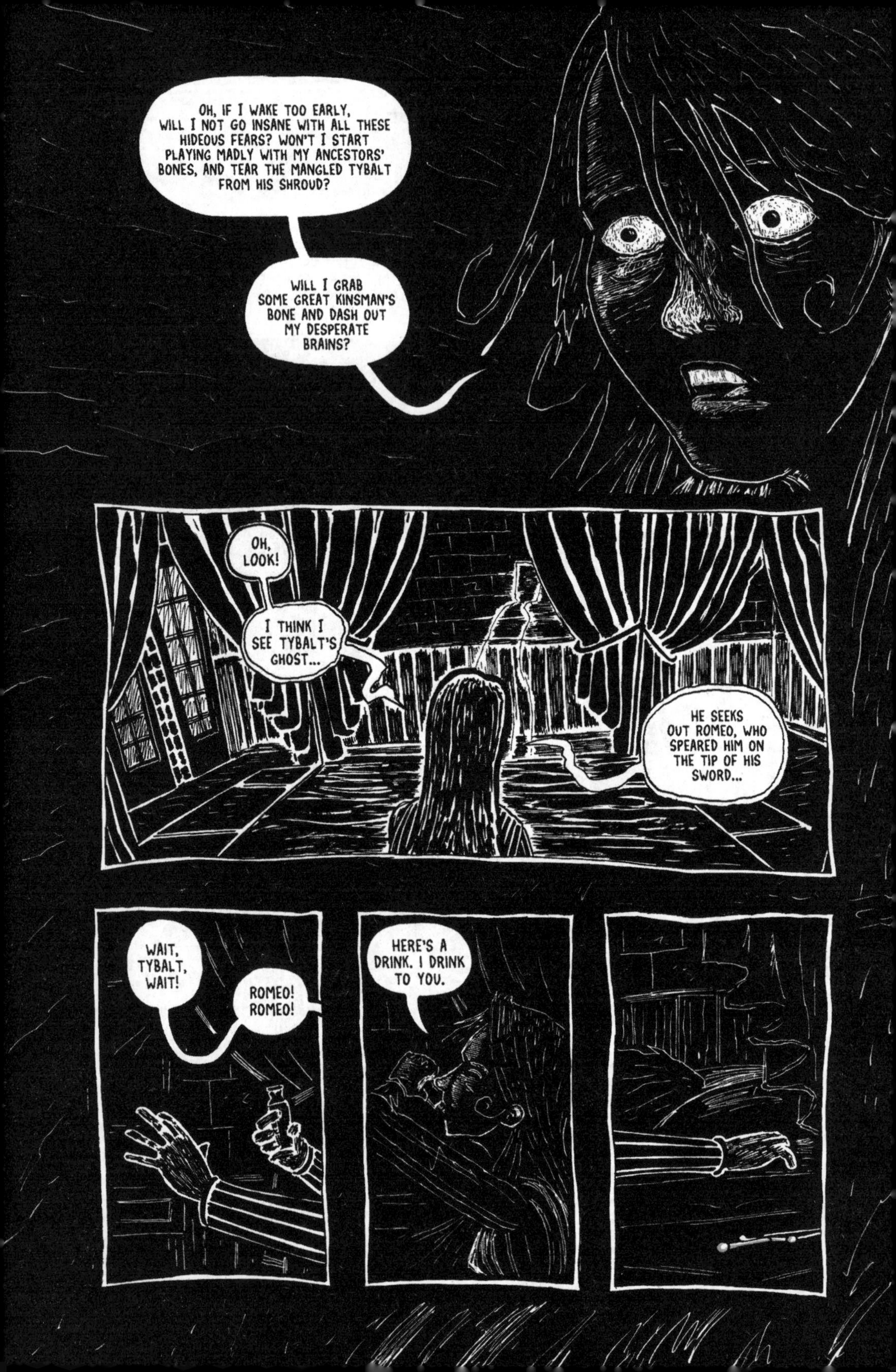
OH, IF I WAKE TOO EARLY, WILL I NOT GO INSANE WITH ALL THESE HIDEOUS FEARS? WON'T I START PLAYING MADLY WITH MY ANCESTORS' BONES, AND TEAR THE MANGLED TYBALT FROM HIS SHROUD?
WILL I GRAB SOME GREAT KINSMAN'S BONE AND DASH OUT MY DESPERATE BRAINS?
OH, LOOK!
I THINK I SEE TYBALT'S GHOST...
HE SEEKS OUT ROMEO, WHO SPEARED HIM ON THE TIP OF HIS SWORD...
WAIT, TYBALT, WAIT!
ROMEO! ROMEO!
HERE'S A DRINK. I DRINK TO YOU.

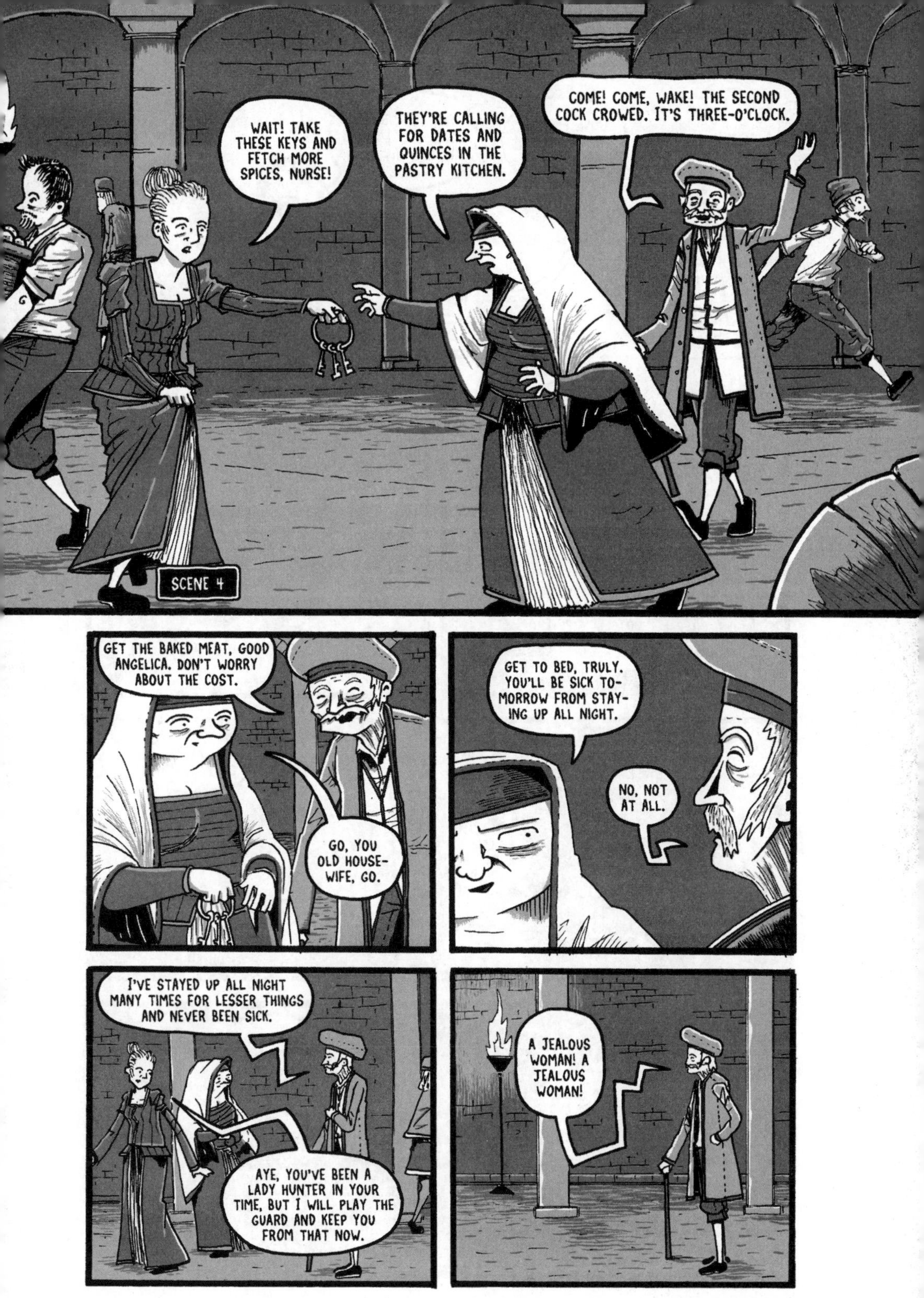
WAIT! TAKE THESE KEYS AND FETCH MORE SPICES, NURSE!
THEY'RE CALLING FOR DATES AND QUINCES IN THE PASTRY KITCHEN.
COME! COME, WAKE! THE SECOND COCK CROWED. IT'S THREE-O'CLOCK.
SCENE 4
GET THE BAKED MEAT, GOOD ANGELICA. DON'T WORRY ABOUT THE COST.
GO, YOU OLD HOUSE-WIFE, GO.
GET TO BED, TRULY. YOU'LL BE SICK TO-MORROW FROM STAY-ING UP ALL NIGHT.
NO, NOT AT ALL.
I'VE STAYED UP ALL NIGHT MANY TIMES FOR LESSER THINGS AND NEVER BEEN SICK.
AYE, YOU'VE BEEN A LADY HUNTER IN YOUR TIME, BUT I WILL PLAY THE GUARD AND KEEP YOU FROM THAT NOW.
A JEALOUS WOMAN! A JEALOUS WOMAN!

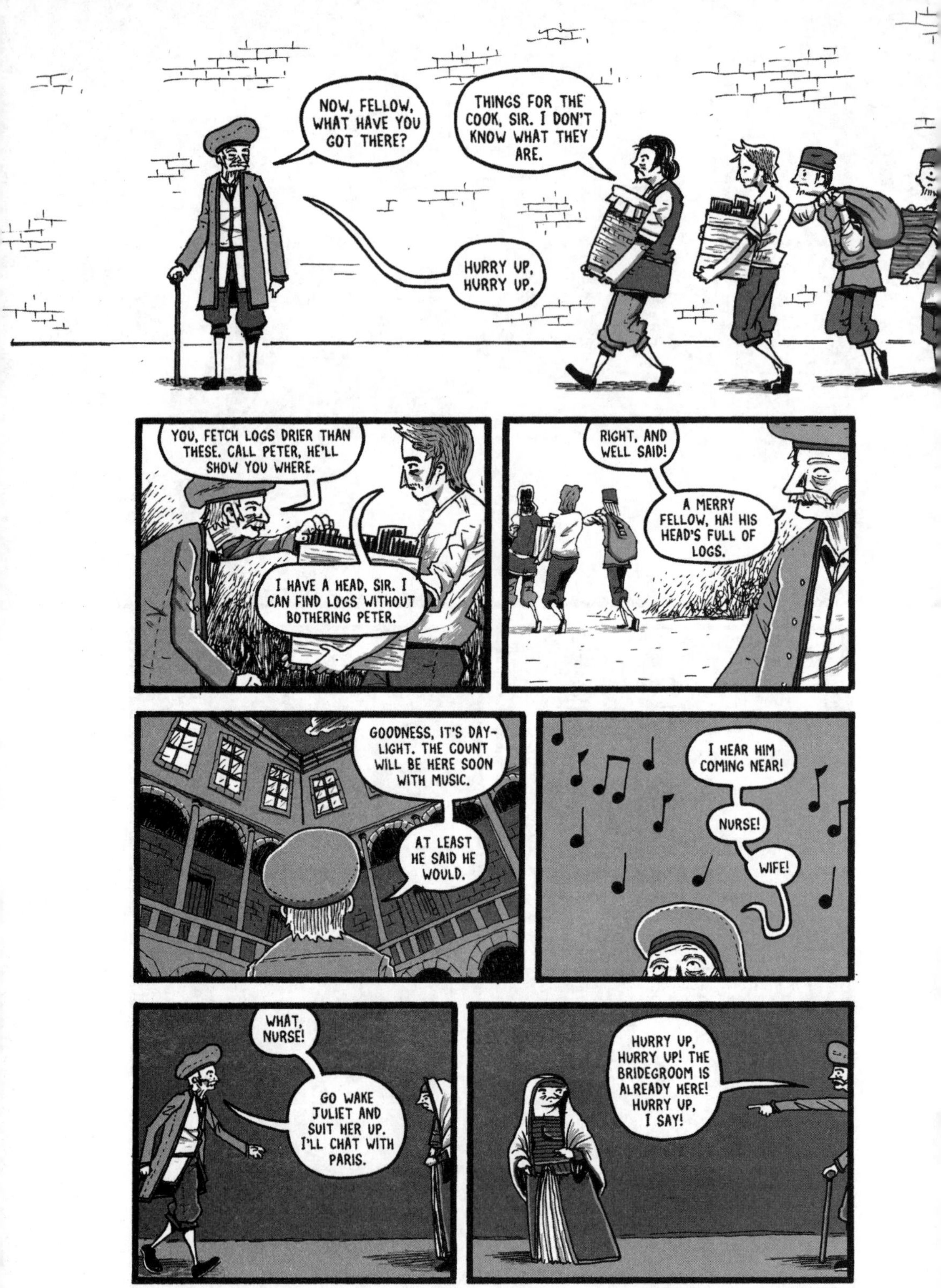
NOW, FELLOW, WHAT HAVE YOU GOT THERE?
THINGS FOR THE COOK, SIR. I DON'T KNOW WHAT THEY ARE.
HURRY UP, HURRY UP.
YOU, FETCH LOGS DRIER THAN THESE. CALL PETER, HE'LL SHOW YOU WHERE.
I HAVE A HEAD, SIR. I CAN FIND LOGS WITHOUT BOTHERING PETER.
RIGHT, AND WELL SAID!
A MERRY FELLOW, HA! HIS HEAD'S FULL OF LOGS.
GOODNESS, IT'S DAYLIGHT. THE COUNT WILL BE HERE SOON WITH MUSIC.
AT LEAST HE SAID HE WOULD.
I HEAR HIM COMING NEAR!
NURSE!
WIFE!
WHAT, NURSE!
GO WAKE JULIET AND SUIT HER UP. I'LL CHAT WITH PARIS.
HURRY UP, HURRY UP! THE BRIDEGROOM IS ALREADY HERE! HURRY UP, I SAY!

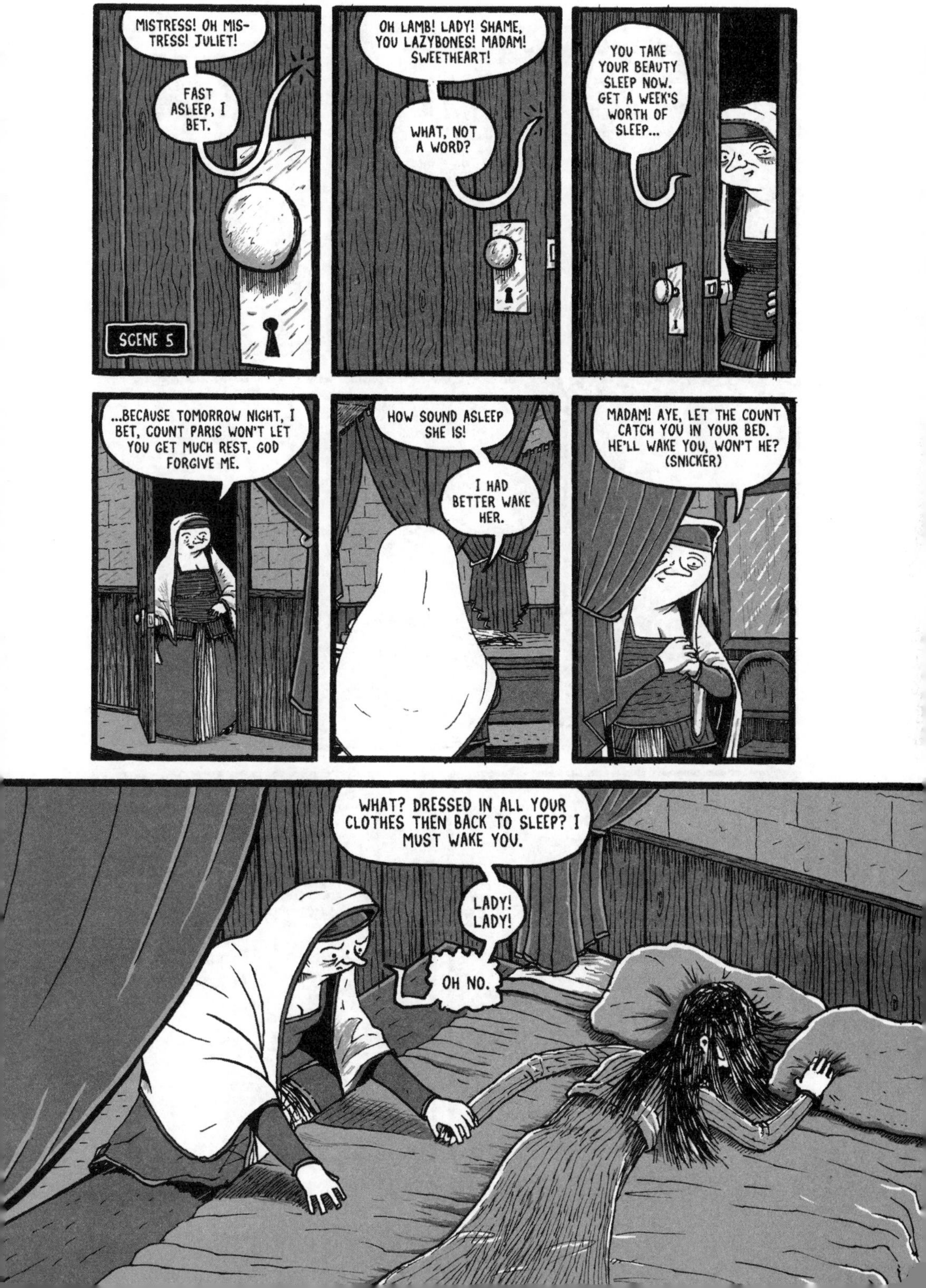
MISTRESS! OH MIS-TRESS! JULIET!
FAST ASLEEP, I BET.
SCENE 5
OH LAMB! LADY! SHAME, YOU LAZYBONES! MADAM! SWEETHEART!
WHAT, NOT A WORD?
YOU TAKE YOUR BEAUTY SLEEP NOW. GET A WEEK'S WORTH OF SLEEP...
...BECAUSE TOMORROW NIGHT, I BET, COUNT PARIS WON'T LET YOU GET MUCH REST, GOD FORGIVE ME.
HOW SOUND ASLEEP SHE IS!
I HAD BETTER WAKE HER.
MADAM! AYE, LET THE COUNT CATCH YOU IN YOUR BED. HE'LL WAKE YOU, WON'T HE? (SNICKER)
WHAT? DRESSED IN ALL YOUR CLOTHES THEN BACK TO SLEEP? I MUST WAKE YOU.
LADY! LADY!
OH NO.

HELP! HELP! MY LADY'S DEAD! OH, CURSE THE DAY I WAS BORN!
OH! GET ME SOME BRANDY!
MY LORD! MILADY!
WHAT'S ALL THE NOISE IN HERE?
OH, SAD DAY!
WHAT'S THE MATTER?
LOOK, LOOK! OH, WRETCHED DAY!
OH ME, OH ME! MY CHILD, MY ONLY LIFE! WAKE UP! LOOK UP, OR I WILL DIE WITH YOU!
HELP! HELP! CALL FOR HELP!

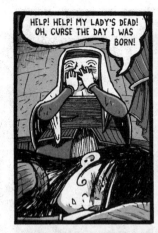

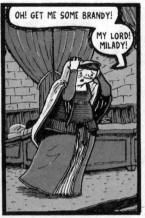

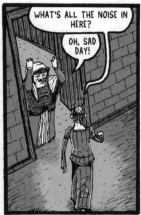

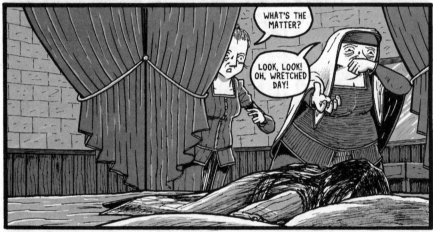

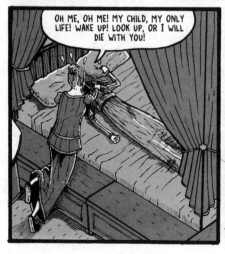

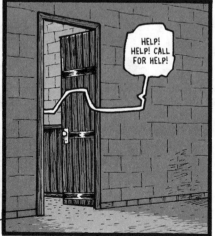

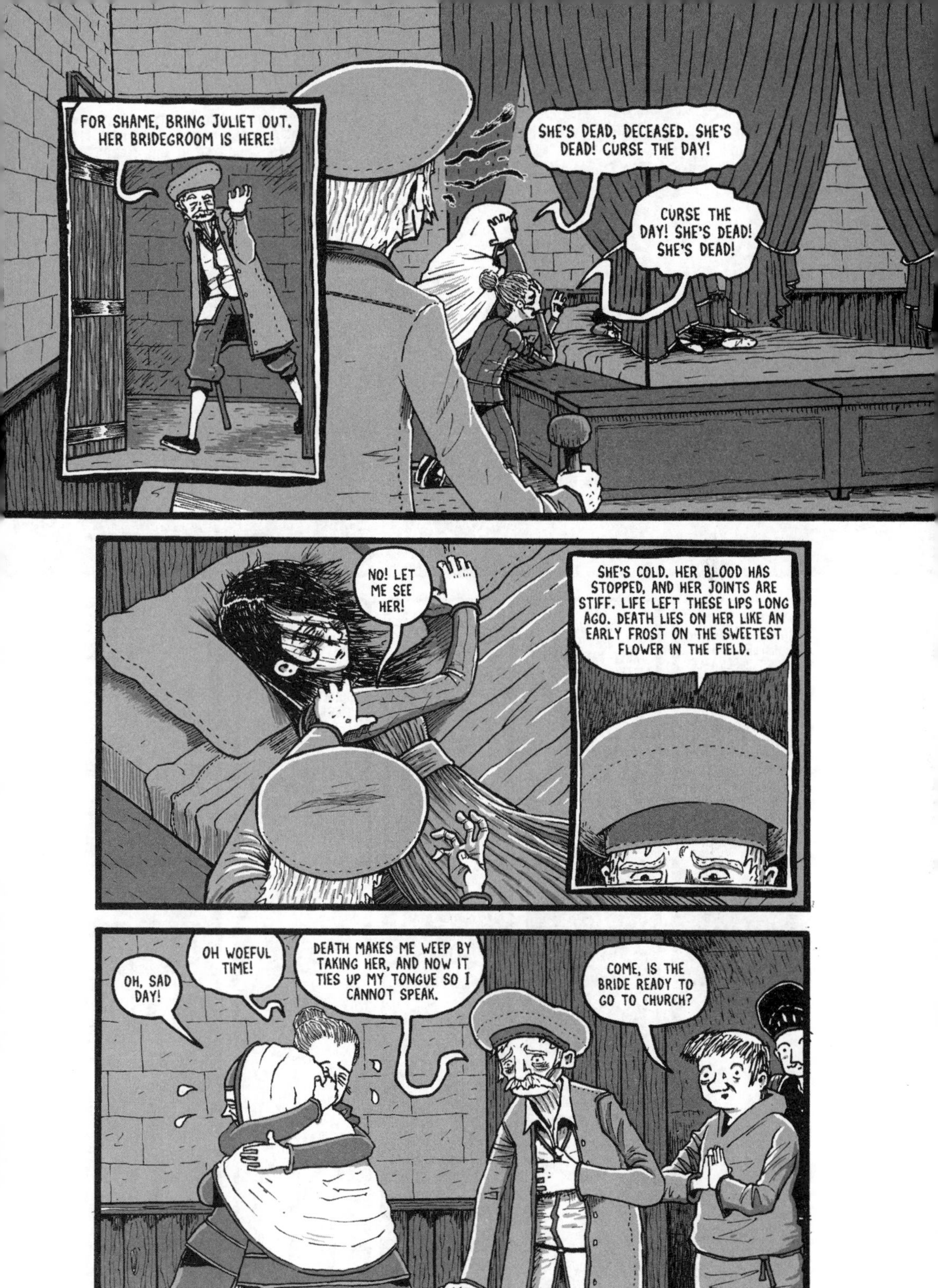

FOR SHAME, BRING JULIET OUT. HER BRIDEGROOM IS HERE!
SHE'S DEAD, DECEASED. SHE'S DEAD! CURSE THE DAY!
CURSE THE DAY! SHE'S DEAD! SHE'S DEAD!
NO! LET ME SEE HER!
SHE'S COLD. HER BLOOD HAS STOPPED, AND HER JOINTS ARE STIFF. LIFE LEFT THESE LIPS LONG AGO. DEATH LIES ON HER LIKE AN EARLY FROST ON THE SWEETEST FLOWER IN THE FIELD.
OH, SAD DAY!
OH WOEFUL TIME!
DEATH MAKES ME WEEP BY TAKING HER, AND NOW IT TIES UP MY TONGUE SO I CANNOT SPEAK.
COME, IS THE BRIDE READY TO GO TO CHURCH?

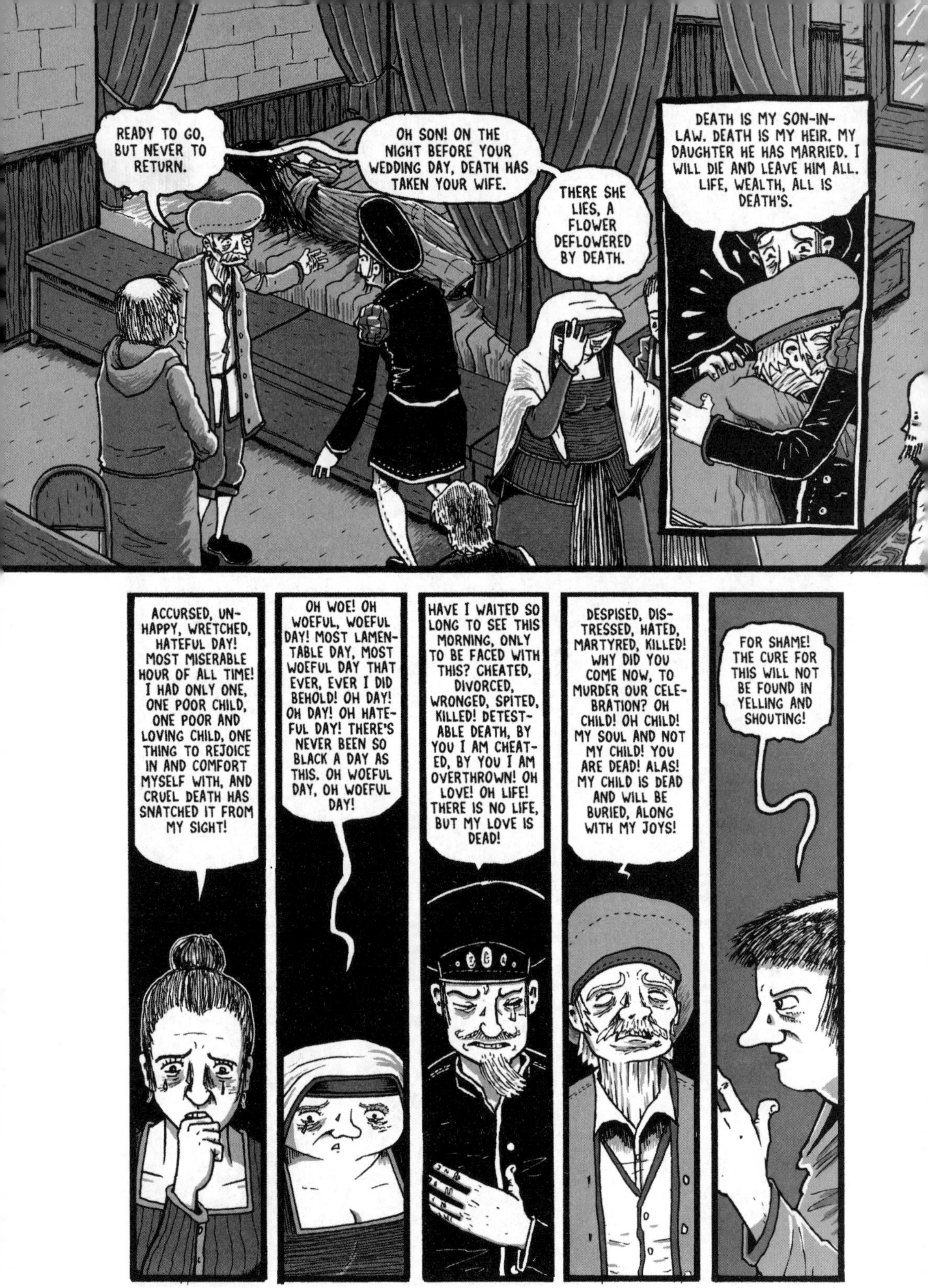
READY TO GO, BUT NEVER TO RETURN.
OH SON! ON THE NIGHT BEFORE YOUR WEDDING DAY, DEATH HAS TAKEN YOUR WIFE.
THERE SHE LIES, A FLOWER DEFLOWERED BY DEATH.
DEATH IS MY SON-IN-LAW. DEATH IS MY HEIR. MY DAUGHTER HE HAS MARRIED. I WILL DIE AND LEAVE HIM ALL. LIFE, WEALTH, ALL IS DEATH'S.
ACCURSED, UNHAPPY, WRETCHED, HATEFUL DAY! MOST MISERABLE HOUR OF ALL TIME! I HAD ONLY ONE, ONE POOR CHILD, ONE POOR AND LOVING CHILD, ONE THING TO REJOICE IN AND COMFORT MYSELF WITH, AND CRUEL DEATH HAS SNATCHED IT FROM MY SIGHT!
OH WOE! OH WOEFUL, WOEFUL DAY! MOST LAMENTABLE DAY, MOST WOEFUL DAY THAT EVER, EVER I DID BEHOLD! OH DAY! OH DAY! OH HATEFUL DAY! THERE'S NEVER BEEN SO BLACK A DAY AS THIS. OH WOEFUL DAY, OH WOEFUL DAY!
HAVE I WAITED SO LONG TO SEE THIS MORNING, ONLY TO BE FACED WITH THIS? CHEATED, DIVORCED, WRONGED, SPITED, KILLED! DETESTABLE DEATH, BY YOU I AM CHEATED, BY YOU I AM OVERTHROWN! OH LOVE! OH LIFE! THERE IS NO LIFE, BUT MY LOVE IS DEAD!
DESPISED, DISTRESSED, HATED, MARTYRED, KILLED! WHY DID YOU COME NOW, TO MURDER OUR CELEBRATION? OH CHILD! OH CHILD! MY SOUL AND NOT MY CHILD! YOU ARE DEAD! ALAS! MY CHILD IS DEAD AND WILL BE BURIED, ALONG WITH MY JOYS!
FOR SHAME! THE CURE FOR THIS WILL NOT BE FOUND IN YELLING AND SHOUTING!

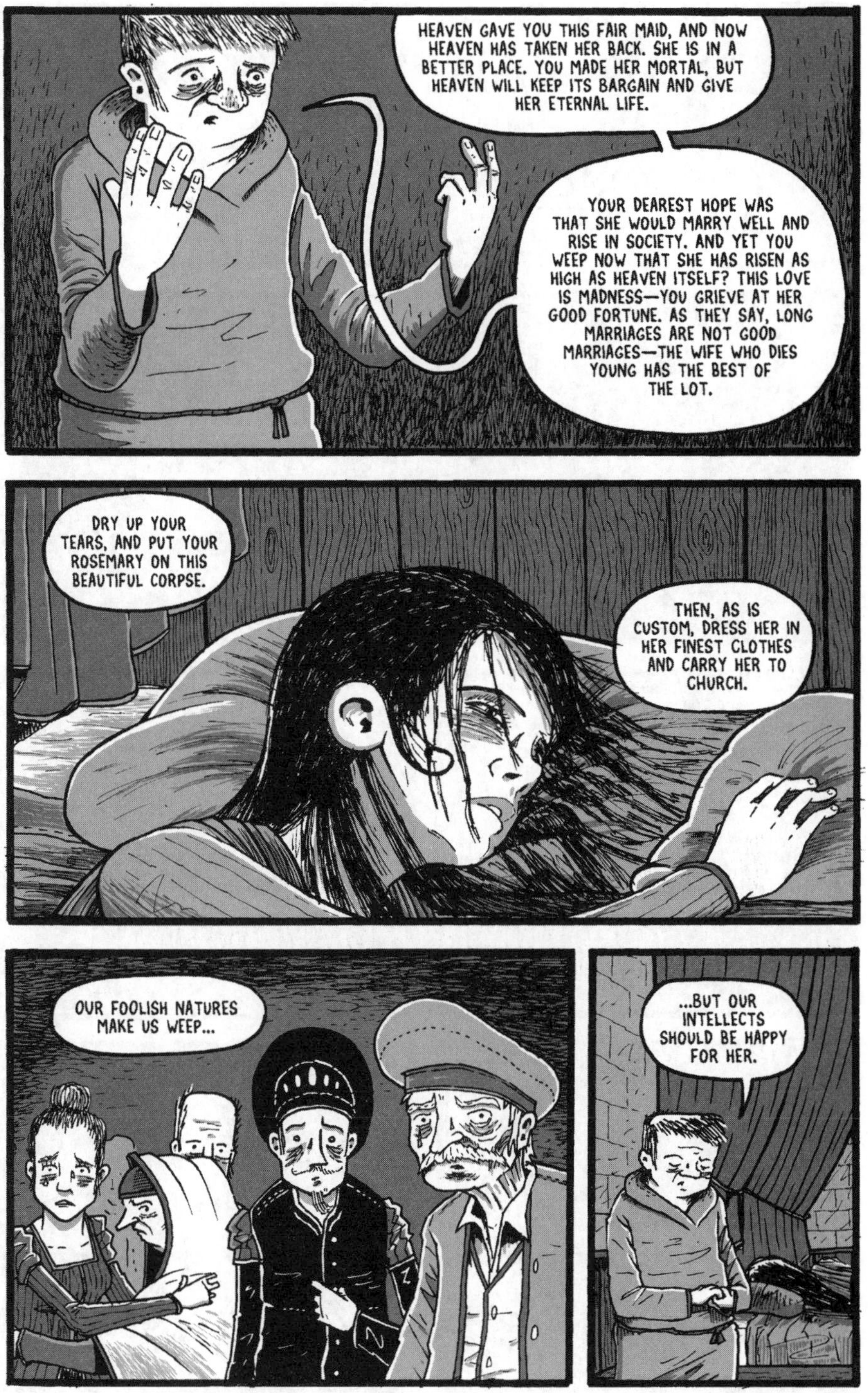
HEAVEN GAVE YOU THIS FAIR MAID, AND NOW HEAVEN HAS TAKEN HER BACK. SHE IS IN A BETTER PLACE. YOU MADE HER MORTAL, BUT HEAVEN WILL KEEP ITS BARGAIN AND GIVE HER ETERNAL LIFE.
YOUR DEAREST HOPE WAS THAT SHE WOULD MARRY WELL AND RISE IN SOCIETY. AND YET YOU WEEP NOW THAT SHE HAS RISEN AS HIGH AS HEAVEN ITSELF? THIS LOVE IS MADNESS—YOU GRIEVE AT HER GOOD FORTUNE. AS THEY SAY, LONG MARRIAGES ARE NOT GOOD MARRIAGES—THE WIFE WHO DIES YOUNG HAS THE BEST OF THE LOT.
DRY UP YOUR TEARS, AND PUT YOUR ROSEMARY ON THIS BEAUTIFUL CORPSE.
THEN, AS IS CUSTOM, DRESS HER IN HER FINEST CLOTHES AND CARRY HER TO CHURCH.
OUR FOOLISH NATURES MAKE US WEEP...
...BUT OUR INTELLECTS SHOULD BE HAPPY FOR HER.

ALL THE THINGS WE PREPARED FOR THIS FESTIVAL MUST NOW SERVE US AT A FUNERAL.

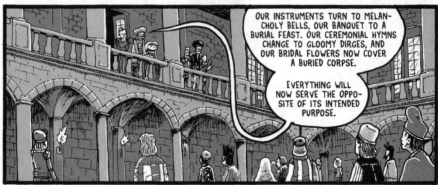

OUR INSTRUMENTS TURN TO MELANCHOLY BELLS, OUR BANQUET TO A BURIAL FEAST. OUR CEREMONIAL HYMNS CHANGE TO GLOOMY DIRGES, AND OUR BRIDAL FLOWERS NOW COVER A BURIED CORPSE.

EVERYTHING WILL NOW SERVE THE OPPOSITE OF ITS INTENDED PURPOSE.

SIR, GO IN, AND MADAM, GO WITH HIM. AND YOU, SIR PARIS. PREPARE YOURSELVES TO FOLLOW THIS FAIR CORPSE TO HER GRAVE.

THE HEAVENS THREATEN AND SCOWL AT YOU FOR SOME PAST SIN. DON'T DISTURB THEM FURTHER BY CROSSING THEM AGAIN.

WELL, WE CAN PUT AWAY OUR PIPES AND BE GONE.

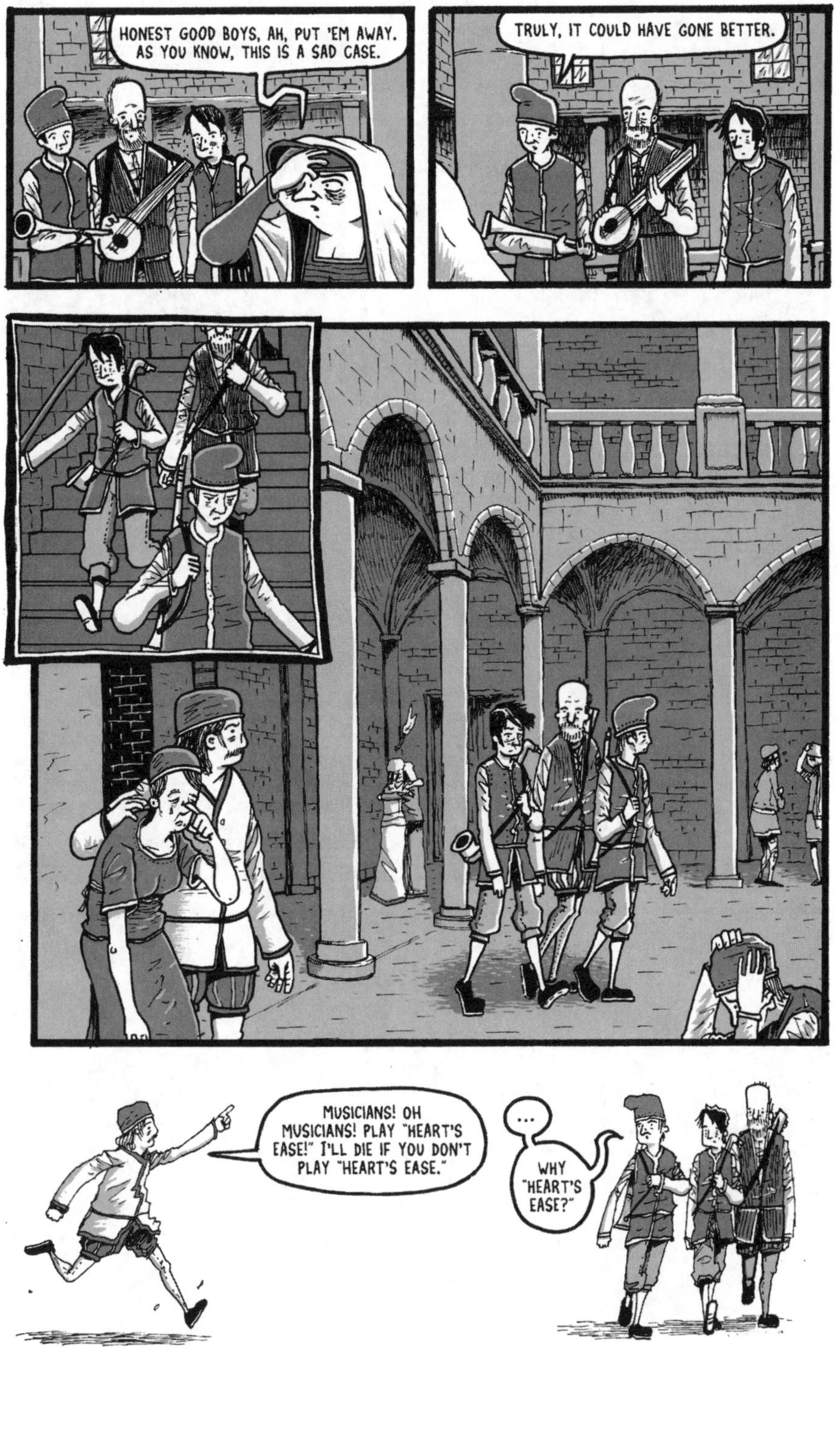
HONEST GOOD BOYS, AH, PUT 'EM AWAY. AS YOU KNOW, THIS IS A SAD CASE.
TRULY, IT COULD HAVE GONE BETTER.
MUSICIANS! OH MUSICIANS! PLAY "HEART'S EASE!" I'LL DIE IF YOU DON'T PLAY "HEART'S EASE."
...
WHY "HEART'S EASE?"

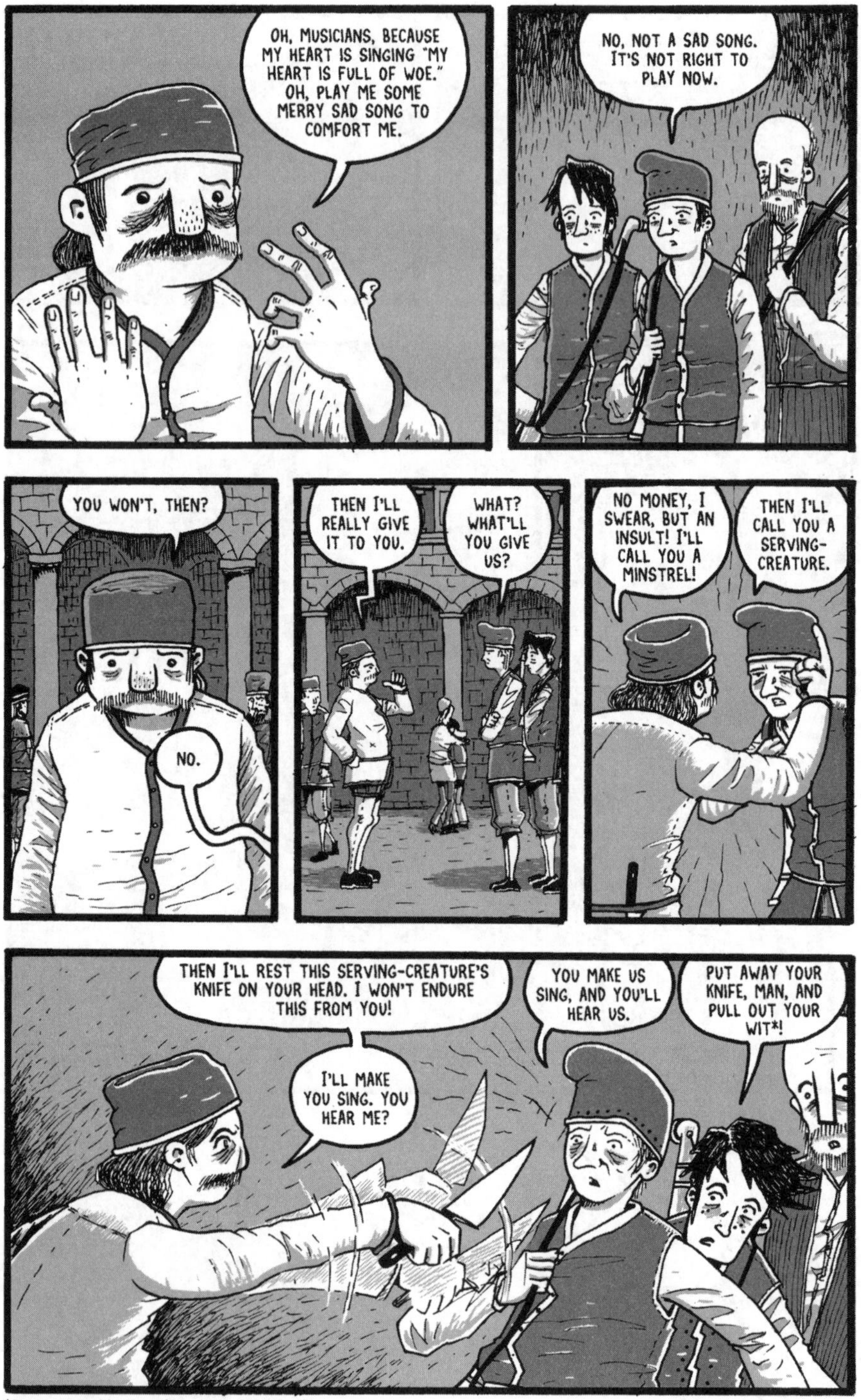
OH, MUSICIANS, BECAUSE MY HEART IS SINGING "MY HEART IS FULL OF WOE." OH, PLAY ME SOME MERRY SAD SONG TO COMFORT ME.
NO, NOT A SAD SONG. IT'S NOT RIGHT TO PLAY NOW.
YOU WON'T, THEN?
NO.
THEN I'LL REALLY GIVE IT TO YOU.
WHAT? WHAT'LL YOU GIVE US?
NO MONEY, I SWEAR, BUT AN INSULT! I'LL CALL YOU A MINSTREL!
THEN I'LL CALL YOU A SERVING-CREATURE.
THEN I'LL REST THIS SERVING-CREATURE'S KNIFE ON YOUR HEAD. I WON'T ENDURE THIS FROM YOU!
I'LL MAKE YOU SING. YOU HEAR ME?
YOU MAKE US SING, AND YOU'LL HEAR US.
PUT AWAY YOUR KNIFE, MAN, AND PULL OUT YOUR WIT*!

*"PULL OUT YOUR WIT!" = "ACT SENSIBLY!"

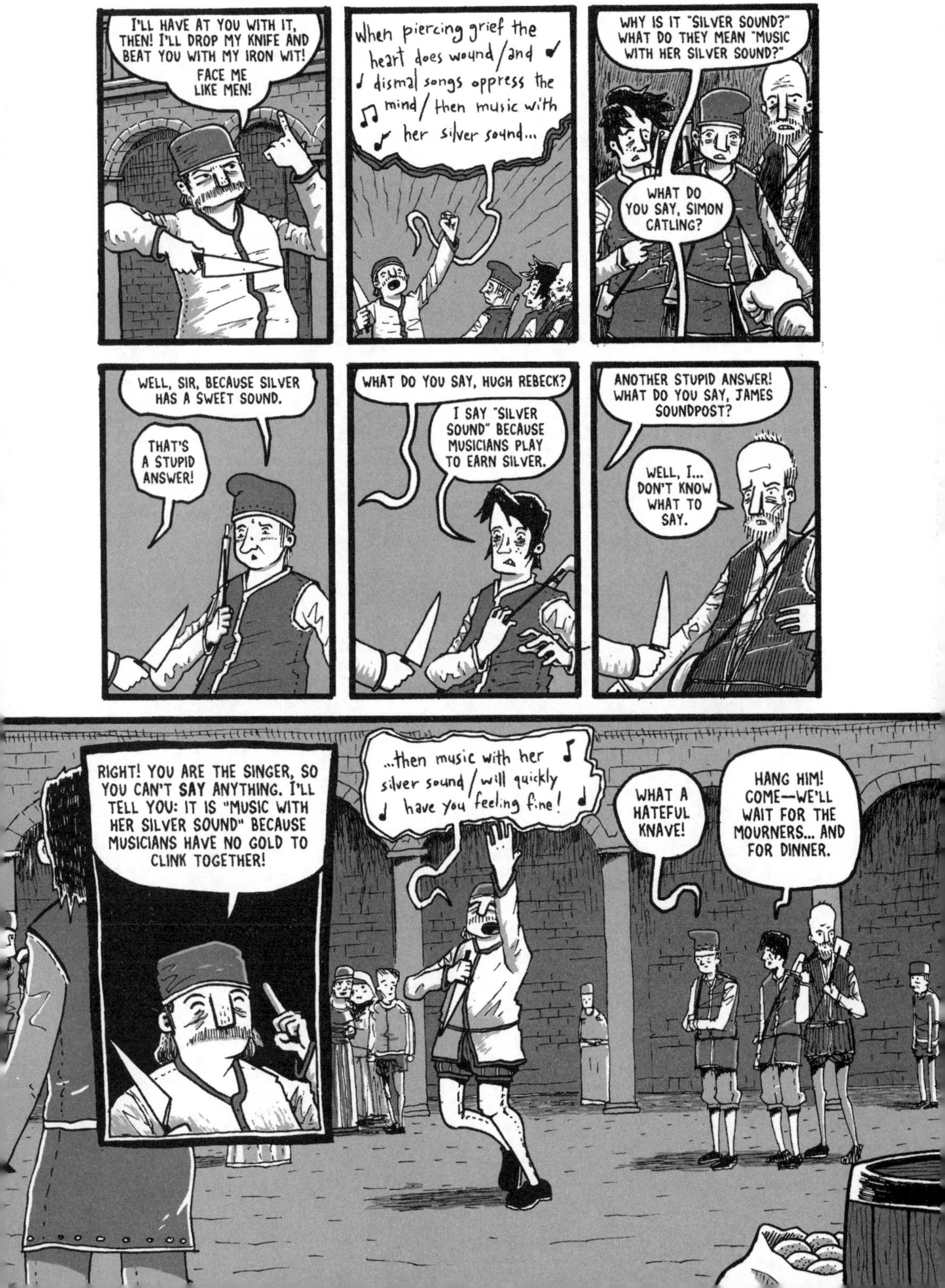
I'LL HAVE AT YOU WITH IT, THEN! I'LL DROP MY KNIFE AND BEAT YOU WITH MY IRON WIT!
FACE ME LIKE MEN!
When piercing grief the heart does wound / and dismal songs oppress the mind / then music with her silver sound...
WHY IS IT "SILVER SOUND?" WHAT DO THEY MEAN "MUSIC WITH HER SILVER SOUND?"
WHAT DO YOU SAY, SIMON CATLING?
WELL, SIR, BECAUSE SILVER HAS A SWEET SOUND.
THAT'S A STUPID ANSWER!
WHAT DO YOU SAY, HUGH REBECK?
I SAY "SILVER SOUND" BECAUSE MUSICIANS PLAY TO EARN SILVER.
ANOTHER STUPID ANSWER! WHAT DO YOU SAY, JAMES SOUNDPOST?
WELL, I... DON'T KNOW WHAT TO SAY.
RIGHT! YOU ARE THE SINGER, SO YOU CAN'T SAY ANYTHING. I'LL TELL YOU: IT IS "MUSIC WITH HER SILVER SOUND" BECAUSE MUSICIANS HAVE NO GOLD TO CLINK TOGETHER!
...then music with her silver sound / will quickly have you feeling fine!
WHAT A HATEFUL KNAVE!
HANG HIM! COME—WE'LL WAIT FOR THE MOURNERS... AND FOR DINNER.

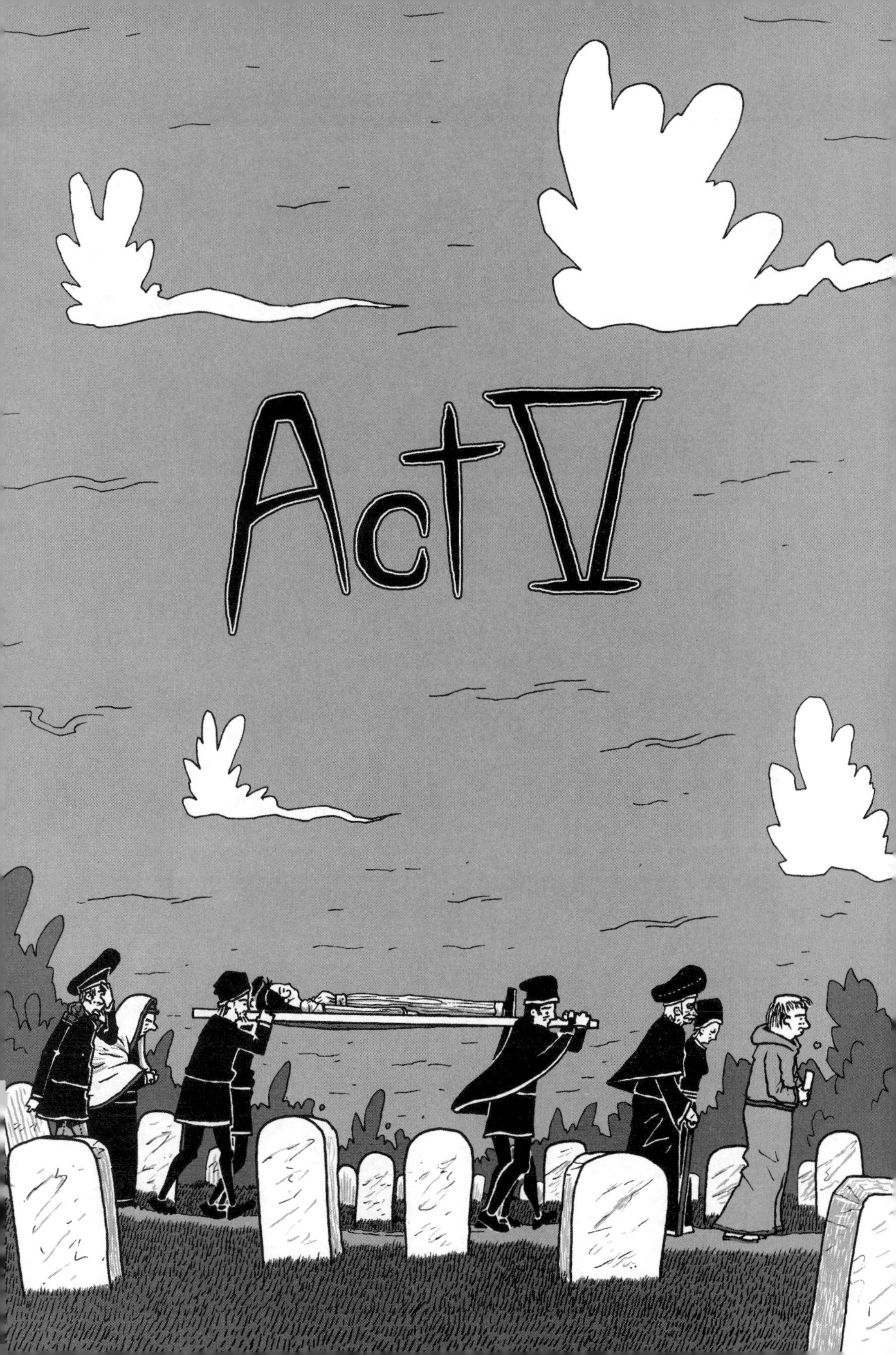
Act V

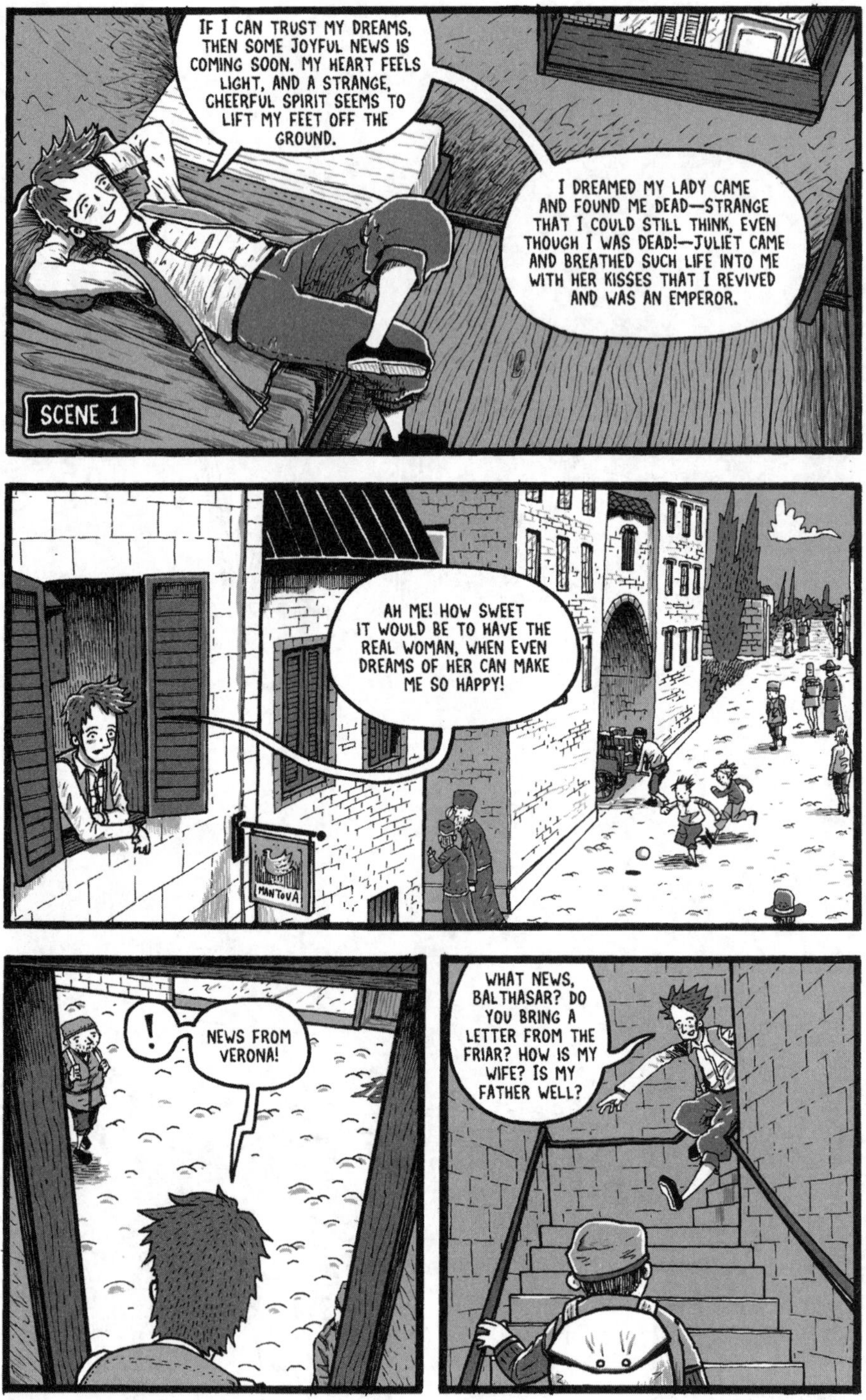
IF I CAN TRUST MY DREAMS, THEN SOME JOYFUL NEWS IS COMING SOON. MY HEART FEELS LIGHT, AND A STRANGE, CHEERFUL SPIRIT SEEMS TO LIFT MY FEET OFF THE GROUND.
I DREAMED MY LADY CAME AND FOUND ME DEAD—STRANGE THAT I COULD STILL THINK, EVEN THOUGH I WAS DEAD!—JULIET CAME AND BREATHED SUCH LIFE INTO ME WITH HER KISSES THAT I REVIVED AND WAS AN EMPEROR.
SCENE 1
AH ME! HOW SWEET IT WOULD BE TO HAVE THE REAL WOMAN, WHEN EVEN DREAMS OF HER CAN MAKE ME SO HAPPY!
MANTOVA
!
NEWS FROM VERONA!
WHAT NEWS, BALTHASAR? DO YOU BRING A LETTER FROM THE FRIAR? HOW IS MY WIFE? IS MY FATHER WELL?

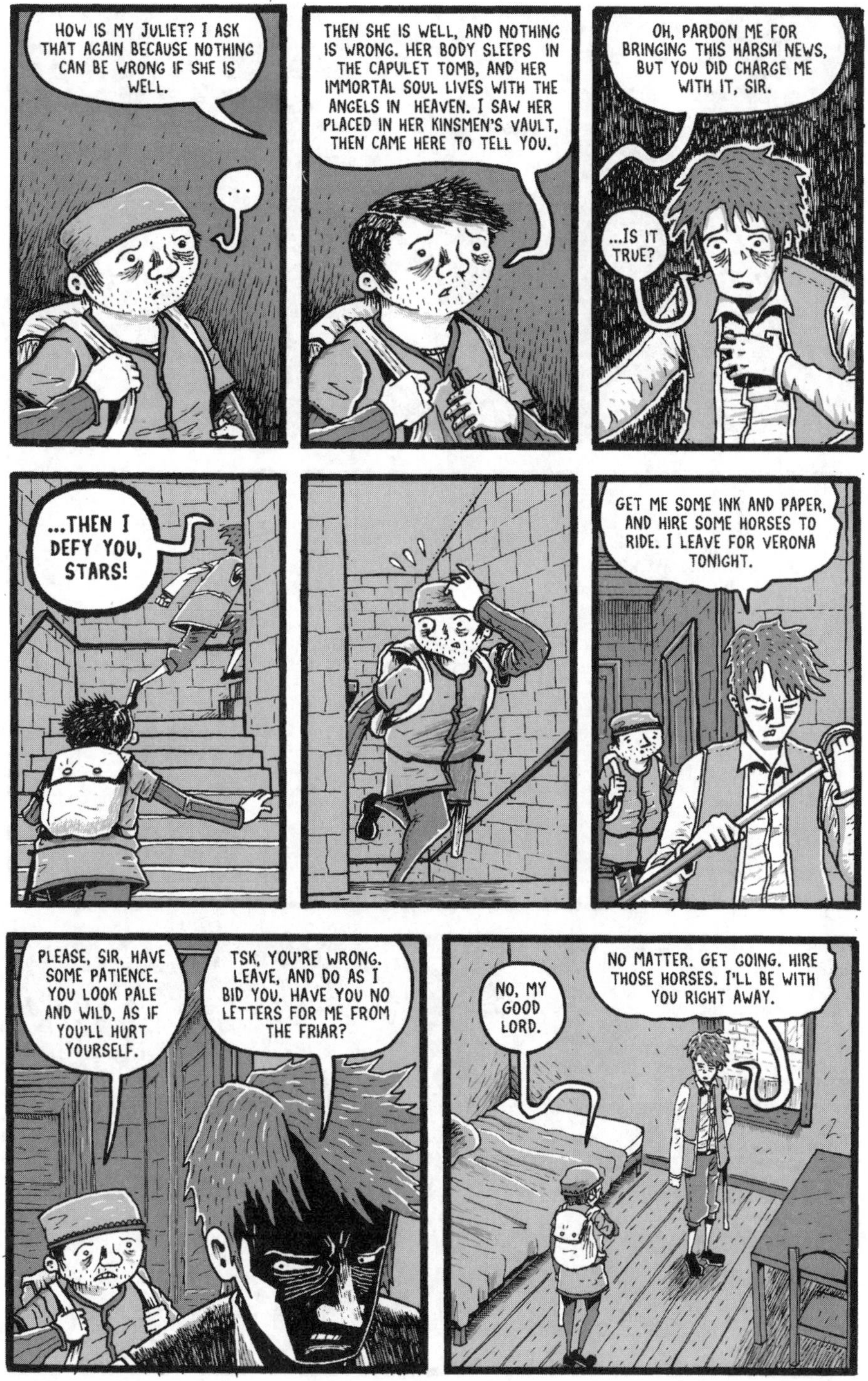
HOW IS MY JULIET? I ASK THAT AGAIN BECAUSE NOTHING CAN BE WRONG IF SHE IS WELL.
...
THEN SHE IS WELL, AND NOTHING IS WRONG. HER BODY SLEEPS IN THE CAPULET TOMB, AND HER IMMORTAL SOUL LIVES WITH THE ANGELS IN HEAVEN. I SAW HER PLACED IN HER KINSMEN'S VAULT, THEN CAME HERE TO TELL YOU.
OH, PARDON ME FOR BRINGING THIS HARSH NEWS, BUT YOU DID CHARGE ME WITH IT, SIR.
...IS IT TRUE?
...THEN I DEFY YOU, STARS!
GET ME SOME INK AND PAPER, AND HIRE SOME HORSES TO RIDE. I LEAVE FOR VERONA TONIGHT.
PLEASE, SIR, HAVE SOME PATIENCE. YOU LOOK PALE AND WILD, AS IF YOU'LL HURT YOURSELF.
TSK, YOU'RE WRONG. LEAVE, AND DO AS I BID YOU. HAVE YOU NO LETTERS FOR ME FROM THE FRIAR?
NO, MY GOOD LORD.
NO MATTER. GET GOING. HIRE THOSE HORSES. I'LL BE WITH YOU RIGHT AWAY.

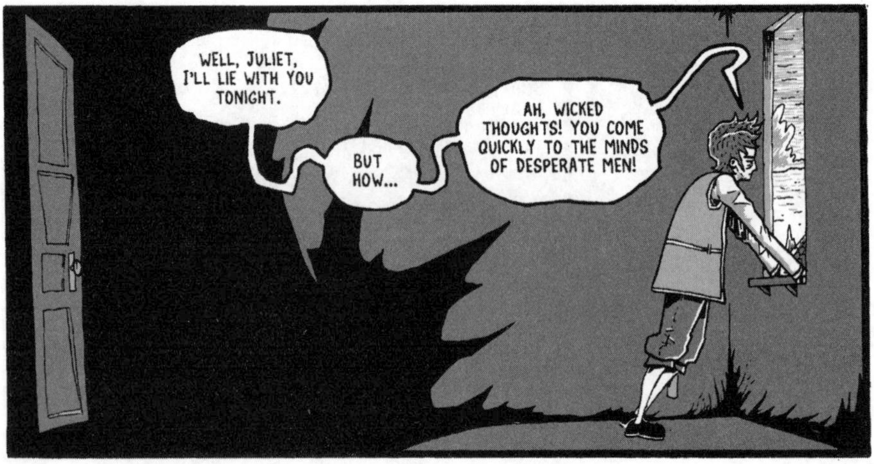
WELL, JULIET, I'LL LIE WITH YOU TONIGHT.
BUT HOW...
AH, WICKED THOUGHTS! YOU COME QUICKLY TO THE MINDS OF DESPERATE MEN!

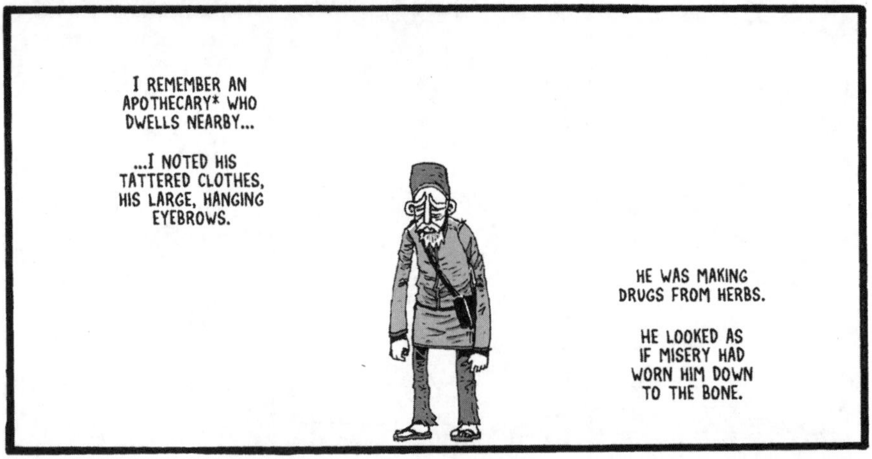
I REMEMBER AN APOTHECARY* WHO DWELLS NEARBY...
...I NOTED HIS TATTERED CLOTHES, HIS LARGE, HANGING EYEBROWS.
HE WAS MAKING DRUGS FROM HERBS.
HE LOOKED AS IF MISERY HAD WORN HIM DOWN TO THE BONE.

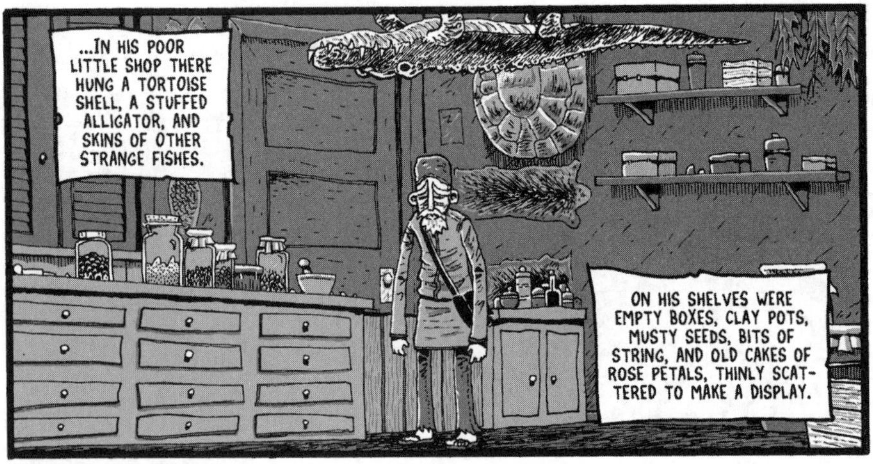
...IN HIS POOR LITTLE SHOP THERE HUNG A TORTOISE SHELL, A STUFFED ALLIGATOR, AND SKINS OF OTHER STRANGE FISHES.
ON HIS SHELVES WERE EMPTY BOXES, CLAY POTS, MUSTY SEEDS, BITS OF STRING, AND OLD CAKES OF ROSE PETALS, THINLY SCATTERED TO MAKE A DISPLAY.

*APOTHECARY = PHARMACIST

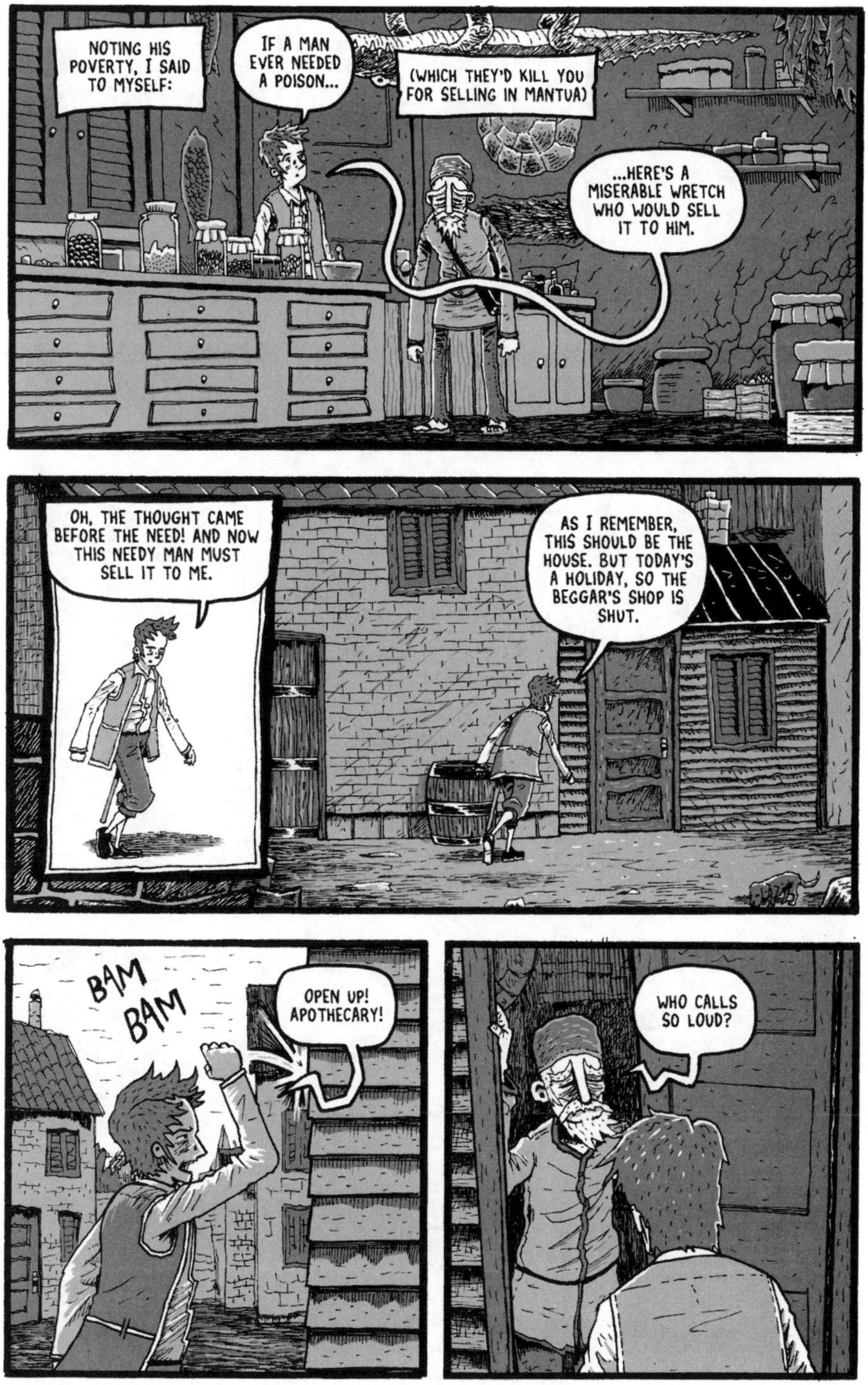
NOTING HIS POVERTY, I SAID TO MYSELF:
IF A MAN EVER NEEDED A POISON...
(WHICH THEY'D KILL YOU FOR SELLING IN MANTUA)
...HERE'S A MISERABLE WRETCH WHO WOULD SELL IT TO HIM.
OH, THE THOUGHT CAME BEFORE THE NEED! AND NOW THIS NEEDY MAN MUST SELL IT TO ME.
AS I REMEMBER, THIS SHOULD BE THE HOUSE. BUT TODAY'S A HOLIDAY, SO THE BEGGAR'S SHOP IS SHUT.
BAM BAM
OPEN UP! APOTHECARY!
WHO CALLS SO LOUD?

COME HERE, MAN, I SEE THAT YOU ARE POOR. HERE IS FORTY DUCATS. LET ME HAVE A SHOT OF POISON.

...SOMETHING THAT SPEEDS SO QUICKLY THROUGH THE VEINS THAT THE DRINKER FALLS DEAD IMMEDIATELY.

I HAVE SUCH POISONS, BUT MANTUA LAW PROMISES DEATH TO THE MAN WHO SELLS THEM.

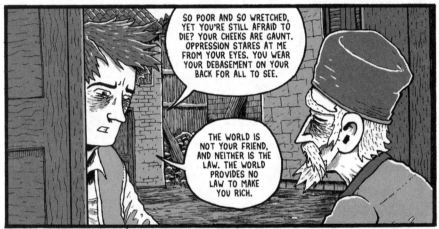

SO POOR AND SO WRETCHED, YET YOU'RE STILL AFRAID TO DIE? YOUR CHEEKS ARE GAUNT. OPPRESSION STARES AT ME FROM YOUR EYES. YOU WEAR YOUR DEBASEMENT ON YOUR BACK FOR ALL TO SEE.

THE WORLD IS NOT YOUR FRIEND, AND NEITHER IS THE LAW. THE WORLD PROVIDES NO LAW TO MAKE YOU RICH.

SO DON'T BE POOR. BREAK THE LAW AND TAKE THIS MONEY.

...MY POVERTY MAKES ME DO THIS AGAINST MY WILL.

I PAY YOUR POVERTY AND NOT YOUR WILL.

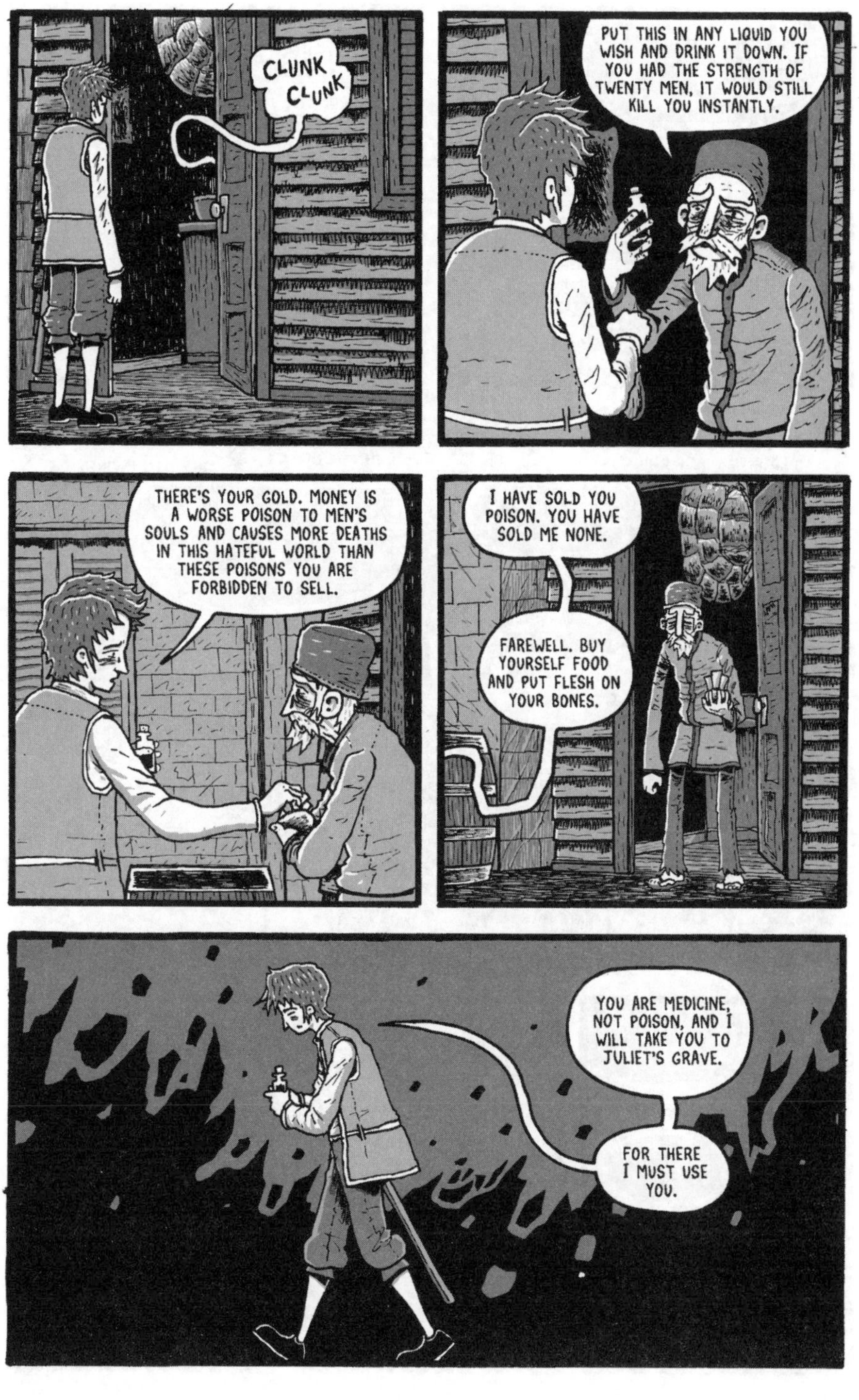
CLUNK
CLUNK
PUT THIS IN ANY LIQUID YOU WISH AND DRINK IT DOWN. IF YOU HAD THE STRENGTH OF TWENTY MEN, IT WOULD STILL KILL YOU INSTANTLY.
THERE'S YOUR GOLD. MONEY IS A WORSE POISON TO MEN'S SOULS AND CAUSES MORE DEATHS IN THIS HATEFUL WORLD THAN THESE POISONS YOU ARE FORBIDDEN TO SELL.
I HAVE SOLD YOU POISON. YOU HAVE SOLD ME NONE.
FAREWELL. BUY YOURSELF FOOD AND PUT FLESH ON YOUR BONES.
YOU ARE MEDICINE, NOT POISON, AND I WILL TAKE YOU TO JULIET'S GRAVE.
FOR THERE I MUST USE YOU.

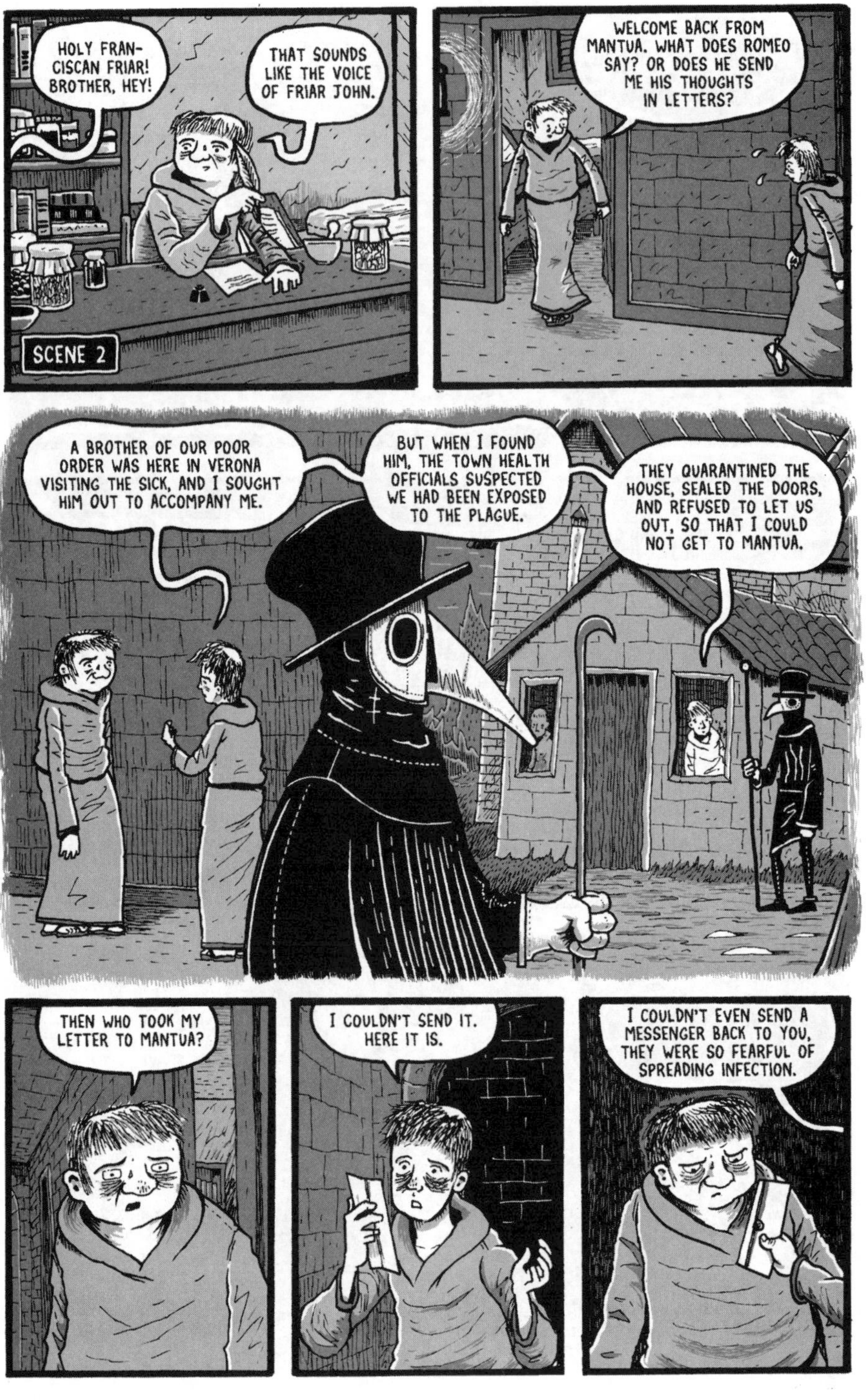

HOLY FRAN-CISCAN FRIAR! BROTHER, HEY!
THAT SOUNDS LIKE THE VOICE OF FRIAR JOHN.
SCENE 2
WELCOME BACK FROM MANTUA. WHAT DOES ROMEO SAY? OR DOES HE SEND ME HIS THOUGHTS IN LETTERS?
A BROTHER OF OUR POOR ORDER WAS HERE IN VERONA VISITING THE SICK, AND I SOUGHT HIM OUT TO ACCOMPANY ME.
BUT WHEN I FOUND HIM, THE TOWN HEALTH OFFICIALS SUSPECTED WE HAD BEEN EXPOSED TO THE PLAGUE.
THEY QUARANTINED THE HOUSE, SEALED THE DOORS, AND REFUSED TO LET US OUT, SO THAT I COULD NOT GET TO MANTUA.
THEN WHO TOOK MY LETTER TO MANTUA?
I COULDN'T SEND IT. HERE IT IS.
I COULDN'T EVEN SEND A MESSENGER BACK TO YOU, THEY WERE SO FEARFUL OF SPREADING INFECTION.

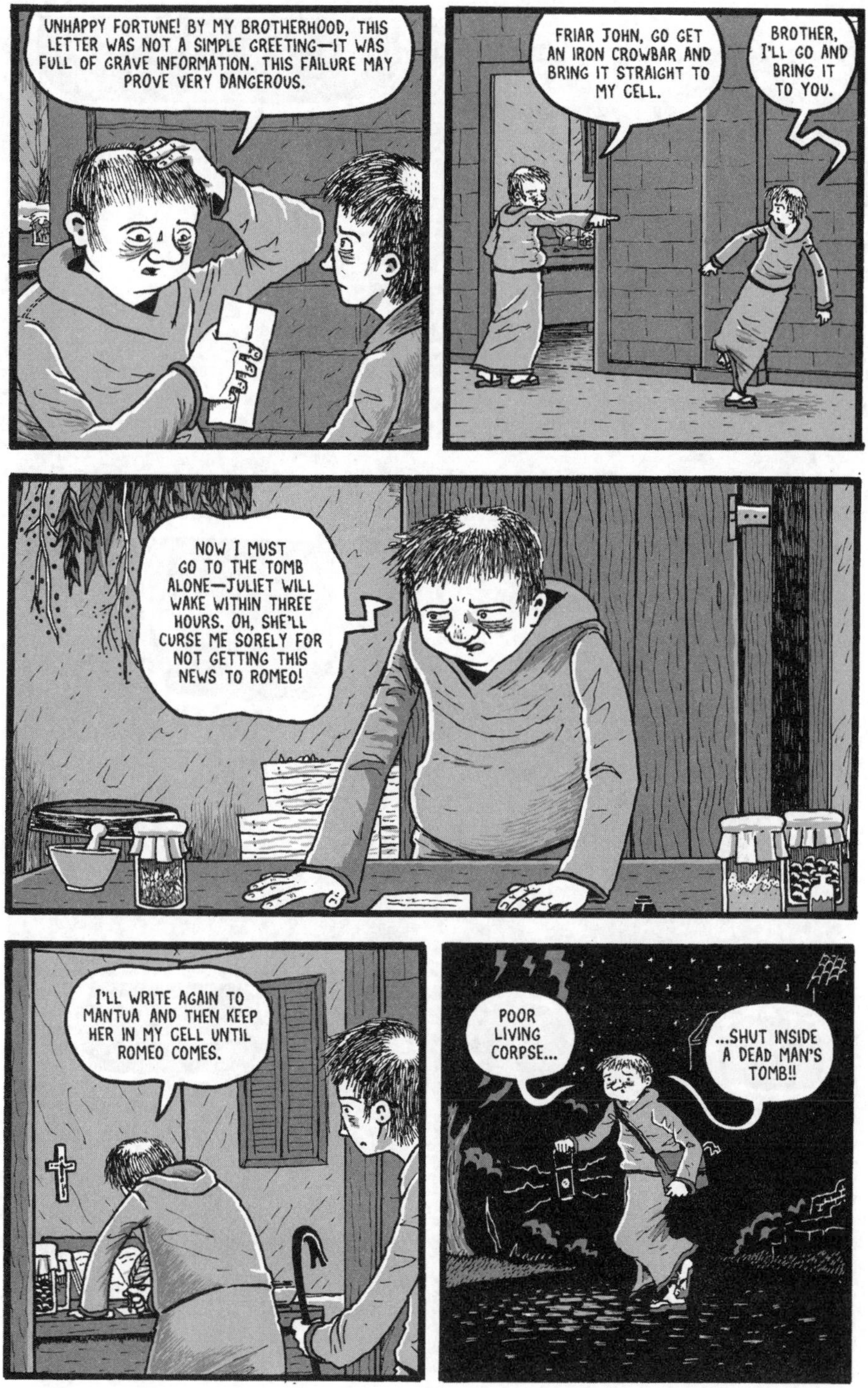
UNHAPPY FORTUNE! BY MY BROTHERHOOD, THIS LETTER WAS NOT A SIMPLE GREETING—IT WAS FULL OF GRAVE INFORMATION. THIS FAILURE MAY PROVE VERY DANGEROUS.
FRIAR JOHN, GO GET AN IRON CROWBAR AND BRING IT STRAIGHT TO MY CELL.
BROTHER, I'LL GO AND BRING IT TO YOU.
NOW I MUST GO TO THE TOMB ALONE—JULIET WILL WAKE WITHIN THREE HOURS. OH, SHE'LL CURSE ME SORELY FOR NOT GETTING THIS NEWS TO ROMEO!
I'LL WRITE AGAIN TO MANTUA AND THEN KEEP HER IN MY CELL UNTIL ROMEO COMES.
POOR LIVING CORPSE...
...SHUT INSIDE A DEAD MAN'S TOMB!!

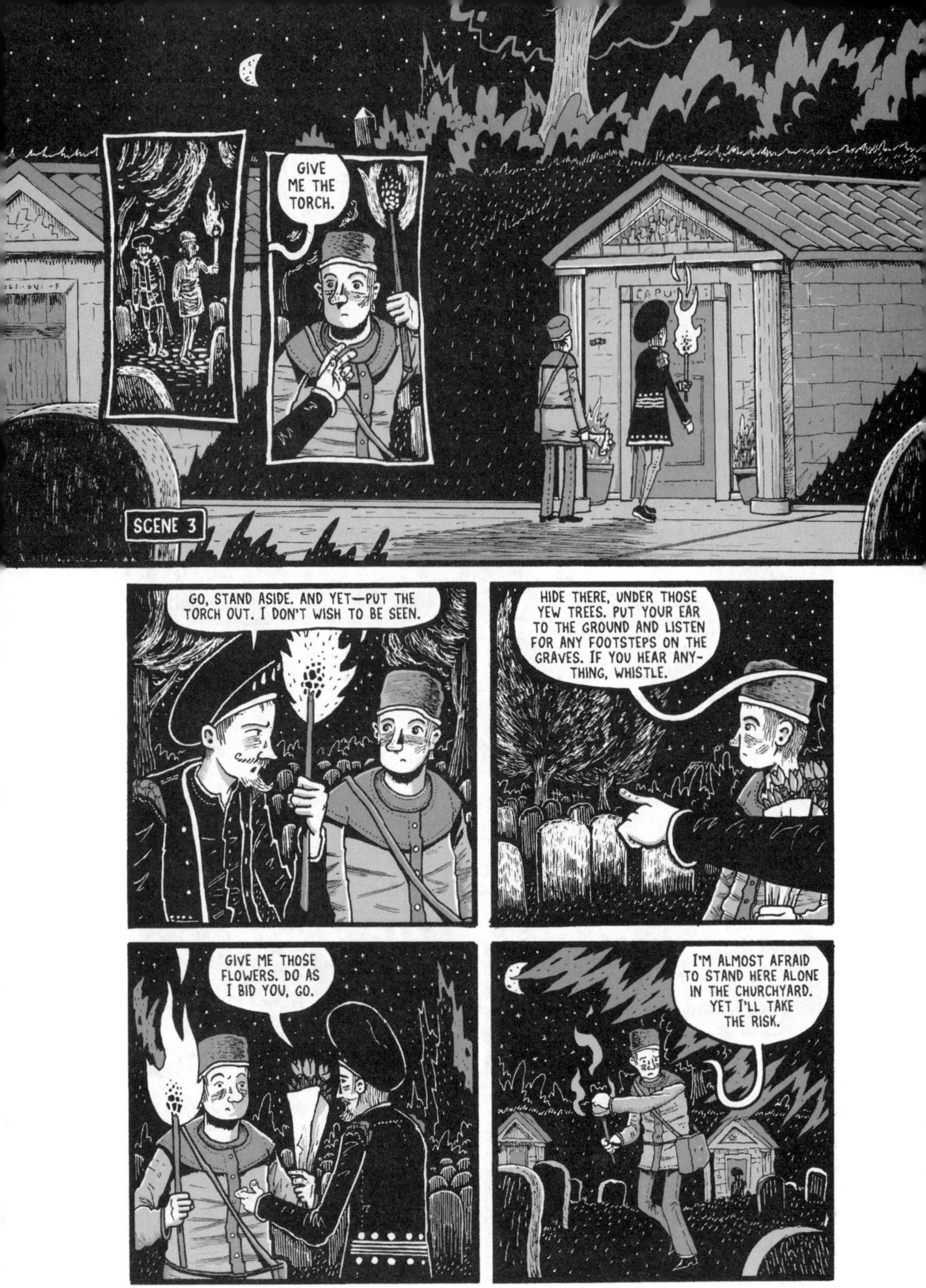
GIVE ME THE TORCH.
SCENE 3
GO, STAND ASIDE. AND YET—PUT THE TORCH OUT. I DON'T WISH TO BE SEEN.
HIDE THERE, UNDER THOSE YEW TREES. PUT YOUR EAR TO THE GROUND AND LISTEN FOR ANY FOOTSTEPS ON THE GRAVES. IF YOU HEAR ANYTHING, WHISTLE.
GIVE ME THOSE FLOWERS. DO AS I BID YOU, GO.
I'M ALMOST AFRAID TO STAND HERE ALONE IN THE CHURCHYARD. YET I'LL TAKE THE RISK.

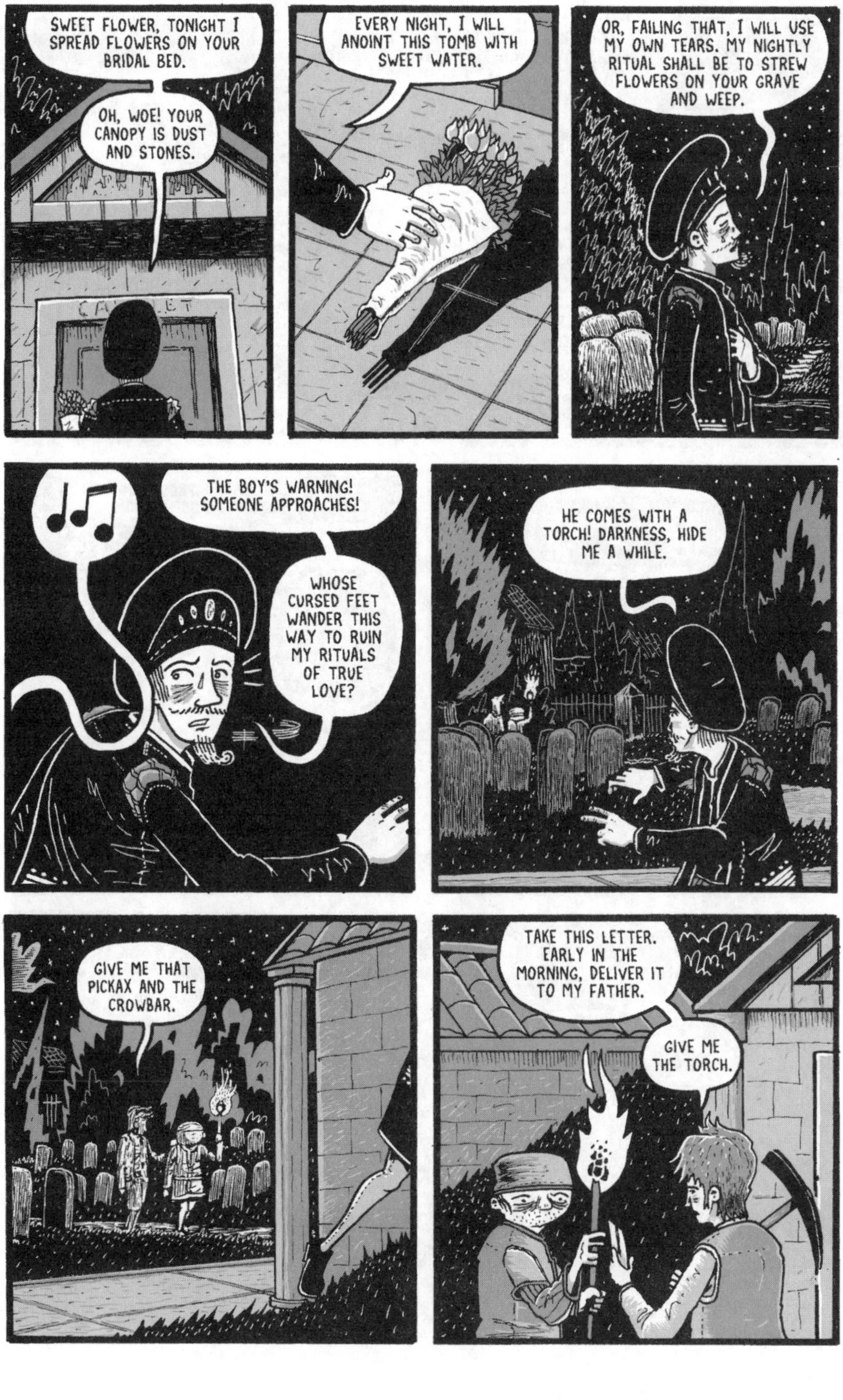
SWEET FLOWER, TONIGHT I SPREAD FLOWERS ON YOUR BRIDAL BED.
OH, WOE! YOUR CANOPY IS DUST AND STONES.
EVERY NIGHT, I WILL ANOINT THIS TOMB WITH SWEET WATER.
OR, FAILING THAT, I WILL USE MY OWN TEARS. MY NIGHTLY RITUAL SHALL BE TO STREW FLOWERS ON YOUR GRAVE AND WEEP.
THE BOY'S WARNING! SOMEONE APPROACHES!
WHOSE CURSED FEET WANDER THIS WAY TO RUIN MY RITUALS OF TRUE LOVE?
HE COMES WITH A TORCH! DARKNESS, HIDE ME A WHILE.
GIVE ME THAT PICKAX AND THE CROWBAR.
TAKE THIS LETTER. EARLY IN THE MORNING, DELIVER IT TO MY FATHER.
GIVE ME THE TORCH.

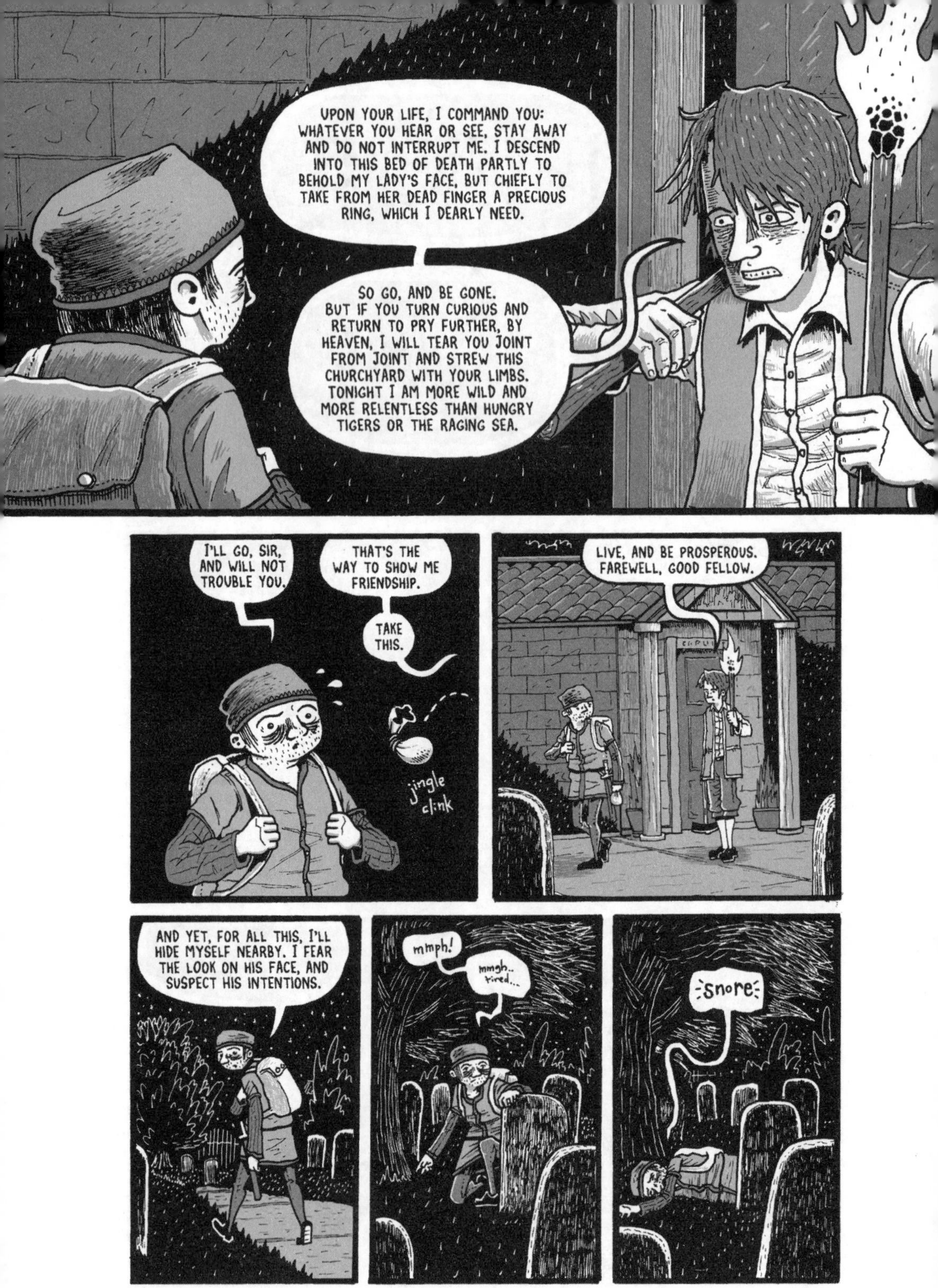
UPON YOUR LIFE, I COMMAND YOU: WHATEVER YOU HEAR OR SEE, STAY AWAY AND DO NOT INTERRUPT ME. I DESCEND INTO THIS BED OF DEATH PARTLY TO BEHOLD MY LADY'S FACE, BUT CHIEFLY TO TAKE FROM HER DEAD FINGER A PRECIOUS RING, WHICH I DEARLY NEED.
SO GO, AND BE GONE. BUT IF YOU TURN CURIOUS AND RETURN TO PRY FURTHER, BY HEAVEN, I WILL TEAR YOU JOINT FROM JOINT AND STREW THIS CHURCHYARD WITH YOUR LIMBS. TONIGHT I AM MORE WILD AND MORE RELENTLESS THAN HUNGRY TIGERS OR THE RAGING SEA.
I'LL GO, SIR, AND WILL NOT TROUBLE YOU.
THAT'S THE WAY TO SHOW ME FRIENDSHIP.
TAKE THIS.
jingle
clink
LIVE, AND BE PROSPEROUS. FAREWELL, GOOD FELLOW.
AND YET, FOR ALL THIS, I'LL HIDE MYSELF NEARBY. I FEAR THE LOOK ON HIS FACE, AND SUSPECT HIS INTENTIONS.
mmph!
mmgh.. tired...
snore

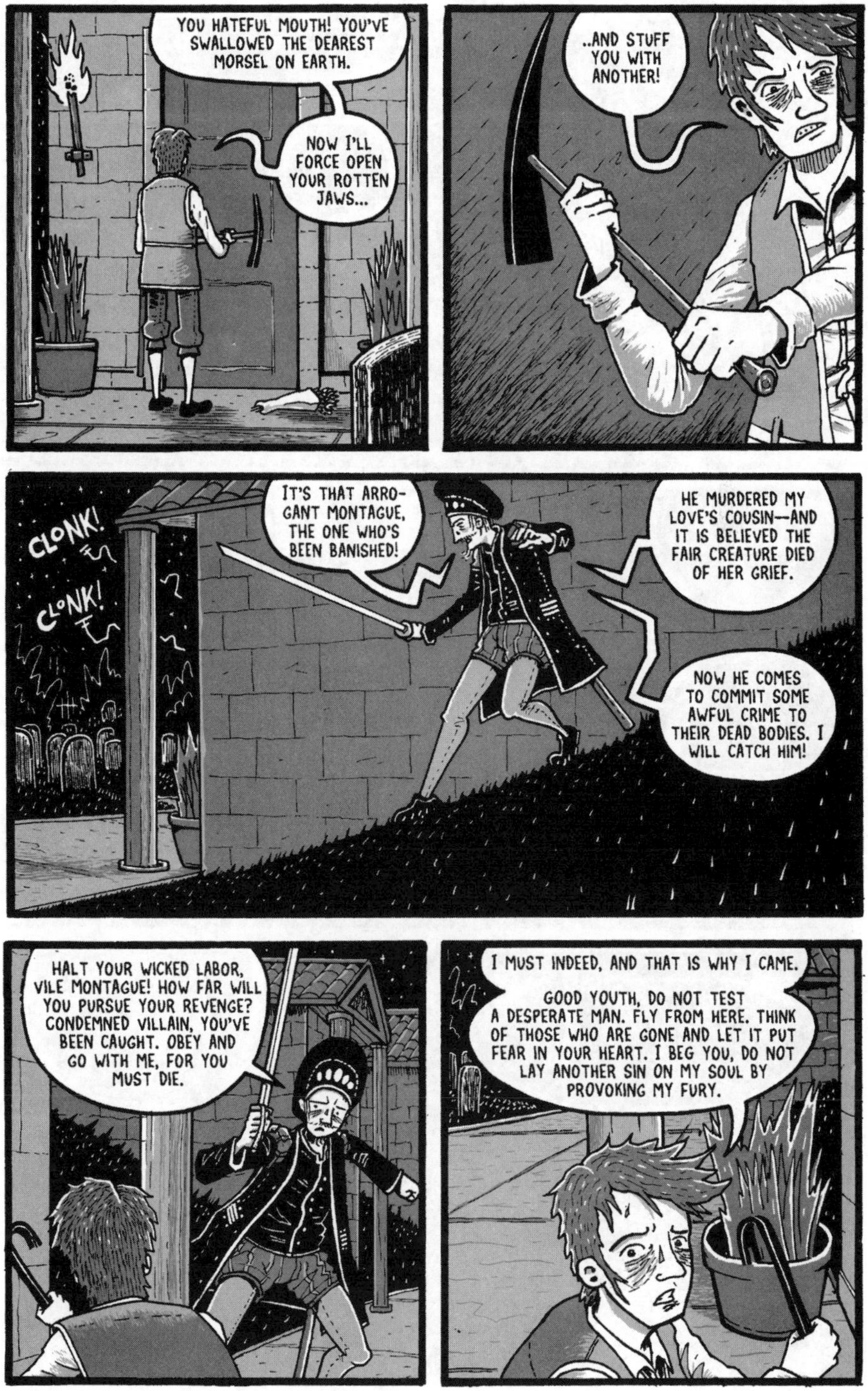
YOU HATEFUL MOUTH! YOU'VE SWALLOWED THE DEAREST MORSEL ON EARTH.
NOW I'LL FORCE OPEN YOUR ROTTEN JAWS...
..AND STUFF YOU WITH ANOTHER!
CLONK!
CLONK!
IT'S THAT ARRO-GANT MONTAGUE, THE ONE WHO'S BEEN BANISHED!
HE MURDERED MY LOVE'S COUSIN--AND IT IS BELIEVED THE FAIR CREATURE DIED OF HER GRIEF.
NOW HE COMES TO COMMIT SOME AWFUL CRIME TO THEIR DEAD BODIES. I WILL CATCH HIM!
HALT YOUR WICKED LABOR, VILE MONTAGUE! HOW FAR WILL YOU PURSUE YOUR REVENGE? CONDEMNED VILLAIN, YOU'VE BEEN CAUGHT. OBEY AND GO WITH ME, FOR YOU MUST DIE.
I MUST INDEED, AND THAT IS WHY I CAME.
GOOD YOUTH, DO NOT TEST A DESPERATE MAN. FLY FROM HERE. THINK OF THOSE WHO ARE GONE AND LET IT PUT FEAR IN YOUR HEART. I BEG YOU, DO NOT LAY ANOTHER SIN ON MY SOUL BY PROVOKING MY FURY.

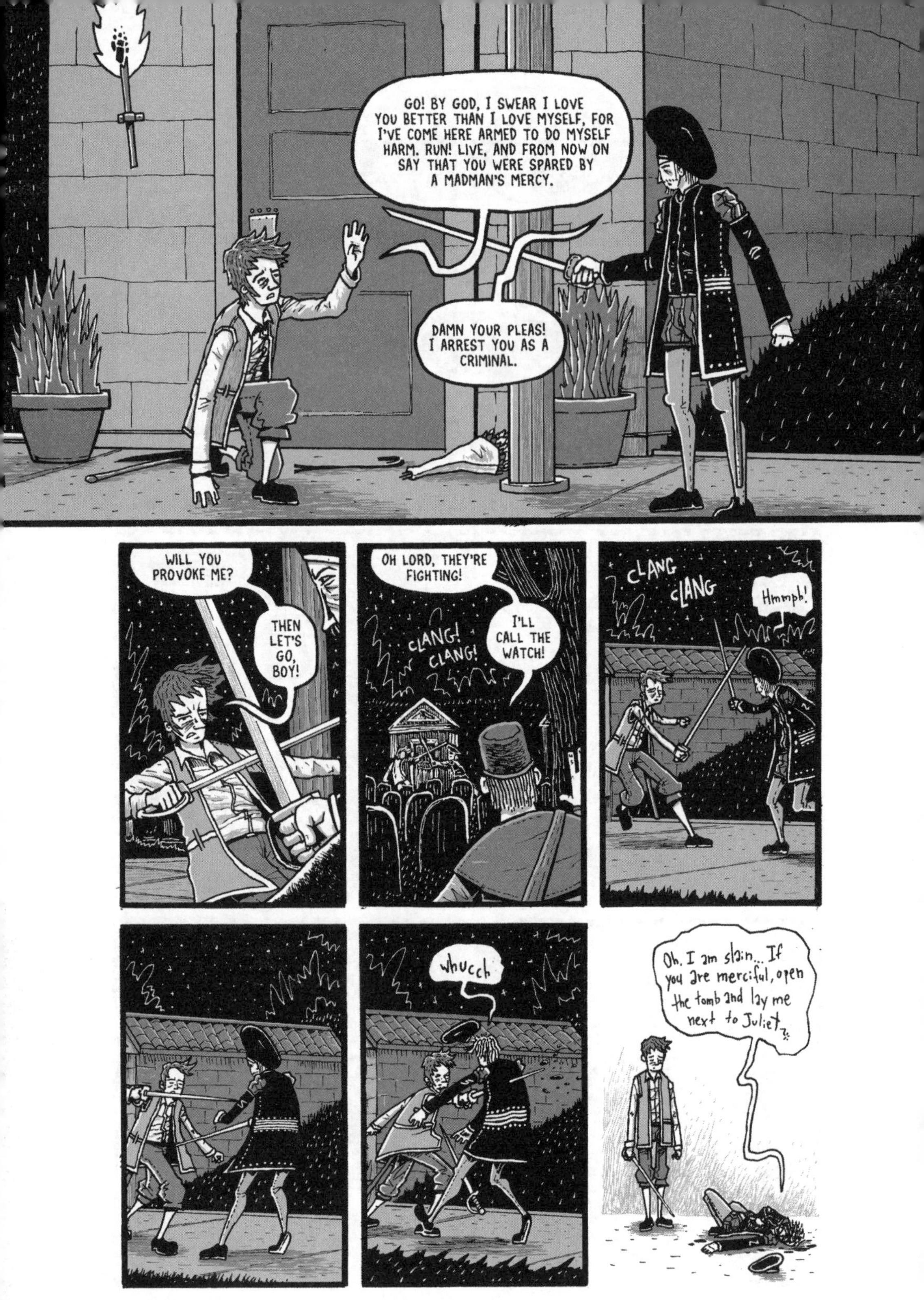
GO! BY GOD, I SWEAR I LOVE YOU BETTER THAN I LOVE MYSELF, FOR I'VE COME HERE ARMED TO DO MYSELF HARM. RUN! LIVE, AND FROM NOW ON SAY THAT YOU WERE SPARED BY A MADMAN'S MERCY.
DAMN YOUR PLEAS! I ARREST YOU AS A CRIMINAL.
WILL YOU PROVOKE ME?
THEN LET'S GO, BOY!
OH LORD, THEY'RE FIGHTING!
CLANG! CLANG!
I'LL CALL THE WATCH!
CLANG
CLANG
Hmmph!
whucch
Oh. I am slain... If you are merciful, open the tomb and lay me next to Juliet...

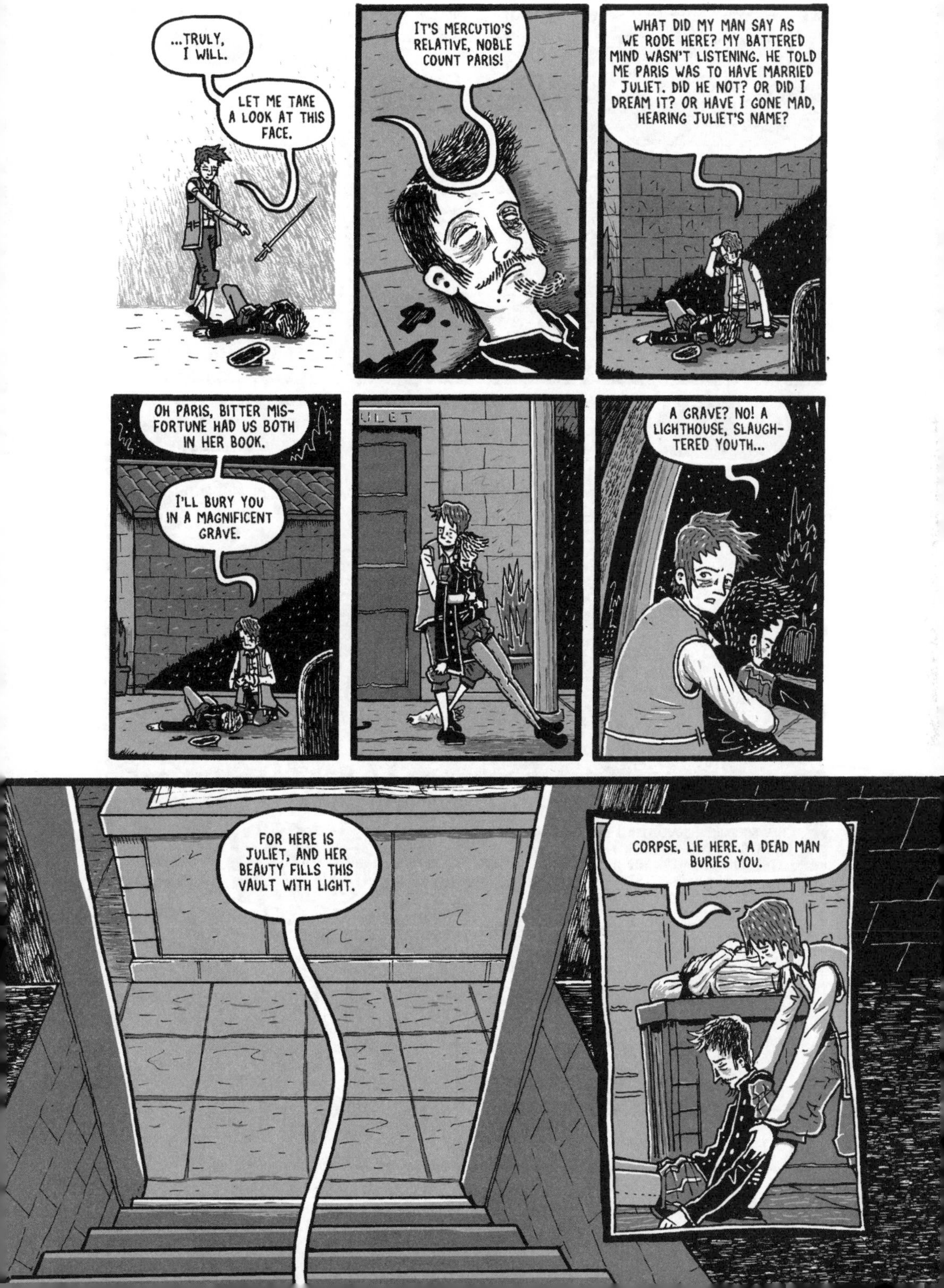
...TRULY, I WILL.
LET ME TAKE A LOOK AT THIS FACE.
IT'S MERCUTIO'S RELATIVE, NOBLE COUNT PARIS!
WHAT DID MY MAN SAY AS WE RODE HERE? MY BATTERED MIND WASN'T LISTENING. HE TOLD ME PARIS WAS TO HAVE MARRIED JULIET. DID HE NOT? OR DID I DREAM IT? OR HAVE I GONE MAD, HEARING JULIET'S NAME?
OH PARIS, BITTER MISFORTUNE HAD US BOTH IN HER BOOK.
I'LL BURY YOU IN A MAGNIFICENT GRAVE.
ULET
A GRAVE? NO! A LIGHTHOUSE, SLAUGHTERED YOUTH...
FOR HERE IS JULIET, AND HER BEAUTY FILLS THIS VAULT WITH LIGHT.
CORPSE, LIE HERE. A DEAD MAN BURIES YOU.

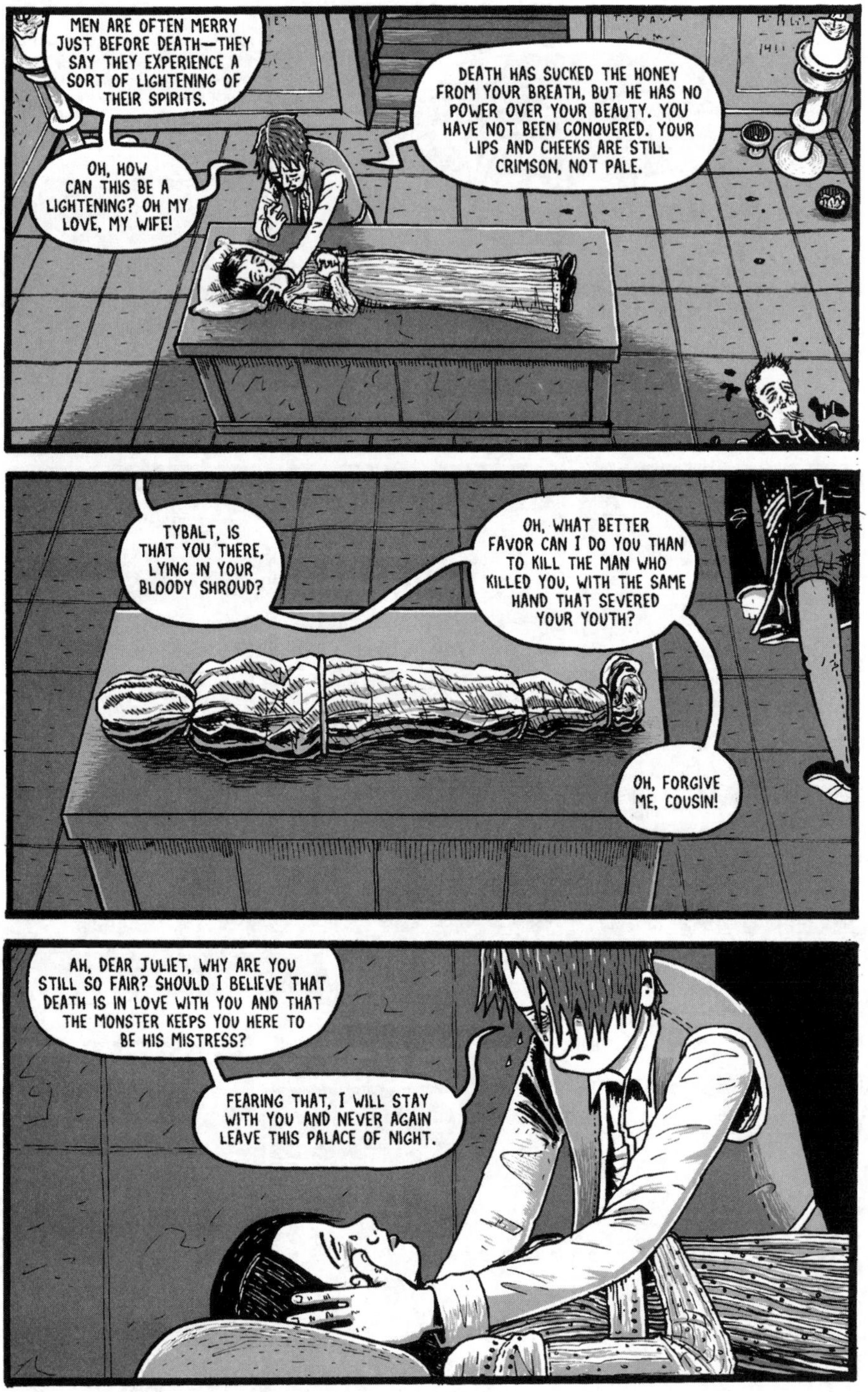
MEN ARE OFTEN MERRY JUST BEFORE DEATH—THEY SAY THEY EXPERIENCE A SORT OF LIGHTENING OF THEIR SPIRITS.
OH, HOW CAN THIS BE A LIGHTENING? OH MY LOVE, MY WIFE!
DEATH HAS SUCKED THE HONEY FROM YOUR BREATH, BUT HE HAS NO POWER OVER YOUR BEAUTY. YOU HAVE NOT BEEN CONQUERED. YOUR LIPS AND CHEEKS ARE STILL CRIMSON, NOT PALE.
TYBALT, IS THAT YOU THERE, LYING IN YOUR BLOODY SHROUD?
OH, WHAT BETTER FAVOR CAN I DO YOU THAN TO KILL THE MAN WHO KILLED YOU, WITH THE SAME HAND THAT SEVERED YOUR YOUTH?
OH, FORGIVE ME, COUSIN!
AH, DEAR JULIET, WHY ARE YOU STILL SO FAIR? SHOULD I BELIEVE THAT DEATH IS IN LOVE WITH YOU AND THAT THE MONSTER KEEPS YOU HERE TO BE HIS MISTRESS?
FEARING THAT, I WILL STAY WITH YOU AND NEVER AGAIN LEAVE THIS PALACE OF NIGHT.

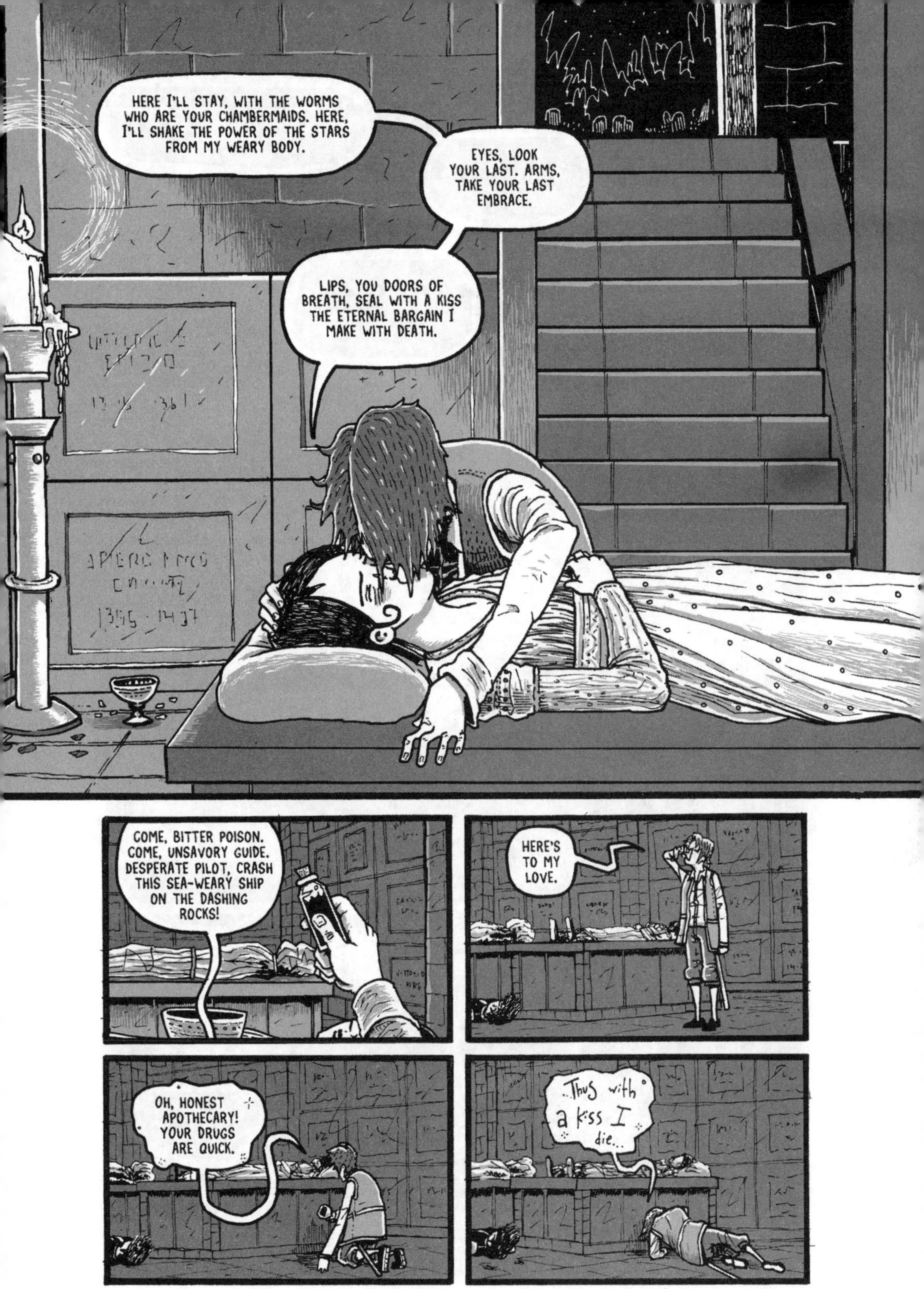
HERE I'LL STAY, WITH THE WORMS WHO ARE YOUR CHAMBERMAIDS. HERE, I'LL SHAKE THE POWER OF THE STARS FROM MY WEARY BODY.
EYES, LOOK YOUR LAST. ARMS, TAKE YOUR LAST EMBRACE.
LIPS, YOU DOORS OF BREATH, SEAL WITH A KISS THE ETERNAL BARGAIN I MAKE WITH DEATH.
COME, BITTER POISON. COME, UNSAVORY GUIDE. DESPERATE PILOT, CRASH THIS SEA-WEARY SHIP ON THE DASHING ROCKS!
HERE'S TO MY LOVE.
OH, HONEST APOTHECARY! YOUR DRUGS ARE QUICK.
..Thus with a kiss I die...

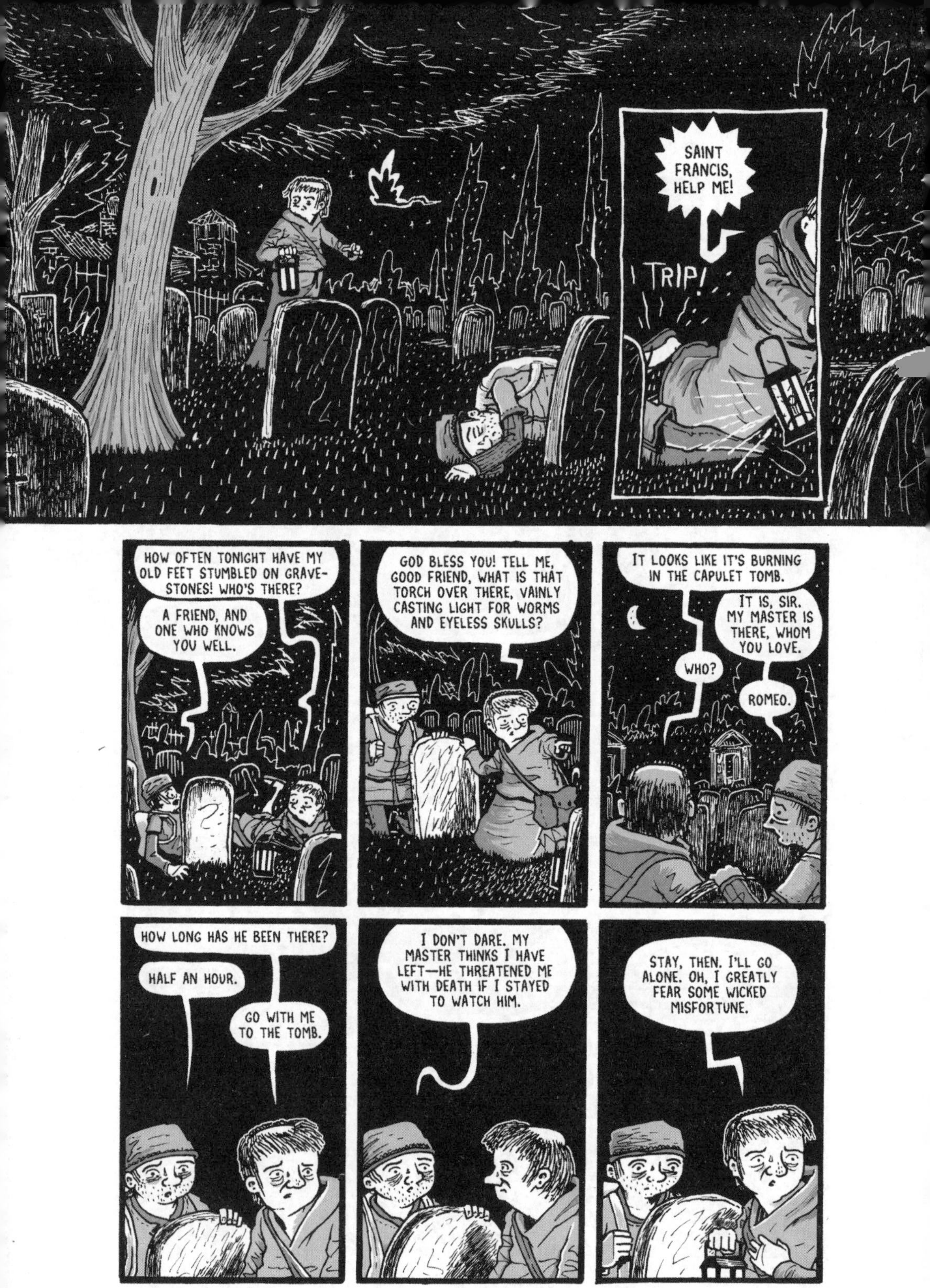

SAINT FRANCIS, HELP ME!
TRIP!
HOW OFTEN TONIGHT HAVE MY OLD FEET STUMBLED ON GRAVESTONES! WHO'S THERE?
A FRIEND, AND ONE WHO KNOWS YOU WELL.
GOD BLESS YOU! TELL ME, GOOD FRIEND, WHAT IS THAT TORCH OVER THERE, VAINLY CASTING LIGHT FOR WORMS AND EYELESS SKULLS?
IT LOOKS LIKE IT'S BURNING IN THE CAPULET TOMB.
IT IS, SIR. MY MASTER IS THERE, WHOM YOU LOVE.
WHO?
ROMEO.
HOW LONG HAS HE BEEN THERE?
HALF AN HOUR.
GO WITH ME TO THE TOMB.
I DON'T DARE. MY MASTER THINKS I HAVE LEFT—HE THREATENED ME WITH DEATH IF I STAYED TO WATCH HIM.
STAY, THEN. I'LL GO ALONE. OH, I GREATLY FEAR SOME WICKED MISFORTUNE.

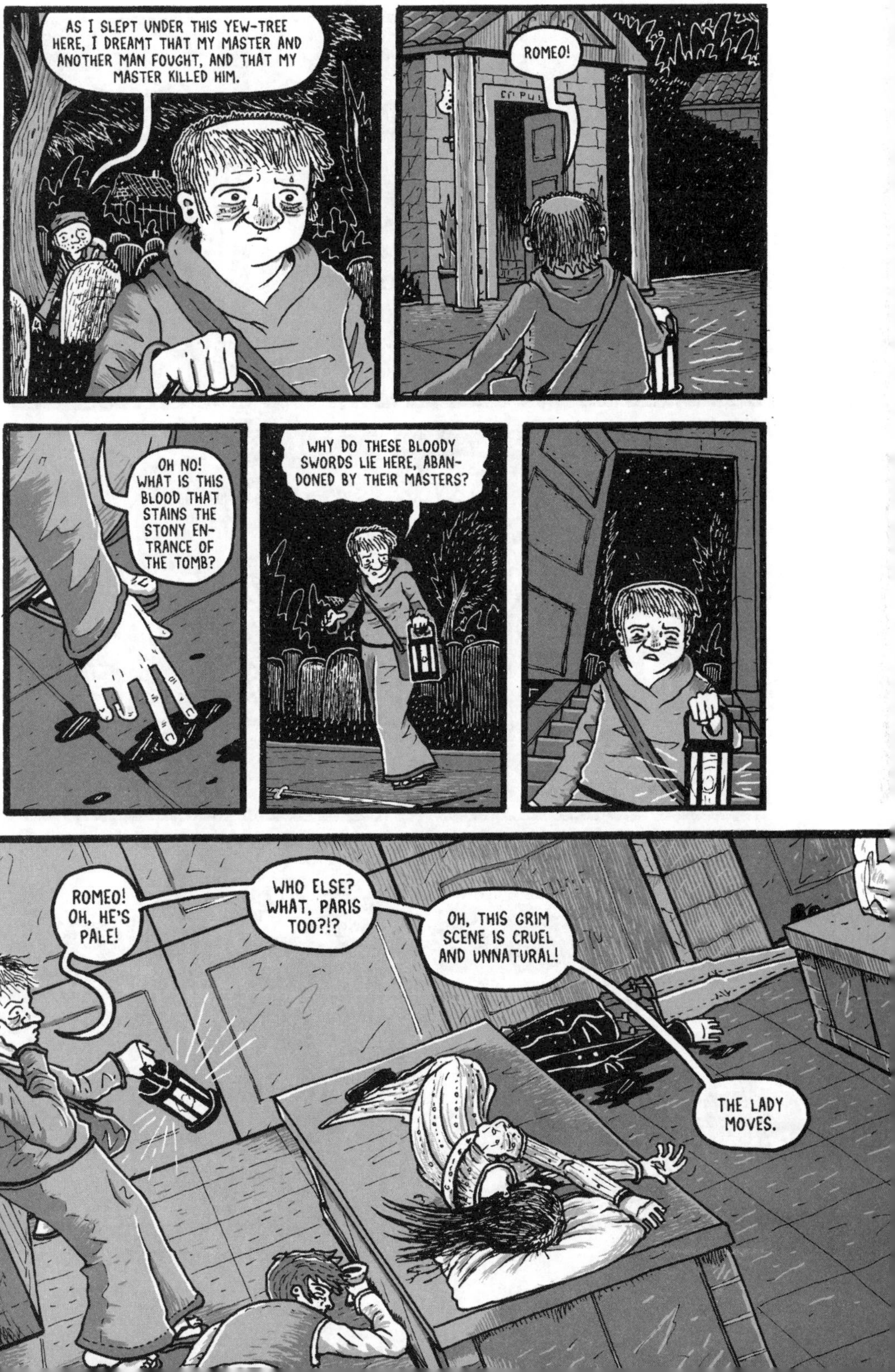
AS I SLEPT UNDER THIS YEW-TREE HERE, I DREAMT THAT MY MASTER AND ANOTHER MAN FOUGHT, AND THAT MY MASTER KILLED HIM.
ROMEO!
OH NO! WHAT IS THIS BLOOD THAT STAINS THE STONY ENTRANCE OF THE TOMB?
WHY DO THESE BLOODY SWORDS LIE HERE, ABANDONED BY THEIR MASTERS?
ROMEO! OH, HE'S PALE!
WHO ELSE? WHAT, PARIS TOO?!?
OH, THIS GRIM SCENE IS CRUEL AND UNNATURAL!
THE LADY MOVES.

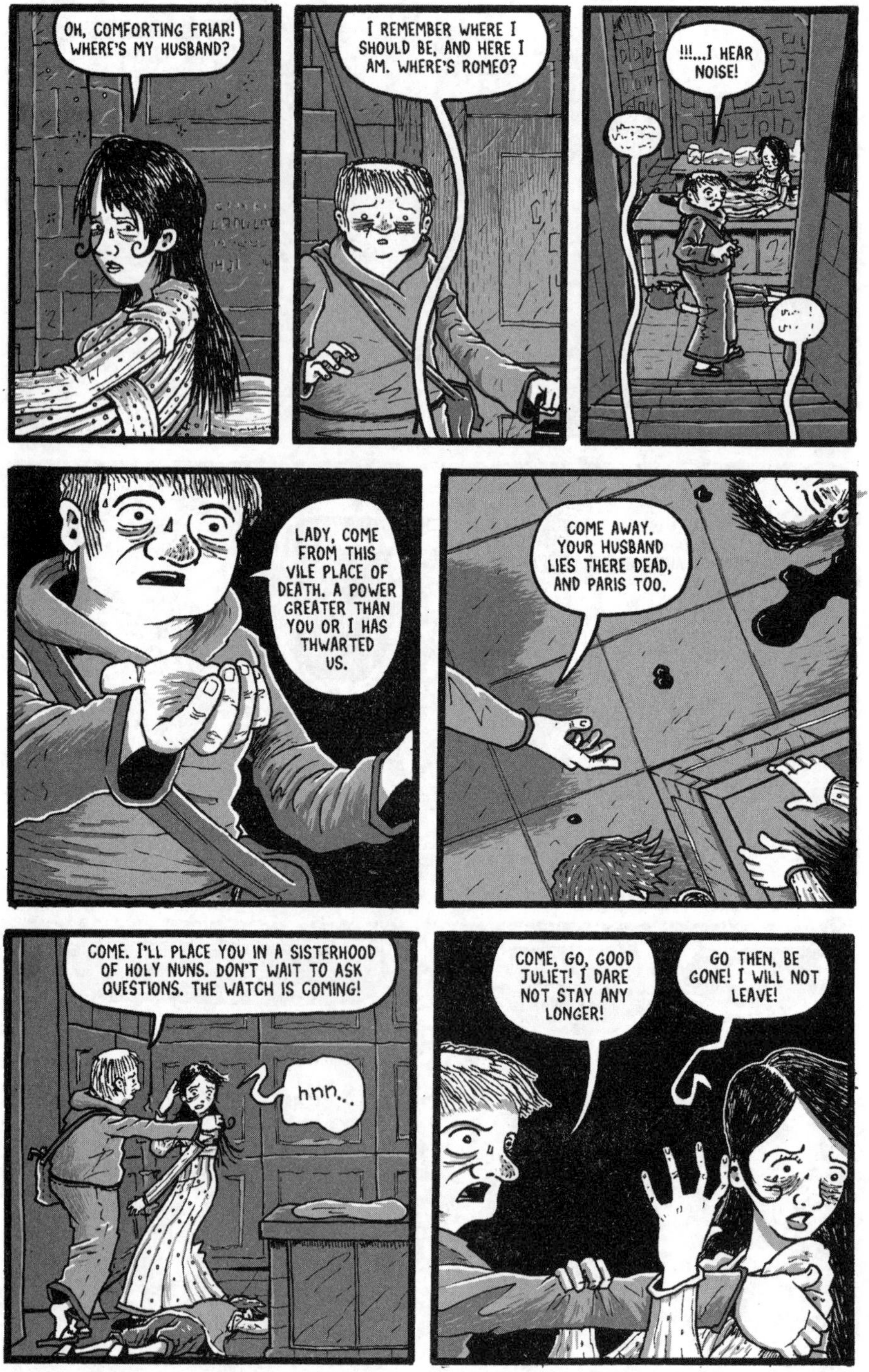
OH, COMFORTING FRIAR! WHERE'S MY HUSBAND?
I REMEMBER WHERE I SHOULD BE, AND HERE I AM. WHERE'S ROMEO?
!!!...I HEAR NOISE!
LADY, COME FROM THIS VILE PLACE OF DEATH. A POWER GREATER THAN YOU OR I HAS THWARTED US.
COME AWAY. YOUR HUSBAND LIES THERE DEAD, AND PARIS TOO.
COME. I'LL PLACE YOU IN A SISTERHOOD OF HOLY NUNS. DON'T WAIT TO ASK QUESTIONS. THE WATCH IS COMING!
hnn...
COME, GO, GOOD JULIET! I DARE NOT STAY ANY LONGER!
GO THEN, BE GONE! I WILL NOT LEAVE!

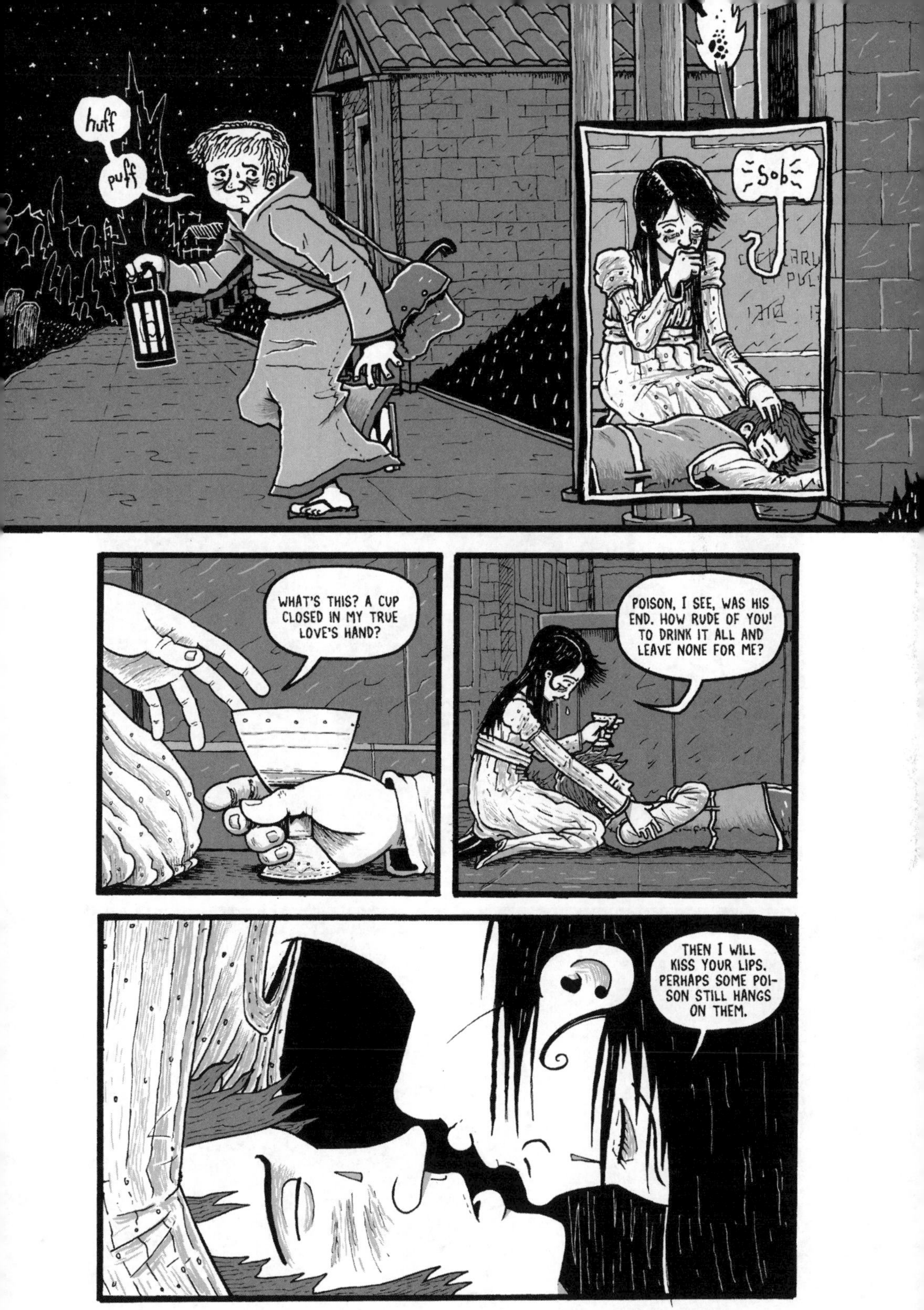
huff
puff
Sob
WHAT'S THIS? A CUP CLOSED IN MY TRUE LOVE'S HAND?
POISON, I SEE, WAS HIS END. HOW RUDE OF YOU! TO DRINK IT ALL AND LEAVE NONE FOR ME?
THEN I WILL KISS YOUR LIPS. PERHAPS SOME POISON STILL HANGS ON THEM.

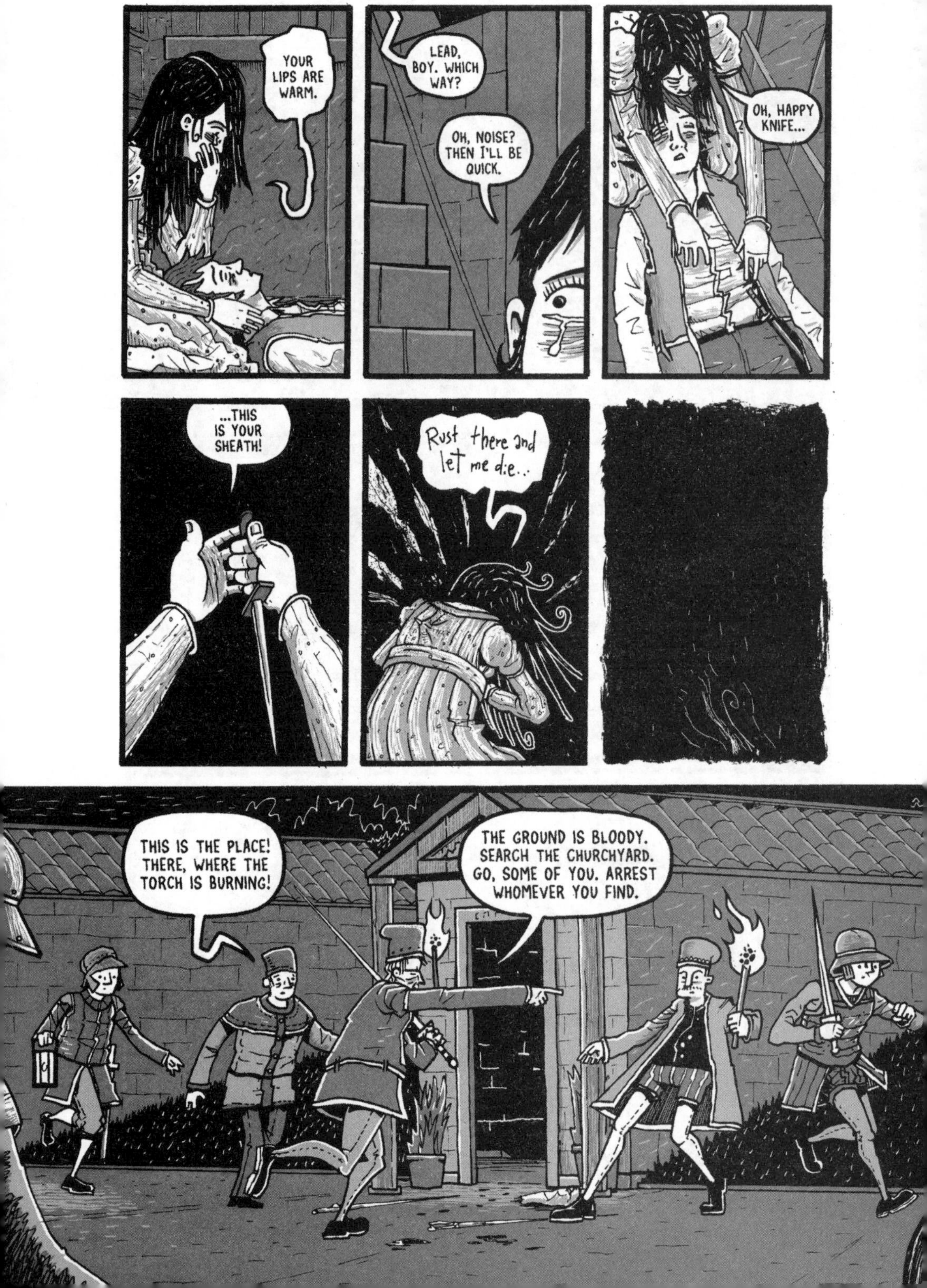
YOUR LIPS ARE WARM.
LEAD, BOY. WHICH WAY?
OH, NOISE? THEN I'LL BE QUICK.
OH, HAPPY KNIFE...
...THIS IS YOUR SHEATH!
Rust there and let me die...
THIS IS THE PLACE! THERE, WHERE THE TORCH IS BURNING!
THE GROUND IS BLOODY. SEARCH THE CHURCHYARD. GO, SOME OF YOU. ARREST WHOMEVER YOU FIND.

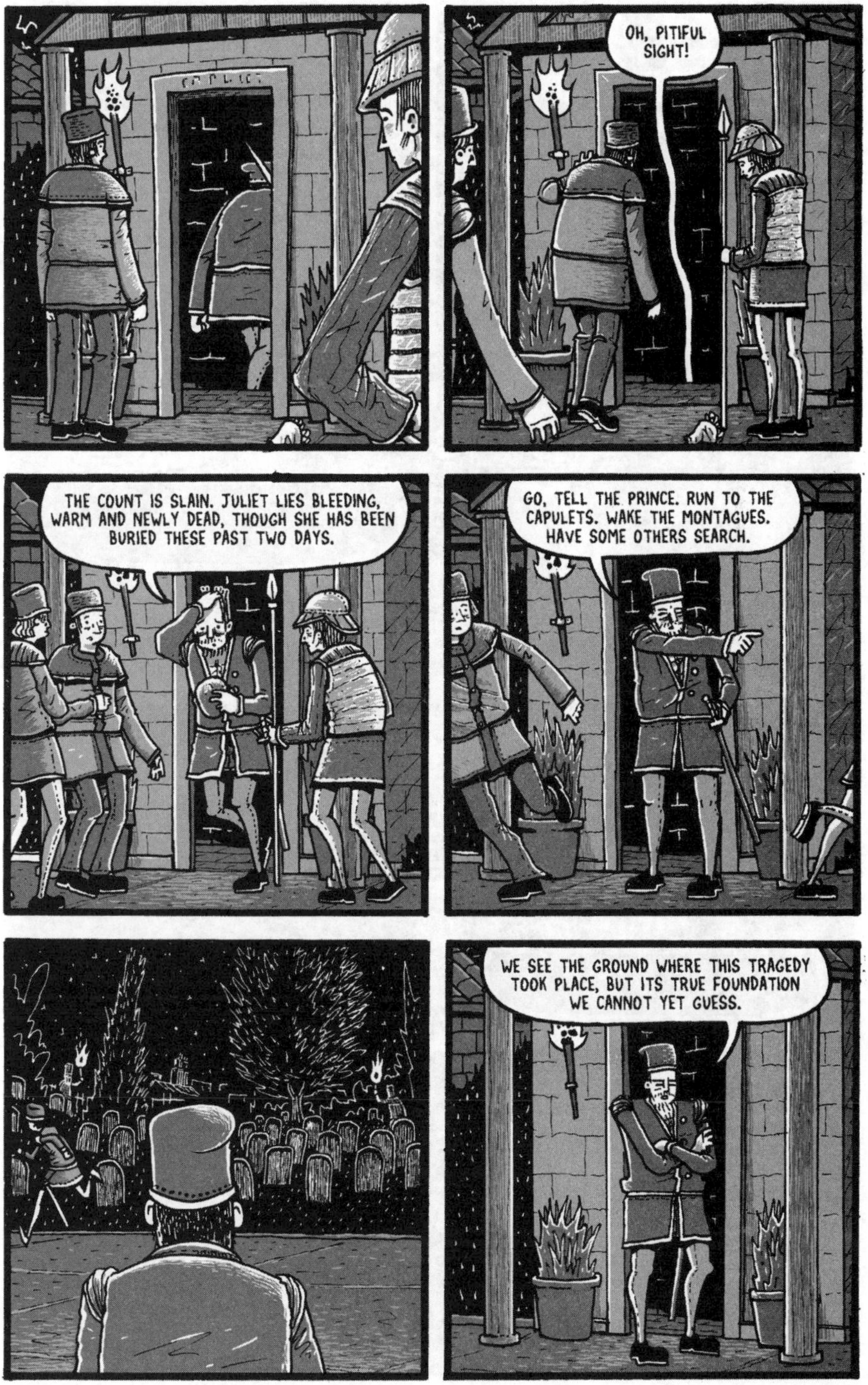
OH, PITIFUL SIGHT!
THE COUNT IS SLAIN. JULIET LIES BLEEDING, WARM AND NEWLY DEAD, THOUGH SHE HAS BEEN BURIED THESE PAST TWO DAYS.
GO, TELL THE PRINCE. RUN TO THE CAPULETS. WAKE THE MONTAGUES. HAVE SOME OTHERS SEARCH.
WE SEE THE GROUND WHERE THIS TRAGEDY TOOK PLACE, BUT ITS TRUE FOUNDATION WE CANNOT YET GUESS.

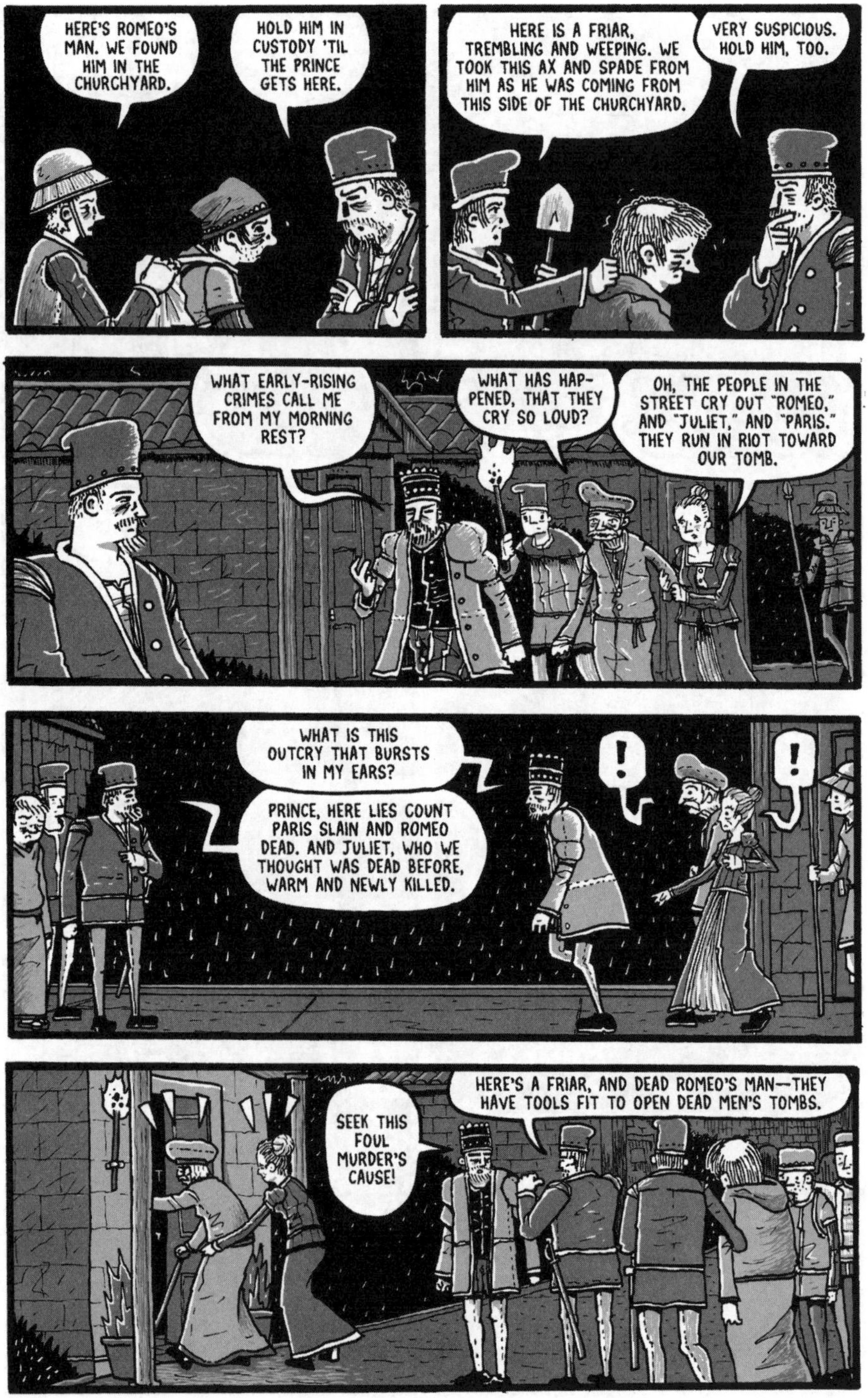
HERE'S ROMEO'S MAN. WE FOUND HIM IN THE CHURCHYARD.
HOLD HIM IN CUSTODY 'TIL THE PRINCE GETS HERE.
HERE IS A FRIAR, TREMBLING AND WEEPING. WE TOOK THIS AX AND SPADE FROM HIM AS HE WAS COMING FROM THIS SIDE OF THE CHURCHYARD.
VERY SUSPICIOUS. HOLD HIM, TOO.
WHAT EARLY-RISING CRIMES CALL ME FROM MY MORNING REST?
WHAT HAS HAPPENED, THAT THEY CRY SO LOUD?
OH, THE PEOPLE IN THE STREET CRY OUT "ROMEO," AND "JULIET," AND "PARIS." THEY RUN IN RIOT TOWARD OUR TOMB.
WHAT IS THIS OUTCRY THAT BURSTS IN MY EARS?
PRINCE, HERE LIES COUNT PARIS SLAIN AND ROMEO DEAD. AND JULIET, WHO WE THOUGHT WAS DEAD BEFORE, WARM AND NEWLY KILLED.
!
!
SEEK THIS FOUL MURDER'S CAUSE!
HERE'S A FRIAR, AND DEAD ROMEO'S MAN—THEY HAVE TOOLS FIT TO OPEN DEAD MEN'S TOMBS.

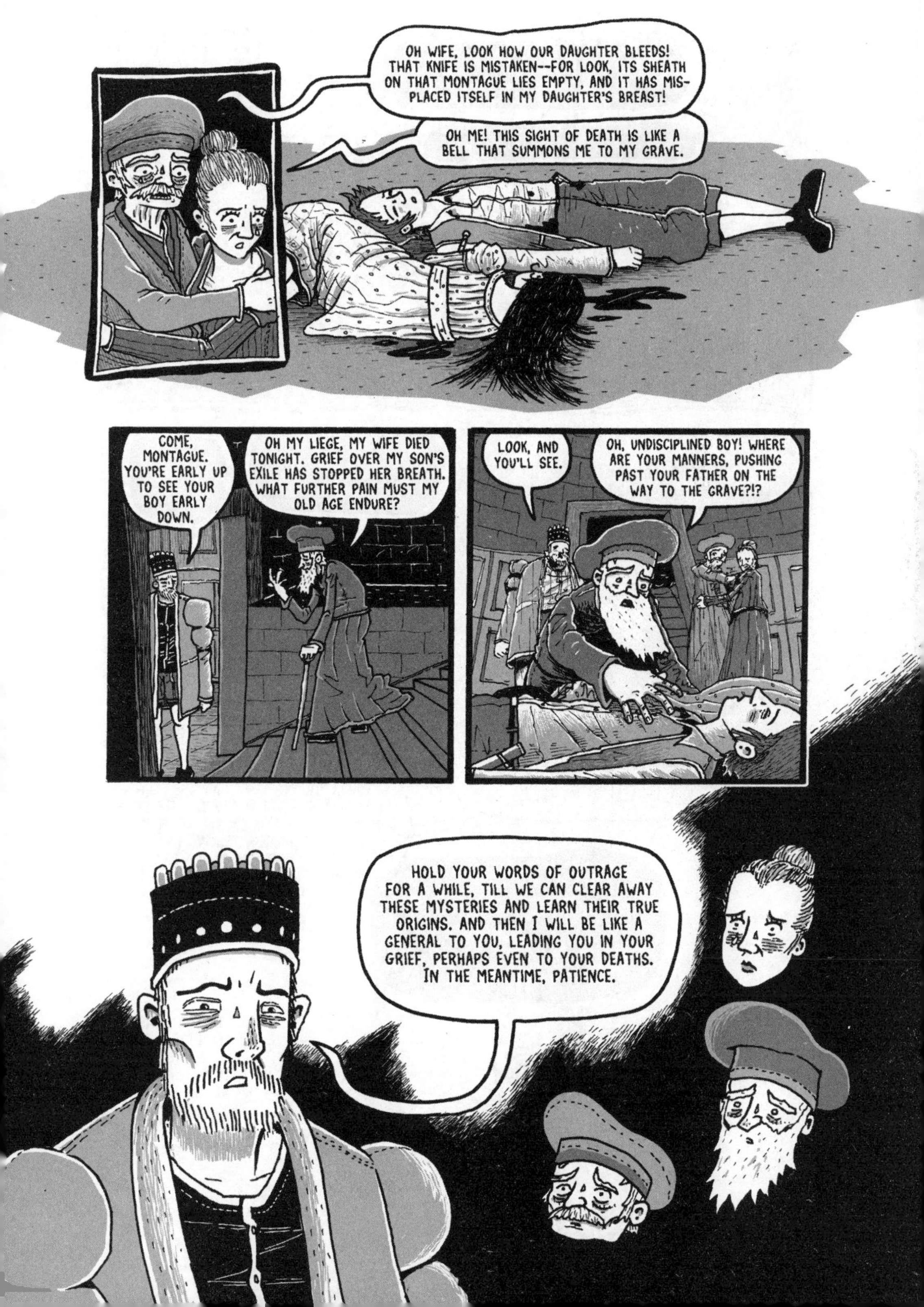

OH WIFE, LOOK HOW OUR DAUGHTER BLEEDS! THAT KNIFE IS MISTAKEN--FOR LOOK, ITS SHEATH ON THAT MONTAGUE LIES EMPTY, AND IT HAS MISPLACED ITSELF IN MY DAUGHTER'S BREAST!
OH ME! THIS SIGHT OF DEATH IS LIKE A BELL THAT SUMMONS ME TO MY GRAVE.
COME, MONTAGUE. YOU'RE EARLY UP TO SEE YOUR BOY EARLY DOWN.
OH MY LIEGE, MY WIFE DIED TONIGHT. GRIEF OVER MY SON'S EXILE HAS STOPPED HER BREATH. WHAT FURTHER PAIN MUST MY OLD AGE ENDURE?
LOOK, AND YOU'LL SEE.
OH, UNDISCIPLINED BOY! WHERE ARE YOUR MANNERS, PUSHING PAST YOUR FATHER ON THE WAY TO THE GRAVE?!?
HOLD YOUR WORDS OF OUTRAGE FOR A WHILE, TILL WE CAN CLEAR AWAY THESE MYSTERIES AND LEARN THEIR TRUE ORIGINS. AND THEN I WILL BE LIKE A GENERAL TO YOU, LEADING YOU IN YOUR GRIEF, PERHAPS EVEN TO YOUR DEATHS. IN THE MEANTIME, PATIENCE.

BRING FORTH THE MEN UNDER SUSPICION.

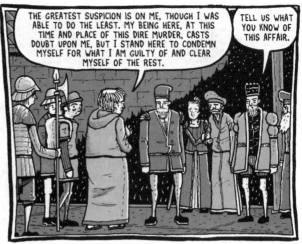

THE GREATEST SUSPICION IS ON ME, THOUGH I WAS ABLE TO DO THE LEAST. MY BEING HERE, AT THIS TIME AND PLACE OF THIS DIRE MURDER, CASTS DOUBT UPON ME, BUT I STAND HERE TO CONDEMN MYSELF FOR WHAT I AM GUILTY OF AND CLEAR MYSELF OF THE REST.

TELL US WHAT YOU KNOW OF THIS AFFAIR.

I WILL BE BRIEF, FOR THE LITTLE THAT'S LEFT OF MY LIFE IS NOT SO LONG AS A TEDIOUS TALE. ROMEO, THERE DEAD, WAS HUSBAND TO THAT JULIET. AND SHE, THERE DEAD, WAS ROMEO'S FAITHFUL WIFE.

I MARRIED THEM—THEIR SECRET WEDDING DAY WAS THE SAME DAY TYBALT DIED. HIS UNTIMELY DEATH CAUSED THE NEW-MADE BRIDEGROOM TO BE BANISHED. JULIET MOURNED FOR HIM, NOT FOR TYBALT.

TO LIFT HER GRIEF, YOU CAPULETS BETROTHED HER TO PARIS AND WOULD HAVE FORCED THE MARRIAGE. SHE CAME TO ME THEN, AND WITH A WILD LOOK BEGGED ME TO DEVISE SOME WAY TO ESCAPE THIS SECOND MARRIAGE—OR ELSE SHE WOULD KILL HERSELF IN MY CELL.

I GAVE HER A SLEEPING POTION, WHICH I MIXED USING MY MEDICAL TRAINING—IT HAD THE EFFECT I'D INTENDED, FOR IT TURNED HER INTO AN IMAGE OF DEATH. IN THE MEANTIME, I WROTE TO ROMEO, TELLING HIM TO COME HERE THIS DIRE NIGHT TO HELP TAKE HER FROM HER BORROWED GRAVE WHEN THE POTION WORE OFF.

BUT THE MAN WHO BORE MY LETTER, FRIAR JOHN, WAS PREVENTED FROM LEAVING, AND LAST NIGHT HE RETURNED MY LETTER TO ME.

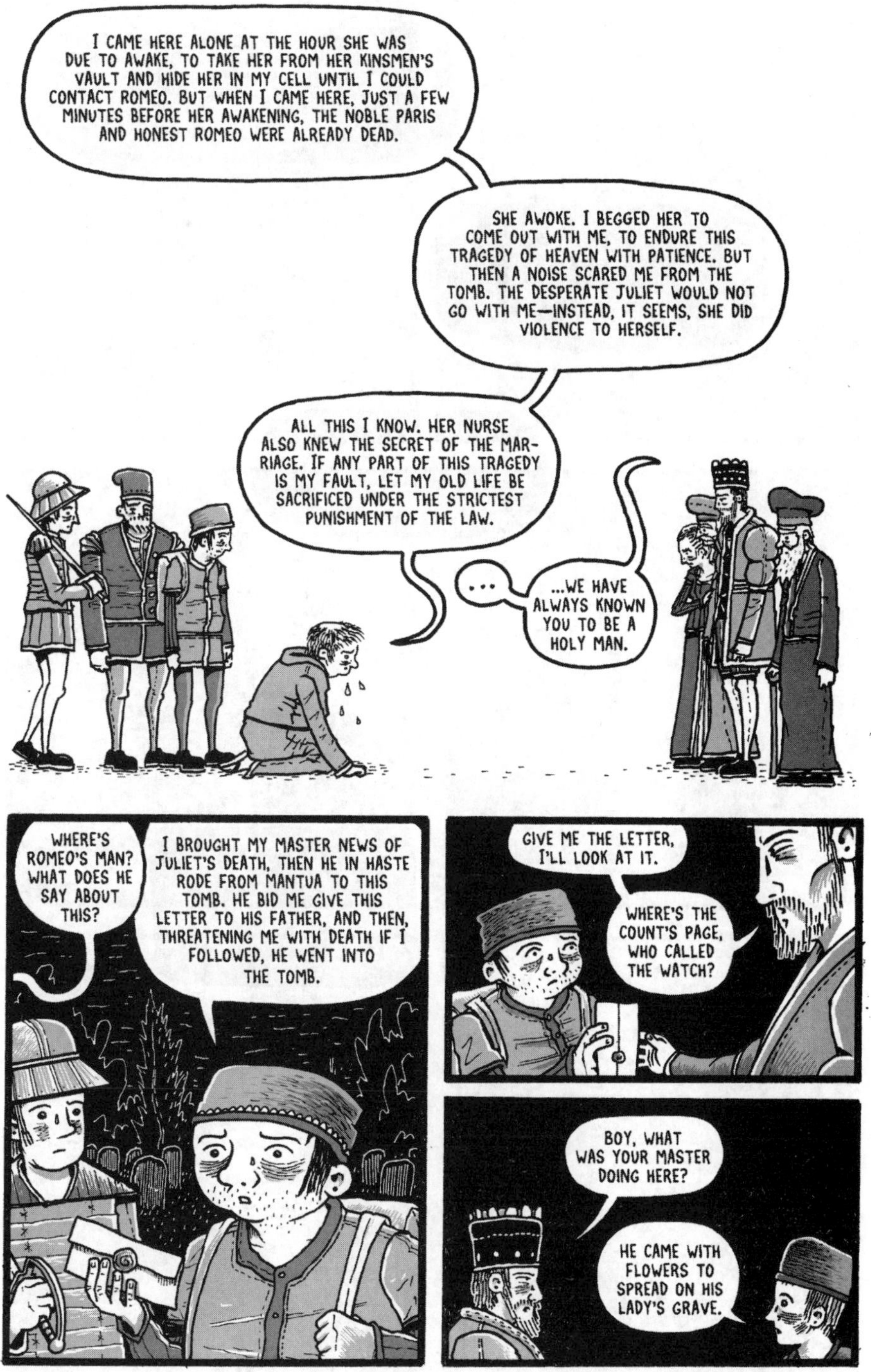
I CAME HERE ALONE AT THE HOUR SHE WAS DUE TO AWAKE, TO TAKE HER FROM HER KINSMEN'S VAULT AND HIDE HER IN MY CELL UNTIL I COULD CONTACT ROMEO. BUT WHEN I CAME HERE, JUST A FEW MINUTES BEFORE HER AWAKENING, THE NOBLE PARIS AND HONEST ROMEO WERE ALREADY DEAD.
SHE AWOKE. I BEGGED HER TO COME OUT WITH ME, TO ENDURE THIS TRAGEDY OF HEAVEN WITH PATIENCE. BUT THEN A NOISE SCARED ME FROM THE TOMB. THE DESPERATE JULIET WOULD NOT GO WITH ME—INSTEAD, IT SEEMS, SHE DID VIOLENCE TO HERSELF.
ALL THIS I KNOW. HER NURSE ALSO KNEW THE SECRET OF THE MARRIAGE. IF ANY PART OF THIS TRAGEDY IS MY FAULT, LET MY OLD LIFE BE SACRIFICED UNDER THE STRICTEST PUNISHMENT OF THE LAW.
...
...WE HAVE ALWAYS KNOWN YOU TO BE A HOLY MAN.
WHERE'S ROMEO'S MAN? WHAT DOES HE SAY ABOUT THIS?
I BROUGHT MY MASTER NEWS OF JULIET'S DEATH, THEN HE IN HASTE RODE FROM MANTUA TO THIS TOMB. HE BID ME GIVE THIS LETTER TO HIS FATHER, AND THEN, THREATENING ME WITH DEATH IF I FOLLOWED, HE WENT INTO THE TOMB.
GIVE ME THE LETTER, I'LL LOOK AT IT.
WHERE'S THE COUNT'S PAGE, WHO CALLED THE WATCH?
BOY, WHAT WAS YOUR MASTER DOING HERE?
HE CAME WITH FLOWERS TO SPREAD ON HIS LADY'S GRAVE.

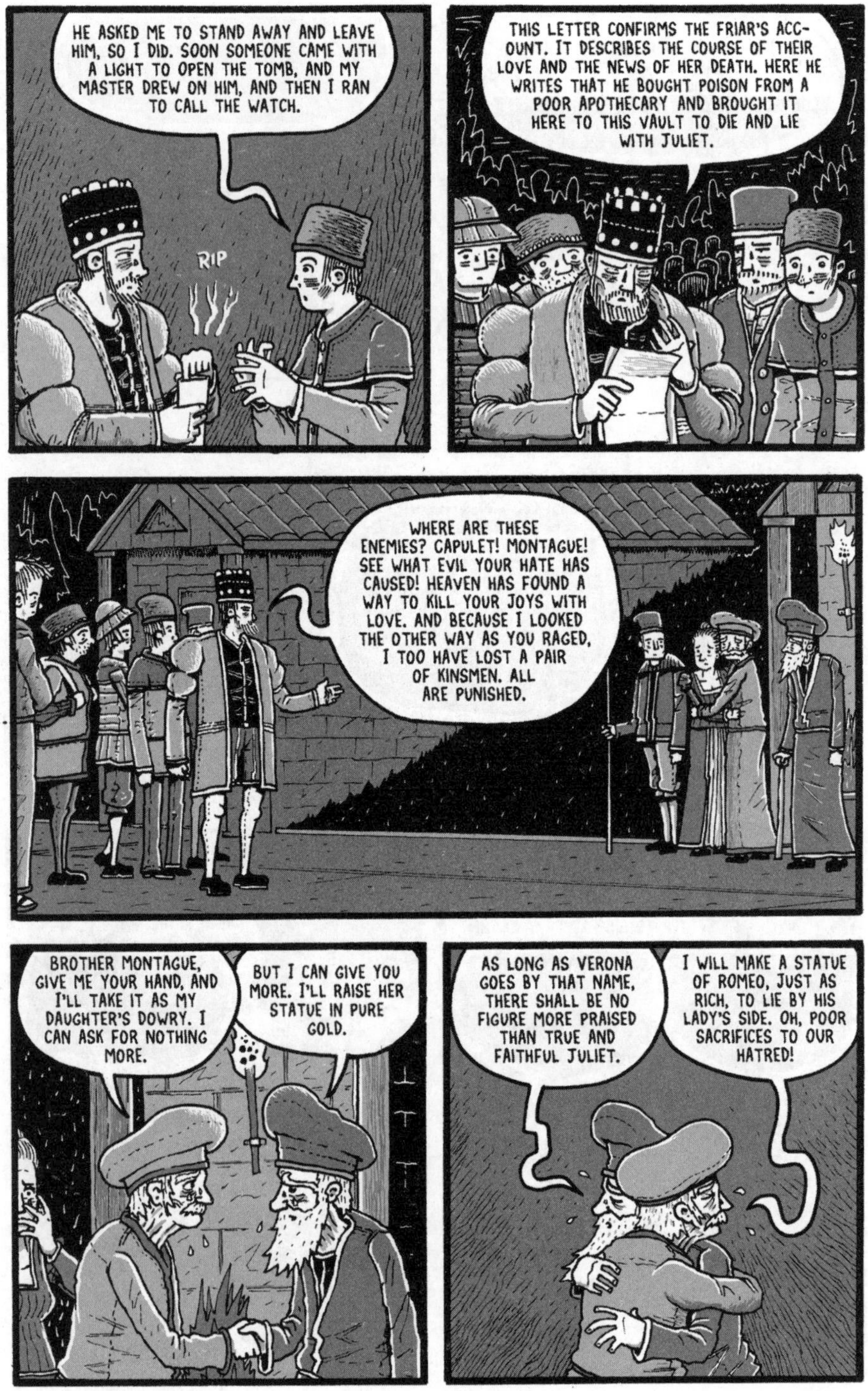
HE ASKED ME TO STAND AWAY AND LEAVE HIM, SO I DID. SOON SOMEONE CAME WITH A LIGHT TO OPEN THE TOMB, AND MY MASTER DREW ON HIM, AND THEN I RAN TO CALL THE WATCH.
RIP
THIS LETTER CONFIRMS THE FRIAR'S ACCOUNT. IT DESCRIBES THE COURSE OF THEIR LOVE AND THE NEWS OF HER DEATH. HERE HE WRITES THAT HE BOUGHT POISON FROM A POOR APOTHECARY AND BROUGHT IT HERE TO THIS VAULT TO DIE AND LIE WITH JULIET.
WHERE ARE THESE ENEMIES? CAPULET! MONTAGUE! SEE WHAT EVIL YOUR HATE HAS CAUSED! HEAVEN HAS FOUND A WAY TO KILL YOUR JOYS WITH LOVE. AND BECAUSE I LOOKED THE OTHER WAY AS YOU RAGED, I TOO HAVE LOST A PAIR OF KINSMEN. ALL ARE PUNISHED.
BROTHER MONTAGUE, GIVE ME YOUR HAND, AND I'LL TAKE IT AS MY DAUGHTER'S DOWRY. I CAN ASK FOR NOTHING MORE.
BUT I CAN GIVE YOU MORE. I'LL RAISE HER STATUE IN PURE GOLD.
AS LONG AS VERONA GOES BY THAT NAME, THERE SHALL BE NO FIGURE MORE PRAISED THAN TRUE AND FAITHFUL JULIET.
I WILL MAKE A STATUE OF ROMEO, JUST AS RICH, TO LIE BY HIS LADY'S SIDE. OH, POOR SACRIFICES TO OUR HATRED!

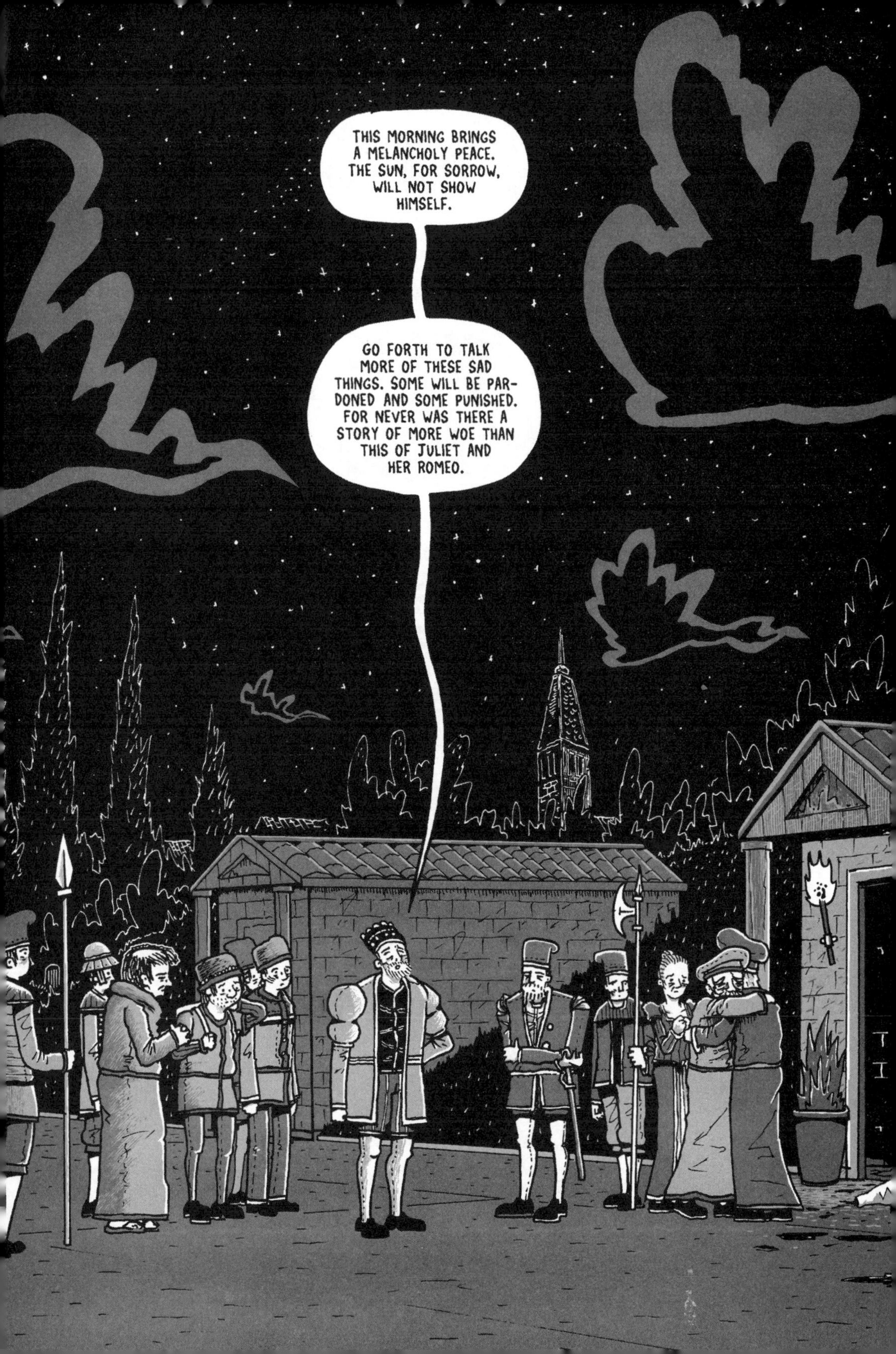
THIS MORNING BRINGS A MELANCHOLY PEACE. THE SUN, FOR SORROW, WILL NOT SHOW HIMSELF.
GO FORTH TO TALK MORE OF THESE SAD THINGS. SOME WILL BE PARDONED AND SOME PUNISHED. FOR NEVER WAS THERE A STORY OF MORE WOE THAN THIS OF JULIET AND HER ROMEO.